Jurists: Profiles in Legal Theory

General Editors:
William Twining
Neil MacCormick

Ronald Dworkin

Stephen Guest

STANFORD UNIVERSITY PRESS
Stanford, California

Stanford University Press
Stanford, California
© 1991 Stephen Guest
Originating publisher: Edinburgh
    University Press, Edinburgh
First published in the USA by
    Stanford University Press, 1991
Printed in Great Britain
Cloth ISBN 0-8047-1997-7
Paper ISBN 0-8047-2019-3
LC 91-75060
This book is printed on acid-free paper

Contents

Preface

My aim in this work has been to advance a comprehensive and coherent interpretation of Dworkin's positions in legal and political philosophy. I have considered many of the main criticisms that have been levelled against them, as well as others, and offer an interpretation that provides, in general, what I believe to be a good defence. I am very fortunate to have been able to draw upon some of Ronald Dworkin's unpublished papers.

Like Dworkin, I am convinced that a theory of law known as legal positivism incorrectly characterises law and legal argument. A widely accepted version of positivism, which Dworkin refers to as the 'plain fact' theory of law, is that law is clearly or plainly identifiable as a matter of, ultimately, agreement among public officials. Thus identified by the facts of agreement, and not personal moral convictions, law is identifiable independently of its moral content.

The plain fact quality of law was its attraction to me when, as a legal positivist, I first came across Dworkin's ideas. I thought that viewing the law in this way was supported by the important moral reason that people should be *clear* in seeing the difference between their own moral convictions and what the state demanded of them in the name of law.

I do not now accept that law and morality should be so distinct. People are amenable to engaging in moral argument and my view is that, at least in the Anglo-American jurisdictions, little is to be gained by denying moral arguments about the use of a community's formal coercive powers the status of *law*. The lawyer's job is better seen as advancing good moral arguments in order to persuade judges. Much, of course, is contained here in what is meant by a good moral argument, but it is a contention of this work that the apparent 'subjectivity' of this approach is illusory, and that opponents of Dworkin misunderstand his views about the objective nature of legal argument.

Standard accounts of Dworkin's work have unhelpfully tended to overstress his attacks on positivism. My view is that Dworkin is right both in his characterisation of the 'plain fact' view of law and in its underpinning by the idea of what he calls 'conventionalism'. But I think, too, that the legal theory of Dworkin's intellectual protagonist, Herbert Hart, can be rescued from Dworkin's claim that it is simply a semantic version of a plain fact theory.

I am particularly grateful to the Series editors, William Twining and Neil MacCormick, for their patient reading of various drafts and their detailed comments. I have gained a lot from many discussions with Sheldon Leader, who has also commented on most of the chapters. David Richards, Michael Freeman, Nigel Simmonds and Roger Cotterrell have been extremely helpful in their comments on early drafts. I am, too, conscious of the debt I owe to Ronald Dworkin, who has kindly provided me with several of his unpublished papers, and has also been kind enough to read and comment on various parts of different drafts. I am very grateful for numerous conversations with him over the years. I also wish to thank Simon Grégoire for his painstaking work in compiling a bibliography and David Brooke for his help in checking the footnotes. The financial support I received from the University College London Department of Laws Research Committee was also of great assistance.

Stephen Guest
London

1

A preliminary sketch

Ronald Dworkin's legal and political theories have a complexity, novelty and moral power that have excited a wide range of academic and political thinkers. He writes about the political and legal thought of the Western democratic legal systems, in particular those of the United States and the United Kingdom. His views are developing and are by no means settled, particularly his views about the nature of justice. But the enormous output of books and papers he has produced, along with the formidable profusion of lectures and seminars he has delivered in many places in the world, have given him a very wide reputation as a highly original thinker, with much of importance to say. He is cited in legal, political, philosophical and economics books and journals and writers who disagree or agree with him are united in thinking that the ideas he has are of sufficient significance to require serious consideration.

In short, Dworkin's theory of *law* is that the nature of legal argument lies in the best moral interpretation of existing social practices. His theory of *justice* is that all political judgments ought to rest ultimately upon the injunction that people are equal as human beings, irrespective of the circumstances in which they are born.

But this is highly compressed and it is my task in this work to try to make his theory clearer and more accessible than it has so far been. I have attempted to make the best sense of his theory as a whole. His writing is not easy to many, including myself. And because he writes for a number of audiences, sometimes the general public, sometimes for academic lawyers, sometimes for philosophers and economists, it is an especially hard task to dig out the different strands of thought.

Some background notes

We should join this sketch of Dworkin's theory with some background to his own life and times. Dworkin is an American. He was born in 1931, in Worcester, Massachusetts. His initial interest was philosophy. He studied for the AB at Harvard College before studying for the B.A. in Jurisprudence at Oxford University where, at Magdalen College, he was a student of the late Sir Rupert Cross. It was there, as he said to Brian Magee, in Magee's *Men of Ideas* programme on British television in the late 1970s, that he discovered his real interest. He then went to Harvard Law School to study law and, after graduating, became a law clerk to the great American judge Learned Hand in the period 1957–8. He became a member of the New York bar and was an associate of the New York law firm of Sullivan and Cromwell from 1958 to 1962. In 1962 he became a professor of law at Yale University, in 1968 becoming holder of the Wesley N. Hohfeld Chair of Jurisprudence.

In 1969, Dworkin was appointed to the distinguished Chair of Jurisprudence at Oxford and is still there today, although from 1975, as a professor of law at New York University, he has spent the Fall term of each year teaching in the New York University school of law. He has also, at various times, held other professorships at Harvard, Cornell and Princeton universities. He has been a visiting professor at University College London since 1984.

His first article was on the topic of judicial discretion, published in the *Journal of Philosophy* in 1963,[1] and there were several other articles, mainly review articles.[2] They are interesting chiefly for two reasons. First, they display the anti-utilitarian strain then beginning to emerge from the wilderness of Anglo-American political philosophy. In particular, it is possible to detect the influence of Rawls's very influential article 'Two Concepts of Rules' published in 1955.[3] Second, they display a sophisticated awareness of the nuances of legal and political reasoning.

But it was the publication of 'Is Law a System of Rules?' in the *University of Chicago Law Review* that made his reputation.[4] This article has three notable features. It is very well written, having energy and journalistic clarity, it contains a brilliant summary of the main tenets of Herbert Hart's *The Concept of Law* and above all, it presents a sustained and constructive attack on the thesis contained in that book. The article, now appearing as Chapter 2 of *Taking Rights Seriously*, has not lost its initial force. It is the best article to encourage students to read first. Although, in later years, some emphases have changed, the emerging thesis is clear.

It was two years after the publication of this article that, in 1969, Dworkin succeeded Hart to the Chair of Jurisprudence in Oxford. That Chair had previously had an American holder, Arthur Goodhart, who had held it for some years until Hart came to it in 1952. English jurisprudence was then in the doldrums. As Neil MacCormick, speaking of the time, says in his book on Hart, 'Lawyers had stopped being interested in philosophy, philosophers in law. Jurisprudence in the universities had become a routine reading and re-reading of a canon of texts and text-books.'[5]

Political theory was also in the doldrums. The first really rigorous and exciting piece of writing, perhaps giving a foretaste of the good writing that was to come, was T.D. Weldon's *The Vocabulary of Politics* published in 1953.[6]

It is important, I think, to appreciate how the position in Britain had improved in both fields by the time of Dworkin's appointment. Hart had an enormous impact on a generation of lawyers and philosophers. He is a distinguished philosopher who is well versed in the developments inspired by Wittgenstein and the 'ordinary language' school of philosophy. He was also a barrister who had practised for some years at the Chancery Bar. In his inaugural lecture 'Definition and Theory in Jurisprudence' he introduced not just the methods of contemporary philosophy, in particular linguistic philosophy, but a particular kind of rigour, one distinguished by a remarkable clarity. That clarity is still a mark of good English jurisprudence.

Several other publications were of some importance in the field in the 1950s. People were beginning to assimilate Julius Stone's massive and important three volume work, published earlier in 1946, entitled *The Province and Function of Law*. Others were the works, remarkable for their clarity and breadth of thought, *Law and Social Change in Contemporary Britain* (1951) by Wolfgang Friedman, followed by his *Legal Theory* (1967). Also helpful was Dennis Lloyd's *Introduction to Jurisprudence* (1959), which provided a clear and readable summary of the major schools of jurisprudence and, most importantly, included a large number of readings from diversely published works of jurists. Although these readings were relatively common in the United States, it widened access to primary sources in jurisprudence to law students in Britain. It was followed, shortly afterwards, by his lucid summary of major issues in *The Idea of Law*.[7]

A transitional work was *Oxford Essays in Jurisprudence*, a selection of papers on jurisprudence, edited by A.G. Guest in 1961.[8] The standard of writing was very high, although the essays now seem curiously dated. But the tone set by the volume was eclectic, consisting of varying analyses of 'concepts', and the writers deal with topics such as 'ownership', 'logic in the law' and 'entitlements'. With the publication of *The Concept of Law* in 1961, it seemed that the Oxford jurisprudential die was cast. Rigour, clarity, analysis and close attention to language were its hallmarks. There was a growing interest in the subject, too, partly because of the growth in the numbers of students of law at the universities.

The United States was not immune from these developments. But the traditions in its law schools, at least for the past thirty or so years, were different. In United States law schools there is considerably more interest shown in the mechanics of legal argument in the courts. Part of the reason for this interest was the great movement in American law schools in the early part of this century towards being 'realistic' about what 'actually' went on in courts and away from what was perceived to be a 'formalistic' tinkering with legal 'doctrine'.

That interest, coupled with the interest, natural to citizens in the United States, in the enormous constitutional power wielded by the Supreme Court to strike down legislation, set a different tone to American jurisprudence. It is not surprising that the term, used by United States lawyers, a 'hard case', meaning by that an intellectually difficult case, is late in gaining ground here. That term does have, of course, the connotation in the United States of 'hard cases make bad law'. But it does, too, retain a connection with the case which is 'worth appealing', as Karl Llewellyn put it.[9] If the idea does gain ground here it will be largely through Dworkin's references to it. But the idea has long been part of United States law. There is no British equivalent.

So, when *The Concept of Law* was published in 1961, Dworkin's background was both of Oxford jurisprudence, when there had been big changes, and of the jurisprudential traditions of the United States. But the 1960s were times also of social transformation. It is not possible here to explore the causes of the particular spirit of liberalism generated in that time. The civil rights movement was already in existence, but there were greater changes impending. One impetus must have been the Vietnam war. In the 1960s a witless United States administration did things which were wrong, and cruel, in ways that were difficult to articulate. That administration's actions seemed to be supported by a majority of people and seemed to be done with the intention of promoting the interests of decency. Further, those within the civil rights movement were split over the issue. It would be understating the position to say that the United States public were merely divided on the issue. It was more than that. It created fissures among American people the traces of which still exist.

I think the Vietnam war had this result. It was a major cause of the strong feeling among thinking people of the need for coherently articulated principles of governmental conduct. That, in turn, provided an impetus towards the reinterpretation and analysis of concepts such as 'rights' in a more overtly political sense. Political philosophy of this sort took off and, in 1971, John Rawls finally published his enormously influential *A Theory of Justice*, parts of the manuscript of which had been circulating privately for some time.

The theme of this book is grand, in the style of earlier writers such as Hobbes and Rousseau on the idea of a social 'contract', and is avowedly anti-utilitarian. The work pays close attention to methodology, in particular the idea that we should work towards a 'reflective equilibrium' between our intuitions and an articulated set of propositions that could unite all intuitions in one coherent whole.

Also, there is in Rawls's work a serious attention paid to the question of the relationship between theories of economics and political philosophy.

This is, briefly, the setting in which we may view Dworkin's work. The impression various thinkers have made upon his own writings is not entirely clear. Rawls and Hart have obviously made a deep impression. The milieu of legal and political theorising in which Dworkin writes is largely their creation. Rawls's *A Theory of Justice* is a stunning articulation of political principles, especially given that it broke new ground. And the same can be said of Hart in legal philosophy. But Dworkin has, I venture to say, a more abstract grasp of the requirements of political justification than Rawls. For example, although Dworkin uses Rawls's idea of 'reflective equilibrium', he is more direct and explicit than Rawls in employing it as a method of 'constructing' moral argument, not finding it. Dworkin is also like Hart, sensitive to the uses of language and is fully versed in the intricacies of linguistic philosophy. But he has transcended that methodology completely in his development of 'interpretive' understandings of various of our social practices, notably those constituting law.

People are inclined to say that he has been heavily influenced by Lon Fuller and there are, too, distinct traces of what Dworkin says in the works of the American realist, John Dickinson, whose 'The Law behind Law', published in 1929, draws distinctions similar to the rules and principles distinction that permeates Dworkin's work.[10] Further parallels might be drawn between Dworkin's work and the methods employed in the collection of materials widely used in United States law schools of Hart and Sacks.[11] Interestingly, while Fuller was the Carter Professor of Jurisprudence at Harvard when Dworkin was studying law at Harvard law school, Dworkin himself did not take jurisprudence as one of his subjects and there was little contact between them. In that period, too, in the late 1950s, Hart visited Harvard and the outcome was the well-known Hart–Fuller debate on the status of legal positivism.[12]

There are parallels between Fuller's ideas of the 'inner morality of law' and the integrity of which Dworkin writes. But I am inclined to regard the close drawing of influences in this way with some suspicion. There *is* a tradition of jurisprudential thinking in the United States which expects theorising about what happens in difficult or 'hard' cases, whether the difficulties are created by vague rules or by evil legal systems. I do not think it useful to say that Dworkin was particularly 'influenced' by any particular jurist, in the same way that it would be wrong to say that Hart was greatly 'influenced' by Bentham. It would be wrong, of course, to say that Bentham exerted no influence on Hart at all.

I think that the chief contributors besides Rawls and Hart to the milieu from which Dworkin derives intellectual support have been philosophers who write in the mainstream of philosophy (and, perhaps, economics) rather than jurists. Probably the greatest background contribution, drawn from the cast of post-war American philosophy, would have been Quine. Quine taught that philosophy was practically oriented and constrained by logic and rationality. Certainly, it is a strong blend of practicality and logic that informs Dworkin's work. I should say, too, that I think Bernard Williams has made some noticeable impression. The origins of the development of Dworkin's ideas on equality and utilitarianism are in Williams' writings on these subjects.[13]

Another philosopher, Gareth Evans, should be mentioned. Gareth Evans was a highly gifted philosopher who tragically died in 1980, at the age of 31. He was capable in many different fields of philosophy, including epistemology and ethics.[14] In the period 1973–5, he and Dworkin gave a series of seminars in Oxford on the topic of objectivity in law and morality, which I attended. These seminars were the anvil at which many ideas were forged.[15]

I remember two things in particular. One was a highly empirical approach to the problems. After some sessions, the idea that truth might 'exceed its demonstrability' was finally clarified. This idea, as you will see, is vital to understanding Dworkin's use of the concepts of essential contestability, interpretation, rival conceptions and, I think, reflective equilibrium. Evans and Dworkin then invited a number of people, on separate occasions, from other disciplines and, after explaining the problem, subjected them to the most exacting cross-examination. The point was to see whether the idea was accepted in other disciplines that propositions could be true without demonstration or proof. I remember one bewildered mathematician, pleased, though, because he had given answers that were apparently satisfactory to Evans and Dworkin.

Evans forced Dworkin to be clearer. He had an irreverent style which exactly suited this stage of the development of Dworkin's thought. Much of what was said in that period by Dworkin I recognised in published form over the following ten years. A particular memory I have is when Evans forced Dworkin to say what the connection was between the justification of decisions in hard cases and the ordinary rules that make up the bulk of the law. A sudden dawning of understanding, apparent in everyone, occurred when Dworkin informed us that the justification was the same as the justification of the settled rules. Evans made a great noise of contentment.

The force of that memory will seem trite to those familiar with Dworkin's subsequent publications. But these were before the publication, in 1977, of his collection of essays, *Taking Rights Seriously* and, more significantly, in a time when it sounded perverse to say that democratic principles had anything to do with justifying legal decisions. When I encountered Dworkin at the first seminar he was giving in a series on legal rights (again with Gareth Evans) I was fascinated to hear him announce that '[a]s you will know, my view is that there are natural legal rights'. To a positivist, as many who were not American were then, this sounded wrong in many ways. We knew what a 'natural' lawyer was. He may have believed in 'natural rights' but would more likely have disapproved of the idea of 'rights' at all. But *legal* rights – that could *only* have been a positivist assertion. So Dworkin's statement could not be fitted into any category which I had encountered. And even now, the hold of these categories is strong. Each year a student will say to me, 'I found your lecture on Dworkin interesting, but please tell me, in a nutshell, is he a positivist or a natural lawyer?' For a long time, at a higher academic level, interpretation of Dworkin was marked by an assumption that he must be one or the other, an assumption that should have been rendered unnecessary by the publication of *Law's Empire* in 1986.

There are other contemporary influences. Thomas Nagel, who is also a professor of law and philosophy at New York University law school, runs a seminar with Dworkin and a number of other legal and political philosophers. In Oxford, there has been a regular seminar which he attends, with Derek Parfit, Joseph Raz, John Finnis, Gerry Cohen and the economist Amartya Sen. I think, however, that a search for origins in Dworkin's case is fruitless. He is a philosopher by nature. By that I mean he goes straight to the problem without relentless enquiry into what other people say. He has an intense concern for the effect of philosophy. He wants what he says to be understood and acted upon. He means what he says, which, extraordinarily, people find idiosyncratic, perhaps particularly in the United Kingdom. An example is the criticism, which is frequently made of Dworkin's model for the ideal judge, whom he calls 'Hercules', that Hercules is really Dworkin himself. But how could this possibly be a criticism? Of course, Dworkin will put into Hercules' mouth what he, Dworkin, thinks Hercules should say. It would be strange if he did *not*. Again, a criticism is made that Dworkin's views are those broadly of the liberal left. That is true, but why is that fact itself a criticism?

Dworkin is not a scholar in the usual sense. You do not find in Dworkin's writings detailed analyses of what other philosophers have said, although there is an impressive breadth of background knowledge ranging through theories of ethics, aesthetics, economics, language and logic. Although he has published prolifically in the past ten years, the best way to make headway with understanding his thoughts is to hear him philosophise in person. He has the style somewhat of the continental café philosophers. He has the extraordinary capacity to deliver a complicated but logically structured argument without recourse to any form of notes. His Maccabean lecture to the British Academy, delivered in 1977, was such a performance. It was well over an hour long and, for you to judge, the resulting lecture is published, practically verbatim, as Chapter 1 of his collection of essays, published in 1985, *A Matter of Principle*.[16]

Let me return to the short and compressed characterisation of Dworkin's thought that I have provided by way of introduction. You will note that I have described his direct concern with 'legal argument'. This concern is prevalent in his work, especially his legal theory, and it is helpful to understand at the outset his intention to cultivate in us an *argumentative* attitude to law. In fact, it is useful for understanding his work to think of him as a lawyer, or a judge, who is busy spelling out all the arguments pertaining to his function. He is different from the ordinary lawyer, however, because he has set himself the task of *fully* justifying all the conceivable arguments. And, on top of that, at the end of the day, he wants the best possible justification for making some decision that affects people. I accept his aim, as you will see throughout this work. To me, any account of law that relegates the question of justification to minor status misses one of the most important points about understanding law.

Accounts of law that underplay or deny the force of justification are perfectly possible. There is no problem in understanding a comparative history of repressive legal systems, in which the justification of the law is absent, for example. But the disconnection between that history and the strong sense in which both you and I understand a lawyer's plea in court is vast. You must ask yourself whether, for you, a satisfactory account of the *nature* of law could possibly be provided solely by a history of repressive legal systems.[17]

Let us keep this picture of legal argument as a central focus of Dworkin's work. It provides a useful angle of comparison with other legal philosophers, some of whom saw themselves as providing only a descriptive account of how social practices just simply happen to be. I shall explore some of these theories in the course of this book.

Dworkin's idea of interpretation is also important. He does not think that we can get very much sense out of just describing 'what law is like'. Our whole perception of all those rules and institutions, including courts and legislatures, police, and so on – what may loosely be described as 'the social practice of law' – must be coloured by our judgment. What we must do is sharpen that judgment. We must try to make 'the best sense' of these social practices. Dworkin develops the idea of interpretation fairly late in the elaboration of his work. But it makes clearer a number of his earlier doctrines, in particular his well-known distinction between rules and principles. The basic idea is simply that you make the best of what you have before you. It is a very simple and appealing idea, I have found, to practising lawyers.

For Dworkin it is a short step from the idea of 'making the best sense' of something to morality. His perspective on law is that of justification. We must interpret the law so as to make the best 'moral' sense of it. In other words, we must always assume when we try to work out what the law requires or permits that it makes *moral* sense. Why? Because it supplies sense to law. What is the point of justifying action in the name of law unless that action has also a moral justification?

And we go from this idea of making moral sense of the law directly to what this 'morality' is. It is the major concern of Dworkin's moral and political theory and rests upon what we might call his foundational principle that people should be treated with equal concern and respect. When we are making sense of law, we must assume that its best sense expresses an equal concern for people.

You should be able to see the critical power this theory has for practice. Which of two rival interpretations of a rule of law is better? For Dworkin, the one that more closely accords with the foundational principle. But, contrary to a popular and wrong understanding of Dworkin, this does not mean that, in order to work out the law, you merely make law into whatever is necessary to treat people as equals.

Why not? If we are allowed to read law as subject to the foundational principle that all people be treated as equals, it seems that almost anything could count as law. This is the thrust of many of my students who say that Dworkin makes the law irredeemably 'subjective'.

Dworkin has detailed answers to this objection. But it is important to see that these answers are not part of his theory. Dworkin thinks that his theory of law is right, which is natural. He offers reasons to support his theory. He looks for criticisms. What he regards as a side issue is the seemingly more abstract and important question of whether any kind of 'objective' argument is possible for law. Instead, he asks you to tell him where he has made mistakes in the arguments. Objectivity involves nothing more startling, in his view, than the possibility of seeking better or best answers. And that does not mean, for him, thundering knockdown arguments.

In fact, Dworkin is pleasingly candid in his approach to methodology. His approach is intuitive and practical, in a thoroughly lawyer-like way. Of course, intuition alone is not enough, as most of us would agree. But Dworkin provides us with many of his intuitive insights, mixed with attempts to explain them in a structured account.

This method bothers some people. Why should we be introduced to another person's intuitions? We either accept them or we do not. We want arguments. But this is too simple. Arguments cause us to change our intuitions; our intuitions cause us to change our arguments. It is a two way process which works and describes the actual arguments that we have in daily life. So it should not appear so strange.

Dworkin's theory is a massive project which he has been developing for over twenty years. It is ambitious. The legal part of it is fairly settled now, with the publication in 1986 of *Law's Empire*. But it is part of his idea that legal and political philosophy – and legal argument – cannot be wholly separated. So it is necessary to keep an eye to his political philosophy and, in particular, his development of the idea of equality. That is still in the stages of formation.

In the light of the general sketch which I have just given, I can now explain some of the terms with which he has become associated. His theory of *discretion* is simply that judges are legally constrained in their exercise of their power of final decision. Even although the existing legal practices might not supply a definitive answer, the judge must nevertheless make a substantive judgment about what decision best, as a matter of equality, *fits* the settled law. So the judge is bound by law and is not permitted to use his power of decision-making in a stronger sense.

In the *hard cases*, which are those where the existing legal practices do not supply a definitive answer, the judge cannot rely on *rules* because, by hypothesis, there are no rules. Instead, he must rely on standards of legal argument which Dworkin calls *principles*, paramount among which, of course, is the foundational principle that people must be treated as equals. Principles, unlike rules, do not apply in an 'all-or-nothing' sense, but require argument and justification of a more extensive, controversial sort.

As a matter of justice, people have *rights* to treatment as equals. That means, for Dworkin, that the foundational principle cannot be compromised. You cannot say: if we end up with most people better off, that would justify our not treating some people as equals. So Dworkin would disallow the pursuit of community goals which overrode these rights to treatment as equals. In other words, to take rights seriously, we must view rights as *trumping* community goals.

We could not interpret our actually existing legal practices so that they accorded with justice as equality in an ideal world. That could not amount to an interpretation of the *law*. But it is true, too, that the best interpretation of the real law could not succeed in showing that all laws were fair, say. A proper interpretation of the law, according to Dworkin, lies in the idea of *integrity*. Through this idea we must personify the law – treat it as having its own integrity – so that it takes on a moral character, one that consistently treats people as equals. Legislative and judicial events of the past relate to decisions of the present by being part of one integral picture: the community's *equal* commitment to its citizens.

Above all, law is an argumentative attitude which rises out of a concern with the extent of the coercive power of the law. 'Law's empire', Dworkin says, is 'defined by attitude'. That attitude '... is constructive: it aims, in the interpretive spirit, to lay principle over practice to show the best route to a better future, keeping the right faith with the past'.[18]

You should see now that, for Dworkin, questions of law are questions of morality about the legal institutions and practices we have. At the same time, his theory is intended to be practical, in the obvious and appealing sense, and it denies any importance in the distinction between the mundane and the abstract.

Legal theory

Dworkin's contribution to jurisprudence in the past twenty years is marked by his sustained criticism of a particular way of viewing law and legal argument. In particular, he is critical of a widely influential idea, known as legal positivism which, briefly, asserts that morality is irrelevant to the identification of law. That doctrine began in Thomas Hobbes[19] and there are contemporary sophisticated forms, those of Hart and Joseph Raz, for example. Dworkin's attack has been too sustained and too powerful for any easy answers. One of his achievements has been his insistence on the *practical* reasons why we should accept legal positivism.

But, we might ask, had no one really thought of the *practical* reasons for adopting one view of law over another? The answer is that some had, but the position is complex and requires some explanation. Long before legal positivism, Aristotle and Aquinas, to name only the most distinguished, asked practical questions about the way we should view law, and they supplied answers. But the legal positivists were just unclear about the matter. There is a distinct ambiguity present in Bentham and this ambiguity continues through other thinkers to Hart. That ambiguity hovers between the following two strands of thought.

First, there is a sense in which some legal positivists intended simply to describe what law is. Law is simply *there*, as a complex of social facts. That may have been the opinion of Jeremy Bentham. It certainly was that of John Austin, his disciple, and, albeit in a highly qualified sense, of the German legal philosopher Hans Kelsen. Hart's brilliant work *The Concept of Law* certainly begins in that way, with its well-known affirmation in the Preface that, among other aims, he intended a 'descriptive sociology' of the law.[20]

That is one strand of legal positivism. It is this sort of idea of law that is behind our comparative account of repressive legal systems. Such an account can, of course, serve practical purposes, such as those of historians, or dictators, or anthropologists in search of differences between legal systems.

The other strand is practical in, I suggest, a more obvious and appealing sense. It is that positivism is a *liberal* doctrine. It is not a coincidence that the growth of positivism paralleled the growth of liberalism in the early nineteenth century. Why was it liberal? The positivists emphasised the point in different ways. Essentially it is that the law must be identifiable by means of clearly identifiable and public criteria to enable the citizen to keep distinct the demands of his conscience and the demands of the state. Hart spoke for this strand of positivism when he said in *The Concept of Law*:

> What surely is most needed in order to make men clear sighted in confronting the official abuse of power, is that they should preserve the sense that the certification of something as legally valid is not conclusive of the question of obedience, and that, however great the aura of majesty or authority which the official system may have, its demands must in the end be submitted to a moral scrutiny.[21]

The idea is explicit in Bentham's distinction between 'expository' and 'censorial' jurisprudence,[22] Austin's claim 'The existence of law is one thing; its merit or demerit is another',[23] and Kelsen's promotion of law as 'science' to counteract tyranny.[24]

Ronald Dworkin's theory of law is a liberal theory, too. It is infused with the liberal idea that the state must protect personal autonomy. But the theory allows the highly abstract and liberal idea of 'the right to be treated with equal concern and respect' to be debated, in the form of different and controversial conceptions of that idea, as a matter of *law*. It is here that Dworkin's theory parts company with positivism. But notice that he nevertheless insists upon the requirement of what he calls the 'articulate consistency' of public officials.[25] This is in part what he means by decisions being made in accordance with principle. And to this extent, his theory shares the public criterion requirement of the positivists.[26]

I believe that positivism can be a good liberal theory, but whether it works depends on the type of community in which it has sufficiently widespread acceptance. Its strong point is to pronounce the limits of state requirements. It tells us where the law 'stops' and 'ideology' starts. So, in a culture where there is less homogeneity of political opinion and where there are irreconcilable ideological or fundamentalist conflicts of view, positivism will be attractive for liberalism. According to positivism, since there can be little controversy about what the state requires, ideology cannot be smuggled within the name of law. In parts of continental Europe, and in Latin America, this feature of positivism is thought to be its virtue.

But the culture of a political community is not necessarily submerged by conflict. The existence of competing ideas and interests can be *part* of a culture. For example, people can unite through an understanding that people can differ in their views. An existing consensus might be that convictions of certain kinds *matter*, say, convictions about democracy, or equality, or rights, *and* that arguments about these issues just happen to be controversial.

I think this more sophisticated homogeneity is true of both the United States and the United Kingdom. It is a good thing. It needs to be protected. It allows for the possibility of a more sophisticated way of viewing law. In communities where people accept that their views compete rather than conflict, legal positivism's stark declaration that law starts where ideology ends is unnecessary.

In the United States, the homogeneity largely arises through a strong history of democracy and through the strong central force in argument of the publicly known and written constitution. In the United Kingdom, sophisticated homogeneity has, perhaps, grown in more homely ways. There is less by way of a publicly understood set of principles regulating the political constitution of the United Kingdom. On the other hand, the culture is less diversified than the United States and there is a strong tradition of tolerance and informed and articulate argument.

Hart has said, and I believe it to be true, that if Dworkin's theory does not succeed in catching on, it will be because people will not accept the idea that there can be right answers to legal questions when there is no means of *showing*, or *demonstrating*, what the right answers are.[27] Dworkin's theory of law must also allow for this possibility because, for him, a legal theory must be 'interpretive' of a prevailing political and legal culture. If it interprets a culture in which people just do not accept that there is competition of principles, only conflict, then positivism might be the only liberal legal theory that can make sense of – be interpretive of – that culture.

But Hart's comment does not amount to a serious criticism. Dworkin's theory better describes the Anglo-American legal and political culture. Indeed, the arguments of descriptive 'fit' that he provides equal, in my view, his arguments of moral substance. My own experience with practising lawyers, and with students, at least in the United Kingdom, is that his theory describes better than any other theory what they actually conceive themselves to be doing.

I suggest that a day in court will convince you if you think otherwise. Let us take the English High Court, although any appeal court in the United States will throw up a situation that is very similar. Two barristers begin the day with various provisions of the Factories Act 1961 before them. In an hour's time they will face each other before a judge. Each will supply an argument, one to support the truth of a proposition that the defendant, in the particular circumstances of the case, had a legal duty to fence dangerous machinery, the other to say that the proposition is false. Each side will have the same cases and will be familiar with their contents. Each knows that the defendant has a right to a fair hearing. Each knows that there is no 'answer' waiting in a statute, or in a case, and that the answer lies in the best interpretation of the statutory provisions and the cases. They know that the judge will try to get the answer 'right'. They know that they and the judge could be mistaken. They believe that what they are doing is not a nonsense. They believe, in advancing their arguments, that these are *legal* arguments.

It is difficult to give a general characterisation of Dworkin's thought. Richard Posner has wondered whether Dworkin is a 'genuine Kantian' or a 'utilitarian of the egalitarian school'.[28] In the idea that people have rights to treatment with equal concern and respect, he *is* Kantian. This very abstract principle in Dworkin's thought asserts the importance of people as ends and not means. It asserts too, I suppose, in the idea of equality, Kant's insistence on the universalisable characteristic of moral rules. But there is little else that shows anything in particular in common between Kant and Dworkin.

He has been described by Neil MacCormick as a 'pre-Benthamite', by which MacCormick meant that Dworkin does not share the modern perspective which distinguishes legal fact from legal value, or, in Bentham's terms, does not insist on the separation of 'expository' from 'censorial' jurisprudence.[29] But there are *some* strains of Bentham. Contrary to a common belief, Dworkin is not wholly dismissive of utilitarianism. Since his political theory relies extensively on the idea of the interpretation of existing political practices, many of which are broadly recognisable as utilitarian, some of his ideas take a background of utilitarianism for granted. Indeed, his central idea of rights depends for its force on its ability to 'trump' background arguments for increasing average utility. But in the ideal world, his abandonment of the idea of welfare as a metric[30] means that Dworkin does not accept utilitarianism, even in the 'egalitarian' form in which he thinks it makes most sense. On the other hand, Bentham's insistence on the importance of a public criterion for law is not far from Dworkin's insistence on publicly articulated principles of official decision-making.

Another philosopher with whom we might hope to spot an affinity is John Stuart Mill. Dworkin's use of the idea of the equality of individuals in the construction of a private sphere of resources publicly protected leaves us with what, at first sight, is a Millian conception. On closer inspection, it turns out that Dworkin's idea of individuality is less private than Mill's. The private sphere is 'parametered' (his word) by justice which is a matter of the public domain and a person's life is to be critically measured by his acting within the parameters.[31] Thus Plato's idea of the 'just man', as opposed to the 'just system', is closer to Dworkin than to Mill.[32] On the other hand, it is a Millian idea that people ought not to be able to have a 'second' count in the utilitarian calculus, when that has an effect on other people's lives.[33] That is very close to Mill's idea of other-regarding action. But Mill was, after all, a welfare utilitarian, and since, as we shall see in Chapter 10, Dworkin abandons welfare as a metric of a just distribution, he is clearly not a utilitarian of the Millian sort.

But these comparisons are unhelpful. Dworkin does not fit into an orthodox category. His theory of law is radical in that it sees legal argument primarily about rights yet conservative in seeing such argument as constrained by history. He is libertarian both in valuing ambition and asserting a right to pornography, yet socialist in believing that no person has a right to a greater share of resources than anyone else. In particular, he advocates a system which would tax people on resources they accumulate solely through their talent alone, as opposed to the exercise of their ambition. Although he makes extensive use of modern economic thinking, he abandons the orthodox criterion of measurement by welfare, for a metric of resources. Finally, he is neither an liberal 'atomist' nor a 'communitarian', thinking that the distinction does not make more than superficial sense.

It is necessary now to turn from background to the detail of Dworkin's legal and political theories. I have said that his legal theory is distinctive both in its attack on legal positivism, as he interprets it, and its merger of legal argument with political and moral argument. I begin with a chapter on his methodology, dealing with his important approach to the idea of understanding certain human practices, in particular, creative practices, and his idea of 'interpretive' concepts.

I then turn to the positive legal theory which finds its expression in the idea of integrity. I examine the idea, especially as it relates to his theory of adjudication, and in Chapter 4, entitled 'Integrity and Community', I examine the link between legal and political obligation, which Dworkin casts in the form of fraternal association, or community. Then, because of the prominence that has been accorded Dworkin's attacks on legal positivism, I examine theories of positivism and his attack on a version of that theory which he calls, in *Law's Empire*, the 'plain fact' view of law. In fact, a chronological understanding of Dworkin begins here, because he developed his theory, in its early stages, by a close criticism of this legal theory, in particular that of Hart. But I have chosen this order of study simply because his attacks on positivism represent only a negative aspect of his overall legal theory.

I consider positivism for another reason, too. The 'plain fact' view of law is one that many people are disposed to accept. The arguments that are used by Dworkin to attack it, accordingly, need careful examination. Linked to this discussion is an examination of the alternative ways in which a positivist might account for the idea of a difficult or 'hard' case in the law.

Although it is necessary to know a certain amount about his political theory for the purposes of his legal theory, it certainly is not necessary to know it all. I have left discussion of this part of the theory to the final chapters. I should say, however, that the idea of the equality of 'resources' has consequences for some legal cases, particularly the economic analyses of negligence and nuisance, and the central idea of the impartiality of political principles has consequences for cases involving matters of personal morality.

The final three chapters introduce more directly what might best be called his 'pure' political theory. The central idea is that of equality of 'concern and respect'. I have reserved two topics of importance for Chapter 9. One is his attack on the economic analysis of law as espoused, in particular, by Richard Posner. The attack Dworkin makes is an obvious one in terms of his adjudicative theory. I have included the debate for an important reason, however, which is to introduce concepts of economics and the important distinction between resources and welfare in the context of the idea of equality. This distinction is central to the final two chapters. I discuss that distinction and Dworkin's affirmation of equality of resources on the ground that only equality of resources mirrors the idea of liberty which, he says, is only another aspect of equality.

In the final chapter, I examine Dworkin's justification for the foundation of the principles of political liberalism. The link with legal reasoning is best understood through the example of state intervention in matters of personal morality, such as sexual morality. In hard cases, the best sense, in terms of justice, is applied to legal practices. That sense is, for Dworkin, supplied by his political theory. It envisages a set of political principles which, flowing from each person's set of moral convictions, provides a principle of toleration towards other people's different moral convictions.

Notes

1. 'Judicial Discretion' (1963) 60 *Journal of Philosophy*, 624–38.
2. See, 'Does Law have a Function? A Comment on the Two-Level Theory of Decision' (1965) 74 *Yale Law Journal* 640–51. This was previously printed under the title 'Wasserstrom: The Judicial Decision' (1964) 75 *Ethics* 47; 'Philosophy, Morality and Law – Observations prompted by Professor Fuller's Novel Claim' (1965) 113 *University of*

Pennsylvania Law Review 668–90; and 'The Elusive Morality of Law' (1965) 10 *Vanderbilt Law Review* 631–9. (This last is a capsule form of 'Philosophy, Morality and Law'.)

3. *Philosophical Review* vol.64 (1955) 3–32. Also in *Theories of Ethics*, ed. Foot, Oxford (1967), p. 144.

4. 'The Model of Rules' (1967) 35 *University of Chicago Law Review* 14–46. This article is reprinted as 'Is Law a System of Rules?' in Summers, ed. *Essays in Legal Philosophy* (1968) Blackwell at p. 25 and as Chapter 2, 'The Model of Rules I', in *Taking Rights Seriously* (1977) Duckworth at p.14, and also appears in Dworkin, ed. *The Philosophy of Law* (1977) Oxford, at p.38.

5. See *Hart* by Neil MacCormick (1981) Edward Arnold, p. 19.

6. Penguin Books.

7. (1964) Penguin.

8. *Oxford Essays in Jurisprudence, 1st Series* (1961) Oxford.

9. See Llewellyn, *The Common Law Tradition* (1960) Boston, Toronto, Little Brown.

10. See *Columbia Law Review* 19 (1929) 113; and 29 (1929) 285. Also 'Legal Rules: Their Function in the Process of Decision' 79 *University of Pennsylvania Law Review* (1931) 833. See also his *Administrative Justice and the Supremacy of Law*, acknowledged by Hart in his *The Concept of Law* as 'the most illuminating general discussion' of the character and relationships between different forms of legal control.

11. See their *The Legal Process* (1958).

12. See 71 *Harvard Law Review* (1958) at 598 for Hart's article, and at 630 for Fuller's reply.

13. See Williams' article, entitled 'The Idea of Equality' in *Philosophy, Politics and Society second series*, ed. Laslett and Runciman (1962) p.110 and his essay on utilitarianism in *Utilitarianism: For and Against* by Smart and Williams, (1977) CUP. There are some early remarks in Williams *Morality* (1972) Cambridge, too, slightly predating Dworkin's work on objectivity. See pp.28–51, particularly, on cultural relativity, pp.34–9, where he claims that relativism is internally inconsistent in using a *non*-relative sense of 'right' to support the truth of its claims.

14. He is thought by many to have solved the problems raised by what is known as the 'causal' theory of knowledge. See Evans *Collected Papers* (1985) Oxford.

15. In 'No Right Answer?', in *Law, Morality and Society: Essays in Honour of H.L.A. Hart*, ed. Hacker and Raz (1977) Oxford, Dworkin thanks Gareth Evans for his contribution in the seminars they held together on objectivity in 1975 in Oxford.

16. 'Political Judges and the Rule of Law', *Maccabean Lecture in Jurisprudence* (1978) 64 *Proceedings of the British Academy*. Reprinted in *A Matter of Principle*, Chapter 1, at pp.9–32.

17. Here is a striking case. Imagine describing a particular scene of torture from every point of view but the view that it is unjustified. It is possible to do that. Someone might aim to discriminate between the different methods of torture used from century to century. But imagine teaching someone what torture *was* simply by handing them the book. All

he will have is a manual on torture. See Finnis, *Natural Law and Natural Rights*, (1980) Clarendon, who thinks that it is the question of justification that distinguishes Dworkin's theory from theories of 'positivism' such as Hart and Raz. For this reason, Dworkin's attack on their theories 'miscarries'. His theory is a 'normative theory of law, offering guidance to the judge as to his judicial duty; theirs is a descriptive theory, offered to historians to enable a discriminating history of legal systems to be written', p. 21.

18. *Law's Empire*, p. 413.
19. Hobbes, *Leviathan*.
20. Hart, *The Concept of Law* (1961) Oxford, Preface.
21. *The Concept of Law*, p. 206.
22. See Bentham, *An Introduction to the Principles of Morals and Legislation*, 1970, ed. Hart and Burns, Athlone, pp. 293–4.
23. See Austin, *The Province of Jurisprudence Determined*, ed. Hart, 1954, Lecture V, p.184.
24. See Kelsen, *General Theory of Law and State*, 1945, trans. Wedberg: 'In social and especially in legal science, there is still no influence to counteract the overwhelming interest that those residing in power, as well as those craving for power, have in a theory pleasing to their wishes, that is, in a political ideology ... The ideal of an objective science of law and State, free from all political ideologies, has a better chance for recognition in a period of social equilibrium' xvii.
25. See *Taking Rights Seriously* (1978) Duckworth, p. 162.
26. See, for example, *Taking Rights Seriously*, p. 162: 'The constructive model [of judicial reasoning] ... demands that decisions taken in the name of justice must never outstrip an official's ability to account for these decisions in a theory of justice ... It demands that we act on principle rather than on faith ... It presupposes that articulated consistency, decisions in accordance with a program that can be made public and followed until changed, is essential to any conception of justice.' The idea is an essential part, I think, of his idea of integrity. See, for example, *Law's Empire*, at p. 413, where he sums up his views about the argumentative nature of law. It is clear that legal argument must draw from a set of *public* principles: 'Law's empire is defined by attitude ... It is an interpretive , self–reflective attitude addressed to politics in the broadest sense. It is a protestant attitude that makes each citizen responsible for imagining what his society's public commitments to principle are ...'
27. See Hart, *Essays in Jurisprudence and Philosophy* (1983) Oxford, 139–40: '... if I may venture a prophecy, I think the chief criticism that it will attract will be of his insistence that, even if there is no way of demonstrating which of two conflicting solutions, both equally well warranted by the existing law, is correct, still there must always be a single correct answer awaiting discovery.'
28. See p. 411, n. 15 of Dworkin's *A Matter of Principle* (1985) for the reference.
29. See Chapter 7 of MacCormick's *Legal Right and Social Democracy* (1982) Oxford: Clarendon Press. Dworkin's reply to this article, in *Ronald Dworkin and Contemporary Jurisprudence*, ed. Cohen (1984) Duckworth,

278–81 is helpful for a restatement of his views on the idea of constructive theorising.

30. See Chapter 10.

31. See Chapters 10 and 11.

32. See Plato's definition of justice in *The Republic*, Chapter 14, as a virtue in the individual, by which he means that justice is an internal order of the soul which will bring about right behaviour. The connection with Plato's view of justice is one which Dworkin suggests in his Tanner lectures on the foundations of liberalism but it is an indirect one, linked through Dworkin's idea of a person's living a 'critical' life. See later, Chapter 10.

33. See Chapter 9, 'Equality and utilitarianism: double counting'.

2

The idea of interpretation

Many of the developments in Dworkin's approach to legal and political philosophy, notably the unfolding of the idea of interpretation, occurred after some of his important theses had become well-known. A helpful understanding of his work is achieved by first taking into account his very important idea of the 'interpretive' understanding of social phenomena in general and then applying that idea to the particular case of law. The interpretation of law, for him, means seeing law as an integrated and coherent body of doctrine.

Interpretation

Dworkin's analysis of the idea of interpretation places his earlier writings in a clearer light. It purports to show what is fundamentally wrong with what he calls the 'plain fact' approach.[1] The analysis represents a breakthrough in legal philosophy. It is an approach sensitive to the difficulties posed in understanding law by the presence of the twin bogeymen of 'objectivity' and 'subjectivity', the special problems of which are examined in Chapter 6. Dworkin's conclusions can be presented as a synthesis of each idea, for interpretation clearly combines elements of each.

It is, however, more rigorous, and more helpful, to regard the idea of interpretation as a different form of social understanding altogether. The ideas of 'objectivity' and 'subjectivity' have done a lot of work in philosophy in general but, unfortunately, they have done it for different people and for different purposes. The result has been that any use of these terms, unless carefully defined, is unhelpfully vague.

The major idea is that interpretation aims at understanding some pre-interpretive social data in the 'best possible light' and that, for law, a theory should strive to make the 'best *moral* sense' of legal phenomena. But this is leaping ahead. What is the problem? What are we doing when we try to work out what law is? We can imagine all sorts of motivation. We have been asked to provide an hour-long talk to a women's institute entitled 'What law is'. Or, we might have been asked to address a group of Marxist students on the same subject. Or, we may just want to satisfy ourselves, from a purely self-interested point of view, on what we are permitted or required to do by law. Or, we may want to know what law is with a view to considering how it fits in, or could contribute to, a more just society. There are all sorts of reason. Even just unanalysed 'interest' is enough.

The question is where should a person start? One response might be that you should begin law school. But that is not wholly satisfactory, for problems about what law is remain, even given acquaintance with a large number of laws. The most acute problems for lawyers arise in the areas of apparent overlap and disjoint between moral questions and legal questions, and in important areas of constitutional law where often the law seems to 'run out'. The question 'What is law?' is notoriously not fully answered by familiarity with legal argument. It is the same with morality. The question 'What is morality?' is not answered by a feeling of relative confidence in encountering moral questions. If you ask yourself that question, you are bothered that just understanding your daily moral dealings does not supply an answer.

Many people would say that the last person to tell you what 'law' was would be a lawyer. Lawyers have a vested interest in obscuring the workings of their trade. In any case, what lawyers do is not the 'real' law. People often advocate being 'realistic' in a search for an answer to the question. They advocate a 'roll up your sleeves and go out and look' approach. Can we do that? Let us examine a policeman questioning a black person in a council estate. I see a man in a blue uniform bullying a black person. Do I need to know any more? Our understanding of law cannot *begin* here, at least. I need to know what a policeman is and what is the extent of his powers, which will require some knowledge of the court system, the system of sanctions and the system of legislation. An easy way to this conclusion is as follows. How would I distinguish the policeman from an imposter, dressed in a police uniform, intent on seeking some sort of retribution? I need some knowledge of the rules by which a policeman is invested with legal status.

What happens when we get down to finding out what the law is in this way? We end up with a set of rules and procedures, many of which relate to the regulation of everybody's behaviour in some way. Many of these are written down on paper and are described in books. Reference to these rules and procedures are the daily stuff of courtroom occurrences, which are in turn invested with legal status. It may be that, after analysis, it is more sensible to turn our attention to the words that are used to define the rules and procedures, which in turn appear to define what is a properly legal decision or action. Our grandly empirical approach into the council estate ends up instead in a plethora of words.

Can we just simply *stipulate* what we believe law to be? We will just set out our beliefs about law, that it is, for example, represented by the policeman's knock on the door, and give that as our lecture. But this will not do at all. If it is your stipulation, you cannot possibly be wrong. It is yours and so why should it be of any use to anyone else? After all, they want to know what law *is*, not what you have just stipulated it to be.

This is a simple point. Your stipulation will only be of interest to another if it matches at least something similar in that other's experience. The point can be made abundantly clear by your lecture consisting only of an assertion that law is 'making leather sandals'. No one would know what was going on. People could reasonably ask what leather sandal making had to do with law. At the very least, people would say, law has to do with policemen, rules, prisons, courts, legislatures and so on, and they would want to know the connection. There is that much in common, and probably a good deal more.[2]

To the person who says, as Humpty-Dumpty said, 'a word means anything you want it to mean', the answer is 'not quite'. Even where we stipulate meanings as in a wartime code, for example, that stipulation must be translatable into something *someone* understands.

Would a dictionary help? Notoriously not. We know the type of schoolboy debate on justice in which each protagonist quotes different dictionary meanings. The *Oxford English Dictionary*, for example, gives 'giving each his due' and 'fairness' as alternative definitions. Each one suggests a vast array of different arguments, different in profound and difficult ways. (We might look to Aristotle for the first and Rawls for the second, for example.) But the dictionary gives us no guide at all. Why? Because it simply records how people *in fact* use the word. The women's institute, or the Marxist students, are not looking for dictionary definitions. They know, in this simple sense, how to use the word 'law'.

But, of course, we can make ourselves and other people *more* aware of the way we understand language which expresses the law. We could, therefore, use the dictionary as a start in this direction. We might follow up all the words that relate to law, like 'obligation' and 'police' and 'courts' and 'rule'. Then, we could test all the possible uses of these words, trying them in different sentences and different contexts. We could also contrast law-related words with other kinds of words that appear in the same sorts of contexts as these words, such as 'morals', or 'custom'. In this sort of project, we will be refining our sense of what amounts to correct and incorrect use of language.

Good examples can be drawn from one of the masters of this kind of approach, Herbert Hart. Our perception of our use of law-related language such as 'being under obligation' is sharpened by his pointing out that the sort of situation to which it refers is different from the situation properly described as one where a person is 'obliged' to do something.[3] This kind of process of analysis is very useful. It delves deeply into the linguistic practices that we already have, and so it can have the satisfying result of telling us, as so much philosophical thought does, what, in one sense, we already know.

But there are drawbacks to this approach. It is parasitic entirely upon how things actually are between us. That is, it aims at securing agreement. There is a student in my classes who, each year, cannot see the difference between the use of the phrases 'being under an obligation' and 'being obliged'. He fails in his ability to discriminate among the linguistic practices we share.

But there is another student who makes a different point. He appreciates the difference in our linguistic practices but he says something else. He is unwilling to say that law is fundamentally different from naked coercion. He is not keen to affirm that it has any connection with the idea of obligation. He will produce an argument, say, a Marxian one, that law only *appears* to have legitimacy because a dominant class of people has encouraged such a view to further its own economic interest.

This sort of argument cannot be met by citing language. It makes a point beyond that of showing our agreement in linguistic practice. It is *most* significant that Hart, whose theory is central to some of the debates examined in this book, has recognised the serious limitations of this form of approach in an admission in the Preface to his book of essays, published in 1983, entitled *Essays in Jurisprudence and Philosophy*.

> The methods of linguistic philosophy which are neutral between moral and political principles and silent about different points of view which might endow one feature rather than another of legal phenomena with significance ... are not suitable for resolving or clarifying those controversies which arise, as many of the central problems of legal philosophy do, from the divergence between partly overlapping concepts reflecting a divergence of basic point of view or values or background theory, or which arise from conflict or incompleteness of legal rules. For such cases what is needed is first, the identification of the latent conflicting points of view which led to the choice of formation of divergent concepts, and secondly, reasoned argument directed to establishing the merits of conflicting theories, divergent concepts or rules, or to showing how these could be made compatible by some suitable restriction of their scope.[4]

What are we left with? Dworkin suggests a new approach, one which transcends the shared meanings of law-related terms. This he calls the 'interpretive' approach. It is, in a nutshell, that we should 'make the best sense' of all those things that we call, in some relatively uncontroversial way, 'law'. This approach gives us the freedom to say what we like about law without being pulled up by a stern reminder that we are not using law-related language correctly. The Marxian student is now permitted to say that, despite there being a difference in use between 'being under an obligation' and 'being obliged', the distinction has *no significance*, in a proper understanding of law. That freedom comes with a sting, however. We must have an argument about what is the best way to understand what we commonly refer to as law. But before we come to that, it is necessary to explore some distinctions.

Interpretation versus descriptivity and 'normativity'

Let us first contrast the ideas of description and 'normativity'. The question is whether we can *describe* things. I think it is clear that we can. The description of occurrences that are known by observation – 'empirically' known – is the most obvious sort. We can describe the chairs or blackboards in the lecture theatre or the style and colour of the lawyer's gown, or the latest model Ford car, or the weather, or the shape and colour of a person's face.

Normative statements have a different sort of character, which is to ask us to do something. They have a different purpose from descriptive statements. They tell us what we should have done, or what we ought to do. A normative statement may, for example, tell us about a possible utopia, not existing in present society, but one which we should, perhaps, attempt to bring about. Or it may be a statement of law or morality, expressed as a conclusion about our own, or others', acts. Normative statements would include exhortations to universal vegetarianism, or the abolition of personal property and so on.

But descriptive statements do not apply only to the present and past, or only to empirical concepts, and normative statements do not apply only to the future or the past. We can describe things that will exist or that do not exist, such as cars that run by nuclear fusion, or colonies on Mars, without exhortation or approval or disapproval. And, of course, we can make normative statements about existing things, say, when we condemn or support the current arrangements for private health care, or the political system of apartheid.

Dworkin's idea of interpretation is not intended to dispense with these ideas of descriptivity and normativity. Rather, he wishes us to accept the idea that it is in the nature of some concepts that they are not fully understood unless in an interpretive way. They are concepts which need to be invested with some meaning that a simple description cannot supply. Normative statements, on the other hand, because they may only refer to non-existing states of affairs, do not invest existing things with point. Crudely, the thing to be interpreted is nevertheless a *thing*.

The quickest way to interpretive concepts is through the idea of something 'having a point'. Note that we can describe a practice without making any statement about the point or purpose of the practice. Thus a solely descriptive account of playing chess might take a number of forms, say, at its lowest, 'the pushing of pieces of wood over a board' or, the more sophisticated 'the moving of pieces of wood in accordance with a particular set of rules'. A description such as this tells us that this is chess, rather than say, draughts, but stops short of describing what many of us might consider to be some vital features of the game.

Do we fall short of a 'true' description here? Is more needed? What extra ingredients would be required to make the description of 'the game of chess' an appropriate, or 'true' one? What would satisfy people? If I provided the details of the rules and then said that the point of the game was to win, many people would agree. But I could, as people do, go further and say that the game was an intellectual one that required only intellectual strategies, and not ones such as causing an opponent to lose through upsetting him by wearing an obviously false beard, for example. Or, I could say that the point of chess is to develop the players' intellectual powers and that winning was only incidental to that purpose. I could offer many descriptions, in other words, of the 'true' point of chess.

Dworkin does not analyse the idea of description to any great depth. For him, I think, it refers to a level of description which incurs relatively little controversy. He provides an example of a social practice of courtesy in which hats are doffed to social superiors. It is clear that this 'pre-interpretive' data *can* be understood as a matter of description because it is uncontroversially held to be correct. In other words, for the society in which the practice occurs, it is simply understood that hats should be doffed to superiors. When Dworkin concedes that even this pre-interpretive data is itself subject to interpretation, he makes it clear that, for interpretive concepts, the distinction between description and interpretation relates primarily to the *degree* of acceptance.[5] It is quite clear that Dworkin has no views such as, for example, that description refers to 'brute' facts, namely facts which stand apart from us 'out there' in the world somewhere.[6] We can draw a distinction, readily apparent in ordinary discourse, between describing something and ascribing to that thing a point.

When it is pushed away from the 'description of brute fact', description becomes closer to the idea of 'point'. It is difficult to give a complete description of the game of chess without reference to some point, say, that it is a game (which, in turn, is a portmanteau word for a number of 'points'). Can we really 'describe' a piece of abstract art, say, by Mondrian, as 'a rectangle divided into four white smaller rectangles (of precise dimensions) and two red squares (of precise dimensions) by vertical and horizontal black lines? There is a very significant sense in which this kind of description is banal because it makes no attempt to ascribe point. It would be going too far, though, to say that this kind of description *cannot* be made. It may be sufficient for two people, uninterested in anything other than identification, say, where they have to collect the painting for delivery.

Here we come to the most difficult aspect of interpretation. This is that the idea of interpretation is, as Dworkin puts it, an interpretive idea itself. Put in terms of point, it is a matter open for interpretation whether a 'thing' has point or not, quite apart from the consideration of what that point is. So people might reasonably differ as to whether a Mondrian painting may be given the above description, or whether a game such as chess has any point, or even whether law must have a point.

In other words, the reason description seems to merge into interpretation once we abandon the idea of some sort of 'brute' fact out there in the world somewhere, is that the distinction itself is one that requires an interpretive explanation. A demand for a more concrete way of drawing the distinction can only be met by saying that the demand itself must have point.

We should now turn to the question of the relationship between *interpretation* and normativity. They are presumably alike in the following way. If we interpret something, we recommend or endorse a particular understanding of that thing. We do not merely record some observation we have made. We are 'offering an interpretation', one that we are prepared to encourage others to accept. On the other hand, a 'purely' normative statement may be made which does not refer to an understanding of a 'thing'. The best example may be drawn from law. It is possible to make an interpretation of the law but at the same time say that the law is not as it should be. A anti-abortionist may interpret the law so as to agree that it provides for legal abortions in a certain category of case and, at the same time, urge that the law 'ought to be changed'. Or a judge may decide that the best interpretation of the common law he can produce is one which does not produce the 'best' result. He may reluctantly conclude that nevertheless this is what the law is, but that the law ought to be changed.[7]

It is the idea of a 'thing' or activity to be interpreted that is important. Take, for example, Hart's theory of law. It is sometimes taken as providing both a description of a modern municipal legal system ('an essay in descriptive sociology') as well as a *normative* account of how law should be. It is thought to provide, in other words, a justification of the way things actually are, by way of an endorsement of its description of law as centrally the union of 'primary' and 'secondary' rules.[8]

According to this theory, the primary rules are rules of obligation

and the secondary rules are those rules concerned with the primary
rules, chiefly through their conferring various kinds of *powers*. What
Hart really gives, in *Law's Empire*'s terms, is an exhaustive account of
the pre-interpretive model for law. He *then* considers whether it is
preferable to restrict that model to cases of morally acceptable rules
(what he calls the 'narrow conception' of law[9]) and he concludes, on
normative grounds, that it is not.

Note that one of the aims of Hart's theory is to preserve the
distinction between a person's moral conscience and the demands
made on him in the name of law.[10] I think it is wrong to suppose that
Hart's aim here is normative and not interpretive. Let us imagine that
his theory of law in which, in his words, the 'key to jurisprudence' lay
in the 'union of primary and secondary rules' is a special set of
measures, a 'package', invented to enable men to live in a civilised way
in society. Perhaps we could think of this package of measures as we
might regard an inventor who makes something entirely new which
makes life easier or more pleasant. It would then make sense to
encourage members of other societies, say, societies composed of
extreme religious fundamentalists, to adopt the social device, for the
supposed civilising reasons contained in the device (in Hart's case, the
preservation of individual moral judgment against the incursions of the
State).

But the inventor and the jurist are different. The inventor is not
selling a version, as it were, of something. The 'thing' is new. But Hart
recommends a version of *law*. He does this by investing that idea with
a particular point, located in the generic ideas of clarity and objectivity.
His endorsement of this version has a strongly moral quality, but this is
the result of his *interpretation* of law.

The thing interpreted

Let us now examine Dworkin's analysis of interpretation. The
essential idea in interpretation is making 'the best' of something that it
can be, and this very abstract idea is to be applied to the idea of law. A
number of ways can be used to describe the idea of 'making the best' of
something. I have suggested that the quickest way to the idea is
through the idea of a thing 'having point', for example. But another
metaphor is that of 'placing a thing in its best light', whereby we
assume that 'the thing' has some point and we examine it as
thoroughly as we can to see what is the most sensible way of viewing it.

Why would anyone wish to place something in its best light? Try to
see it in terms of point. Someone produces an argument which you
think is a bad one. You want to avoid the accusation that, in
representing that argument so that you can show how poor it is, you
have missed its point. In order to destroy the argument, in other

words, you have, as it were, to be 'fair' to it. Then you are protected against the accusation. If, when you make the other side's argument the best it can be, it stands on its own as a very poor argument, then you have given the best argument of all for showing that it *is* poor.

Everything is contained in the idea of 'best', and this may strike some people as begging the question. But that would be wrong. It is simply the case that we do understand what poor interpretations are ('*Hamlet* is a play about courtly manners', for example, or 'Beethoven's fifth symphony consists of some rollicking good tunes but not much besides') and that good interpretations are to be preferred to interpretations of this sort. A common objection is that sometimes we should try to place things, not in the best light, but in poorer light, or even in the worst light. Sometimes, we may think that the sensible way to portray something is to paint the worst possible picture of it. But there is nothing in the idea of the best interpretation of the rise of Adolf Hitler, for example, that compels us to show him as morally good. Painting the best possible picture of him is compatible with showing him to be the worst possible monster.[11] In the requisite sense of 'best', the best interpretation of Hitler would not be achieved by the suppression of facts, or only understanding events from his point of view, or by confining interpretation only to historical materials in the possession, say, of the *Wehrmacht*.

But it is a difficult and controversial question what the criteria of interpretation of historical events are, and Dworkin, who argues that 'best' in the case of the interpretation of law means 'morally best', does not enter that debate. There is no difficulty in saying that a better interpretation of historical events is to be preferred to a worse one. That only sounds tautological because the idea of what is best is so abstract.

Dworkin's idea that interpretation requires placing things – or activities – in their best light is so abstract that it should command fairly widespread acceptance. People do, after all, have their own views about what 'the best light' is and so they do not have to agree on any particular interpretation. The abstract nature of interpretation is appealing because it abstracts from the substantial arguments about what is the best interpretation and shows that two participants, offering rival interpretations, can have a plateau of agreement, namely, that they are arguing about what amounts to the best interpretation.[12]

Interpretation and law

How does interpretation apply to social practices? Dworkin says that we may understand a social practice in three analytical attitudes, the pre-interpretive, the interpretive and the post-interpretive. These important ideas can be described by the use of a simple example. Take the pre-interpretive attitude first. Imagine a society in which there is a social practice requiring that men doff their hats to women. In this society, no attitude is struck towards the value of the rule. No point is ascribed to it. Members of the society just accept it in an unquestioning way. It is not just that men doff their hats out of habit. It is not that they merely do it 'as a rule'. It is rather that there is an actual rule of courtesy that requires it.[13]

An 'interpretive' step may now be described. Analytically, the pre-interpretive and interpretive stages may be distinguished as two ways of understanding the existing social practice, or rule. We can now imagine that, after a while, people begin to ask questions about this practice of courtesy and what the reasons are for conforming to it. It is easy to imagine, too, that people will differ about their understanding of it and will argue among themselves about what the practice requires in particular cases.

There will therefore be two parts to the introduction of this 'interpretive' phase, one where there is an attitude of questioning, and giving of 'meaning', to the social rule of courtesy, and a second where the question arises about the extension of this meaning to particular cases. We can test these distinctions by reference to games, such as cricket, in which a description of the rules is distinguishable from a discussion of its point (is it fun? does it test skill? is it competitive? is it educational? does it make money?), which in turn is distinguishable from the way particular rules are to be interpreted (does 'bowling' include throwing? or underarm bowling? and so on).

The analytical move from the pre-interpretive to the interpretive phase is a significant one in legal philosophy. It says that a necessary part of understanding law is to understand its point. Dworkin's move can be usefully likened to the move in Hart's *The Concept of Law* from the pre-legal to the legal society. For Hart, the analytical, 'pre-legal', society consisted of the bare rules of obligation alone. It was only by the addition of the secondary, or power-conferring, rules that the functional apparatus of the modern municipal legal system could be characterised.

This interpretive account rescues Hart from the charge that his theory is descriptive only. The secondary rules prevent 'vendettas' (Hart's word) by creating a court structure, allow for progress by creating a legislature, and make life relatively secure for the citizen by creating criteria of identification of law in the rules of recognition.[14] Hart's two-fold criticism of the command theory, that it ignored the character of rules and largely ignored the function of power-conferring rules, resulted in the positing of some point to the description. But it relied on the empirical fact identification of reasons for regarding certain criteria as determining what the law was. It could not, therefore, go further than merely pointing to the empirical facts that officials accepted certain reasons as so determinative of what the law was.

Here we must be careful. Hart's account is a good one of the pre-interpretive stage, because it is an account which people would (and do) accept as a fairly accurate description of law. But it is interpretive, too, in the sense I have just outlined, and it may then be thought to be an unsuitable candidate for providing a pre-interpretive account.

I do not think there is a difficulty, however. Dworkin's theory of interpretation requires that there be something 'there' to be interpreted and Hart's account, in what might be called its descriptive aspect, can do that. What is special about Hart's account is that it appears only to offer a description of the way law is, and this description is immediately, if only superficially, appealing.

But Dworkin does not hold any view that there are facts 'out there' (say, expressed in characteristic uses of law-related language) by virtue of which a descriptive account of law is true. He instead distinguishes, as between the pre-interpretive and the interpretive stage, between two *levels* of interpretation. The pre-interpretive stage constitutes the formal structure against which interpretive substantive judgments must be made. That way of looking at things is not contradictory or even odd, as, for example, Stanley Fish has claimed.[15]

The drawing of a distinction between substance and form (or, as Dworkin calls it, 'fit') is itself an interpretive act, one which, I think, is implicit in Hart's account. This is what I meant when I suggested that Hart might have had moral reasons for drawing a distinction between questions of legal validity and morality.

Let us test this idea further, because it causes enormous difficulties for understanding Dworkin. Dworkin steers between the pure objectivity of the 'out there' approach to law, the approach which no one would accept without reasons at least of the Hartian sort, and the pure subjectivity of the sort that ignores completely what people regard as law. It helps to distinguish here between questions concerning the nature of law, which I think might be ascribed to Hart, and professional questions, often described as the question 'of justification',[16] with which Dworkin is concerned.

Hart's answer to the question of *nature* ('What is law? – the union of primary and secondary rules') suits the pre-interpretive attitude because it describes a consensus of thinking about law. Dworkin's theory requires an interpretive understanding of this answer, at this level. But we have to bear in mind, too, that his theory will also require an interpretive understanding of particular laws, in particular legal systems, where those laws are identifiable by some local test. Hart provides a method for the identification of such laws. You look to what he calls the 'rule of recognition'[17] – the identifying rule – and see whether it validates any purported rule. If it does, that rule is a valid legal rule in that legal system.

Interpretation will thus occur both at the level of questions about the nature of law and the level of questions about professional problems. Hart's theory is thus of use as a basis for Dworkin to make interpretive claims and it is open to Hart to disagree at the interpretive level as to which account, his or Dworkin's, is correct.

Let us return to the analytical tool of imagining the pre-interpretive stage of the social practice of courtesy. We now imagine that after a while people begin to ask questions about the practice of courtesy, about what the reasons are for conforming to it. It is easy to imagine, too, that people will differ about their understanding of it and will argue among themselves about what the practice requires in cases of hat-doffing that are not so clear.

There will therefore be two parts to the introduction of this 'interpretive' phase, one where there is an attitude of questioning, and a giving of 'meaning', to the social rule of hat-doffing, and a second where there is consideration of what the rule requires in difficult cases. For example, some people might take the view that hat-doffing to women shows respect for the 'weaker' sex, while others believe that it shows a more genuine respect for the ability of women to bear children.

The second interpretive stage occurs when people extend their understandings of the meaning of the rule to unclear cases. Those who think that the rule embodies respect for the 'weaker' sex may not think that hat-doffing by men is necessary when a woman is doing a 'man's' job, or when the woman is a lesbian, for example. Someone who thinks that hat-doffing is a mark of respect for people who have the capacity to bear children may not think the rule should extend to a spinster or the wife of a childless couple.

At this point, Dworkin posits the existence of a third, 'post-interpretive' phase. This will be where, as he says, interpretation 'folds back into itself' and has the effect of changing the original rule. So, in our example, some people, perhaps through argument and discussion, will come to have an altered perception of the original rule and this altered perception will lead them to modify it. Those who saw the rule as marking a respect for the 'weaker' sex may now see the rule in terms of respect for those who have served society in some deferential but faithful way. They may now want to see a change to a rule so that it includes a smaller class of women (exclusion of lesbians, say), but a wider class of people (including old servants, say). Those who saw the rule as marking a respect for child-bearing ability may now see the rule as one that should recognise certain other abilities, such as the ability to contribute to society in other ways, say, through leadership. These people might take the view that the rule only requires hat-doffing to women who have actually borne children but extends to the more important political leaders, for example.

Dworkin says that the interpretation of social practices is like 'artistic' interpretation, which interprets the thing – the work of art – created by people and separate from them. He distinguishes it from 'scientific' interpretation, which interprets things *not* created by people. Nor does he think it is like 'conversational' interpretation, which interprets what people say. He says that artistic interpretation is 'creative' interpretation because 'A participant interpreting a social practice ... proposes value for the practice by describing some scheme of interests or goals or principles the practice can be taken to serve or express or exemplify.'[18]

The contrast with scientific and conversational interpretation is instructive. The important distinction appears to be that neither of these two sorts of interpretation requires proposing human interests or goals or principles. That is clear in the case of scientific interpretation. I think it is right, too, to say that it is the scientific conception of interpretation that some positivists would endorse. Scientifically interpreting the law is interpreting what the plain facts of law 'out there' are.[19]

The case of conversational interpretation is more difficult because the 'thing' to be interpreted is not clearly independent of the purposes and practices of language. In order to interpret what a person means we have to make sense of the human purposes inherent in language. But it is unlike artistic interpretation because the interpreter is not so free to place his own construction upon what the speaker said. The criterion of what the speaker meant, in conversational interpretation, is what he actually intended his words to mean. If we deny this point, we must deny the distinction between the artistic use of language and its ordinary day-to-day use in communicating.

Dworkin nevertheless says that both scientific and conversational interpretation may be drawn under the umbrella of 'constructive' interpretation by saying that all kinds of interpretation strive 'to make an object the best it can be, as an instance of some assumed enterprise ...'.[20] He does this by using the idea in conversational interpretation of *charity*, whereby we make the best of a person's communication to understand what he said, and the idea, for scientific interpretation, of the standards of theory construction, such as simplicity, elegance and verifiability.

Making the best moral sense of law

I suggested that Dworkin's idea of interpretation is so abstract that it is difficult not to accept. I also introduced his idea of the interpretation of courtesy. How, though, does interpretation apply to *law*?

The rules of law constitute the social practices which are the 'thing' to be interpreted in the constructive or artistic way. But what does it mean to say that we must show the legal practices in their best light? Dworkin is less explicit about this, although the idea is central to his anti-positivist position that moral argument is an essential ingredient of legal argument. But it is clear that he takes the existence of law to be a moral justification for state coercion and claims that the concept of law we share is one through which we understand the point of law to be that of constraining and licensing governmental coercion:

> Law insists that force not be used or withheld, no matter how useful that would be to ends in view, no matter how beneficial or noble these ends, except as licensed or required by individual rights and responsibilities flowing from past political decisions about when collective force is justified.[21]

Is this a reasonable thing to say? Dworkin has certainly described a common view of law. If we are to understand the meaning of, to interpret, these social practices we understand in that way, is it not natural to suppose that we must understand them in their best *moral* light? What other light should we see them in?

There are some obvious objections. For example, the idea of law expressed here has, built into it, we might argue, the idea of moral justification. Law, according to this account, begs the question of its own justification. A further objection is that the definition just given endorses itself as a peculiarly bourgeois idea: the invocation of something as law means that the state has some interest in preserving or enhancing or forbidding certain kinds of conduct as against others. In other words, the committed anarchist will find no joy in this idea of law.

But there are confusions in these sorts of argument. We cannot advance the positivist idea of law in its own support, for that, too, is begging the question. That is, we cannot be suspicious of the assertion that law must be cast in its best moral light solely on the ground that we have a belief that law and morality are 'conceptually' distinct. Ask yourself, if you doubt the argument here: how should we make sense of those social practices that license the very considerable and pervasive powers of the courts?

Try, for example, other sorts of lights: the most elegant light? the most consistent light? the most socially divisive light? the most economically efficient light? the most religious light? And – very important – if someone wishes to argue that the idea of law makes most sense in terms of preserving a bourgeois state of affairs, we can always ask ourselves: is that the best moral light in which it can be cast?

Concepts and conceptions of law

Dworkin makes frequent use of a distinction between concepts and conceptions. The distinction is used and understood in contemporary philosophy. In particular, it is openly adopted by Rawls in *A Theory of Justice*[22] and its use is widespread among political philosophers. It is, too, common in ordinary discourse. It is helpful in unpicking the strands in argumentative subjects such as politics and law.

The idea is this. People can have different conceptions of something and they can, and often do, argue with others about which conception of it is the better conception. You will note the obvious analogy with rival interpretations of a 'thing'. In the context of conceptions, this 'thing' is the 'concept' and it is constituted by a level of abstraction about which there is agreement on a discrete set of ideas, and which is employed in all interpretations. A conception, on the other hand, will take up some controversy that, according to Dworkin, is 'latent' in the concept.

Let us use an example. Democracy is a concept which in some obvious sense we understand. There are ideas that we understand to be 'democratic' ideas, such as free elections, the equality and freedom of people, the rule of law. There are other ideas we would probably agree on. Perhaps the only agreement we will reach is the idea that democracy is, very broadly, government by consent. And, clearly, people have different *conceptions* about the force and scope of the idea of consent. We may, for example, disagree on the *kind* of consent required. Consent as evidenced by proportional representation, or by the system of the non-transferable vote? Some people endorse block voting for trade unions to ensure 'workers' democratic rights'. Take the idea of equality, for many people think that idea is expressed in the phrase 'one man, one vote'. A conception of that idea was once that it could not include women. Others view democracy as a system of procedural, majority rule only, while others view it in a substantive way, as essentially about the protection of minority interests and rights. Others view democracy as a restraint on decision-making at all levels rather than any particular scheme of government. Others, in East European and other countries, have found democracy in the idea of the one party state.

All these ideas can, and are, debated, on, I suggest, the common ground that democracy is about government 'by consent', and probably on wider grounds, involving those discrete propositions about equality, freedom, representation and government, which 'have to do with' democracy.

The seminal analysis of the distinction between concepts and conceptions is to be found in an article by Gallie, entitled 'Essentially Contested Concepts'.[23] This idea was taken up by many political philosophers, notably Rawls, as I have said, in *A Theory of Justice*. Gallie argues that some concepts, such as art, democracy, social justice and 'the Christian life', are, by their nature, ideas which can only be understood as involving controversial argument. He lists a number of conditions which are part descriptions of any 'essentially contested' concept and these entail, I think, the idea that such concepts are understood through different conceptions.

These are that the concept must be 'appraisive' (i.e. critical), 'internally complex' and 'variously describable'; it must also admit of 'considerable modification in the light of changing circumstances' and that 'to use an essentially contested concept means to use it against other uses and to recognize that one's own use of it has to be maintained against these other uses'.[24] And, in order to distinguish such concepts from 'radically confused' concepts, Gallie says that users of such concepts must recognise the 'authority' of an 'original exemplar' of the concept and the competition among users must enable 'the original exemplar's achievement to be sustained and/or developed in optimum fashion'.[25]

It is instructive to apply the distinction between concepts and conceptions to Hart's *The Concept of Law*. I have already suggested that Hart's book is about one particular interpretation of law, and it is one which comes closest to what Dworkin has called the 'conventionalist' account, which preserves the ideal of protected expectations, and which I examine in Chapter 8.[26] To employ the terminology, Hart's theory is his *conception* of the *concept* of law.

On the other hand, we can, as I have heard Dworkin do at times, refer to Hart's theory as a description of the 'pre-interpretive' data of law. In the language of concepts and conceptions, seen in this way, Hart's work, in Dworkin's view, describes the set of discrete ideas 'uncontroversially employed in all interpretations'.[27]

Gallie's analysis is, I think, not to be exactly equated with Dworkin's use of the idea of interpretation and the distinction between concepts and conceptions. It rather amounts to a sociology of a form of argument to be found in political philosophy but gives little, if any, thought to the important question of the justification for the existence of essentially contestable concepts.

Dworkin provides a justification that is an important part of his approach to interpretive questions. In short, it is that we have a responsibility to 'construct' answers to this sort of question, and that it is a reneging of responsibility to stand off and assume that there just is an answer 'out there' which, maybe, is in the powers of someone else, or even nobody, to resolve.[28]

Is this abstract philosophy removed from the realities of the courtroom? No. It directly describes what happens. Take the famous United Kingdom case of *Donoghue* v. *Stevenson,* for example.[29] In this case, the House of Lords devised a new relationship of liability between the ultimate manufacturer, a maker of fizzy drinks, and the ultimate consumer, a woman who became ill after eating a decomposed snail in one of the manufacturer's drinks. Lord Atkin argued that the manufacturer was liable because of a general duty in tort law upon those whose acts could reasonably be seen to affect others (known as the 'neighbour' principle of tortious liability), whereas Lord Buckmaster's view was that liability in this sort of case was limited to categories already existing in tort. Since there were none to cover the case, and there was no contractual relationship between the parties, the woman's case had to fail.

Does not the language of concept and conception exactly describe the differences, say, between Lord Atkin and Lord Buckmaster? It is illuminating to say that each had a different conception of the same concept of tortious liability. The important point is that both judges were on the same plateau of argument about tort. They were not talking, as it were, past each other. They each shared the idea that tortious liability was the basis for common law compensation for wrongs committed outside the confines of contract. They each shared the idea that such liability should arise from a relationship between the parties. It happened that Lord Atkin's conception of the concept of tortious liability in this case was a wider one than Lord Buckmaster's. And we might want to go further and say that, along with many commentators on this well-known decision, Lord Atkin's conception was the superior one because, by creating the neighbour principle, it brought together several strands of separate heads of liability in a coherent and principled way.

We need not take only the great and famous cases as examples. After all, those cases are not typical. But I suggest that even in the mundane, day-to-day cases of legal argument the distinction between concept and conceptions is apparent. Take a typical case involving the interpretation of some section of a Factory Act. The concept in question, the discrete set of ideas around which agreement collects, is that of the duty on the part of the employer to fence dangerous machinery. The factory owner's lawyer argues for the conception of that duty which absolves the factory owner from criminal liability when an employee has been negligent. The inspector's lawyer argues for a different conception under which owners have duties to guard even against negligence. It is not necessary to go further with this example, for as lawyers will know, the arguments for each conception (and several more) are contained at great length in the law reports. I think that the distinction between concepts and conceptions is of great help in describing the differences between the factory owner and the factory inspector, and between Lord Atkin and Lord Buckmaster.

Ultimately, the two sides under this account are arguing within a consensus that they must accept the best interpretation of the rule that an employer has a duty to fence. And even if we do not feel disposed to accept that 'best' means 'morally best', given everything else about the legal system, the distinction between concepts and conceptions is helpful in understanding the above differences.

The concept of law

What, for Dworkin, is the concept, as opposed to the correct conception, of law? The central idea is that of justification. When we talk of law, the 'discrete' collection of ideas which we uncontroversially accept concerns the justification of the use of state power. Thus, he says, 'legal argument takes place on a plateau of rough consensus that if law exists it provides a justification for the use of collective power against individual citizens or groups'.[30] It is, as I have suggested, difficult to deny and accepting it does not mean that we are bound to accept Dworkin's conception of law.

The descriptive side to Hart's theory at first sight seems antagonistic to the concept, but only because its attraction lies in its immediate clarity and simplicity. Seeing it as interpretive allows us to see it as one of a cluster of conceptions of the concept of state coercive power. It requires judges to be 'neutral' on such questions, as we saw, and for Hart, I suggested, the importance of distinguishing law from morality lay in the preservation of individual conscience against the state's demands.

The compromise between justice and fairness

So far, the drive of this chapter has been descriptive of Dworkin's methodology. But we can now turn to his legal theory directly.

A part-summing up will help us. Remember that Dworkin is concerned with the justification of claims made in the name of law. His theory must, therefore, be responsive to real legal arguments: we must be able to test it against the actual arguments judges use. Further, the background must always be the best moral sense that can be made of the legal materials, for his theory is a theory of *law*, not of how things in the ideal world morally should be. So bear in mind always with Dworkin's theory of law that there will be a constant tension between what the legal materials say and what is the morally best way to interpret them.

The moral judgments required here are of the political sort. The best interpretation of the legal materials must draw upon the best moral theory of the legal system. Dworkin is thus required to provide a theory of morality which casts our legal practices in their best light. The very important connection between what we may characterise as his twin abstract principles of interpretation and equality should now be appreciated.

Morality, which, in his view, is based upon the idea that people should be treated as equals, supplies the light in which we are to cast the legal practices. Thus, summing up, Dworkin's theory is that legal practices are only to make sense against the background of a moral theory based on the idea of equality.[31]

The meld between the legal materials and moral theory is achieved in the idea of *integrity* which requires that law cohere in a way that is distinct from justice, according to which the right state of affairs exists in society, and distinct from fairness, a conception of equality according to which 'each point of view must be allowed a voice in the process of deliberation'.[32] It means, in short, that law should always be created, or interpreted, so as to form an integral whole. This injunction expresses the virtue of integrity, which is distinct from, but, according to Dworkin, on the same plane as, the twin virtues of justice and fairness.

Dworkin characterises justice and fairness in general terms as follows:

> Justice ... is a matter of the right outcome of the political system: the right distribution of goods, opportunities, and other resources. Fairness is a matter of the right structure for that system, the structure that distributes influence over political decisions in the right way.[33]

Let us suppose that the most just society would outlaw abortion. Let us also say that the fairest society gives each person a voice in the process of decision. Imagine a society in which a majority of people want, and vote for, legalised abortion in specified circumstances. Obviously, if we accept the initial premises we are bound to conclude that there is a conflict.

Dworkin now tests our intuitions. Imagine the following situation. The legislature adopts a compromise between justice and fairness by granting rights of abortion to women in proportion to the number of pro-abortion legislative votes. Let us say that there was a two-thirds majority vote against and one-third for abortion. The legislation now allocates permissions for abortions at the rate of one to every three requests (with some request system). To be fair, it allocates them randomly, by means of a lottery system, or some other random method, perhaps by date of birth, or randomly specified months of conception.

There is a nod in the directions of both fairness and justice. We do not know conclusively whether abortion is just or not, but we do know that there will be some justice done (because either justice permits abortions in the specified circumstances or it does not), and that justice is apportioned according to the fairness of allowing 'each point of view its voice in the process'.

The point is: what do our intuitions say on the matter? Is the result a satisfactory one? Most people are disinclined to accept it because it does not seem 'principled', even although the requirements of justice and fairness have been considered. These sorts of compromise solutions have been tried before.[34] Legislative requirements such as these have become known as 'checkerboard' statutes because they produce a result which is both contrasting (different outcomes for different individuals) and symmetrical (the law is general).

Dworkin uses our intuitive response here in positing the existence of the virtue of integrity. He compares his argument with the discovery of the planet Neptune, whose existence was confirmed, not by a direct sighting but by noticing that the effects of gravitational pull on nearby planets could only be explained by positing the existence of another planet not directly observed. We notice the virtue of integrity by noting its pull on justice and fairness, he says, and it is this virtue which makes us think that the law should 'speak with one voice', in one coherent and principled way.

The idea of integrity appears first in *Law's Empire* and is the fundamental virtue in Dworkin's *legal* philosophy. But the idea is present throughout Dworkin's earlier work in the idea of justifying decisions in hard cases. There the general scheme for arguing for decisions was to argue in terms of value, in particular by arguing and asserting matters of principle.[35] The easy cases themselves were justified by the arguments of principle that were underpinning them, and it was from these arguments that arguments should be drawn, in his view, to argue in the hard cases.

A word on 'coherence'

Coherence is an idea that often suggests more than it can deliver. The requirement of coherence in the law is more than just consistency or, what Dworkin prefers to call it, 'bare consistency'. Bare consistency just amounts to the absence of logical contradiction between two statements of law. Coherence must, rather, be consistency 'in principle', that is, it must 'express a single and comprehensive vision of justice'.[36] We think this way, I suggest, about legal argument. True, we must produce arguments that are consistent with previous decisions and statutes, and with arguments that have been used in the past. But it is not just consistency that is at work here.[37]

Bare consistency, for example, is an impossible requirement because we all accept, as properly characteristic of legal argument, that some previous decisions are mistaken. We deal with mistakes by justifying their unique position with arguments that are much richer than bare consistency can permit. We might, for example, be prepared to put forward an argument for overturning a line of cases, not on the grounds that they are inconsistent with other cases. There may be none. Or, if there are, under bare consistency, the argument for retaining them is just as good as for abandoning them by declaring them to be mistakes.

Coherency captures the logical tone of consistency but permits other criteria of right and wrong. The incoherent account a child gives of his afternoon's activities goes further than inconsistency. For his account to be coherent it must 'make sense', not just be consistent. On the other hand, coherency describes a situation at a highly abstracted level, where we are reduced to saying that things must make sense, or 'hang together' without being much more specific. Coherency is only fully understandable in a particular context. Take the sorts of arguments that were used in *Donoghue* v. *Stevenson*, the decomposed snail case. Lord Atkin, I suggested, was trying to make coherent the idea of liability for negligence, by finding an abstract way of expressing various forms of existing liability in contract and tort. He thought, as many others have since thought, that the principled way was through the neighbour principle. His argument, I suggest, had the virtue of coherence. It makes sense, or 'hangs together', because it provides a way of arguing from the facts of that particular set of circumstances, to all sorts of other circumstances, by means of a principle – the neighbour principle – in a way which clearly shows why the previous cases were justly decided and why it would be wrong to restrict liability in negligence only to certain categories of case (as Lord Buckmaster did).

But we can be quicker in argument than all this. Ask yourself: do you think that good legal arguments should be coherent and justified in principle, producing a single vision of justice? The answer is simple. Of course you do.

Dworkin sees the special virtue of the 'single vision of justice' as representing the ideal of community or, as he prefers to call it, the ideal of 'fraternity'. This ideal he believes to be resident in the idea of law as the background justification for personifying the state in a way that the ideal of integrity must assume. I shall turn to his development of the idea of community, which is his liberal and individualist response to the conservative 'communitarians', in Chapter 4. In short, his view is that one's *being an individual* gives rise to certain public virtues, among which is the duty the state has (and the duty the individual has to uphold) to ensure that people are treated as equals. The arguments for this distinction between duties of the private and the public sphere now occupies much of Dworkin's time.

The ideal ideal world and the ideal real world

The connection between integrity and the ideal of equality is crucial to Dworkin. It is through the single vision that the law must present, he says, that the state treats its citizens as equals. Service to the virtue of integrity strives towards keeping the state speaking with one voice to all of its citizens. That voice is not just that of consistency in dealing, which is, as Hart has pointed out,[38] 'compatible with great iniquity', but incorporates the idea of treating people as equal.

Integrity is the principal virtue of legal argument and it is a moral virtue in the political sphere. Thus, legal and moral argument cannot be separated. Legal argument must, according to Dworkin, characteristically refer to the right each person has to be treated as an equal.

But there are all sorts of problems here. Dworkin takes us through a number of worlds. In what he calls the 'ideal ideal' world, there is no need for the virtue of integrity. Imagine the perfect world where everyone behaves as they should. The perfectly just legislative decision is made in the abortion case, referred to above, and everyone votes for it. In any case, the legislation is not needed as everybody does what is morally right. Here, the legislators are not torn between the issue of substantive justice and the issue of fairness. Everyone concurs, and rightly. Since the state, by hypothesis, treats everyone as equals, there is no need, in the ideal world, for the separate virtue of integrity. This is so because it is a corrective concept, one which is only necessary when there is a tension between justice and fairness.

Another way of putting it is to say that Dworkin's use of the idea of integrity is designed to construct an ideal judicial system, where trade-offs are perfectly made by judges. The judges have a correct conception of justice with which they work, but they are able (also correctly) to trade it off against other factors arising in the real world.

This argument establishes, I think, the unique nature of integrity. Its function is to constrain states in the real world, where decisions are often unjust but fair. Since its function, its special virtue, is to *constrain*, it is, too, an *ideal* but one that exists in the 'ideal *real*' world. In other words, in the 'real real' world, the one you and I live in, legislators, and lawyers and judges, must aim at the ideal of making all laws form a coherent whole, one that makes the state speak to all citizens equally.[39]

Notes

1. See Chapter 5.
2. I am not suggesting there could not possibly be a connection.
Perhaps an argument along the lines of a connection between
sandal-wearing and anarchic hippiedom of the 1960s could be made. But
the point is that the connection would have to be made. If there is none
argued and none imaginable, the audience is justified in saying that the
lecturer is not talking 'about law'.
3. See *The Concept of Law* (1961) Oxford, Chapter 2.
4. *Essays in Jurisprudence and Philosophy* (1983) Oxford. Introduction,
p.6.
5. I think this becomes clear, too, from his discussion of paradigms of
law. These are the uncontroversial descriptions of standard understandings
of law. They are paradigms because of uncontroverted acceptance of them
so as to make deviations clear mistakes. On the other hand, they are not
uncontrovertible, given the appropriate argument. They are not wholly, or
'conceptually', distinct, therefore, from interpretations.
6. See, for the contrast with facts of an institutional type such as legal
facts, MacCormick, 'Law as Institutional Fact' 90 *Law Quarterly Review* 102
(1974).
7. As Lord Simon and Lord Kilbrandon do, for example, in the House
of Lords case on the defence of duress in the criminal law of *Lynch* v. *D.P.P.*
[1975] 1 All E.R. 913. Both judges dissented from the majority judgment in
this case. Lord Simon says (939): 'I am all for recognising frankly that
judges do make law. And I am all for judges exercising this responsibility
boldly at the proper time and place - that is, where they can feel confident of
having in mind, and correctly weighed, all the implications of their decision
and [emphasis added] *where matters of social policy are not involved which the
collective wisdom of Parliament is better suited to resolve.*' Lord Kilbrandon's
remarks are stronger. He emphasises a judicial duty not to step outside a
judicial function, which is a different ground from that of just whether
judges are sufficiently knowledgeable to make the decision. At 942, he says:
'... the grounds on which the majority propose that the conviction of the
appellant be set aside involve changes in the law which are outside the
proper functions of your Lordships in your judicial capacity ... An alteration
in a fundamental doctrine of law, such as this appeal proposes, could not
properly be given effect to save after the widest reference to interests both
social and intellectual for transcending those available in the judicial
committee of your Lordships' House ... modern society rightly prefers to
exercise that function for itself, and this it conveniently does through those
who represent it in Parliament.'
8. See Hart's *The Concept of Law*, Chapter 5.
9. See *The Concept of Law*, pp. 204-6.
10. 'What surely is most needed in order to make men clear sighted in
confronting the official abuse of power, is that they should preserve the
sense that the certification of something as legally valid is not conclusive of
the question of obedience, and that, however great the aura of majesty or
authority which the official system may have, its demands must in the end

be submitted to a moral scrutiny.' *The Concept of Law*, 206. See, too, the surrounding discussion about the reasons for choosing the 'wider', positivistic, concept of law over the 'narrower' concept that excludes morally iniquitous rules.

11. There *are* other ways of interpreting events or actions, but Dworkin's point is that, at the least in the case of law, this is a normal, or paradigmatic, way of interpreting. Thus he says: 'I do not mean that every kind of activity we call interpretation aims to make the best of what it interprets - a 'scientific' interpretation of the Holocaust would not try to show Hitler's motives in the most attractive light, nor would someone trying to show the sexist effects of a comic strip strain to find a nonsexist reading - but only that this is so in the normal or paradigm cases of creative interpretation.' *Law's Empire*, 421, n. 12. William Twining takes issue with my defence of Dworkin on this point. What would the best interpretation of the rise and fall of Adolf Hitler then be, he asks. To this it just seems to me that the answer that I am uncertain is sufficient. Dworkin does not offer an account of what counts as good historical interpretation in general, only what counts as the best, namely, the moral, interpretation of law. I do not think it follows, and Dworkin presumably agrees, that if differing perspectives determine different historical interpretations, moral or not, that law can be interpreted properly in these differing ways, too. Again: it would not follow from there being valid historical interpretations devoid of moral point that *there could be interpretations of law that are equally valid although devoid of moral point*. A comparative study of evil legal systems would only provide an account of law in a derivative - non-paradigmatic - kind of way. The derivative moral point could be to draw attention to what can go wrong. But ignoring this derivative interest, what would be the point of the study? What would be the criterion of interest that connects one evil legal system with another? Why is it that 'evil' legal systems are chosen?

12. Skipping ahead, it is useful to see the connection with Dworkin's other very abstract principle that the state has a duty to treat its citizens with 'equal concern and respect'. The two ideas together generate the ruling concepts of his legal and political theory.

13. Hart's analysis of rule-following provides a neat account here. See *The Concept of Law*, pp. 79-88. That there is such a social rule of courtesy means that men regularly doff their hats when meeting women. This behaviour is coupled with the consistent criticism of deviations from this pattern. A further necessary feature is that this criticism is based upon reasons accepted by at least some members of the society that courtesy is so required. When we assert the existence of this social rule, without reference to its point, Dworkin says that this shows a pre-interpretive understanding of the assertion that a social rule about courtesy to women exists.

14. See *The Concept of Law*, Chapter 5.

15. Stanley Fish, 'Working on the Chain Gang: Interpretation in Law and Literature' 60 *Texas Law Review* 373 (1982); 'Wrong Again' 62 *Texas Law Review* 299 (1983).

16. See Finnis, *Natural Law and Natural Rights* (1980) Oxford, Chapter 1.

17. See Hart's *The Concept of Law* (1961) Oxford, pp. 97–107.

18. *Law's Empire*, p. 52.

19. I suggested, in the last chapter, that elements of this idea are perhaps present in Bentham, and certainly in the works of John Austin. For Dworkin, the idea of a 'scientific' interpretation of the law will ultimately be unsuccessful, as we shall see from his discussion of conventionalism in Chapter 8. It requires, in hard cases, the construction of more and more abstract conventions, the culmination of which is the idea of soft conventionalism resting on a 'consensus' among officials that the best interpretation be sought. That would amount, I presume, for Dworkin, to the same as saying that kind of interpretation is creative, not scientific.

20. See Dworkin, *Law's Empire*, p. 53.

21. *Law's Empire*, p. 93.

22. See his *A Theory of Justice* (1971) Harvard, Chapter 5. Note also the use of the idea in Hart *The Concept of Law* (1961) Oxford, pp. 155–9.

23. *Proceedings of the Aristotelian Society* Vol.56 (1965) 167.

24. *Proceedings of the Aristotelian Society* Vol.56 (1965) 167, 171–2.

25. *Proceedings of the Aristotelian Society* Vol.56 (1965) 167, 171–2, 180.

26. Dworkin has told me that he now regrets not having begun his chapter entitled 'Conventionalism' in *Law's Empire* with a general statement that he regarded Hart's theory of law as best understood as a conventionalist theory.

27. See *Law's Empire*, p. 71.

28. See Chapter 6, 'The Duty to Construct'.

29. [1932] A.C. 562. For a detailed, and jurisprudentially friendly, discussion of this case see MacCormick's *Legal Reasoning and Legal Theory* (1978) Oxford.

30. See Dworkin, *Law's Empire* pp. 108–9. See also Raz, 'Authority, Law and Morality' in 68 *The Monist* 295 (July 1985).

31. It should be added that it does not follow that, if Dworkin's view that morality in the political sphere of the justification of law is fundamentally concerned with equality is wrong, his theory of interpretation is wrong. They are separate theories.

32. *Law's Empire*, p. 179.

33. *Law's Empire*, p. 404.

34. Dworkin uses as an example the US Constitution which originally compromised slavery by counting three-fifths of a state's slaves in determining the state's representation in Congress. See *Law's Empire*, p. 184. But it is not a good example, because the solution there was to treat slaves *neither* as persons, who had a full vote, *nor* as non-persons, because some account was taken of them. It was not the sort of solution where some people, but not others, received justice.

35. See Chapters 7 and 8.

36. *Law's Empire*, p. 134.

37. MacCormick, N. 'The Role of Coherence in Legal Justification' in Peszenick, ed. *Theory of Legal Science*.

38. See Hart, *Essays in Jurisprudence and Philosophy*, Chapter 15.

39. It means that integrity represents a striving, in the real world, for a justice which, Dworkin says, 'abstracts' from institutions. 'Pure' integrity, he says 'declares how the community's practices must be reformed to serve more coherently and comprehensively a vision of social justice it has partly

adopted, but it does not declare which officer has which office in that grand project' (*Law's Empire*, p. 407).

3

Integrity and legal argument

The ideal judge – Hercules

Integrity exists at two levels. It is both a legislative principle which tells legislators that simple trade-offs between justice and fairness are wrong, and an adjudicative principle which tells judges, and therefore lawyers, to make their decisions and arguments integrate with the body of existing law. So far as legal philosophy is concerned, it is the adjudicative principle that is of most interest. The idea is best captured by examining Dworkin's well-known model of the ideal judge, a judge who is superintelligent and exceedingly hard-working, whom he calls 'Hercules'.

We need to get several things clear about Hercules. Many people, in particular lawyers, who are introduced to Hercules in Dworkin's article 'Hard Cases' simply dismiss him by saying that no such judge ever existed. But this is too superficial. Hercules is a model against which, like any other ideal, legal arguments are to judged. Take, for example, the idea of the ideal market. It would be silly, because off the point, to say that the ideal market does not exist (or that the model of the atom, or the DNA molecule, does not exist). To *say* that is to recognise the idea of the ideal, in any case. The point of the ideal market, about which economists (and practical-minded politicians) argue vociferously, is to show how, in the real world, there are imperfections. Against the model of the ideal market, we see that monopolies and other restrictive practices are 'bad', that transaction costs and imperfect knowledge 'distort' the real market, and so on.

Why, then, should we not hypothesise the existence of an ideal judge, against whom we can measure bad or distorted legal arguments? There is no reason to suppose that we cannot. But it is worth trying to explore the reasons why people make the mistake of saying, in effect, that there cannot be ideal arguments in the law. The problem is one of superficiality, I think, no more. People like to think of law as historic fact. They do not like to think of legal argument as something as shifting and as controversial as moral argument.

It is necessary for Dworkin to posit an ideal judge because his theory is not that law is a discrete set of rules but, rather, that law concentrates centrally on the idea of argument. He can only, therefore, provide a *scheme* of argument which, among other things, is sufficiently abstract to allow for controversial argument. He cannot provide a set of premises from which conclusions may be drawn by, say, the use of formal syllogisms. His is not that sort of theory. In fact, he is highly critical of that sort of theory. He thinks it paints a simplistic picture of legal reasoning. In order for him to describe the inherently controversial nature of hard cases, he can only provide the general scheme of argument.

The model of Hercules is intended to point the way to correct legal argument. It is not that there is a method which will come up with the right answer, there, uncontroversially for all of us to see. If a problem is raised about whether there *could* be such a right answer, it is one about the objectivity of legal argument, not a criticism of the ideal model of Hercules.

How then does Hercules decide a hard case? The key is the following idea:

If a judge accepts the settled practice of his legal system – if he accepts, that is, the autonomy provided by its distinct constitutive and regulative rules – then he must, according the doctrine of political responsibility, accept some general political theory that justifies these practices.[1]

What does this really mean? Look at the position of the judge. He has some ideas about his role, his duties as defined by his judicial oath and by other sources. If he did not, it would certainly be surprising. He has an idea about legislative purpose and principles of the common law.

In this, United States and United Kingdom judges differ. In the United States, judges are more aware of their role as public 'protectors' of the Constitution and they are more explicit (both to themselves and the public) about their position within the separation of powers doctrine and their duties to protect the rights of the individual. United Kingdom judges are, for cultural reasons to do with background and education, more diffident about such matters.[2]

Dworkin's point is relatively simple. It just does not make sense to suppose that judging occurs within a vacuum of justification. For Hercules to make sense of his position, he must be able to make general statements about what judging entails, and it will not be enough for him simply to declare that he accepts a set of rules without providing any explanation, or justification, for why he accepts them.

This point of Dworkin's must be right. We only to have to think of the magnitude of the coercive powers of judges to appreciate the force of the requirement for justification. It is just naïve to say that there are no reasons of political morality that 'underlie' or are 'embedded' in the settled practices of the legal system. Put in another way: it is eminently reasonable to say that we should assume that there is a rationale behind the business of judging.

What does Hercules do when constructing the arguments in all the hard cases put before him? We can assume, says Dworkin, that he accepts most of the settled rules of his jurisdiction, rules which lay out for us what are the familiar characteristics of the law. For example, the constitutive and regulative rules that grant the legislature the powers of legislation give judges the powers of adjudication and the duties to follow previous cases, as well as all the settled rules of the various areas of law, such as tort, contract and so on.

But Hercules can go further. He can produce theories underlying all these rules. Democracy, in some form, clearly underlies the United States and the United Kingdom jurisdictions. So we have there a basic justification for judicial coercion in accordance with what the legislature has required. But this is only the beginning. The justification for the common law doctrine of precedent lies in the idea of *fairness*, the idea of treating people in a consistent way. The justification for particular applications of statutes and the common law lies within more elaborately worked out theories, or reasons, such as (and I give random examples) a theory of responsibility in the criminal law (and attendant theories about *mens rea* and the idea of recklessness), a theory of relevance in the law of evidence, a theory of the division of capital and income in the law of taxation, a theory of consideration in the law of contract. The list is huge and is familiar to anyone who has studied law for long enough.

And even this is not enough. Each theory has its sub-theories. To take just one example, consider responsibility in the field of the defence in the criminal law of duress. Among just the enunciated theories of duress is a theory that duress is a *justification* for action (self-preservation) and another that says it is, instead, an *excuse* absolving a defendant from blame, as a recognition of human weakness in dire circumstances. There are further theories over what constitutes 'dire' circumstances, whether, for example, duress should extend as a defence to murder in the first degree. There is a further theory that there is a *moral* difference between first and second degree murder which justifies extending the defence to second degree murderers but not to first degree murderers.

We can examine all the possibilities just mentioned in the law reports and academic writings. And these are not exhaustive. We can develop our own theories or, if we prefer, our own arguments. Dworkin's use of Hercules is intended to show the general form – the scheme – of the types of arguments that may be used. We can imagine Hercules producing all the theories, with their attendant sub-theories, for all areas of the law. In each topic, he will have to justify the particular settled rules with the substantive theories he has devised.

He will also have to do more. The division by topic will itself be a matter for justification, which will proceed by way of looking to the settled rules for topic demarcation (say, the division between tortious and contractual liability[3]) and devising a theory which explains that division. He might decide that, for some special cases, the importance of the division may be outweighed, as Lord Atkin thought it was, but not Lord Buckmaster, in *Donoghue* v. *Stevenson*.

The question of his jurisdiction to decide might also be a matter for theoretical justification. In the case of duress, for example, he might come to the following conclusion. Because the settled law is clear that duress does not extend to first degree murder, *and* that the question of duress is a *moral* matter, *and* that there is no moral distinction between second and first degree murder, the law is clear that duress is not a defence to second degree murder. And other judges might disagree, in a number of differing ways, where the disagreement stems from various points in the web of tacit or express moral positions on any of these three points, or others not mentioned.

We should note, too, this example as one of a judge drawing a conclusion about the 'clear' law in a way different from merely 'reading off' the law. He might, for example, conclude from this fact that he would be exceeding his judicial powers if he 'departed from' the clear law and 'extended' the defence of duress. He might express himself, as Lord Kilbrandon did in a case involving just this point, by warning that a decision to so extend the law would step 'outside the proper functions' of the court.[4] His view in this case is expressed just as a political philosopher might express a statement about the separation of judicial and legislative powers. The essence of the statement is expressed in different ways from time to time by judges.[5]

The chain novel

Legal argument, for Dworkin, in most hard cases, will develop as the result of a tension between two dimensions of argument, one that argues towards a 'fit' with what is accepted as 'settled' law, the other that argues towards substantive issues of political morality. While the twin abstract injunctions in Dworkin 'to make the best sense' of law, and 'to treat people as equals', propels his legal and political philosophy, it is the distinction between 'substance' and 'fit' that forms the cutting edge, for him, of legal argument.

As a preliminary to getting into the idea, we may employ Dworkin's idea of the chain novel. A number of novelists agree to write a chapter each of a proposed novel. The first chapter is written by one, the second by another, the third by another, and so on. We can see that there will be certain constraints of 'fit' upon the author of the second chapter, and even more on the author of the third chapter, and so on. These constraints will be such things as the names of the characters ('Keith' in the first chapter cannot, with no reason given, have the name 'Nicola' in the second chapter, for example), plot (again, without explanation, a novel set in the eighteenth century cannot move to the twentieth), and language (something would be wrong if the first chapter were in English but the second in Maori).

Many more lines of fit could be proposed. Is there fit with style, descriptiveness, thematic material, dialect and so on? The important point is that if certain things are accepted as settled within the text of the first chapter, later creativity is constrained by that acceptance, in order for the later chapters to be part of the novel.

There are familiar responses to this description of 'fit'. It is a matter of argument (or 'opinion'), people say, as to what constitutes 'fit'. It is too 'wooden' to assert that novels cannot allow for the change of name, sex, century, and geography. But what follows from this? That everything and, therefore, nothing, counts as 'fit'? Of course not. It is uncontroversial that we hold some framework assumptions, or constraints, constant while we allow others to vary.

Nevertheless, in Dworkin's terminology, the question of 'fit' is itself an interpretive question. For example, the acceptance of the genre of 'novel' for the chain novel is itself open to interpretation. A second chapter novelist might, for example, decide that the first chapter is a political tract about conservatism and best seen as the first chapter of a political manifesto. This interpretive judgment might constrain the way he continued to write the second chapter. If he did so, perhaps if the chain novel writing project was a commercial one to produce a radio serial, his contract as a chain novelist would be terminated. But there is no reason holding back the *possibility* of making that interpretive judgment, although, of course, his judgment that the first chapter was the first chapter of a political manifesto might be difficult to justify.

Stanley Fish has attacked Dworkin's analogy of the chain novel but misses the point contained in the previous paragraph.[6] He wrongly has taken Dworkin to be asserting that judgments of 'fit' are judgments about what is 'given' or 'there'. He thinks that it is an absurdity for Dworkin to suppose that 'interpreting a novel' is an interpretation of something about which an interpretive judgment has not already been made. This is that it is a matter of judgment that *we are in the 'novel' genre*.

But we have seen that, when Dworkin distinguished between the 'pre-interpretive' and the 'interpretive' phrase, he allowed for some work of interpretation to have been done in isolating the pre-interpretive materials. Fish raises the important question of whether Dworkin is allowed to make this move, which we shall examine in a moment. But Fish goes further. He says that because there are no requirements of fit, the only constraints are those imposed by the community of interpreters. Everything is open to interpretation so, he says, the only possible common ground is agreement, and that will only be possible among a group of similarly-minded interpreters. There will, therefore, be no possibility of discourse between different communities of interpreters for they will, in effect, be speaking different languages.

But Fish makes a number of mistakes here.[7] In the first place, arguments *within* communities of interpretation (the 'Jane Austen society'? the 'Cambridge Post-Structuralists'? the 'Dickens Club'?) are understood to be controversial despite this division of interpreters into 'interpretive communities' was supposed to solve. Interpreters of Shakespeare readily understand the various claims of 'fit'. Holding different interpretations themselves, they understand, and know how to argue for and against, such claims as that Hamlet was 'just neurotic', or that the play is 'just a ghost story' or that *The Merchant of Venice* is an 'anti-semitic tract', or *Macbeth* a play about an oversexed woman.

Secondly, Fish misunderstands the possibilities of translation. Language is rich enough to enable everyone to join the arcane group of interpreters. It can cross any boundaries that Fish invents. If he wants to maintain that there could be no objectivity outside a particular community, then, since he has no objectivity of the sort he requires within the community, it is not clear what he requires by way of objectivity. I fancy he has in mind *agreement* within the community. But that is too restrictive – especially so in the field of literature – to make any sense.

I said that Fish raises the important question of whether Dworkin can continue to draw the distinction between 'fit' and 'substance' once he admits that whether a matter is one of 'fit' is itself an interpretive matter, so subject to similar, if not identical, vagaries as to questions of substance. Both 'fit' and 'substance' are interpretive questions. So is there a distinction worth saving here?

The answer is yes. Our judgments about interpretive matters, such as literature, and law, are complex, containing many elements of constraint. Overall judgments we make are the result of various sorts of judgments, some of which are independent judgments acting as a constraint on others. Dworkin is bound to hold this view, because any kind of constraint on the sorts of judgments we make cannot be of a plain fact, 'out there' kind. The constraints must themselves issue from judgment. In his words:

It is a familiar part of our cognitive experience that some of our beliefs and convictions operate as checks in deciding how far we can or should accept or give effect to others, and the check is effective even when the constraining beliefs and attitudes are controversial.[8]

Let us turn now to the question of 'substance'. In the chain novel example, there may be a number of different ways in which the novel could develop, each of which fits equally well with the constraints accepted as existing in the first (and subsequent) chapters. In these cases, the chain novelists will have to make a different sort of judgment about how the novel should develop. This judgment will be one about the novel's substance. Which development would make the novel *better* as a novel, for example?

The answer to this question is, again, an interpretive one. The novelist may decide that it would make a better novel if a character's diffidence is emphasised rather than diminished, say, where this trait is shown to be particularly human in the face of important events. She might, for example, decide that it would be a lesser novel if diffidence were shown to be cowardly, or to be a good quality for a poker player. Although such decisions would each 'fit' with the character's diffidence in the earlier chapters, a substantive judgment about the novel's direction and worth would have to be made about the character's development.

You must bear in mind the controversial nature, or 'essential contestability' of all of these claims. There is no getting away from it. But the characterisation of the arguments can only be achieved in this schematic way. None of the following arguments is denied as possible by the scheme of literary creation described here although, of course, we would want to examine the arguments for each claim closely. 'It is not a novel but a political tract'; '"diffidence" is a weak and feminine trait and so should not be ascribed to a man'; 'it is unimportant to emphasise human qualities in novels'; '*all* novels are political statements'; the list is endless.

The point is that under Dworkin's abstract portrayal of interpretation, all these statements are possible ones. But it does not follow as, I think, Fish thinks it does, that each one is *as good as the other*. I know many people disagree with Dworkin on this point and it is important to isolate the reasons for this. 'Fit' is something people understand. The reason is simply the brute, rational pull of bare consistency.

Let us try it. Let us take Dworkin's literary analogy and broaden it to encompass art and music. What if Dickens, in the second chapter of *David Copperfield*, had begun to call David 'Goliath', had transported the Murdstones (now called the Plantagenets) to Abu Dhabi, where Mrs Murdstone, resurrected from the dead, ran a fish-processing business? It is absurd, in the absence of some link, to say that this second chapter is a chapter of *David Copperfield*. And even in this reworking there are some recognisable links ('Goliath' is recognisable as the former 'David'; the 'Murdstones' are common to both chapters). If there were *no* links, no 'fit', clearly Dickens has begun a new story.

Or take art. It is by virtue of lack of 'fit' that we can say that my abstract painting of 'red blobs against a green background with white triangles' is not a representation of the Mona Lisa. There is just nothing to connect them. And calling it the 'Mona Lisa', or painting it with the intention of its being a representation, will not do the trick, either. Again, however, there is no plain fact of the matter that says it is *not* such a representation; that, too, we must remember. Maybe, the blobs and triangles, the blended shades of green, in my painting, capture just the right mood – or whatever – of the Mona Lisa. But the connection will be tenuous if not downright implausible, and the strain will be to find the link of fit, the link that makes the argument possible, albeit tenuous.

What about music? Let us take a musicologist who completes the Schubert Unfinished Symphony, of which Schubert only wrote two complete movements. The new movement is four hours in length, and consists of a 1,000-strong choir of Fijian men plus twenty bass guitarists and an amplified Australian didgeridoo. It is in twelve tone. The effect from a distance is impressive. It is music of a kind. But the link with the first and second movements of the Schubert symphony are non-existent. Again, we must be wary. We must not be arrogant. Of course, it may be that the substance of the music captures something 'inherent' in the Schubert piece. But the pull of the requirement of connection by way of 'fit' is too strong for the argument to be very convincing.

Substance and fit in the law

The literary analogies annoy many.[9] What have literature, and so on, to do with law? The answer is in the idea of interpretation. If both literature and law are interpretive activities then an examination of the meaning of interpretation in both is highly relevant. What is so different about the interpretation of law that makes the literary analogy misleading? One common answer is that 'law is a practical subject concerned with decision-making'. But should that make a difference? Why, for example, should any interpretive activity not be concerned with decision-making?[10]

Can we imagine a society, more leisured than ours, in which laws assume a lesser practical role in society's affairs than art and literature? It is difficult but not, I think, impossible. Perhaps it is a society in which people are sufficiently virtuous, and without complicated desires, so as to require a minimum of law. Let us then imagine tribunals of art which are *required* to make decisions about what constitutes the best way to finish a novel, or a symphony, say, organised on the same lines as literary panels of judges such as the Booker prize judges. There is nothing unintelligible, at least, about having such decision-making importance hanging upon a particular interpretation of art.

Let us, however, turn to the issues of fit and substance in the law and use Dworkin's example in *Taking Rights Seriously*. Imagine that in Hercules' jurisdiction the written constitution forbids the establishment of a religion. The legislature passes a statute that appears to allow free busing to children who go to schools of a favoured religion. Does a child have a right to free busing by virtue of this statute? What theory underlies the constitution's prohibition on the establishment of a religion? Dworkin suggests two. Hercules might decide that it is grounded in the state's duty to prevent great social tension or disorder, which the establishment of a religion might have. Another possibility is that the prohibition is best understood as confirming a general right to religious liberty. Each of these theories justifying the prohibition has equal fit with the prohibition in the constitution.

Hercules will then have to see whether either of these two theories makes a 'smoother' fit with the remaining rules of the constitution. Let us say that the right to religious liberty does this (it fits more easily various other rights of freedoms, for example). But there will still be problems that cannot be solved by reference to institutional fit. What is religious liberty? Does religious liberty mean that taxes should never be spent on supporting religion? Or does it mean that taxes should never be spent on supporting religion at the expense of another? The right to free busing to the religious school of your choice is, of course, ruled out by the first conception, because that right uses public money. But the second conception does not necessarily rule out free busing because no other religion need be compromised.[11]

Since there is no question of 'fit' here, Dworkin says that the question of substance is one of political philosophy. In *Taking Rights Seriously* he says:

> At some point in his career Hercules must therefore consider the question not just as an issue of fit between a theory and the rules of the institution, but as an issue of political philosophy as well. He must decide which conception is a more satisfactory elaboration of the general idea of religious liberty.[12]

Here is the cutting edge of law for Dworkin, as I have said. But it is here, too, that Dworkin's theory is often met with perplexity. How, people reasonably ask, can there be anything more to legal argument, according to Dworkin's account, when, by his own admission, there are areas of the law where there is no objective requirement of fit, but only the subjective requirement of political morality?

We may now have objectors who are prepared to go along with Dworkin's arguments because they can see a link between clear rules and the arguments appropriate in hard cases. In other words, they find force in the idea that the rationale of the clear rules plays a part justifying extensions to those rules. But they might now not be able to take Dworkin's appeal to an argument of 'substance', an appeal directly to arguments of political morality. Where, in the absence of 'fit', is there an anchor providing a stability for argument? What is *wrong* under this theory with a judicial decision either way on the question of religious liberty? Is it not just simply the case of Dworkin 'building into' the law *his own personal moral views*, when institutional fit runs out?

The criticism forces out the question of the nature of legal reasoning. But Dworkin's answer is relatively simple and it is implicit in his article 'Hard Cases' and explicit in *Law's Empire*.[13] Hercules must decide on the basis of integrity, whose spirit, he says, is located in the idea of fraternity. In other words, the rationale granting the legal institutions their role in legal argument of providing arguments of 'fit' is the same rationale behind the extension to arguments of substance.

What does that mean? If we accept that judgments of law must fit with institutional practices, we must accept that they do for a reason. What is the reason? According to Dworkin, our judgments must 'fit' with institutional practices not only because we must assume that our community speaks with one voice, but because that voice, too, speaks in a 'principled' way. This much must be true from his drawing the important distinction between 'bare' and 'strategic' consistency.

Dworkin is a little obscure about the appeal to integrity in arguments of substance, as opposed to fit, given that substance is so prominent at the cutting edge of legal argument. But the nerve of his point is in the following paragraph of *Law's Empire*:[14]

The spirit of integrity, which we located in fraternity, would be outraged if Hercules were to make his decision in any way other than by choosing the interpretation that he believes best from the standpoint of political morality as a whole. We accept integrity as a political ideal because we want to treat our political community as one of principle, and the citizens of a community of principle aim not simply at common principles, as if uniformity were all they wanted, but the best common principles politics can find. Integrity is distinct from justice and fairness, but it is bound to them in that way: integrity makes no sense except among people who want fairness and justice as well. So Hercules' final choice of the interpretation he believes sounder on the whole – fairer and more just in the right relation – flows from his initial commitment to integrity. He makes that choice at the moment and by the way integrity both

permits and requires, and it is therefore deeply misleading to say
that he has abandoned the ideal at just that point.

Let us get into this in the following way. Why should we be bothered
about institutional fit? Dworkin's answer seems to be that we are not
concerned with uniformity ('mere elegance'). The distinction he
draws between 'bare' and 'strategic' consistency is obviously important to him here. It follows, I think, that we should not be concerned
with fairness alone, for that presumably would be satisfied by uniformity. Nor, it is clear, are we concerned with justice alone, for that would
clearly not be satisfied by uniformity.

What, then, is special about integrity? 'Principle' cannot do the
desired work because we can use that term in contexts where fairness
and justice are completely absent, as when we talk of the principles of
torturing and poisoning.

It becomes obvious that the important and relevant connection is
with the idea of fraternity, or community. I shall explore that idea in
the following chapter, but for present purposes it is sufficient to
employ Dworkin's characterisation as follows. The best understanding
of the Anglo-American society sees itself based upon communal obligations of an 'associative' sort. It is an interpretive idea, interpretive of
the kind of society we live in (and so the idea is itself subject to
criticisms of the 'fit' and 'substance' sort). These obligations, among
others, require that the group's practices must show an equal concern
for all members.[15]

The presence behind the scenes of the most abstract of Dworkin's
propositions of political morality should not cause surprise. The state
must, through its laws, as through other means, treat people as equals.
That idea is the force which, through the idea of community, drives
integrity.

Does this get us anywhere? Does it mean that judgments of fit are
judgments about how the state ought to treat people as equals? And
that when previous decisions do not treat people as equals (as when,
for example, it exempts barristers, but no one else, from liability in
professional negligence[16]) integrity requires us to depart from previous
decisions? This, in my view, is the right way to read Dworkin. Legal
argument must proceed on the basis that the best way to make sense of
law must be to read it so that it represents the state's striving to treat
people as equals.

This interpretation makes sense of the idea of institutional fit
without, at least directly, using the ideas of fairness and justice. In
metaphorical terms: has the state spoken with one voice? Yes, in the
sense that it has been assumed it has acted in accordance with the
principle that it treat all citizens as equals. Is that the same as treating
all citizens uniformly? No, because that is not the same thing as

treating citizens as equals. It is, instead, the very different idea of delivering equal treatment to all citizens, and this is compatible with great iniquity.[17]

The present discussion brings us back to the relationship between justice, fairness and integrity. Integrity is, as you will remember, a virtue only required in the real world where it is unavoidable that there are to be unjust outcomes and unfair decisions. Presumably, for Dworkin, the ideally just and fair society would be the one where all citizens are always treated with equal respect. And there would be no need for the constraint, or check, of integrity because, by hypothesis, the society is just.

We can assume, therefore, that the virtue of integrity is related to justice in the sense that it is the second best we can hope for, because we recognise that we live in a less than ideal world, a world in which it is necessary to have institutions for making decisions about what is just.

The common law and 'gravitational force': the drive behind analogy

How does Hercules decide the common law? In 'Hard Cases', Dworkin proposed the thesis that previous decisions exerted a 'gravitational force' of fairness, so that Hercules would be bound to consider previous cases as to whether he had, in fairness, to decide in accordance with them, to the extent, anyway, that those previous decisions exerted 'force'.

This thesis has many attractions. Its main one lies in its demonstrating how only certain features of a previous decision are relevant to a decision. While Dworkin does not say so, he offers an enhanced and, I think, better account of the *ratio decidendi* of a decision. Why is it relevant that, in a previous case, a judge awarded damages against an ultimate manufacturer, but irrelevant that the defendant's name was Smith, or that he was black? The relevance can only be that of fairness or, it may be, a similar virtue, such as treating people as equals. Distinctions on the basis of name or skin are unfair.

Someone might object that we are not abstracting the right proposition from the previous case, one which would distance itself from particularities of name and race. This is a better objection than first appears. It may be part of the *nature* of rules that they apply to a wider class of people than that constituted by one person. We feel that there would be something fundamentally wrong with a rule that applied to a particular place and time. For example, distinguishing a previous decision on the ground solely that it was decided on 1 April 1920, suggests that there could have been no rule created by that case.

But these are relatively trivial analytical matters. There is no reason in logic, as opposed to fairness or justice, why rules should not be created which confine themselves to people of a particular race, as many have, or who even have a particular name as, for example, a law that requires those whose names have been drawn out of a hat to report for military service.[18]

The idea that it is fairness to which appeal is made in legal argument about decided cases would clearly mean that arguments of value are intrinsic to legal argument. When, for example, we say to a judge that the case of *Donoghue* v. *Stevenson* applies to our client's case, we are, according to Dworkin, saying that it would be *unfair* for the judge to decide otherwise. Why? Because Mrs Donoghue had been treated in relevantly the same way as we are urging our client should be treated.

This characterisation makes good sense of the extensive use of arguments by analogy. Such arguments, when used by judges, cannot be arguments of logic alone, because they would include arguments such as the absurd ones that I referred to before, such as 'this analogy is not relevant, because it refers to a defendant with the name of Stevenson, not Smith', for example. Arguments by analogy, when not underpinned by arguments of fairness, do not succeed because they are, in this case, prone to the fact which Hart, in a similar context, pointed out, namely that 'logic does not classify particulars'. It is only by appeal to arguments of moral weight that we can make sense of arguments which purport to dismiss characteristics of precedents as 'irrelevant'.

Joseph Raz and Neil MacCormick both stress the importance of analogical arguments in the law. Raz, for example, says that 'Dworkin's theory of adjudication is the most extreme case of total faith in analogical arguments'.[19] MacCormick, throughout his work on legal reasoning, *Legal Reasoning and Legal Theory*, shows in patient detail the extent to which judges rely on such arguments.[20] Both jurists emphasise the constraining role of analogy, allowing the judge only to come to a conclusion which does not, in Raz's terms, introduce 'new discordant and conflicting purposes or values in the law'.[21]

Both Raz's and MacCormick's analyses are compatible with Dworkin's view. But the emphasis in Dworkin is laid directly upon the *moral* point of such arguments and this is where is account differs sharply from their views. To put the question bluntly: why should we be persuaded by an argument from analogy? We must, in Dworkin's view, make the best *moral* sense of the arguments. If there is no moral sense in an argument by analogy, what sense is there left? And so it is not surprising that he takes the moral force of precedent to be one which generates arguments of *fairness*, the 'gravitational force' of precedents varying exactly in accordance with the strength or weakness of the analogy.

The thesis about gravitational force in 'Hard Cases' undergoes some reorganisation in *Law's Empire*. A less convincing thing about the idea that it is fairness *simpliciter* that is behind the doctrine of precedent is the example of the criminal law. Is it 'fair' to the state for a defendant to be convicted on the basis that precedent declared that he had no defence of duress to murder in the first degree? Under the common law, to whom is the judge being fair? Fairness does not seem appropriate here, or if it is, it is submerged within some other more dominant principle.[22]

It is at this point that we can see most clearly a distinction Dworkin draws between 'fairness', which he characterises as 'the matter of the right structure' for the system, and 'procedural due process', which he characterises instead as 'a matter of the right procedures for enforcing rules and regulations the system has produced'.[23]

The common law is concerned with 'procedural due process' which is that form of fairness (for I take it to be a form of fairness) which protects the citizen who relies on pronouncements by judges. In Dworkin's words:

> Strict doctrines of precedent, the practices of legislative history ... are largely, though in different ways, matters of procedural due process because they encourage citizens to rely on doctrinal pronouncements and assumptions that it would be wrong to betray in judging them after the fact.[24]

This articulation suggests more than it can support. It is, independently of integrity, the stand-by, familiar in legal argument, of 'certainty', or the right to have one's reasonable expectations fulfilled. But it is important to distinguish it from fairness in 'the matter of the right structure' for the system. This refers to the fairness underpinning the legislature's right to legislate.

The majority's right to legislate is the rationale behind the application by Hercules of statutes. We see this rationale referred to by judges on various occasions, expressed in terms of the relationship between the judiciary and the legislature as, for example, in the injunction that the judiciary ought not to 'usurp the function of the legislature'. This phrase can only make sense if the legislature is thought to have some justification for having its legislation made effective by the judiciary. Otherwise, why should not a judge ignore a statute whenever he wants?

The distinction between the 'due process' conception of fairness and the 'majority will' conception throws into relief the virtue of codification of the criminal law. It is not just clarity of a code which is important, although that is of undoubted value, but the kind of fairness that is involved in the application of criminal law. It seems untrue to say that people conduct their lives so that, for example, they have a reasonable expectation that first degree murderers may not escape conviction on the basis of a defence of duress. It is, at least, an odd way of putting the argument for the prosecution. (Which is why the 'gravitational force' argument in 'Hard Cases' is not sufficiently analysed in that article.) A more secure footing for the argument that it is fair that duress should not be extended to first degree murder is that it is fair to recognise the legislature's right to legislate and the code did not contain that defence.

Principles and policies

Dworkin is well known for the distinction he drew between arguments of principle, which are arguments about a person's rights, and arguments of policy, which are arguments about community goals. The distinction is important to Dworkin for a number of reasons. First, it is intended to be largely descriptive of distinctions that in fact are drawn by lawyers. Secondly, it represents for him the line to be drawn between the legitimate jurisdictional activities of judges as required by a properly understood democratic separation of legislative and judicial powers. Thirdly, and most importantly for him, it represents his main assault on the most popularly understood version of the moral theory known as utilitarianism.

It is most important to understand the role of the language in the terms he uses. 'Principle' and 'policy' are terms of art for him. Technically, that means he has stipulated meanings for them. He gives definitions for them as follows in Chapters 2 and 4 of *Taking Rights Seriously* and in *Law's Empire* he accepts these definitions without modification.[25]

> I call a 'principle' a standard that is to be observed, not because it will advance or secure an economic, political, or social situation deemed desirable, but because it is a requirement of justice or fairness or some other dimension of morality.[26]
>
> I call a 'policy' that kind of standard that sets out a goal to be reached, generally an improvement in some economic, political, or social feature of the community.[27]
>
> Principles are propositions that describe rights; policies are propositions that describe goals.[28]
>
> A political right is an individuated political aim. An individual has a right to some opportunity or resource or liberty if it counts in favor of a political decision that the decision is likely to advance or protect the state of affairs in which he enjoys the right, even when no other political aim is served and some political aim is disserved thereby, and counts against that decision that it will retard or endanger that state of affairs, even when some other political aim is thereby served.[29]

True, these are stipulations, but it happens that, in his view, these stipulated meanings do correspond very closely to actual usage. It is because of a lack of appreciation of this use by him of the terms as terms of art that fruitless criticism has been made that lawyers some-times mean different things by the word 'policy'. It is the word 'policy' that gives the most difficulty. I think that lawyers (and others) are straightforward about what they mean by an argument of 'principle'. Indeed, saying that 'this is a matter of principle' has at least the following very definite meaning given here, in my view. To make something a 'matter of principle' means being prepared to act upon something *irrespective* of the consequences, because it represents a matter of importance in the dimension of fairness, or morality. In the lawyers' case, it is a small step to say that making a case one of principle is making it one whose moral importance consists in the assertion of a legal right. There is certainly no problem in the United States from jumping from statements of principle to statements about rights. And, I suggest, the only problem in the United Kingdom is that judges tend to be more diffident about these matters, not that there is any more fundamental difference.

'Policy' causes difficulties for different reasons, none of which strikes at Dworkin's thesis. First, I shall make the bald statement that judges, and lawyers, and law students, *know* they should not decide, or argue, on the kinds of grounds that Dworkin calls 'policy' grounds. They *know* that judges have a function specific to the litigants, specific to determining the rights of those litigants. They know, too, I suggest, that the kinds of arguments relevant to making such determinations are different from those which aim at some goal independent of the litigants' rights.

Why the problem? First, there is the simple philosophical one of the existence of penumbral meanings of 'principle' and 'policy' whereby some principles seem indistinguishable from policies and vice versa. But the way out of that problem is easy: some cases are hard. In Hart's terms, '... even if there are borderlines, there must first be lines'.[30] The argument that we have cases that do not fall easily into the categories of principle and policy does not mean that those categories are non-existent.

Secondly, it is clear from Dworkin's definitions (and he says it[31]) that the distinction is not one of content, but of form. This means that for one person a political state of affairs could be a matter of principle and for another it could be a matter of policy. In this way, the distinction stands clear of differences of political opinion. An example should make this clear. George and Emma both believe that the policy of allowing police to detain people indefinitely without trial in North-ern Ireland is unjustified. George believes it on the ground that in the long run this will lead to more violence. In Dworkin's terms, therefore, he believes that indefinite detention without trial is a bad policy. He dislikes it on policy grounds. Emma, on the other hand, is uninterested in the policy question. It is not relevant to her whether indefinite detention without trial will or will not reduce violence in Northern Ireland. She thinks that, as a matter of principle, as a matter of what rights people have, indefinite detention without trial is unjustified. She has a different attitude to the police powers, which is reflected in the formal distinction between principles and policies.

It may be that George is not swayed by the question of rights at all. He may see everything in terms of the policies they serve. He might deny the distinction, in fact, between policies and principles by saying that any matter of principle is able to be converted into a matter of policy. It would mean that he would have to say that there is no sense in the expression 'Damn the consequences, this is a matter of principle'. It would mean, too, that he would have to say that people (including innocent people, of course) had no right to protection from indefinite detention without trial, wherever terrorist violence would be reduced as a result.

It follows from this argument that the distinction is one of form *only* in the sense that it defines the setting in which rival conceptions of what is politically justified may be argued. But it is a distinction of substance, too, in the sense that it requires a strong, separate sense in which principles are not reducible to policies. This is borne out by Dworkin's well-known statement that rights 'trump' utilitarian goals.[32]

Thirdly, critics become bothered by the fact that it is easy to imagine circumstances in which only goals seem to be important, and where rights are of no consequence. Most people, for example, accept the situation in wartime when civilian rights are suspended. Martial law is accepted as a possible option whenever its imposition warrants the pursuit of the desirable goal of winning a war. The problem is thought to be that if there can be situations where there are justifiably *no* rights, or principles, because of the importance of the goal, what criteria could there possibly be for defining principles independently of goals?

The problem is, like the first one, philosophical. There is no problem in logic with having a special category of case where principles are subservient to policies. Martial law is such a category of case. Is there a justification in morality for having such a category? Yes. Principles are subservient to policies whose aim is to preserve or regain a political state of affairs *in which principled decisions would not otherwise be a possibility*. This category of case is obviously justified only by emergencies or catastrophes where rights have to suspended because that is the only way rights will in the future be reinstated.

This special category of emergency is well-catalogued in our moral, political and legal thinking. Martial law is 'martial' law. Its imposition is only justified in wartime, when war is 'raging'.[33] Our concern about the suspension of civilian rights under martial law is characteristically about whether there was a situation which justified its imposition. Many people, for example, felt that the situation in Poland in 1981, although bad, was not bad enough to justify the Polish government in imposing martial law. Many felt that it was being imposed, not because it was necessary to preserve the existence of civilian rights, but to protect a particular political system from change, perceived as undesirable.

But mistake compounds mistake. Some judges are innovative (in the United States, 'activist') in the chain novel sense to which I have already referred. Sometimes, rather self-consciously, they will refer to their decisions as decisions of 'policy'. A good example is Lord Denning in the *Spartan Steel* case, referred to by Dworkin in *Taking Rights Seriously*:

> At bottom I think the question of recovering economic loss is one of policy. Whenever the courts draw a line to mark out the bounds of *duty*, they do it as a matter of policy so as to limit the responsibility of the defendant. Whenever the courts set bounds to the *damages* recoverable ... they do it a matter of policy so as to limit the liability of the defendant.[34]

But it is clear from other remarks that he makes that at least some of his reasons for his judgment attach to the particular parties and do not look to future general impact. He thought the matter should be decided on the basis of relationship of the parties. If other relevantly similar bodies were excused liability (in this case by statute), in Lord Denning's view, this was a strong argument for excusing the defendant.[35] The argument was not helped, in other words, by appealing to *a novel way of arguing*.

And yet other judges (Lord Denning fits into all of the categories, representing different stages of his career) are blatant. They *do* decide policy, in Dworkin's sense, but disguise it. A good example is *DPP* v. *Majewski*,[36] in which the House of Lords interpreted the following words of the Criminal Justice Act 1967 as excluding evidence offered by a defendant as to whether he intended or foresaw a particular result in a criminal case relating to drink or drugs:

> 'A court or jury, in determining whether a person has committed an offence ... shall decide whether he did intend or foresee that result by reference to *all* the evidence ...'[37]

One of the arguments used was that Parliament could not have intended to overturn a clear rule of exclusion in the common law. But this was a *criminal* case and there is an equally clear common rule that criminal statutes should be construed in favour of the defendant. It was argued that s.8 was 'only' a rule of evidence but this was evasive and unconvincing. The sense of the decision was that the judges knew the havoc that would be created by allowing defendants to plead drunkenness as an excuse rather than as only a mitigating circumstance.[38]

Rights and utilitarianism

I think the connection between rights and utilitarianism is relatively clear in Dworkin. He is anti-utilitarian in a sense which gains wide acceptance. The most well-known sense of utilitarianism trades wrongs done to individuals with improvements to general welfare. There are standard examples. The innocent man who is punished (and the fact of his innocence successfully hidden) in order to avert general law-breaking is often used, or the justification of euthanasia on the unmarried orphan tramp on a desert island. Our intuitions about these examples is that there is more to the moral choice than simply the totting up of the overall welfare (the conviction of an innocent person *versus* widespread civil disorder; one killing *versus* personal unhappiness and cost). We intuit that there is something intrinsically wrong in these cases that goes beyond a mere assumption that the consequences would always be bad if these acts were carried out.[39] We intuit that there is a violation of something to do with the people involved that is simply part of the fact that they are people. We can call it an attack on a right to humanity or dignity, or whatever. The point is that this widely understood version of utilitarianism really does not have any conception of a person, other than a 'container' of welfare.

Dworkin's attack on utilitarianism is an attack on this version. From his writing to date, however, it seems that he is prepared to accept utilitarianism in some conception which incorporates an egalitarian premise. Indeed, I shall argue in Chapters 9 and 10 that the version he will be constrained to accept will arise from his understanding of the right people have to be treated as equals. For it does seem to follow from that idea that people may choose the kind of consequences they want for their lives. Why not, then, by combination? What combinatorial principles are consistent with the right to be treated as equals? Democratic principles? It seems right to say that the consequences brought about by a large agglomeration of choices are still consistent with the right of each to be treated as an equal, and thus may properly be used as a justification for political action. Dworkin's discussion of the reverse discrimination principles and his 'right to pornography' discussion particularly bear this out.[40] In *Taking Rights Seriously*, he announces:

> Utilitarian arguments of policy ... seem not to oppose but on the
> contrary to embody the fundamental right of equal concern and
> respect, because they treat the wishes of each member of the
> community on a par with the wishes of any other ...[41]

But the attack on the popular version is fairly straightforward. It is that
utilitarian arguments do not exhaust the position of rights. More
strongly, utilitarianism does not take rights seriously because any claim
of right can be submerged by appeal to the overall consequences. So
Dworkin's criticism of popular utilitarianism amounts to saying that
claims of right are not defeated by a simple appeal to a marginal
increase of welfare. (I say 'marginal' here, to avoid the problems raised
by the cases of catastrophe and emergency.) 'What is important', he
says, 'is the commitment to a scheme of government that makes an
appeal to the right decisive in particular cases.'[42] To take my Northern
Ireland example, the Dworkinian understanding of a right allows the
right not to be detained indefinitely without trial to defeat the argument that a policy of giving such powers to the police will have the
result of reducing the violence by some margin. In his words, arguments of right will 'trump' arguments of policy, meaning by that that in
cases of conflict they have a priority.

I have simplified Dworkin's argument to some degree for the sake of
clarity. The ideas I have just described form a part of his major thesis in
Taking Rights Seriously. In his later writings, he appears to relate claims
of rights to what he calls 'background' justifications for communal
goals. Prominent among these 'background' justifications, of which
there are a number, are utilitarian theories.[43] The idea of rights
'trumping' goals assumes, therefore, a wider significance than is first to
be understood from *Taking Rights Seriously*. It is now not obviously
anti-utilitarian in strain.

I think the reason is simple. Dworkin's development of the idea of
interpretation requires him to see rights arguments as interpretive. It
only makes sense of interpretation to say that it is interpretive of
something. What? The practices of justifications for communal goals.
So the assertion of rights attaches to the background justification (itself
to be interpretively understood) of a particular community.

There is a difficulty and a subtlety here. It helps to go back to the
idea of integrity which, as we saw, was distinguishable from justice and
fairness. It is out of a concern for justice and fairness that integrity,
however, acquires its gravity. But it does not follow that a decision
made in accordance with the requirements of integrity is the best in
terms of justice or fairness. To remind ourselves, we live, not in the
ideal world, but in the real world. It follows that being interpretive
about the background justification in a community about communal
goals does not carry with it *ideal* endorsement.

It is this point that Hart does not appreciate in his criticism of Dworkin for being unable to give an account of rights in either brutal totalitarian regimes, where no interpretation could yield a background justification for communal goals, or a society where people are perfect, like angels. Dworkin only needs to reply that these communities are not ones with the appropriate background justifications for rights.[44]

Dworkin denies that rights are 'timeless' and 'fixed by human nature'. They are a relative idea, relative to the background justification. They 'figure in complex packages of political theory':

> I am anxious to show how rights fit into different packages, so that I want to see, for example, which rights should be accepted as trumps over utility if utility is accepted, as many people think it should be accepted, as the proper background justification ... But it does not follow from this investigation that I must endorse ... the package of utilitarianism together with the rights that utilitarianism requires as the best package that can be constructed. I do not. Though rights are relative to packages, one package might still be chosen over others as better, and I doubt that in the end any package based on any familiar form of utilitarianism will turn out to be best.[45]

The different kinds of rights

Dworkin produces a useful taxonomy of the forms of right-based arguments in his article 'Hard Cases'. The different forms of rights he describes cross political theories and the use and emphasis laid on each will reflect each kind of political theory. He distinguishes, for example, between 'absolute' rights, ones that withstand no competition (as in theories that posit, for example, an 'absolute' right to life), and rights that are less than absolute. The important point is, remember, that the idea of a right is defined by its ability to withstand competition against non-urgent goals (for example, 'any of the ordinary routine goals of political administration'[46]).

We may distinguish between 'background' rights and 'institutional' rights. 'Background' rights are those rights which argue towards some state of affairs without referring to the right some institution has to make a decision. An example would be where someone proposes that we have a right, when no such right is contained in legislation or in the constitution. Someone might argue that we have a 'background' right to another person's property if we need more. That statement can be understood without reference to any legislation or constitutional principle in the Anglo-American jurisdiction. It is a statement that can be understood, nevertheless, as making sense.

Many people will disagree that statements of rights, not referring to the actual institutions of state coercion, make sense. What is the point of such statements? What is there to them but empty statements of political rhetoric? Such is the substance of Bentham's criticisms of the rights proclaimed by the defenders of the French revolution, that they were 'nonsense on stilts'. Again, though, appeal to common sense. It *does* make sense to claim, whether or not you agree with the moral substance, that a foetus has a 'right to life', or that people have the right not to be detained by the state indefinitely without trial. It is side-stepping the issue to say that such statements ought to be rewritten in the form, for example, that 'a foetus *ought* to have the right to life'. If it is rewritten in that way, the argument is still one urging a political state of affairs that should obtain, independently of the rights that can be identified as part of an institution.

The foregoing argument does not, in my view, alter the distinction of type between 'background' and 'institutional' arguments. The point is that there are (at least) two different sorts of argument, each independent of arguments concerning unindividuated goals (the 'policy' arguments) which urge a political state of affairs. One is drawn from institutions, the other not. Arguments which deny the existence of rights independent from institutions, but allow for arguments urging changes in those institutions, clearly employ the distinction Dworkin recommends. If the arguments quarrel with the idea of *rights*, they are relevant to Dworkin's attempt at distinguishing rights from policies, not to the distinction between background and institutional type arguments.

Dworkin draws a further distinction between 'abstract' and 'concrete' rights. 'Abstract' rights are the grand statements of rights such as that 'people have a right to free speech' or to 'dignity' and so on, which are 'abstract' because they do not spell out the impact which they are intended to have on any actual social situation, or how such rights are supposed to be compromised against other rights. On the other hand, 'concrete' rights are more or less definite about such matters as, for example, when we might say that people have a right to publish defence plans classified as secret provided that this publication will not create an immediate physical danger to troops. This right is a 'concretisation', as it were, of the abstract right to free speech.

The interpretive character of the common law

Dworkin's theory of law is interpretive, as we have seen. It is not, therefore, fully responsive to descriptive criticisms which take the form: this is not actually how judges behave. A common criticism of Dworkin proceeds by pointing out cases in which judges have decided an issue by a clear reference to a mode of reasoning that Dworkin would accept to be policy-making. There is no doubt that it happens. But that proves, in itself, nothing. What if judges and lawyers (including academic lawyers) characteristically criticise such modes of reasoning (as they do)? Then, as a part of a proper description of the law, we must include such modes of criticism as part of the law. Only in that way will we properly describe what judges *characteristically* do.

By failing to tackle this point, John Bell's long and thoughtful study of Dworkin's legal theory in the United Kingdom misfires.[47] Bell points out the well-known cases where courts have decided in a way characterised by Dworkin as 'policy decisions' but does not join them to a description of how many of those cases have met with *characteristic* criticism. In a narrowly historical sense it is 'descriptively' true to say that the House of Lords and the Court of Appeal have made or contemplated decisions on the basis of Dworkin's conception of policy. But it is equally true that such decisions, actual or envisaged, are frequently condemned by lawyers. Random examples are Lord Parker's warning against the usurpation of the legislative function by the judiciary (itself a theoretical, interpretive, statement about the judicial role), in *Fisher* v. *Bell*,[48] Lord Simon's similar warning in *DPP* v. *Lynch*,[49] the House of Lords statement that it is for Parliament and not the courts to create new exceptions to the hearsay rule,[50] and Lord Scarman's statement in *McLoughlin* v. *O'Brian*[51] that it is for the legislature, not the judiciary, to decide matters of policy.

Academic lawyers, too, fill journals and books with statements criticising what they believe be wrong decisions in law. Imagine taking well-known textbooks such as *Treitel on Contract* or *Cross on Evidence* and attempting to remove the 'prescriptive' bits so as to leave only the 'descriptive' bits. It would be a pointless task. We should note, too, the rapport which exists between public attitudes and constitutional arrangements. This requires explanation in terms of something more sophisticated than simple description. For example, significant public criticism of the decision in *Shaw* v. *DPP*[52] centred on the assumption made by the judges, thought by the public to be wrong, that they had the power to create new criminal offences, as a matter of judicial policy, independently from Parliament.

When we draw up a list of cases in which it has appeared that judges have decided on policy grounds, we discover that these cases stick out for that very reason. It is not enough, for example, to say that *Shaw* v. *DPP* was a case which shows Dworkin to be wrong. On the contrary, it shows him to be *right*. The extensive criticisms levelled at the decision in that case are Dworkinian ones. This was a case of retrospectively enforced legislation untouched by considerations of the rights of the defendant.

Many of the cases which are used to show that policy decisions are characteristic of the legal system are those in which Lord Denning was involved. But his position in the judicial world has to be treated with great care. He was a great judge. Many of his decisions are Herculean in the best sense. Imaginative, innovatory and just. His judgments reveal the creative possibilities inherent *within* the judicial role. Many lawyers viewed his decisions with great suspicion because they felt that he was underemphasising, or even ignoring, the role of rights of only a particular sort, those which create certainty by giving rise to reasonable expectations. And, I think, that at times Lord Denning frankly legislated.[53] We should not let this fact blind us to the innovatory sorts of genuine legal judgments he made, however.

The right to damages for emotional distress

We have now the means to follow Dworkin's analysis of the case decided in the House of Lords, that of *McLoughlin* v. *O'Brian*.[54] This should be instructive as to how he views legal argument. Remember that, in his view, substantial arguments (relating to the right people have to be treated as equals) have to be matched to fit (the already existing case law).

Mrs McLoughlin learned that her husband and children were involved in a car accident. She set out for the hospital some miles away, and when she got there she was told her daughter was dead and she saw that her husband and other children were seriously injured. She suffered severe shock and she sued, among others, the driver of the vehicle, whose negligence caused the accident.

How should the case have been decided? It was a hard case, because in all the previous cases, the facts involved people suffering nervous shock almost immediately upon the accident occurring and more or less at its scene. In these cases, the people suffering shock were allowed to recover.[55]

Dworkin suggests how Hercules might decide this case. He says that Hercules might begin by considering the following six possible interpretations of the case law:

1. *Success (for the victim) only where there is physical injury.* But we can rule this out immediately because it does not fit the law of tort. It is clear that damages may be obtained for *nervous* shock.

2. *Success only where the emotional injury occurs at the accident, not later.* But, says Dworkin, this would just draw a morally arbitrary line.

3. *Success only where a practice of awarding someone like Mrs McLoughlin would be economically efficient.* If this were simply a matter of economic *policy*, Dworkin would reject it because it does not respect 'the ambition integrity assumes, the ambition to be a community of principle'.[56] The argument is, in other words, to be rejected because it is one of naked policy, ignoring Mrs McLoughlin's right to be treated as an equal.

There is, however, an ambiguity which Dworkin says is inherent in the idea that a community should aim at efficiency. It may be that people have a *right* to a certain amount of redistribution under some system which aims at economic efficiency. But I leave this for Chapters 9 and 10, where I discuss it at some length. Dworkin leaves a developed discussion of the idea (which first appears in a very obscure fashion in his article 'Hard Cases'[57]) to Chapter 8 of *Law's Empire*, in a highly compressed and difficult chapter.[58] But for present purposes, it is true to say that Dworkin rejects the economic pursuit of economic efficiency in this sort of case where it consists solely of the pursuit of overall (unindividuated) communal wealth.

4.   *Success only where the injury, whether physical or emotional, is the* direct *consequence of the accident.* But this interpretation has to be ruled out because it is contrary to fit: it contradicts the clear case law, where there is a test of foreseeability which limits the liability of the person who causes the accident.

5.   *Success only where the injury is foreseeable.*

6.   *Success for foreseeable injury, except where an unfair financial burden is placed on the person who causes the accident.* ('Unfair' meaning 'disproportionate to the moral blame for causing the accident'.)

According to Dworkin, 5 and 6 are the best contenders. 1 and 4 are ruled out because they contradict 'fit'. They simply cannot be made to cohere with the previous legal decisions. 2 is ruled out because it is an interpretation that relies on an arbitrary assertion that people at the scene can recover, those who are not cannot. 3 is ruled out because it relies on policy, not principle.

How do we assess Dworkin's discussion of possibilities 1–4? It is not clear whether they are either matters of fit or substance, but I do not think that matters. Certainly, arbitrariness is not an attribute of a good judicial decision. Most lawyers would agree with that, and to that extent we can say that arbitrariness as a feature of the common law just does not 'fit'. But it is also a matter of substance. Being arbitrary – making decisions without reasons being thought necessary – constitutes a substantial wrong. We see as wrong, as 'arbitrary', for example, a discrimination between people on the basis that some have black skins.[59]

Dworkin can argue, too, both from fit and from substance to rule out policy decisions by judges. As I have argued, judges *characteristically* say that policy matters are for the legislature and, in *McLoughlin* v. *O'Brian*, Lord Scarman said:

> ... in this branch of the law it is not for the courts but for the legislature to set limits, if any be needed, to the law's development ... The problem is one of social, economic, and financial policy. The considerations relevant to a decision are not such as to be capable of being handled within the limits of the forensic process.[60]

Of course, there were statements from the other judges, notably Lord Bridge, that oppose Lord Scarman's idea. On the other hand, Dworkin provides a full theory, based on rights, from which he can criticise the majority's views (as many others have). That theory supports a distinction between what a judge should do and what the powers and responsibilities of the legislature are. As we have seen, that theory proposes that a working distinction be drawn between decisions based on principle and decisions that further policies.

Let us now examine interpretations 5 and 6. 'Which story', he asks, 'shows the community in a better light, all things considered, from the standpoint of political morality?' Suppose that interpretations 5 and 6 equally 'fit' the precedents. Dworkin says that Hercules should construct two abstract principles. First, that community sympathy towards individuals who are suddenly required to pay large amounts for accidents they cause is an argument in support of public insurance schemes, safety regulations and so on. This is a principle of 'collective sympathy', he says. Second, that it is right that people who are at fault should pay for the consequences of their fault and so costs should be apportioned between private individuals.

These are two principles of exactly the sort that a lawyer could produce in court. If the 'private apportioning' principle should prevail of these two, then interpretation 5 is the correct one. Mrs McLoughlin wins just because Mr O'Brian was at fault. If, on the other hand, the 'collective sympathy' principle prevails, Mrs McLoughlin loses. Why? Because Mrs McLoughlin's injury, while foreseeable, was so remote as to place an unfair burden upon Mr O'Brian in proportion to his fault.

Which interpretation should be preferred? Dworkin thinks that Mrs McLoughlin should have won, favouring interpretation 5, at least in automobile accident cases when there is a widely available and sensible liability insurance available privately.

Law as an argumentative attitude

A good way to gain an understanding of Dworkin's theory of law is to appreciate the importance he places upon legal argument. Do not think of law as a set of rules, to be 'learned', and that is it. Think of law as an attitude of mind. This, I think, is the most important and attractive feature of Dworkin's work in legal philosophy. In the final chapter of *Law's Empire*, Dworkin rather grandly says:

> Law is not exhausted by any catalogue of rules or principles, each with its own dominion over some discrete theater of behaviour. Nor by any roster of officials and their powers each over part of our lives.

Law's empire is defined by attitude, not territory or power or process.[61]

This idea, that law is primarily about an argumentative attitude towards our legal institutions, understood in the broadest sense, is particularly well understood by lawyers used to court practice. Observe some lawyers at work here. Arguments are what make or break their day. The invention of a new argument that 'makes sense', that works, is what an advocate thrives on, what a judge understands and, very importantly, what a law student studies.

Legal education

Dworkin's theory has great significance for understanding the point of legal education, especially in England. English lawyers are more suspicious of 'theory' than lawyers in the United States. Although in England there has been an increase in the theoretical content of some academic law courses over the past decade, much of this has been marked by a lack of rigour in thinking about what 'theory' means. To some it means economics and to others just a critical attitude. Some law teachers think, quite wrongly, that our knowledge of theoretical issues is so far developed that we need now *only* have separate 'theories' of, for example, contract, tort, labour law and so on.[62]

In some limited ways, of course, it is true to say that a theoretical understanding of the skills we possess is not always required. We do not have to understand theories about the frictional properties of laces in order to tie our shoes. Gifted lawyers produce sophisticated and complex arguments because they have learned the 'feel' of their appropriateness.

Sometimes, too, creative efforts in many fields of expression exceed and appear to defy theoretical explanation. Indeed, our acceptance of this possibility explains why we think of certain relatively rare kinds of innovation as 'ahead of their time'. In art, what to many seemed scrappy and unfinished works by the impressionists are now widely understood as artistic expression which exploited the dimension of light to a greater degree than previously.

Law is similar. Landmark judgments have been provided with later and widely accepted theoretical explanations. Examples are the 'High Trees' principle, now understood as reasonable reliance,[62] and Lord Denning's famous dissenting judgment in *Candler* v. *Crane, Christmas & Co.*, now seen as an important early statement of the principles of liability for negligently induced economic loss.[63]

But to seize upon this gap between theory and practice as evidence of the fruitlessness of theoretical understanding would be wrong. Law students are better equipped if they are, early on, inculcated with an awareness from the beginning of what they are supposed to do – of what counts as appropriate legal argument. And among skilled and experienced lawyers at the other end of the profession, there is a strong need for a theoretical structure where the sense of appropriateness begins to fray in difficult cases, very particularly in constitutional cases.

Some of the most widely known cases in recent years have been of this hard sort. Accounts by United Kingdom judges of the powers and duties of government officials such as the Attorney-General,[64] or the roles of the local authorities,[65] or the limits of censorship,[66] show a distinct and unhealthy diffidence toward engaging in constructive political theorising. The judiciary and the legislature are, after all, *political* institutions and their respective political dress is not *just there* for judges to observe. Judgment is required.

It should be much more widely appreciated that the decisions in these sorts of cases require justifications that are not 'subjective' only, nor 'descriptive' of the law 'as it happens to be'. These decisions require full-blooded, normative accounts of why the very considerable powers of state coercion should, or should not, be used in various specific occasions.

In the United States, not only are judges more generally aware of the different theories of constitutional interpretation but theoretical issues actually enter the domain of public discussion. The original intention theory of constitutional interpretation in the United States is a good example. It was discussed in the popular press extensively during the Robert Bork nomination hearings in Senate in late 1987, for example. I can remember actually discussing the issue with a New York taxi driver, at the time. It is a bleak truth that *there is no equivalent understanding of constitutional issues in the United Kingdom corresponding to this level.*

Part of the reason must be legal education. The differences between the United States and the United Kingdom (with more emphasis on England) are enormous and well known. Teaching law students legal argument beyond the citing of relevant statutes and precedents is impossible without some sort of theoretical structure within which, or against which, arguments can be compared, weighed, criticised, adopted or dropped. Regrettably, the bulk of legal education in England goes little further than the stockpiling of rules. Yet, if this is the objective of legal education, a level is achieved no higher than that, say, of learning history by noting only dates, names and events, or learning works of literature by simply following the plots, or learning to play musically by paying attention only to the key and time signatures. This focus of legal education is career-directed in the meanest sense. It carries little, if any, vestige of a conception of service to public argument and of contribution to public virtues.

It is the idea of the *point* of integrity that links the discussion here of

legal education with the subject of the next chapter. For, according to
Dworkin, legal argument must aim at the coherence demanded by
integrity for a special reason. It is that integrity should reflect a
commitment by the community to treating all of its citizens as equals.
For him, legal argument is fundamentally concerned with public
argument. We turn, then, to consider the relationship between the
idea of integrity and community.

Notes

1. *Taking Rights Seriously*, p. 105.
2. A distinguished English judge told me recently (and he was not being
flippant) that courts had 'nothing to do with rights' and that the separation
of powers was 'history' if it was even that, and that he saw his task as only to
do what the 'public's sense of justice' required.
3. What Dworkin calls 'compartmentalisation' and the problem of
'local priority'. He thinks that the practice of legal compartmentalisation is
an interpretive one and that integrity, on the whole, condemns it because
the aim of integrity is to make the law coherent as a whole. Nevertheless,
'Dividing departments of law ... promotes predictability and guards against
sudden official reinterpretations that uproot large areas of law ...' *Law's
Empire* p. 252.
4. *Lynch* v. *D.P.P.* [1975] 1 All E.R. 913, 942.
5. See, for example, Lord Diplock's remark in *Fisher* v. *Bell* [1961] 1
Q.B. 394, 400 that the judiciary must not usurp the function of the
legislature. And see the references in the next chapter in the discussion on
the descriptive nature of Dworkin's distinction between principles and
policies.
6. See 'Working on the Chain Gang: Interpretation in Law and
Literature' 60 *Texas Law Review* 551 (1982) and 'Wrong Again' 62 *Texas
Law Review* 299 (1983).
7. He displays all the mistakes about objectivity which I examine in
Chapter 6, too, which I do not deal with here.
8. *Law's Empire*, p. 235.
9. The professor of jurisprudence at Belfast University accuses Dworkin
of being a 'culture vulture', for example. See Lee *Judging Judges* (1988)
Faber at p.30.
10. Neil MacCormick says that the imaginary society I posit here would
bring about a corruption of art. It would change it, he says. It is simply not
clear to me that it would, as long as the idea that the judges (of art) were not
right *because* they were invested with that authority to judge. In my view,
that would be an equally corrupting idea in our society in relation to judges
of law.
11. See *Everson* v. *Board of Education* 330 U.S. 1 (1947).
12. *Taking Rights Seriously*, p. 107.
13. *Taking Rights Seriously*, pp. 254–8.
14. *Taking Rights Seriously*, p. 263.

15. Even if they are hierarchical, says Dworkin, as long as they are not class based. For example, 'Armies may be fraternal organizations if that condition is met. But caste systems that count some members as inherently less worthy than others are not fraternal ...' *Law's Empire*, p. 201.

16. See Dworkin's discussion in *Law's Empire*, pp. 219–20, and the restriction on this immunity placed by the House of Lords in *Saif Ali* v. *Sydney Mitchell & Co.* [1980] A.C. 198.

17. See the discussion in Chapter 9 on equality.

18. See Hart's useful discussion about the formal quality of rules in *The Concept of Law* particularly Chapter 9.

19. See his *The Authority of Law* (1979) Clarendon Press, Chapter 10, p. 205, n. 19.

20. See *Legal Rights and Legal Reasoning* (1978) Clarendon, particularly Chapter 7.

21. *The Authority of Law*, p. 204.

22. See *Taking Rights Seriously*, p. 100, where Dworkin acknowledges, rather than explains, the different 'geometry' of civil and criminal cases.

23. *Law's Empire*, pp. 404–5.

24. *Law's Empire*, p. 405.

25. See *Law's Empire*, p. 438, n. 30.

26. *Taking Rights Seriously*, p. 22.

27. *Taking Rights Seriously*, p. 22.

28. *Taking Rights Seriously*, p. 90.

29. *Taking Rights Seriously*, p. 91.

30. See Hart, *Essays in Jurisprudence and Philosophy* (1983) Clarendon, Chapter 2, p. 71.

31. *Taking Rights Seriously*, p. 90.

32. *Taking Rights Seriously*, Introduction p. xv.

33. See *R. (Garde)* v. *Strickland* [1921] 2 I.R. 317.

34. *Spartan Steel* v. *Martin & Co.* [1973] 1 Q.B. 27 at 36.

35. See pp. 37-8.

36. [1977] A.C. 443.

37. S.8.

38. My interpretation of this decision is supported in *Jaggard* v. *Dickinson* [1981] Q.B. 527.

Good examples of the various uses of the word 'policy', in Dworkin's sense and others, are to be found in John Bell's excellent study *Policy Arguments in Judicial Decisions* (1983) Oxford.

39. What is often referred to as a 'side effects' argument for utilitarianism. See Glover *Causing Death and Saving Lives* (1977) Penguin pp. 40–1.

40. See also Dworkin's 'What Is Equality ? Part I: Equality of Welfare' (1981) 10 *Philosophy and Public Affairs* 185–246, particularly towards the end. Further important discussions are to be found in *Taking Rights Seriously* pp. 94–100 and 272–8; and in *A Matter of Principle* pp. 359–72.

41. *Taking Rights Seriously*, p. 275.

42. *Taking Rights Seriously*, p. 96.

43. See *A Matter of Principle*, p. 359.

44. Hart's article, entitled 'Between Utility and Rights', which contains a

brilliantly clear résumé of various of both Nozick and Dworkin's positions in political philosophy, is to be found in Hart's *Essays in Jurisprudence and Philosophy* (1983) Oxford, Chapter 9, p. 198, and esp. pp. 208–21. The article is also to be found in *Ronald Dworkin and Contemporary Jurisprudence* ed. Cohen (1984) Duckworth p. 214. Dworkin's reply to the article is in the Cohen volume, at p. 282. See also *A Matter of Principle* pp. 353-72.

45. *A Matter of Principle*, p. 370.

46. *Taking Rights Seriously*, p. 13.

47. See John Bell, *Policy Arguments in Judicial Decisions* (1983) Oxford.

48. [1961] 1 Q.B. 394, 400.

49. [1975] A.C. 653, 695–6.

50. *Myers* v. *DPP* [1964] 2 All E.R. 881 per Lord Hodson at 893: 'There is not in my opinion any justification for endeavouring to extend the rule ... Hedge the extension about with safeguards as you will, this surely would be judicial legislation with a vengeance in an attempt to introduce reform of the law of evidence which, if needed, can properly be dealt with only by the legislature.' The history is that Parliament, very shortly after this judgment and in response to criticisms of its result, enacted the *Criminal Evidence Act* 1965, which made admissible those statements contained in business records of the type adduced in *Myers*.

51. [1983] A.C. 410, 431.

52. [1962] A.C. 200.

53. I think Lord Denning legislated when he tried, famously, to create a married woman's 'equity' by virtue only of her status as a wife in order to bind third parties so that she could remain in the house. He was overruled by the House of Lords in *National Provincial Bank, Ltd.* v. *Ainsworth* [1965] A.C. 1175. Lord Upjohn, in the House of Lords, said at 1239: 'I am of opinion with all respect to the Master of the Rolls' statement of her rights ... her mere equity not amounting to an equitable interest nor being ancillary to or dependent upon an equitable interest does not bind purchasers.' Of course, *that* Lord Upjohn said this does not *mean* that the Court of Appeal legislated. It is a matter of interpretation of the law. But I use this as an example of a case famous for a common interpretation that Lord Denning was departing from law, although moved by a considerable feeling for the justice of the result he produced. The situation now is that that justice is provided for in statute. (See The Matrimonial Homes Act 1983.)

This case can be contrasted with Lord Denning's equally famous judgment which confirmed the principle of 'promissory estoppel', *Central London Property Trust, Ltd.* v. *High Trees House, Ltd.* [1947] 1 K.B. 130. More commentators are prepared to say, about that case, that it was a highly imaginative and bold decision *but in accordance with legal principle*. There are many other such judgments in Lord Denning's career. My point is to say that in making judgments about his role in cases, we do employ a distinction between creative decisions which are outside the judicial role and those that are within it.

The English law is scattered with other examples where creative decisions of Lord Denning's appear on either side of the border between adjudicative and legislative function. For example, see *Lim* v. *Camden Health Authority* [1979] 2 All E.R. 910, where Lord Scarman, in the House of Lords, made the following remark (913–4): 'Lord Denning MR in the Court of Appeal declared that a radical reappraisal of the law is needed. I agree. But I part company with him on ways and means. Lord Denning MR believes it can be done by the judges, whereas I would suggest to your Lordships that such a reappraisal calls for social, financial, economic and administrative decisions which only the legislature can take.'

54. See *Law's Empire* pp. 238–50.

55. See *Marshall* v. *Lionel Enterprises Inc.* [1972] O.R 177; *Chadwick* v. *British Transport* [1967] 1 W.L.R. 912.

56. *Law's Empire*, p. 243.

57. See *Taking Rights Seriously*, pp. 98-100.

58. See later, Chapter 10, in the section entitled 'The neighbour principle and the law of tort'.

59. See 'Lord Devlin and the Enforcement of Morals' (1966) 75 *Yale Law Journal* 986–1,005. It is reprinted in *Taking Rights Seriously* at pp.240–58 and in Wasserstrom, R., *Morality and the Law* (Belmont: Wadsworth, 1971) at pp.55–72. See later in Chapter 6 the section entitled 'Objectivity and morality'.

60. *McLouglin* v. *O'Brian* [1982] 2 All E.R. 310–11.

61. *Law's Empire*, p. 413.

62. See, for example, Hunt, 'Jurisprudence, Philosophy and Legal Education - Against Foundationalism' (1986) 6 *Legal Studies* 292. It is not clear what principles he thinks should determine the categories of subject for which theorising is appropriate. Why not further sub-divisions? Why not 'a theory of offer and acceptance' or 'a theory of attestation' to supplant grander theories? The position reaches absurdity if applied to mechanics. A theory of 'car'; of 'bicycle'; of 'mousetrap'?

63. See Atiyah, 'Contracts, Promises, and the Law of Obligations', in his *Essays on Contract* (1986) Oxford. He says there, for example, '... cases of benefits received or of action in reliance, are more common than is suggested by our conventional image of the legal world', p. 22. See also Fried, *Contract as Promise* (1981) Harvard: 'The connection between contract and the expectation principle is so palpable that there is reason to doubt that its legal recognition is a relatively recent invention,' p. 21.

64. [1951] 2 K.B. 164, 181. In the House of Lords in *Hedley Byrne* v. *Heller and Partners* [1964] A.C. 465 at 530 Lord Devlin, approving of Lord Denning's decision in *Candler*, said: '... in so far as your Lordships describe the circumstances in which an implication will ordinarily be drawn, I am prepared to adopt any one of your Lordships' statements as showing the general rule; and I pay the same respect to the statement by Denning L.J. in his dissenting judgment in *Candler, Crane, Christmas and Co.* about the circumstances in which he says a duty to use care in making a statement exists.' Lord Pearce referred to Lord Denning's judgment, too, saying 'I agree with those words. In my opinion, they are consonant with the earlier cases ...' (539).

65. See *Gouriet* v. *Union of Post Office Workers* [1978] A.C. 435.

66. See the 'Fares fair' case of *Bromley London Borough Council* v. *Greater London Council* [1983] A.C. 768; *Secretary of State for Education and Science* v. *Thameside Metropolitan Borough Council* [1977] 1014.

67. See the 'Spycatcher' case of *Attorney-General* v. *Guardian Newspapers No. 2* [1988] 3 All E.R. 545; and *R.* v. *Secretary of State for the Home Department, ex parte Brind* (1990) W.L.R. 787 (Court of Appeal, awaiting appeal to the House of Lords). The most notorious is, I think, the Clive Ponting case, found as *R.* v. *Ponting* [1985] *Crim. L.R.* 318. Ponting was charged with an offence under s.2(1) of The Official Secrets Act 1911. Ponting, a civil servant, leaked two Ministry of Defence documents to a Labour MP. These documents related to Parliamentary inquiries about the sinking of the Argentinian battleship the *General Belgrano* during the Falklands war. The first document was unclassified and the second was marked 'confidential'. The important question was the meaning of the words 'in the interest of the State'. The judge simply equated that with the interest of the 'particular government of the day'. The report states: 'It was not ... for the jury to decide what the Government's policy should have been nor was it for them to enter into a political debate. In this case it was not in dispute that the policy of the Government was not to give the information which Mr. Ponting communicated.'

4

Integrity and community

As we have seen, Dworkin means his idea of integrity to be something over and above consistency, the idea of treating like cases alike, or, as he says, mere 'elegance'. Integrity, on the other hand, regards the way people ought to be treated as fundamental and regards rights as both giving rise to and constraining decisions about the community's future. The analogy is with the idea of personal integrity. The community is to be regarded as having a personality that is subject to the same sort of moral criticism that we make of a person who has not acted out of integrity. It will be necessary for us to look at the important idea, for Dworkin, of the personification of the community and the special relationship of agency that exists between a person and his community.

The personification of the community

The community can be personified. We make day-to-day judgments about communities (or governments, or states) in respect of what we perceive their duties to be, whether it is to reduce unemployment, curb crime or keep the streets clean. We criticise communities, too, for their war crimes or their irresponsibility towards their duties under international law.

Two questions arise. First, is the personification of the community merely a metaphor which hides the attachment of responsibilities to particular individuals? Second, if the personification of the community allows responsibility of this sort, is it necessary or desirable to go the step further of requiring the community to act in accordance with the requirements of integrity?

We have little difficulty in ascribing moral responsibility to groups. We talk freely and correctly of the responsibility of corporations, for example, and we mean this to be something over and above the ascription of responsibility to executive members of corporations. If we do criticise individual members of a corporation we do so in at least two ways. We can do so by assuming that those members have done something, such as, for example, intentionally or negligently instituted systematic pollution or taken unjustified risks, which was authorised by the corporation.

Here our criticism will centre on what has been done in the name of the corporation. If we go to court we usually take action against the corporation, and this supports the idea that responsibility may be logically prior to the officials involved. Sometimes, in the case of the criminal law, there can be a prosecution of a corporation by way of identifying who effectively controls it, usually the managing director and his close associates. Such a prosecution is usually expressed in metaphorical terms as a prosecution of the 'mind' or 'brain' of the corporation.[1]

Another way to criticise corporate members is simply to say that what they have done is outside the authority of the corporation. Criticisms of the parliamentary member who does not attend debates, or the council worker who skives, may be either criticisms directed towards the failings of the individual, or a mixture both of that and a criticism about how the offices themselves are run. But these sorts of criticism are capable of supporting prior group responsibility, too.

What is to be gained from asserting that ascriptions of responsibility attach to individuals only? The idea of group responsibility is in our language and our common stock of moral thinking. It plays a significant role in our legal system and it permits a more complex allocation of rights and responsibilities than would otherwise be possible. Does ascribing responsibility to corporations makes them 'faceless' and absolve their members of responsibility? But the members of a corporation are connected to corporate responsibility by a complex web of rights and powers. It is an indirect, but nevertheless vital, relationship. There is that fundamental connection. Consider the alternative. Abolish the idea of corporate identity altogether, and in the case more generally under discussion, abolish the idea of the community. We cannot be ready for that.

The 'inner morality' of law

A more fruitful possibility is the second question I asked, namely, can the idea of integrity be helpfully applied to the community? What is *personal* integrity? It is interesting and important to note that the idea is not one which, in the usual case, directly concerns particular actions. If it is used in this way it takes the form of praising the action because it was that of a person who 'has integrity'. Most often we use the idea by invoking the idea of trust, as for example, we will assure ourselves that Andrew was a 'man of integrity' and would not be 'swayed' by, say, the thought of personal aggrandisement.

The idea of 'acting according to principle' is highly relevant here. Andrew will be a man who takes his decision according to what he considers to be the correct moral view of any matter. Saying that a person acts according to principle is part of saying that a person has integrity and conversely, and more frequently, we say that an 'unprincipled' person 'lacks integrity'. There is a further element, too, of reliability. You can trust someone who acts on principle to be consistent in her judgments, but only to the extent that principle demands this, so that integrity is not the same thing as blind loyalty, with which integrity is sometimes confused.

How do these two ideas of moral principle and consistency fit within the metaphor of the community's integrity? The idea of equality is very important. The community must act according to moral principle and it should, as far as principle demands, be consistent in its dealings with citizens. The metaphor works thus far. But the idea of equality is very important for Dworkin and it is not clear how far the idea of integrity, in general, carries with it the idea of equality. It is not difficult to envisage the integrity of the Nazi stormtrooper, who lives according to Nazi principles of racism among others, and who is to be trusted to act according to those principles against the force of self-interest.

Hart's well-known criticism of Lon Fuller's equally well-known eight principles of the 'inner morality' of law is important here. These principles, which loosely describe requirements of procedural justice, were claimed by Fuller to ensure that a legal system would satisfy the demands of morality, to the extent that a legal system which adhered to all of the principles would explain the all-important idea of 'fidelity to law'. In other words, such a legal system would command obedience with moral justification.

Fuller's key idea is that evil aims lack a 'logic' and 'coherence' that moral aims have. Thus, paying attention to the 'coherence' of the laws ensures their morality. The argument is unfortunate because it does, of course, claim too much. Hart's criticism is that we could, equally, have eight principles of the 'inner morality' of the poisoner's art ('use tasteless, odourless poison', 'use poisons that are fully eliminated from the victim's body' etc). Or we can improvise further. We can talk of the principles of the inner morality of Nazism, for example, or the principles of the inner 'morality' of chess. The point is that the idea of principles in themselves, with the attendant explanation at a general level of what is to be achieved (e.g. elimination of non-Aryan races) plus consistency, is insufficient to establish the moral nature of such practices.

What has been unfortunate about Hart's criticism is that it obscured Fuller's point. This was that there is an important sense of legal justification that claims made in the name of law are morally serious.

At the least, the person who makes a genuine claim for legal justification of an immoral, Nazi-type legal system *must* believe that there is some moral force to his claim. We believe that when we make some claim about our law our claim carries some moral force. It is not enough simply to deny this. At least some explanation is required for our belief that this is so if, in fact, we are wrong.

Evil legal systems

Let us explore Dworkin's clear position on this matter. He distinguishes between what he calls the 'grounds' of law and the 'force' of law. The grounds of law are obtained by looking interpretively at the legal practices of some community from the point of view of a participator in those practices. It would be possible, from this standpoint, to work out how a judge in Nazi Germany might decide a case. We can call him Siegfried, J. Imagine some horrific hard case under the Nuremberg laws, say, to do with sexual relations between Jews and German nationals.[2] We could take account of widely believed theories of racial superiority to provide detailed arguments about which way the case should be decided.[3] We could learn how to argue a case by learning the 'ground rules', as it were, of an evil legal system.

But to produce an argument from the 'grounds' of law is not thereby to endorse it. A full-blooded political theory, according to Dworkin, requires an explanation not only of grounds but of the moral 'force' of law. He adds that philosophies of law are usually unbalanced because they are usually only about the grounds of law. So, we can judge Nazi law from Siegfried, J.'s point of view, in the sense that we can predict what he will do, in the same way as we might imagine how a magistrate, in Roman times, would decide a point of Roman law.

It is easy to fall into traps here. Some critics, Hart notably, have supposed that Dworkin had merely created an amended, and confused, form of positivism. By the addition of 'principles' and 'underlying theories' of law, perhaps to a positivist theory such as Hart's, all that was necessary in order to understand and argue hard cases was to talk of 'Nazi principles' and 'underlying theories of racial superiority'. According to this understanding, because Dworkin unites both legal and moral rights, any rights arising should have a very weak prima-facie moral force which would be overridden by a strong background morality. Thus, with some vehemence, Hart says:

> If all that can be said of the theory or set of principles underlying the system of explicit law is that it is morally the least odious of morally unacceptable principles that fit the explicit evil law this can provide no justification at all. To claim that it does would be like claiming that killing an innocent man without torturing him is morally

justified to some degree because killing with torture would be morally worse.[4]

Dworkin's reply to this is difficult and involves several strands. His main idea appeals to the fact that one problem with law is that we do ascribe some moral force to laws which we believe to be morally bad. Why? Almost any structure of community power will have some moral force, because:

> ... the central power of the community has been administered through an articulate constitutional structure the citizens have been encouraged to obey and treat as a source of rights and duties.[5]

It must follow from this, says Dworkin, that the decision whether a statute gives rise to a moral right is a moral question. 'We need', he says, 'the idea of a legal right, which someone might have in virtue of a bad law, in order to express the conflict between two grounds of political rights that might sometimes conflict.'[6]

The idea is much more easily understood in the later light of the development of Dworkin's theory of law as an interpretive concept. The interpretation of law is addressed to a set of legal practices in a particular culture. The essential point about the interpretation of evil legal systems is that the best moral sense that can be made of them is just that they have no moral force. In an important respect, it distorts this project to say simply that the laws are 'there' but should not be endorsed.

On the other hand, we should realise that our language is not inflexible. The Nazis had laws in a recognisably pre-interpretive sense, even though their laws may be 'immoral' in the interpretive sense. We can distinguish the two questions here in the same way we might ask two questions about a promise. First, we could consider whether it was made and, second, we could consider whether it created an obligation. We could, too, says Dworkin, suspend judgment on the first question, and then make an interpretive judgment on the second by looking at the promise 'from the point of view' of the parties to it.[7]

It might be thought that one way of looking at Dworkin's approach to wicked legal systems is to think of his adopting an 'insider' point of view. In the moral legal system, there is not a problem because your point of view is the moral one. In the immoral system, you adopt, for the 'grounds' of law, the point of view of a judge who morally endorses the system, that is, the point of view of the person who *believes* the system to be moral, or has sworn an oath to uphold the system. But the laws of this system have actually no moral 'force'.

But the 'insider' or 'internal' metaphor is overused in jurisprudence and I suggest that it should not be used here to interpret Dworkin. For many, it will cause confusions in relation to the difference for Dworkin between internal and external scepticism. The judgment that the Nazi legal system has no moral force is not an external one. It is an internal interpretive judgment that, because of the gross immorality of Nazi laws, they did not create rights and duties.

Dworkin's conclusion is only mysterious against the background of several hundred years of jurisprudence. Ignore that. Ask yourself this: is it true that a claim of law is a claim that community coercion be threatened or used on a person's behalf? Yes. Should such a claim have moral justification? Yes. Can a judge, such as a Nazi judge, believe that claims of law in his legal system have moral justification? Can we make out the claim of law from the point of view of the Nazi judge? Yes. Can we make a moral judgment independent of that judge about the moral justification of Nazi claims of law? Yes. Is it possible for us to understand what someone means when they talk of 'Nazi law' without our knowing whether they morally approve it? Again, yes.

It is only when we introduce the history of 'natural' law that problems arise. The history of that idea is a long and muddled one, involving very different theories, many with theological origins. In recent times, it has become a debate about the 'conceptual' connection between different uses we make of language. At times, it centres on the structural nature of legal systems, at others, upon the validity of single rules. It mixes with requirements of the laws of the international community. At times, it reports necessary conditions of 'human flourishing', at others it claims that human attributes are merely accidental.

Nevertheless, there are people who want a clear line on the question whether Dworkin is a 'natural' lawyer. If the question is whether Dworkin believes that making moral judgments is part of the question of determining whether the community has a right or duty to use its coercive powers, then he is a natural lawyer. If the question is whether he believes immoral legal systems are not law, then he is not a natural lawyer. If it means whether he thinks that there is a 'natural' answer, 'out there', which supplies an 'objectivity' to moral and legal argument, he certainly is not a natural lawyer. The message should by now be clear. It is not at all helpful in this area to run together, under the one term 'natural law', so many different kinds of theory.

We must not stop here. Dworkin's solution to the vexed problem of wicked legal systems has great normative significance. For the problem of such legal systems is a real, live one. What should lawyers and judges *do* if they find themselves caught up in such a system? Dworkin has posed the problem as an interpretive one. Lawyers are to treat the problem as one in which they are expected to make moral judgments in interpreting the law. How would lawyers do this?

The Nazi legal system is too glaringly horrible an example. What should be done? It seems that the least of the problems is worrying about the grounds and moral force of the Nuremberg laws. The answer might be for lawyers to lie to protect families and relatives. Or, bravely, to be in a better position to subvert the system. Or, to escape the jurisdiction. These are the pressing problems.

But we might take legal systems, let us say, of 'less extreme wickedness'. Such a legal system may have a number of good points. Its judges are not intimidated and have full independence. The legislature, and in fact, all the institutions of law and government, act in accordance with clear procedural constraints. Large numbers of people have planned their lives in accordance with the laws. But the law, too, institutes racial discrimination, not genocide as with the Nazis, but one that insults and creates unjustifiable differences among people.

In this situation judges and lawyers may be in a position to make interpretive judgments that work. It is wrong to suppose that the 'grounds' and the 'force' of law are unconnected. If there are contradictions in the grounds, say, between racially discriminatory statutes and principles long declared in the courts, the judges should interpret those statutes to resolve the contradictions. Given the idea of interpretation, the judges do not have to accept the 'face value' of discriminatory statutes. Their task is, instead, to make sense of the statute in the full matrix of rights and duties in that legal system. And even an interpretation where there is no escape from interpreting a statute as morally repugnant, just the fact that the very best moral sense that can be made of it *is* that it is morally repugnant, is itself a declaration against that statute and an isolating judgment about the legislature that produced it.[8]

The idea of community

In *Law's Empire*, Dworkin explores what he calls 'the puzzle of legitimacy', in other words, the problem of our political obligations to the community. It is a question about the justification of the duty we have to obey law and, ultimately, the answer to that question will have an important bearing on the way we view the moral importance of integrity. His answer, not surprisingly, lies in the idea of 'fraternity'.

But, further, not only does he wish to provide an answer to the question of legitimacy, he needs, as part of his liberal project, to find a justification for political tolerance. In a later article, 'Liberal Community',[9] he considers the question of how far members of a community, in the name of fraternity, may, or must, take an interest in the way other members lead their lives. A particular reason for his concern on this question, apart from the general difficulties in the idea of tolerance, is the attack made on perceived liberal assumptions by the group of political philosophers known loosely as the 'communitarians'.

The puzzle of legitimacy is directly related to Dworkin's arguments for the sense of integrity, and the anti-communitarian arguments he supplies in 'Liberal Community' are directed at the question of the foundations of political liberalism and its virtues of tolerance and neutrality. These latter arguments are thus part of the political philosophy of the ideal world. But, of course, both sets of arguments are related because Dworkin's general thesis of legal philosophy is that argument about law cannot be detached from questions of political philosophy. Legal practices must be interpreted according to their best moral light, and that means, for Dworkin, in accordance with correct liberal principles. As you will see, the questions of legitimacy and community concern for the quality of the lives its citizens lead arise in cases such as those determining the rights of people to lead unorthodox sexual lives.

The puzzle of legitimacy

Dworkin's treatment of the idea of legitimacy follows a familiar path. He considers and rejects one popular response to why people have an obligation to obey government, or the political structures. The idea is that people have 'tacitly consented' to this, as though they had contracted with other members of their community that certain powers would be exercised in political administration by others on their behalf. Political legitimacy is based, therefore, on the fact that people have consented to the way that they are governed.

But, as is commonly pointed out, there is no real consent. It is just wrong to suppose that people have a choice. We are born into communities and do not choose them. Dworkin's point, although not new, is simple and correct. 'Tacit' consent is not consent. But there is some intuitive appeal to the idea. Perhaps, where the political institutions are just, or where there is an element of 'fair play', according to which citizens receive certain benefits, we should be prepared to say that citizens *ought*, if there had been a chance, to have consented to government. There is something of a contortion in this idea, of course, because it requires imagining as facts something that did not happen. But, in general, grounds of justice and fair play do suggest reasons for consents such as making agreements, entering contracts, promising, and so on.

But Dworkin rejects both justice and fair play as the grounds for political legitimacy. Justice, Dworkin says, is too wide a ground to explain the idea of citizenship, because it extends beyond the requirements arising out of community. What ties my political obligations to the United Kingdom if there are more just political institutions in other communities? Justice is too wide and abstract an idea, too 'conceptually universalistic', says Dworkin, to be personal enough to make sense of the particular duties of citizenship which a person owes to his own community.

Fair play, too, is insufficient. The fair play argument is a common one and says that citizens have a duty to government because they receive benefits from the political system and it is only fair that they suffer some detriment, in the form of obedience, in return. But, asks Dworkin, how do you incur obligations when you receive something you did not ask for? He gives the example of a philosopher who delivers lectures of a interesting and valuable sort from the back of a truck. Do you have a duty to pay him?

Further, it is not clear what sense we can give to the idea that citizens obtain benefits under one political system which make it fair that they give a return by suffering corresponding detriments.[10] What if the benefits would have been better under another political system? The citizen has no answer to that question because he has no chance to test the question of whether his political system is more beneficial to him. Instead of fair play, the argument amounts to saying that the citizen merely has to obey because he happens to have been born into a community, with its particular political practices, and not into another.

Dworkin says that there is a more sophisticated way to approach the fair play argument. If we concentrate on the idea of fairness alone, we may be able to say that the citizen should obey government because it treats him in a way that is *actually* fair 'according to the standards of justice and fairness on which it is constructed'. But that is not a sufficient ground, according to Dworkin, using the same argument as against the benefits and detriment argument. He says that the negative fact that a government has not discriminated against you is not strong enough for you to incur an obligation to government, because a government could be fair in a way that does not guarantee you any further benefits.

The underlying difficulty in both these theories of political obligation for Dworkin, I think, is that they are too dependent on the idea of a citizen's incurring obligations by choice. They fail because they try to ground political obligation in a citizen's 'joining in' for different reasons, and then cannot answer the objections that there is no real choice there.

Dworkin thinks that communal obligations, of which political obligations are a part, are far deeper than the mere idea of choice will allow. They are, instead, 'associative' obligations:

> ... they are an important part of the moral landscape: for most people, responsibilities to family and lovers and friends and union or office colleagues are the most important, the most consequential obligations of all.[11]

It is an interpretive idea, parasitic upon existing communal practices. The central point is that there are many obligations that arise simply out of the existence of certain types of relations, such as the relationship between a parent and a child, and out of the association of friendship. The obligations in such relationships often and characteristically 'transcend' choice and the obligations, like the obligations of the fair play argument, are reciprocal.

Dworkin thinks that political obligation arises in this way, from what he calls its 'fraternal' nature. He analyses this idea as follows. Such obligations consist of special obligations to the group, they are personal in that they run directly from each member to each other member, they involve a concern for the well-being of others and, very importantly, the group's practices must show an equal concern for all members.

This last requirement is important for Dworkin. We must remember the character of interpretation and the moral light in which he here casts practices of group, or communal, obligation. This last equality condition does not rule out all hierarchical communities. Some hierarchical communities will be productive of fraternal obligations. What is important is that the hierarchies must not be class-based, so that an army will be a fraternal organisation if it meets the conditions of equality but caste systems that count some members as inherently less worthy than others will not.

It can now be seen what idea of community Dworkin has in mind. The communities or groups in which 'fraternal' obligations arise are not constituted by genetic or geographical or historical or psychological facts. The idea is the result of a moral judgment made upon actual practices.[12] Dworkin says that arguments about the obligations of people in political communities in this fraternal way are more sophisticated. Communities are more complex and comprise closer relationships than a description of them in terms just of geography and history ('crude nationalism') and a more moral commitment than any idea that communities display 'fair play' or justice between their governments and their citizens.

A proper community, one in which it is fraternal association that provides the justification for political obligation, places weight on concern for well-being and equality. Dworkin calls such a community a 'community of principle'. Such a community fulfils the four conditions of having special obligations to the group, being personal, showing concern for the well-being of others and showing an equal concern for all. The community of principle, he says, makes the responsibilities of citizenship special because each citizen must respect the principles of fairness and justice that are embedded in the political arrangements in his particular community.[13] The community of principle, therefore, provides a better defence of political legitimacy as well as a defence of our own political culture, he says.

> A community of principle ... can claim the authority of a genuine associative community and can therefore claim moral legitimacy – that its collective decisions are matters of obligation and not bare power – in the name of fraternity.[14]

Four conceptions of community

Dworkin's conception of community is important for his conception of legal argument. If, through his idea of interpretation, he is to link moral with legal argument, the idea of communal obligation towards the institutions of law must be sufficiently rich and complex to make the task possible. Let us, then, explore his development of the idea of community. We enter the utopian world. But, of course, that does not matter. It is from the utopian world that the morality comes from which existing social practices are cast in their best moral light.

The connection, for Dworkin, between the rights of individuals and the law lies in the justification of *tolerance*. I have mainly left discussion of this, which is the subject of his current work on the justification of liberalism, to the last chapter. However, it will be better to discuss that part of his argument relating to community here, since it so intimately connects with the idea of integrity and has important implications for the interpretive approach he advocates for hard cases on matters of rights to personal freedom.

Dworkin considers four arguments which attack the liberal idea that communities should be tolerant towards unorthodox minority behaviour. To varying degrees, these ideas all share the same emphasis on the importance of the community.

The first is that a community, as a matter of *justice*, is permitted to act on its own behalf, through the mechanism of majority rule, to intervene to prevent, as far as that is possible, minority conduct of which it disapproves. The argument does not depend upon any idea of the wrongness of the unorthodox conduct. Rather, it depends on the justice or fairness in the majority being permitted to 'have its own way'.

Dworkin is critical of the idea. In the first place, he says, it contradicts what we believe justice and fairness require in a democratic community. Democracy does not allow 'winner take all stakes'. In economic matters, for example, the idea of democracy goes together with the idea of the personal market and appears to contradict the centrally planned economy. The economic environment, in other words, is one which is not to be assigned to a majority. If, in a democracy, we should be free to make private economic decisions, why should we not be free to make decisions, for example, about our private sexual lives? The argument from the justice of the community, or fairness to its majority, is therefore insufficient, he says, to permit intolerance towards a minority, at least in a democracy.

An argument that develops from this defence of tolerance is that a majority's determination of a particular kind of moral environment, say, an alcohol-free one, such as by the imposition of prohibition in the United States, has an effect on the market. It inhibits the liberty of a citizen so that the true cost of resources is unknown to him. An argument from justice to show that the majority can restrict the conduct of a minority would not, therefore, be sufficient. There would have to be additional reasons given to show why an individual should not be permitted to buy and do what he wants.

This additional argument is a difficult one because it draws on Dworkin's complex idea of the justice of the equality of resources. I discuss that theory in Chapter 10. But we should note that Dworkin regards it as the most important argument against the 'community as majority' idea of justice and fairness. The point to appreciate, for present purposes, is that it is not a clear and easy matter to separate moral and economic environments.

The second argument against tolerance speaks to the concern that a community should have for the well-being of its members. A proper community should care for the members which compose it. Tolerance of wrong conduct, in other words, ignores the individual member. Although Dworkin does not use the following analogy between physical health and moral health, I think it makes his argument clearer. No one suggests that a community should ignore, or be 'tolerant' towards, physical illness in its members. The community has a duty towards its members to prevent or cure their diseases. Programmes of disease prevention should be instituted, such as clean water, effective sewerage systems and so on, in order to maintain the physical health of the community's members. So, ought not the community show the same sort of concern for the moral well-being of one of its members?

Dworkin dismisses this argument, too. In a nutshell, his reply is that moral health and physical health are not analogous because you cannot 'cure' morally unorthodox behaviour. When the community steps in to prevent a person, say, having homosexual relations, it is being paternal in a special way (in Dworkin's terms, it is being 'critically' paternal). It cannot make sense to say that the community is trying to encourage the homosexual to do what he 'really wants' to do ('volitionally' paternal), that is, be heterosexual. Instead, it is trying to make the homosexual live the 'right way'.

But what is living the 'right way'? Dworkin says that what is valuable to you in life is that you live in the way you approve. You must, he says, *endorse* the way in which you think your life should be led. But what is the possibility of making the homosexual endorse the new way the community forces him to lead his life? He continues as a homosexual, now miserable because he is not permitted to live it in the way that he himself believes is the *right* way, for him, to live.

Obviously, as Dworkin points out, if the community found a way of 'brainwashing' the homosexual into thinking that he was endorsing his new 'orthodox' life, the whole argument for ensuring morally correct sexual conduct would be self-defeating. It would simply mean that the community had admitted that it could not obtain a genuine endorsement and, therefore, a life of genuine value.

The third form of community argument against toleration has more substance, says Dworkin, because it suggests a closer relationship between a community and its members. It is that people have various sorts of needs which can only be supplied by a community that has a large degree of homogeneity. For example, people need a common language and culture, and many other things,[15] and these can only be supplied by the community in which they live. If there were tolerance of unorthodox behaviour, this would weaken homogeneity and the community would be less able to serve people's needs.

Dworkin thinks that the argument holds generally for material needs, but does not see why a 'moral homogeneity' is required as well. Nor does he see why community intolerance on, say, unorthodox sexual matters would help supply intellectual needs, such as language and culture.

What needs, other than material and intellectual needs, could there be? Dworkin considers two that have been recently suggested. I consider one here because the way in which Dworkin attacks it is characteristic of Dworkin's style. It is Michael Sandel's obscure but passionately argued claim that community supplies people with necessary 'self-identity'.[16]

Dworkin puts Sandel's claim in its best possible light. It can, of course, be reduced to the ridiculously tautologous form of 'in order for me to be an American, I must necessarily be an American'. But it has more substance than that. A Roman Catholic might not be able to distance *himself*, say, from *his being Catholic*. That is a serious way in which Sandel's claim might be taken. Tolerance will be bad for community because it will break down the homogeneity required to give people, in this Catholic sense, a means of self-identity. Removing the identity with community, in the same way as removing the identity with Catholicism, would be a profoundly wrong step, leading to a loss of self-identity.

The following argument, I think, shows Dworkin at his best. He meticulously picks each possible thread of the argument out and cleanly snaps it. His main argument is that the self-identity thesis is wrong simply as a matter of phenomenology. He thinks it is wrong to suppose that a single association of identity could be so fundamental.

that it cannot be detached. We have, in my view, to accept that. Take the Roman Catholic example. It *is* possible for a Roman Catholic to identify himself as a person independently of the Roman Catholic religion. It is simply not a difficult idea. And to accept this is not to deny that Catholicism is important to him, or that Catholicism is something to which he, as a person, is committed. Sandel's point (and that of others) is a point about *self-identity*, and Dworkin is right to take the arguments as they are presented on that point.

Further, Dworkin thinks that, even if the phenomenology were true in the case of single associations, it is wrong to suppose that it would be undetachable for *everyone* in a community. That must be right. And, further, Dworkin thinks it would be wrong to think that it would be conduct of the sexual orthodox kind to which there could be this fundamental and undetachable association. And, even further, he thinks it would be wrong to suppose that, if there were a fundamental, undetachable association with sexually orthodox conduct, it would be shared by the *political* community and not some smaller group.

These arguments are devastating and right. But Dworkin has still to come to his final knockdown. Even if all the preceding arguments for intolerance are right, it would not *follow* that a person would lose his sense of self-identity and suffer personal disintegration:

> ...why should people not be able to reassemble their sense of identity, built around a somewhat different and more tolerant set of conditions, when their faith in the morality they associate with their family or community is for some reason shaken?[17]

Certainly, our experience on these matters may differ. It is not too difficult to imagine circumstances of mental breakdown and trauma as the result of isolation from a familiar pattern of social conventions. But there is not sufficient evidence to suppose that the link between a sense of individuality and attachment to community, especially in sexual matters, is as strong as the communitarian argument would seem to require.

These arguments provide a good laboratory for understanding Dworkin. I find these arguments full of clarity and the good will of analytical rigour. But this way of arguing leaves some people in a state of despair. They say that Dworkin is being unfair. Sandel and the other communitarians *must* be saying something more than this. No one can make mistakes of the magnitude Dworkin suggests. And, in any case, Sandel's argument has a sort of appeal, as had the example with the Roman Catholic. Or, conversely, Dworkin is fighting a 'straw man' because the original thesis is so bad it is not worth attacking.

The despair is brought about by a misunderstanding of what philosophy is. It does not follow from Dworkin's arguments that Sandel's views are wrong, just that he has provided no arguments to support them. Dworkin's criticisms force Sandel to go through his arguments again. Philosophy thus advances. The 'straw man' type of criticism is common, too, because good arguments, once accepted, have an obviousness about them. Dworkin, I believe, has done much in clarifying *the ideas we already intuitively use*. He has to, as part of the continuing process of achieving a 'reflective equilibrium' between our intuitions and arguments which make something coherent of them. To a generation schooled on the idea that law was centrally a set of rules, it was a shock to the system when Dworkin said that law also consisted of principles, that such principles were in competition with one another, and that they, not rules, were the characteristic tools of legal argument in the hard cases.

Dworkin's arguments against the communitarians' plea for intolerance, on the ground of the need for self-identity with the community, shows that the identification of the individual with group morals at best applies to a non-political group of sexually neurotic individuals.[18]

It is the fourth, and final, argument of the communitarians that Dworkin considers has the most content. It says that people are related to, or are to be identified with, their political communities in such a way that the life of the community is part of their own life. I think the health analogy I used to explain the second communitarian argument may be used here, too. The argument was there that, simply, the community should take an interest in the health of any one of its members. Here it is that a person should care about the community's health because that affects her own health. That person's health is part of the health of the community. It is not that the community must take a paternal interest in her health but rather that she must take an interest in the community because that is integrally connected with her own well-being.

This is a richer account of the idea of community, in Dworkin's view, because the life of the member of the community and the community are viewed as integral. So, tolerance of, say, unorthodox sexual conduct undermines the integration of a person's life within the life of the community. In sum, Dworkin's argument is that, despite the important identification of people with their communities which, he says, brings out something that many liberal theories ignore, the fourth communitarian account is mistaken in the character of the communal life. 'It succumbs to anthropomorphism; it supposes that a communal life is the life of an outsize person.' In the particular case of unorthodox sexual conduct, a community does not have a sex life.

But this quick criticism which, you have to admit, is intuitively appealing, needs closer attention. Dworkin uses the idea of agency to make more sense of integration. In his discussion of integrity and, in particular, a view of law which he calls pragmatism, which I discuss in

Chapter 8, his view was that individuals could assume responsibility for things that they, as individuals, had not done, but which communities, considered as their agents, had done. Only in this way, says Dworkin, could we understand the responsibilities of directors for what the corporation had done, or such ideas as contemporary German responsibility for the Nazi atrocities.

It is important to understand the idea of integration properly. It is not the idea that a community is solely composed of its members. It has a life of its own.[19] That must follow from the idea of group responsibility. But it also makes no strange claims such that communities are somehow more genuine entities than individuals, or 'ontologically' or 'metaphysically' prior.

Dworkin borrows Rawls's idea of the difference between the members of an orchestra and the orchestra to give integration more shape. People can see the orchestra in these agency terms. The flautist can take pride in the orchestra's achievement independently of the pride he can take in his own performance which contributes to the orchestra's achievement. His own well-being is tied up with the orchestra's well-being.

What, then, asks Dworkin, are the conditions which give rise to this relationship of agency, whereby the well-being of a member of a community is integrally related to the well-being of the community? It must lie in actually existing social practices of agency, he says. I cannot merely become an agent by a simple declaration. I cannot, for example, by fiat, become an 'ethical' member of the Berlin Philharmonic orchestra and thereby take pride in its performances, even although I can only play the guitar and have never been to Berlin.

Such social practices must recognise certain acts as acts of the particular community – say, the orchestra – rather than those of the community. That must include only acts that have been done self-consciously towards that end. Further, there will be restrictions in relation to the scope of the individual members' roles and the 'dimensions' of the community. The business manager of the Berlin Philharmonic cannot, for example, take musical pride in a particular performance, although he might take 'business' pride in a successful tour. And, further, it follows from this argument that the communal life will be a restricted one. The orchestra's life is a *musical* one. The orchestra has no other life. It is not, as Dworkin says, prone to headaches, or problems with friendships, nor does it have a sex life, although individual musicians will.

Now comes the important question. What are the characteristics of the *political* community? The communal acts of the United States are constituted by practices of officials:

The formal political acts of a political community – the acts of its government through its legislative, executive, and judicial institutions – meet all the conditions of collective agency ... Though the acts of particular people – votes of members of Congress, for example, and commands of generals – constitute these collective acts, this is only because these officials act self-consciously under a constitutional structure that transforms their individual behaviour into national decisions.[20]

What else? Do we have a collective national sex life? Our practices do not include any such life. And the fact that we do not choose to become the citizens of a particular community, unlike the members of a symphony orchestra, seems, further, to restrict any such idea.

Majority rule and democracy

We have seen that Dworkin's legal theory raises the question of the justification of the entire political system which, in the legal systems he endorses, is fundamentally democratic. The problem for legal reasoning is to find out more precisely what democracy actually justifies. It is, at least in the United States, popularly understood as majority rule, yet that idea, on further examination, is not clearly able to explain even some of the most familiar institutions and structural provisions of democracy. Powerful officials, such as judges, or secretaries of state, are not elected, for example, and at first sight, even the existence of entrenched legislative provisions which protect familiar institutions of democracy such as the universal suffrage seem to contradict the idea of majority rule.

There is not an obvious problem in the United Kingdom because it does not have a constitution permitting judges to declare legislation to be unconstitutional and thus of no effect. But there is a great problem in the United States. In its Constitution there are, of course, explicit disabling provisions, pronounced in the form of fundamental rights, such as the forbidding of the abridgement of freedom of speech, the taking of life, liberty or property without due process, and the denial of equal protection of the law. These provisions are declared by critics to be undemocratic, precisely because they allow judges, unaccountable to the majority vote, to overturn legislation passed by even overwhelming majority votes in the state legislatures. So an immediate question Dworkin asks is whether these disabling provisions really are consistent with democracy.

It is important and interesting to compare the position in the United Kingdom. The relationship of democracy to law is sad in comparison because there is no notion of 'fundamental rights'. There is even a fairly widespread ignorance in the United Kingdom of *what democracy is*. On the contrary, in the United States, debates about the nature of democracy are common and the idea of democracy as majority rule is widely regarded as one of the crucial issues. But in the United Kingdom, that idea, unanalysed as it is, takes a relatively background place in debates about the importance of 'sovereignty', especially as against the European community. It is sad because it is largely unnecessary, due mostly to a widespread poverty of thinking.

We can examine the idea of fundamental rights in the United Kingdom by looking at the role of the European Convention on Human Rights. This Convention came into being in 1950. It sets out a number of basic human rights and has been adopted by a large number of the Western European nations. Here is a flavour:

Article 5 Everyone has the right to liberty and security of person. No one shall be deprived of his liberty save in the following cases and in accordance with a procedure prescribed by law:
(a) the lawful detention of a person after conviction by a competent court ...

Article 10 Everyone has the right to freedom of expression. This right shall include freedom to hold opinions and to receive and impart information ...

Article 14 The enjoyment of the rights and freedoms set forth in this Convention shall be secured without discrimination on any ground such as sex, race, colour, language, religion, political or other opinion, national or social origin, association with a national minority, property, birth or other status.

Individual citizens have the right under the Convention to complain to a body known as the European Commission of Human Rights. This body acts as an initial review body which assesses the admissibility of claims lodged with it alleging the violation of human rights.[21] If it holds that the complainant's case is admissible it is empowered to refer the matter to the European Court of Human Rights in Strasbourg. After hearing the case, and deciding that there was a violation, that Court may then order the offending nation to bring its laws into line with the Convention.

The United Kingdom has been a frequent defendant before this court. One reason may be that the United Kingdom has no similar sort of fundamental rights legislation in its internal law. Another reason may be that, unlike one or two of the other Western European nations who thought their internal law not up to the Convention's standard, the United Kingdom has not incorporated the Convention, or some form of it, thus leaving the cumbersome, and time-consuming (and expensive) process of 'going to Europe' whenever a major violation of the sorts envisaged by the Convention occurs. Yet another reason, much closer to the actual practice of United Kingdom lawyers (and there is a relatively high proportion of lawyers in Parliament), is that the style of legislation and written judgments on the Continent differs so radically from that of the United Kingdom. The Continental style is drafted in terms of the general, whereas the United Kingdom is drafted in the style of the particular. To have to apply the Continental style of the judgments of the European Court is extremely difficult in the United Kingdom context.[22]

It is not surprising that pressure groups, notably the 'Charter 88' organisation, argue for incorporation of the Convention. Although bills to make the Convention part of the law of the United Kingdom, enforceable by judges in courts in the United Kingdom, have been introduced in Parliament three times recently, not one has succeeded in getting made into law. The reasons are complex and obscure, having deeply to do with British (and predominantly English) conservatism and a lack of enthusiasm about the idea of rights (in turn and in part brought about by class attitudes). But one reason is very clear. People are scared that judges, unelected and drawn from such a narrow class, would have too much power if they were able to overturn legislation passed by a majority in Parliament. This feeling, in Dworkin's view, is unjustified because it arises as result of making false assumptions about the nature of democracy and the nature of judicial reasoning.

Dworkin, in a book supporting the introduction of a bill of rights for the United Kingdom, entitled *A Bill of Rights for Britain*[23], places some of the blame on the Thatcher government for unwittingly running down what he describes as 'the culture of liberty' in a democracy:

> The Tory government calls itself conservative, but it is wrecking the best part of Britain's legal heritage. Thatcher's people are not despots. But they have a more mundane and corrupting insensitivity to liberty.
>
> ... a culture of liberty ... insists that government may not censor the opinions or expression of its citizens, or dictate their convictions or tastes, or decide what they say or hear or read or write, or deny them a fair trial by historical standards, even when it believes, with however good reason, that infringing these liberties would on balance protect security or promote economy or efficiency or convenience.[24]

Dworkin thinks that constitutional lawyers, both in the United States and the United Kingdom, have concentrated too much on the constitution and not enough on what democracy is. There are, of course, some notable defences of the disabling provisions of the United States constitution, but Dworkin's view is that they do not go far enough.

In particular, Dworkin is critical of John Ely's democratic defence of certain of the disabling provisions of the United States Constitution in his book *Democracy and Distrust*, published in 1980.[25] In that book, Ely argues that those disabling provisions of the Constitution which are necessary to protect the *structure* of democracy, such as the right to free speech, are, therefore, not undemocratic. In other words, although it appears to be anti-democratic that, despite what an over-whelming majority of people *want*, the Constitution should recognise a minority's right to express its views, that recognition is necessary to enable people freely to formulate views and vote as properly participating citizens. But, as Ely acknowledges, he is unable to account for disabling provisions such as those protecting freedom of religion, or the criminal process, because these sorts of provisions do not appear to protect democratic processes. There is a problem, too, with the view, widely accepted, that the Constitution protects private choice in matters of personal morality. Under Ely's account, it would seem to be within the Constitution for a state, for example, to outlaw homosexual conduct, because to do so would not upset the democratic structure. Homosexuals would still be able to vote and form views based on the uncensored exchange of ideas. They would simply lose out because their numbers would be insufficient to win in a fair electoral fight.

Dworkin begins by distinguishing between two conceptions of collective action, each of which might be considered as a candidate for democracy.[26] 'Statistical' collective action simply 'counts heads' and provides a statistical readout of what people want. On this account, a majority rule system is justified. Majority rule is the functional expression of what the individual wants, read over a collection of individuals. Simply, statistics are gathered.

But, employing either Rawls's idea of the symphony orchestra, or the idea of collective German responsibility towards the Jews, we can distinguish another form of group action, that of 'communal' collective action. Dworkin says that he prefers the communal sense. He says that it allows us a better reading of Abraham Lincoln's famous statement that 'democracy is government of the people and by the people and for the people' and gives us a better understanding of Rousseau's idea of the 'general will'.[27]

We can distinguish, too, he says, between two types of communal collective action, the 'integrated' and the 'monolithic'. The integrated type places weight on the importance of the individual while denying that collective action is statistical only. The monolithic view of community is a Hegelian conception whereby the community assumes a more important and independent role. This monolithic version of community collective action is rejected by Dworkin, obviously, because it denies the importance of the individual. But the idea of the integrated community, which does not rely on the idea of a statistical collection of people, he says, is further preferable because it provides a better interpretation of actually existing democratic political communities.

But democracy has an important side to it, namely, the distribution of political power. If, as many of us think, democracy is based upon equality and fairness, Dworkin says that it is an important question whether treating people as equals means giving them equal political power. What does 'equal political power' mean, however? He looks at this in two ways. We could compare citizens 'horizontally', ignoring for the time being the question of political authority, and try to make them equal *vis-à-vis* one another. We could also, he says, compare citizens 'vertically' with the officials of a political system.

Dworkin draws yet another set of distinctions.[28] Political power could be measured by 'impact', which is the difference we are able to make on our own by voting one way or the other. Under this conception, a member of Parliament, or the House of Representatives, will have a much larger impact than all of his constituents, even those who voted him into power, and so a vertical equality of power will not be possible.

We can distinguish this power of 'impact' from political power being measured by 'influence', by which Dworkin means the ability to make a difference by leading or inducing others to believe or vote or choose. In a proper working representative democracy, he says, 'rough vertical equality of influence is achieved'. The idea is that, if things are working properly, each citizen has the same chance to influence the relevant political representative, who will see himself as bound to take all views into account in his decision on which way to vote in the legislative chamber. Each citizen has the power, in other words, to influence the politician, although each citizen will not have the same power of *impact* as that politician.

Equality of impact works for the horizontal comparison of the powers of citizens but only at the expense of abandoning democracy. First, we could make all citizens equal in their political power by giving them virtually no power at all, which would be perfectly compatible with many forms of totalitarianism. But second, says Dworkin, '... it does nothing to justify a central assumption we make about democracy, which is that democracy requires not only widespread suffrage but freedom of speech and association, and other political rights and liberties, as well'.[29] For example, the idea of censoring a person's views only makes sense when we understand the relevant equality to be equality of influence. A censored person can, of course, still have equal impact, provided his vote has not been taken from him.

What is interesting about all this is that Dworkin does not believe in equality of political power. Equality of political power as impact does not make sense and, he says, equality of influence would mean restricting people's convictions and ambitions in a way that would deny them the moral worth they should be accorded in a democracy.

This view is striking because there is, at least as far as horizontal political equality is concerned, a great appeal in the idea of making citizens equal in the amount of political influence they can bring to bear. But Dworkin thinks that this intuition can be explained in other ways. For example, it is simply *unjust* that Rockefeller has so much more money than other people. As a result, he has a disproportionate political influence. This disproportionate amount of political influence arises, not because he has exceeded an equal amount of political influence allotted to him, but because it is disproportionate to the maximum amount of political influence he could have had under a just distribution of resources. That way of putting it allows for an unequal political influence.

Dworkin's central point here is that democracy embodies the idea of treating people as equals. That idea I examine in greater depth in the final three chapters. But, for present purposes, it will suffice to say that Dworkin thinks that a person must exercise his personal convictions in both a private and public way. In a democracy, a person must not be prevented, under some assumed constraint of equality of influence, from pursuing an ambition of 'taking pride in the community', and taking part in the 'communal goal of political activity'.

Principles of democracy

Dworkin concludes that we need more than a 'statistical' governing in a genuine democracy.[30] Rather than thinking of democracy as a stock market sort of institution where individual traders push up the price of the yen, we need 'background institutions and assumptions that elicit and nourish the needed pair of democratic attitudes: collective responsibility and individual judgment'. He says that there are three main principles, those of *participation*, *stake* and *independence*.

The principle of participation, he says, is part of the idea of collective agency. We are not a member of some community or organisation unless we have some role to play. And, in a democracy, we only have a *democratic* role if we are treated as an equal in that role. So, he says, this latter reason shows why an orchestra is not a democracy, because the conductor is assumed to have special merits. It follows from the involvement of the foundational principle, too, that the participation of any member of a democratic community ought not to be limited by assumptions about worth, talent or ability.

Importantly, Dworkin does not think the principle of participation is the basis of our structures of universal suffrage and representation. It is, rather, that it shows historical reasons for their adoption. It is not inconsistent with the principle to treat people as equals by giving them a weighted vote, as in the creation of special voting districts for deprived areas.

The principle of stake requires that there be some sort of reciprocity between those in power and citizens. People should have some sort of 'stake' in their community if their community is properly be regarded, unlike a statistical community, as 'theirs'. If this were not the case, we would be in the absurd position whereby German Jews would have been responsible, as members of the German community, for that community's crimes against them. Those Jews had no *stake* in that community.

It is in his discussion of the principle of stake that Dworkin makes an important concession to the problem of founding the obligations of the citizen to the community in the real world. The integrated conception of community suggests that citizens do not have communal obligations where they do not have a full stake in the community. At least the statistical conception can stand off from this requirement and allow other, perhaps non-democratic, principles to govern the obligations of citizens. Dworkin concedes that the integrated conception is like a 'black hole', into which all other ideals are sucked.

His answer is to modify the principle of stake to require, not that the community must have achieved what equality requires, but that its leaders are *motivated* by that.[31] It means a 'good faith' requirement, whereby if the leaders are acting, in good faith, on the assumption that people should be treated as equals, even if that particular conception is *not* the just one in the ideal world, we can assume all citizens have a stake in that community.[32]

The principle of independence says that a democratic government must not dictate what its citizens should think about politics and ethics:

> Just as it is preposterous for a German Jew to accept collective responsibility for Nazi atrocities, it is preposterous that I should think of myself as sharing integrated collective responsibility within a group that denies my capacity to judge for myself.[33]

From this principle, Dworkin derives structural guarantees of freedom of speech, association and religion, on the basis that people must be allowed to take responsibility for their own personalities and convictions. He also says that the principle prevents the enforcement of morality (although he thinks that it can be defended as a matter of *justice*, too, independently of arguments about the structure of democracy).

It is not strong enough, in his view, to say that the principle of independence only protects a person's *judgment*, so that it is being observed when a homosexual is allowed to vote, although not allowed to have sexual partners of his choice. There is no point to a person's judgment being untouched when he cannot shape his own ethical life in his actions:

> That is why people who object to moralistic legislation say that they want to 'make up their own minds', not have the majority do it for them, even when the legislation leaves them free to think what they like so long as they do what it says.[34]

Judicial review

Dworkin thinks that the 'structural' constraints on majority rule which were justified by Ely on the basis that they were necessary for democracy are much better justified in terms of his own integrative account of democracy. For example, Ely's account (the account that simply 'counts heads', in a statistical manner) allows for freedom of speech only on the ground that the public needs the most informed opinion. But Dworkin says that the integrative account can emphasise the *speaker* side of free speech. 'It is, after all, the speaker's right to speak not the audience's right to hear that the First Amendment protects directly.' More importantly, he claims that the integrative account can justify constitutional constraints that Ely admitted could not be justified under his own theory. Dworkin says that freedom of religion is supported by the principle of independence, so that citizens decide *for themselves* matters of personal conviction and conscience. The protection of the system of criminal procedure is more complicated, he thinks, but is nevertheless part of the principle of stake. The due process requirements ensure, he says, that a criminal suspect belongs 'in a community of responsibility' for as long as possible and the presumption of innocence is a 'presumption of continued membership' in the community.[35]

How, then, do these principles relate to the judicial review of legislation in the United States? Dworkin's approach can be guessed. He says that we should prefer interpretations of the Constitution which accord with democratic principles. We should now see that the communal conception of democracy allows us to understand the disabling provisions of the Constitution 'not as compromising democracy but as an important part of the democratic story.'

We have the principle of participation supporting political liberties such as free speech. The principle of stake is behind the equal protection clause, because it should show whether the government's decision reflects a good faith in equal concern for its citizens or, rather, prejudice and partisanship. Further, the principle of independence governs the idea of a 'right to privacy', by ensuring that people are able to make their own moral judgments about the kind of lives they wish to lead.[36]

A brief conclusion

Dworkin concludes that there is an integrative relationship between a political community and its individual citizens. But it is incorrect to suppose that the relationship is so intimate that the community is monolithically personified. What communal life does he envisage for the political community? He restricts it to formal political decision-making on questions of justice. The integrated citizen, Dworkin says, will regard his own life as diminished by injustices within the community. Thus, he concludes:

> That fusion of political morality and critical self-interest seems to me the true nerve of civic republicanism, the important way in which individual citizens should merge their interests and personality into political community.[37]

This conclusion carries him forward to the question of the foundations of political liberalism and I have left discussion of that for Chapter 11. Since that topic requires a better understanding of the extremely abstract and, for Dworkin, extremely important idea of the 'right to be treated with equal concern and respect', we need to look further into that idea, too.[38]

But something else comes first. Dworkin's theory developed chronologically from an extensive criticism he made of a legal theory as 'positivism'. I have so far in this thesis intentionally concentrated on presenting a coherent account of his own theory without examining his well-known criticisms of legal positivism.

There is a problem. Many of Dworkin's critics disagree with his characterisation of legal positivism. I intend, therefore, to set out the theory he criticises and, following him, I shall label it the 'plain fact' theory of law. Whether *that* theory is the same as positivism (or one of its different versions) can then be safely set aside as a separate question not of Dworkin's concern.

Notes

1. See *Tesco Supermarkets Ltd* v. *Natrass* [1972] A.C.170. In this way, a state of *mens rea* can be attributed to the corporation so that it is not able to avail itself of the defence of lack of *mens rea* in the more serious offences.

2. See the *Law Respecting Reich Citizenship* of 15 September 1935, *Reich Law Gazette*, 1935, Part I, p. 1, 146.

3. See *The Holocaust: the Jewish Tragedy* by Martin Gilbert, Fontana, 1986, p. 50, where he describes a doctoral thesis, by a Hans Pavogel, in which it was argued that an individual's worth in the community 'is measured by his or her racial personality. Only a racially valuable person has a right to exist in the community. A racially inferior or harmful individual must be eliminated.'

4. See *Essays on Bentham*, Oxford, 1982, 'Legal Duty and Obligation', p. 127 at p. 151.

5. See *Ronald Dworkin and Contemporary Jurisprudence*, ed. Marshall Cohen, Duckworth, 1984, p. 259. The answers to Hart are in a reply by Dworkin to an article in the same volume by David Lyons, entitled 'Moral Aspects of Legal Theory', p. 49.

6. Cohen, p. 259.

7. He has made this point to me privately and it represents, I think, some concession to those (such as William Twining) who claim that the idea of 'making the best moral sense' of the law is too restrictive a parameter in discourse about law. Nevertheless, this concession is not a destructive one. Dworkin has never claimed that there were no legitimate divergences of view about law; it is just that he characterises law in a strongly central moral sense.

8. See the debate between Wacks and Dugard on the position of the South African judges. Wacks, 'Judges and Injustice' (1984) 101 *South African Law Journal* 266; Dugard, 'Should Judges Resign? – A Reply to Professor Wacks' (1984) 101 *South African Law Journal* 286. These papers, and some additional ones, are usefully collected together in (1988) *Bulletin of the Australian Society of Legal Philosophy* Vol. 12, entitled 'Should Judges Work in an Unjust Legal System? – A Debate Based on South Africa'.

9. Vol.77 (1989) *California Law Review* 479–504.

10. See, for example, Hart's article 'Are There Any Natural Rights?' in *Political Philosophy* ed. Quinton (1967), p. 53, where he justifies political obligation in these terms.

11. *Law's Empire*, p. 196.

12. And that also means, he says, that for conflicts between people's associative obligations and questions of justice, say, where the demands of 'crude nationalism' are contrary to political obligations, justice must settle the argument: '... the best interpretation of our own political practices disavows that feature ... When and where it is endorsed any conflict between militant nationalism and standards of justice must be resolved in favor of the latter' (*Law's Empire*, p. 206).

13. The model of principle, he says, '... makes the responsibilities of citizenship special: each citizen respects the principles of fairness and justice instinct in the standing political arrangement of his particular community,

which may be different from those of other communities, whether or not he thinks these the best principles from a utopian standpoint'. *Law's Empire*, p. 213.

14. *Law's Empire*, p. 214.

15. The idea that community plays an important role in the enhancement of a person's life, in particular his autonomy, by according to him an 'adequate' range of options is, for example, to be found in Raz, *The Morality of Freedom* (1986) Oxford. See Chapters 8, 14 and 15.

16. See *Liberalism and the Limits of Justice* (1982) Cambridge.

17. 'Liberal Community' 490.

18. Dworkin also considers another of the 'need' type arguments. It is Selznick's claim (see 'The Idea of a Communitarian Morality' 75 *California Law Review* 445, 1987) that a 'background' of shared community convictions is needed to 'anchor' morality by giving it 'objectivity'. It is obvious how Dworkin would deal with such a claim. It cannot be a reference to a psychological 'feeling' of objectivity, because eccentric views are held by people who are characteristically convinced of their objectivity. So it must be the claim that moral objectivity is constituted by moral conventionalism. But, 'paradoxically', as Dworkin says, one thing that people do not share is the idea that the objectivity of morality is constituted by shared views: '... moral judgments cannot be made true or false by consensus, that they have force across cultural boundaries, that they are not, in short, creatures of culture or community but rather judges of them'. See Chapters 5 and 6, and his remarks on Walzer's *Spheres of Influence*, in *A Matter of Principle*, p. 214, entitled 'What Justice Isn't'. I discuss the problem of 'objectivity' in Chapter 6.

19. So, says Dworkin, integration rejects Mill, because it rejects the idea of individuality.

20. 'Liberal Community', 496.

21. For a case which well illustrates the procedure by which the Commission operates see *Open Door Counselling Ltd and Dublin Well Woman Centre Ltd and Others* v. *Ireland*, 6 May 1991 (pending, the European Court of Human Rights). The Commission expressed the opinion, by a majority, that there had been violations of Article 10 in the issuing of injunctions by the Supreme Court of Ireland to prevent counselling, by the applicants, of Irish woman on the obtaining of (legal) abortions in the United Kingdom.

22. I am very grateful to Eleanor Sharpston for reminding me of this point. There is a striking absence of discussion on the difference in general between the structure of the United Kingdom common law system and that of the Continental civil systems. Since civil codes purport to be exhaustive of the law and there is no doctrine of binding precedent as such in civil jurisdictions, Continental judges do not wield the same power as judges do in the United Kingdom. Perhaps a reason behind the overly circumlocutious and cautious legislative drafting in the United Kingdom is that legislative draftsmen (among others) consider that the judiciary must have every point spelled out for them in detail in order to prevent judicial legislation. But it is not clear that judges need every point spelled out to them, or that they would be legislating if they decided according to principle. If legislative drafting in the United Kingdom really is based on the view that the law

exists only in the form of specific rules, then the system belittles the capabilities of our judiciary in deciding issues of principle. An interesting comparison of Continental and United Kingdom legislative drafting is to be found in Sir William Dale's *Legislative Drafting: A New Approach* (1977) Butterworth.

23. *A Bill of Rights for Britain. Why British Liberty Needs Protecting* (1990) Chatto & Windus.

24. *A Bill of Rights for Britain,* pp. 9–10.

25. John Ely, *Democracy and Distrust: A Theory of Judicial Review* (1980) Cambridge, Mass.

26. 'Equality, Democracy, and Constitution: We the People in Court' 28 *Alberta Law Review* (1990) 324–46.

27. See *Law's Empire,* 189: '... many of our political attitudes, collected in our instinct of group responsibility, assume that we are in some sense the authors of the political decisions made by our governors, or at least that we have reason to think of ourselves that way. Kant and Rousseau based their conceptions of freedom on this ideal of self-legislation. The idea needs integrity, however, for a citizen cannot treat himself as the author of a collection of laws that are inconsistent in principle, nor can he see that collection as sponsored by any Rousseaunian general will.'

28. 'What Is Equality? Part IV: Political Equality' (1987) 22 *University of San Francisco Law Review* 1–30.

29. 'Equality, Democracy, and Constitution' 333.

30. See earlier.

31. See Philip Soper *A Theory of Law* (1984) Harvard. I discuss the sense of his claim in my review of the book in (1986) *Law Quarterly Review* 332–5.

32. See later, Chapters 9–11. In the 'good faith' qualification of stake, we find a solution to a difficulty that has plagued a clear understanding of Dworkin's work. I have already referred to Dworkin's idea of rights as embedded in background utilitarian justifications in the real world. (See Chapter 3, 'Rights and utilitarianism'.) In his defence of programmes of reverse discrimination, as we shall discover, Dworkin employs an ideal conception of utilitarianism, namely, an egalitarian version. But, later, we discover that he abandons even this 'uncorrupted' version for what he calls equality of 'resources'.

The resolution of the evident tension here lies squarely in the distinctions between the ideal and real worlds. He clearly thinks, with much evidence on his side, that the actual, Anglo-American, communities he discusses are motivated by some form of utilitarian understanding. But, in the ideal world, justice is not to be equated with any form of utilitarianism.

The connection he draws between egalitarian utilitarianism and the institution of representative democracy is very strong. In his essay on 'Liberalism' (see *A Matter of Principle,* Chapter 8), he asserts, for example, that claims for the protection of freedom of speech or sexual preference are 'democratic' even when the majority want free speech or sexual freedom curtailed.

He clearly believes, too, although, I think, with less evidence on his side, that the intellectual and moral culture of these communities is really capable of sustaining an interpretive understanding of that form of utilitarianism based on his foundational egalitarian principle. In other words, he thinks that our stake in democracy in the real world is based on politicians acting on good faith that egalitarian utilitarianism is the proper test of justice.

33. 'Equality, Democracy, and Constitution' 341.

34. 'Equality, Democracy, and Constitution' 341–2.

35. See also 'Principle, Policy, Procedure' in *Essays in Memory of Sir Rupert Cross* ed. Tapper (1981) Butterworth.

36. It is instructive to see how Dworkin shows arguments drawn from democracy might be used to justify the constitutionality of early abortions. He says that, constitutionally, a foetus is not a person, because if it were, states would be *required*, not just permitted, to make it a criminal offence. The question then arises to what extent states might, by majority rule, enact legislation protecting potential people. Not, says Dworkin, by placing a disproportionate burden upon one of society's members. That would violate the principle of stake: 'An anti-abortion law that operates from conception has savage consequences for women, particularly for poor and poorly educated ones, and such laws are genuine and serious handicaps to financial and social equality for women.' Further, the principle of independence is violated. Democracy requires that each person be responsible for his or her own moral development. To require a person to have such a serious thing as an abortion against her will is a 'flat contradiction' of that principle. (See 'Equality, Democracy, and Constitution', 'The Great Abortion Case' *New York Review of Books* 24 June (1989) vol. 36, no. 11 at 49, and 'The Future of Abortion', *New York Review of Books* 28 September 1989, vol. 36, no. 14 at 47.)

37. 'Equality, Democracy, and Constitution'.

38. See Chapters 9 and 10.

5

The plain fact view of law

An important aspect to a full appreciation of Dworkin's work is understanding a theory of law known as legal positivism. A chronological account of his work would take his famous criticisms of legal positivism as its starting-point since, like Hart, whose theory evolved from his criticism of the command theory of law, Dworkin's theory evolved from his criticism of legal positivism. But too often the force of his own theory has been obscured or misunderstood because of criticisms that he does not characterise positivism fairly.

Here is how I intend to proceed. I think Dworkin rightly attacks a view of law which he calls the 'plain fact' view. I think that this plain fact view is one model of legal positivism and I think, too, that it is a model that can reasonably be extracted from Hart's work, in particular, his *The Concept of Law*.

I also think that there is another strand in Hart's work, which complements the plain fact interpretation, which is identical to what Dworkin calls the 'conventionalist' view, and which I examine in detail in Chapter 8. In this chapter I shall explore the attractions and limitations, as Dworkin sees them, of the plain fact view.

The plain fact view of law has an understandably wide appeal. It asserts simply that the law is identified simply by reference to what the facts are 'out there'. A simple example is the following. The English law of murder requires that the victim die within a year and a day of the cause of death. The 'plain facts' of the English law of murder say that. No one who knows anything about English law could sensibly deny that. It is a *fact* of the English legal system. An examination of this view directs our attention to a serious source of confusion in legal and political philosophy, the idea that there really is a reality 'out there' in the world which makes legal, and perhaps moral, propositions true.

I think that Dworkin brilliantly exposes this confusion with his interpretive idea of 'making the best sense' of law. I should mention, though, an irony in modern legal philosophy that many people who call themselves 'positivists', and take the 'plain fact' view to be a travesty of positivism, criticise the apparent 'objectivity' of Dworkin's theory on the ground that there are no plain facts according 'objective' status to law in hard cases.[1] But I shall leave the question of objectivity, which is connected to the idea of law as 'plain fact', as a separate subject for examination in the next chapter.

The appeal of plain facts

The appeal of 'plain facts' owes much of its present status to David Hume, who declared very vigorously that factual propositions differed fundamentally from evaluative propositions.[2]

But what does Hume's distinction really mean? A proposition of empirical fact is one whose truth can be reached through observation of the world, at least in principle.[3] These propositions purport to describe what the world is like from the standpoint, let us say, of observation. They are the most common kinds of fact. One simple reason for this is that they provide a stable basis for argument. For example, it is a question of empirical fact whether it is raining or not. Or whether Madonna's car is red. Or whether Emily Pankhurst is dead. Or whether Tania's house has twenty windows. Or whether copper sulphate (in specified conditions) is blue. Or whether a certain percentage of adults in the United Kingdom smoke cigarettes. Or whether there are nine Supreme Court justices or ten law lords. These propositions are factual in one important sense because we are agreed on the way that their truth can and should be ascertained, namely by observation.

Values

Contrast these propositions with evaluative propositions. Note that I have specifically not referred to propositions of moral value and only to questions of value. This is highly important for clarity in any discussion about legal positivism. We often talk about questions of value without referring to morality. For example, we can make statements of value about some morally neutral thing such as a game. 'He made a good move in chess', for example, is not, at least, in any ordinary context, a proposition of moral value. Indeed, we can make evaluative statements about matters contrary to morality. 'You get better results with electricity than with a thumbscrew' said by one torturer to another, shows that.

Here are some examples of value propositions, including only some of moral evaluation. 'Eric is a better guitarist than Jimmy'; 'the United States economic position is sound'; 'stealing is wrong'; 'foetuses have rights'; 'the war against Hitler was justified'; 'the recent House of Lords decision was a poor one'; 'reverse discrimination programmes are wrong.' These sorts of proposition are commonplace. They differ from the propositions of empirical fact. Their aim is often to criticise the world just because it is lacking in some way. That people are often light fingered does not alter the force of the injunction 'it is wrong to steal'.

Sometimes the world is as the evaluative proposition would declare it should or should not be. But this does not alter its evaluative nature. 'It is wrong to steal' said in a society where stealing is customary means 'stealing should stop'. Said in a society where there is no stealing at all, it means 'stealing should not start'. Or, we can both say that 'generally, people do not steal' and that '*it is good* that people do not, in general, steal'.

Propositions of value do not need to describe the society we live in, at least in the same way. It is therefore useful to distinguish descriptive propositions from evaluative propositions. We should go further and distinguish those evaluative propositions that are offered as a guide to *conduct*. We can, in accordance with jurisprudential usage, already referred to in Chapter 2, call them 'normative' propositions.

Not all descriptive propositions are of empirical fact, although in the case of positivism it is empirical fact which we must bear in mind. The idea is explicit in Hart. Note what he says about the identification of what he calls 'the rule of recognition', which, for him, is the test by which the laws of our legal system are identified as law:

> ... the rule of recognition exists only as a complex, but normally concordant, practice of the courts, officials, and private persons in identifying the law by reference to certain criteria. Its existence is a matter of fact.[4]

> The question whether a rule of recognition exists and what its content is, i.e. what the criteria of validity in any given legal system are, is regarded throughout this book as an empirical, though complex, question of fact.[5]

Dworkin, I think, views any account of law in terms of empirical, descriptive, propositions, as a 'plain fact' view of law.[6] As I have said, I think this 'plain fact' view has a very wide currency.

Describing values

Note that it is perfectly possible, given all I have said, to *describe* normative propositions. I can simply describe that something should be done by other people, or another person, without accepting the value in question. I can say that a chess player 'should' move her Queen in one way and *just* mean that the rules require it. I can say that logic requires a particular conclusion, given certain premises. I may well think that the chess player 'should' abandon her game, because I am tired of being umpire and want to go outside to enjoy the sun. Or I can say that, according to Hindu custom, a widow should be burned alongside her husband on his funeral pyre. Or, a colleague says, 'the boss says you ought to cut your hair'. Or, being the only bi-lingual prisoner of war, I can describe the orders of the prison commander in translation to my fellow prisoners.[7] Or, I can simply describe, for example, the provisions of the English Theft Act 1968 relating to burglary.

In all these examples, I am simply describing rules or norms subscribed to by other people, whether they are the creators of the international chess rules, or a relative, or a prison governor, or of the United Kingdom Parliament. It is clearly possible, too, to make evaluations (and maybe normative ones) of the normative judgments that people make. This not only follows from the possibility of making descriptive normative propositions but is an essential part of the process of appraisal of law and morality. Thus I can say to my colleague 'the boss *ought not* to say that I ought to cut my hair'. Or, to my fellow prisoners (in English) 'these are the orders but you *ought not* to obey them'. Or, I can say, evaluatively, that the Abortion Act 1967 encourages moral wrongs, or that the old laws on homosexual behaviour were cruel and unjust.[8]

In what follows, then, the 'plain fact' view of the law may include an uncommitted descriptive account of normative judgments about what people 'should' or 'ought' to do, according to law. An appreciation of the distinction between normative and what I have called descriptive normative propositions is crucial to an understanding of modern jurisprudential debate.

The straightforward appeal of plain facts

The theory of law Dworkin attacks is the 'plain fact' view. According to this, laws exist as a matter of plain fact, or they do not exist at all. The laws may or may not be easy to ascertain, according to the complexity of the laws in question. In the end, though, once all the facts are in, the means of their identification will not be open to doubt. One useful way of putting this is to say the identification of law is, at least in the vast majority of cases, not a fundamentally controversial matter.

I agree with Dworkin that the plain fact view of law is, as he says, the 'ruling theory', namely the one that has the most popular acceptance. Its appeal arises from its 'plain fact' nature. The appeal is this. When we refer to 'getting the facts together' we mean ignoring for the time being all that is controversial about some matter so that we have a common base from which to argue. It is a sensible way of ascertaining that the parties are not arguing at cross purposes.

It goes further than that, too. Getting the 'facts' together means separating the issues into those for which further argument is required and those which, depending on the circumstances, end the matter then and there. Farmer Jones and Farmer Giles dispute a boundary line. They are practical men. What are the facts? Does the line run straight from the cowshed to the North West corner of the farmyard. Yes. Is this the cowshed? Yes. Is this a straight line? Yes. Is this the North west corner of the farmyard? Yes. It follows that that is the boundary line.

This might be the straightforward way of settling this matter. But 'straightforward' does not mean simple, here. What the straight line cuts through, and what the North West corner are, may have to be confirmed by a surveyor. That the present cowshed is the cowshed in the map, and that the map is an authentic record, may also have to be checked. But the point of the straightforward 'plain fact' approach is that once all the relevant facts are 'in', there is no more to be disputed.

These sorts of difference have to be taken in turn. If there is more than one cowshed, it is important to know which kind of disagreement will arise. It may be that the answer is the discovery that the farmers are at cross purposes, namely, that one farmer mistakenly thought that 'cowshed' referred to another shed which the map shows was not the right shed. If there is no disagreement between them that the map settles the matter, the farmers can now agree. Here, the disagreement is one merely about correct reference, a problem which may, in principle, easily be settled.

But, in the farmers' example, there may be further disagreement if there is more than one map, say, an ordnance map and an ancient parish map found after diligent search in the local library. Here it is important to notice how the argument continues. If it is a question simply of which map correctly shows which cowshed is the right one, then the farmers do not disagree on which facts are the relevant facts. The map which shows the cowshed correctly is the correct map, in which case the map may not be of any help without extra evidence as to its likelihood of being correct. It may be that there is evidence of fraudulent alteration, or evidence that the draughtsman was given wrong or insufficient information which he used second-hand in drawing the map. But this complication does not alter the character of the argument in a significant way, for there is still agreement between the farmers on the right way of going about settling the issue. It is a matter of historical research into where the cowshed was sited.

A promising charge against the description just given about a dispute being settled by reference to the 'plain facts' is that the idea of 'fact' is here too limited. It is too much tied to the idea of agreement on what is empirically ascertainable. Why? Because we have assumed that the 'plain facts of the matter' are discovered when the parties *agree* what the plain facts are. But because it is possible for people to agree on certain facts when those facts do not obtain, as was the case when it was thought that the world was flat (or stipulated 'facts' or facts forming the basis of a negotiation), the discovery of the 'plain facts' in a dispute does not seem to guarantee the truth of those facts. Further, to tie the idea of fact to that of lack of controversy also seems to require something for facts independent of truth. It was at one stage uncontroversial, too, that the world was flat.

Nevertheless, the bracing effect of the injunction to 'get the facts straight' derives from the possibility of agreement and the avoidance of controversy. That agreement is not a guarantee of truth should not come as too much of a disappointment. After all, a *guarantee* of truth is a lot to ask for. Further, great advances in knowledge can be achieved by way of working from an agreed basis, whether or not that basis rests upon truth.

In other words, we might accept a view of plain fact which does not carry with it the idea that there are, as they are sometimes called, 'brute facts' existing 'out there' in the universe waiting for discovery by us.[9] One point to consider is that it is perhaps from the idea of *other* people being able to agree or disagree with us that we come to understand that our views may be wrong.[10] Secondly, in any case, and this is particularly relevant to dispute settlement, it may be irrelevant for some purposes that our agreed set of 'facts' be true.[11]

Dworkin is frequently criticised for presenting the 'plain fact' view of law as a straw man, easy to knock down. Of course, so the argument goes, the 'reality' of law is so much more sophisticated than that represented by the cowshed dispute. Let us, then, try to tighten up the plain fact view. Are there arguments in its support, more particularly in relation to legal argument, in addition to the examples I have so far given?

Plain facts and legal rules

This above sense of 'fact' is very common and means simply agreement on the means by which the truth of the disputed matters may be settled. The above truisms of 'plain fact' argument in the law cause problems for some critics. The account just given of a standard form of argument seems simple-minded. After all, the emphasis is on simple argument and very few legal arguments are as simple as the examples suggest. What are the 'plain facts' of law? They are clearly rules of one form or another, given a suitably wide definition of a rule. A good way to this conclusion is to consider how legal argument begins to answer the question 'What is the law on this point?' We are now concerned, not with the facts giving rise to a dispute, but with facts *about the law* which tell us what laws will apply in some actual or imagined occasion. The relevant statutes and judicial decisions are discovered as a relatively simple matter of historical research. The lawyer's training is necessary here. He will have at least a general idea of where to start looking. He will then find relevant sections of the statutes and perhaps find cases in which judges have made pronouncements on the correct way to read these sections. The various propositions of law which can be extracted from these materials ('murder requires malice afore-thought' or 'wills require two witnesses', and so on) will constitute the plain facts of the legal argument.

Let us take a lawyer who wishes to find out whether someone commits a crime if he sends a letter to a person threatening to kill him. The lawyer takes the Offences Against the Person Act 1861 from the shelves. S.16 says: 'A person who without lawful excuse makes to another a threat, intending that that other would fear it would be carried out, to kill that other ... person shall be guilty of an offence ...' No excuse is offered, or apparent, and the letter writer admits sending it. The person who receives the letter seemed genuinely afraid. Thus, with a relatively short piece of historical research by the lawyer, the relevant facts point towards a clear – a 'plain fact' – case in law for a successful prosecution.

Perhaps the lawyer wishes to check that a will which only one witness attested is valid and therefore likely to be granted probate. She looks at the Wills Act 1837, and discovers that s.9 clearly requires that wills of the sort on which she is giving advice requires two witnesses. She knows, therefore, that the will is invalid.

But, of course, in the life-threatening case, the letter-sender might have been forced to write the letter by someone else; it might not have been posted, or not posted properly; there might have been a veiled, or ambiguous, and, therefore, doubtful threat; the threat might have been a conditional threat (say, conditional upon the receiver succumbing to senile dementia); the letter might have been from a euthanasia society and the receiver of it might have 'feared' the 'threat' but also approved of it, and indeed requested the threat. The list is endless, and the stuff of law reports. We can easily imagine similar sorts of difficulty with the wills case. Nevertheless, these difficult, peripheral, cases are just that. They are peripheral to the clear, 'plain fact' cases.

It is important to go through the argument here to see what precisely counts as a 'fact of the matter'. It is not the words in the statute, or the words the judge uses, in the sense that the law exists on the pages in which those words appear. It is instead the uncontrover-sial proposition of law, that is, the sense in which the law is that which is prohibited.

There is nothing particularly wrong in saying that the plain facts of the law are the words and sentences of the law, but a distinction would then need to be drawn between the meanings of the words that expressed the uncontroversial propositions of law and those meanings that did not. It is obvious that words and sentences can have a range of meanings, but getting the plain facts of the law together requires being able to find the law in its clear application.

There are, of course, important difficulties that arise from vague or ambiguous expressions of meaning. I nevertheless wish to pursue the central idea of law as 'plain fact', not just because of the hold it has for lawyers, but because it also has an important role in understanding legal argument.

Dworkin's criticisms of law as 'plain fact' are not fuelled by scepticism about matters of fact, nor, at the other extreme, are they dependent on any notion that all facts are the result of ideological conditioning of some sort or another. Plain facts clearly exist and it is rather Dworkin's point that their role in the understanding of law has been overestimated.

I propose to consider three forms of the 'plain fact' theory. The first and second of these, I think, can be shown to be inadequate. The third, however, has sufficient sophistication, and overall plausibility, to describe the view of the law that has the wide currency I have claimed.

The orders theory

This theory is familiar to jurists, and gains fairly wide acceptance among lawyers and lay people, although not under the description of 'theory'. It is simply that the law is, in the final analysis, nothing more than orders made by people who wield more coercive power than anyone else, these orders each carrying behind them the real possibility that disobedience will be met by punishment.

This theory has the robust quality noted above, the quality which is one of the attractive aspects of plain fact theories. It draws our attention to various plain facts of political power, and purports to provide us with a common-sense understanding of what the law is. Laws which do not give rise to a real threat of punishment are thus not laws. Rules binding because of a vague and perhaps tenuous 'obligation' arising through custom or tradition or 'mere positive morality' are not really laws on this account.

The theory has appeal because of this no-nonsense approach. Many people would applaud the approach, including a range of lawyers from first year law students confronted by United Kingdom constitutional law, through to practising commercial lawyers confronted by questions of international law.

Although it is an appealing theory, part of that appeal arises from its cynical denial of the conduct governing – normative – quality of law. We want to know, as a matter of plain fact, where law amounts to coercion. That, in the end, is how law affects us. It states that all laws are, in the final analysis, propositions about the probability of coercive measures being applied. But because it makes this emphasis it collapses into a simple theory of prediction, and the arguments against this sort of theory are considered below.

The predictive theory

Put at its baldest, this theory says that the law consists of, and is no more than, propositions of probability about what judges, or other relevant officials, are going to do. The appeal of this theory again lies in its plain fact quality. The predictive theory makes us consider the actual behaviour of the officials in enforcing orders, making decisions and so on. It focuses only secondarily on talk about rights and duties of the various parties. The prediction of the actual outcome of a judicial decision is the primary concern. And this requires study of not just the laws and so on to be found in statutes and reports, but of the behaviour patterns of judges both in general and in particular, and much more besides.

So, according to this theory, while the rules say that the judge in some case should find for the plaintiff, the facts of the matter may be that he will not. There are prejudices, either conscious or unconsciously assumed, or there may be a complex series of causative reasons, resting in the psychological make-up of all judges or just particular judges, or different sociological reasons. A judge might decide for a plaintiff for simple reasons such as his predilection for tall women with blonde hair, and the plaintiff might in fact be such a woman.

The appeal of this approach is immediate. It describes very well the primary concern of most litigants, and, therefore, of many lawyers, namely, the importance of prediction of the likelihood of the imposition of state power.

When we attend a lawyer's office and ask for advice, what are we *really* doing but asking for such a prediction? Could it really be the case that lawyers do not see this as one of their important concerns? Prediction is particularly important in relation to settlements out of court because there the settlement is a compromise worked out largely on the basis of probability of outcome measured against the costs of litigation or simply to obtain a quick result.

But the predictive theory falls down for the simple reason that it cannot make any sense at all of the way a judge reasons. And since how the judge decides is the crucial focus of the predictive approach, all other forms of legal reasoning will be parasitic upon it. A judge's reasons for his decision include reference to the rights and duties of the parties to litigation. It is impossible to see how these could be understood by him only as pieces of evidence raising or lowering the probability of his coming to a particular decision. (Would he still be amassing evidence five minutes before he has decided? At some stage he has to attend to the reasons that justify his decision.)

Let us look, now, at legal positivism, before coming to consider the question of its connection with the plain fact view. I have chosen Hart's model because it has been particularly influential and widely admired and because Dworkin takes it as his starting-point. As we shall see, it can be interpreted in two ways, both of which are criticised by Dworkin as not providing a sufficiently full account of law.

Legal positivism

Legal positivism declares that morality is irrelevant to the question of what is legally valid. Consider the following words of Hart:

> Here we shall take Legal Positivism to mean the simple contention that it is in no sense a necessary truth that laws reproduce or satisfy certain demands of morality, though in fact they have often done so.[12]

In one straightforward and practical sense legal positivism, as defined here, is true. Even without the training of a lawyer, we can easily think of examples of laws where our ability to identify a rule as a rule of law does not, at first blush, require us to make a moral judgment.

Take as an example a homosexual act between two twenty-year-old consenting men in private. Such an act constitutes a criminal offence. There is no doubt that if it complies with the description of the prohibited act in the English Sexual Offences Act 1956, this act is legally prohibited.[13] No reason other than *being in accordance* with the statute is necessary in order for us to say that these acts are unlawful. Yet there are many who think (perhaps you are one) that the existence of those provisions is morally wrong because they legally prohibit what ought not to be prohibited. But these critics will nevertheless usually agree these rules have a status of law.

Another example. Before the Sexual Offences Act 1967 repealed the English statutory provision which made sexual acts between men punishable by 14 years in prison, there were those who, while affirming the validity of the law, thought also that the law was morally wrong. In fact, a little thought should make us realise that it is because of this perceived distinction between law and morality that it makes sense to campaign to bring about *change* in the law. The idea of being able to change the law so as to make its provisions morally acceptable was, in the history of legal positivism, thought to be one of its major virtues.

'Legal positivism' covers a number of different, though related, theories about how the distinction between law and morality is to be achieved. As I have said, a common, and fruitless, criticism of Dworkin is that he does not characterise 'legal positivism' correctly. So we must be clear what model he criticises and, most importantly, why. There are different models which we can distinguish and which will assist us. But we may bear in mind that Dworkin is on record as attacking the Hartian kind.

What is the methodology of this approach? There are clearly two sorts at work in Hart's *The Concept of Law*. Dworkin points out both of them.[14] First, we can adopt Hart's avowedly linguistic approach, that of digging out the shared meanings of terms. I discussed this early on in Chapter 2. We discover, by careful analysis of the linguistic practice we use when using law-related language, what counts as correct uses of that language. Dworkin calls any such theory a 'semantic' theory. So, we distinguish 'semantic positivism' because of its assumptions about a shared understanding about the way we use language.

We might therefore have a number of semantic theories, each expressing what the theorist believes to be a *correct* account of our linguistic practices. But we will use Hart in this context. His semantic theory appears to result in what we might, following suggestions by Joseph Raz, call a sources based theory.[15] This tells us that our shared linguistic practices show that we regard as laws only those entities that can be identified by reference to a historically locatable *source* of law. And the source of law for Hart is to be found in the conventions of judges, or 'officials' of a legal system, by which they recognise what is to count as law within the system. It is what Hart calls the 'rule of recognition'. Note that it is possible to assert that law is conceptually different from morality without having to accept that law is identified (or that a proposition of law were true) as a matter of its historical source.

But we can, secondly, invest Hartian legal positivism with moral and political significance. We can say that legal positivism has moral force just in making a clear distinction between our legal and moral obligations. This characterisation asserts a practical justification for accepting, say, the sources thesis, because it achieves that distinction in a clear, identifiable way. This account neatly corresponds to the distinction, in my earlier discussion, between the simple plain facts theory and the 'practical, moral' plain facts theory.

Hart, according to the interpretation I have suggested here, characterises law as 'conceptually' distinct from morality and explains the difference by asserting a version of the sources thesis. Law is to be centrally identified by the union of primary and secondary rules. These rules are identified by their connection with a set of criteria, which he calls the rule of recognition, whose identity lies in the facts of official practice. Therefore, law is distinct from morality by virtue of its being ultimately identifiable in the historical facts of official practice. Although Hart allows for the possibility of incorporation of moral judgment in deciding what the law is, that is only so by virtue of being specifically so incorporated by reference to the authoritative sources of law. In other words, it is the source of law that determines its identification, and not its moral content. It is fairly clear that both Bentham and Austin thought that their positivism rested on the identifying of law in the historical source of the command of the sovereign.[16]

Dworkin thinks that both of these forms of positivism are wrong. He denies 'semantic' positivism because he thinks that legal theory is not exhausted by a process of 'digging out' shared meanings of words. He thinks there often are *no shared meanings*. And so, in this context, he sets up 'interpretive' as the rival to 'semantic'. In the important cases, for him, there is important controversy, not shared meanings. In them, judges and lawyers have 'theoretical' disagreements over what the grounds of law are, and not merely disagreements over what the particular sources of law are.[17]

But he also further denies the thesis that there is good moral point to legal positivism. His view is that there is greater moral mileage to be gained from including moral arguments within arguments determining questions of legal validity. He does not deny, however, the distinction between the law *as it is* and the law *as it morally ought to be*. Rather, his denial of 'semantic' positivism attacks the idea that we are only concerned with shared meanings.

Judicial positivism and the rule of recognition

A different version of positivism focuses specifically upon the judge and is a theory of judicial reasoning. In Dworkin's terms, this version is a theory of 'strong' discretion, according to which a judge is not bound by law to come to any decision when the question of law is genuinely controversial.

No positivist has clearly enunciated this theory. It could be a doctrine that happens to be associated with the central core of legal positivism. Or, it might be a necessary consequence of regarding law as identified only through its sources. While Hart notably drew attention to the distinction between the 'core' and 'penumbra' of the expressions of legal rules, he did not deal directly with the question of what the judge was bound to do in the area of his discretion.[18] Both Austin and Kelsen thought that judges had legislative powers but both, too, saw these as confined within wider, legal, principles of constraint. Austin thought that the judges were only empowered in accordance with sovereign intention.[19] Kelsen appears to be dogmatic about the question for he asserts that there are no 'gaps' at all. If a judge is authorised to decide a given dispute where there is no 'general norm' covering the matter, the judge is acting validly in adding to the existing law an 'individual norm'. But this occurs, not because there is a gap, but because the judge considers the present law to be 'legally-politically inadequate'.[20]

But it may follow, as Dworkin says it does, that a theory of strong discretion is entailed by these influential theories of positivism, whether the theorists realise it or not. He thinks that judicial positivism is a consequence of the 'sources' type of positivism.[21] In short, according to Dworkin, these two types of positivism say that the law ends at the beginning of uncertainty about shared meanings or understandings about the identification of law. For Dworkin, sources positivism identifies law with the 'plain facts' of the law to the extent that rules and so on that are not identifiable as a matter of plain fact *cannot, under the theory, be properly called 'law'*.

You will now have guessed the line of argument. One interpretation of Hart's rule of recognition theory is that it is a highly sophisticated model of the plain fact theory. That theory's sophistication arises from its being able to account for the normative character of ideas familiar to law such as 'rights', 'duties' and 'rules'. The theory states that laws are to be identified in the final analysis by reference to an attitude, that of acceptance, by judges and officials. It is not so bald as to require that each law be consciously regarded as law by this official attitude of acceptance. Nevertheless, each law must be identifiable by reference to criteria that are accepted in this way.[22]

The appeal of this theory lies in the non-mysterious way in which it accounts for our ordinary view of law. Dare I say it? It is a much better plain fact account. One reason is that if law is to be merely identified through a process of *logical* relation with the empirically ascertained facts of acceptance by officials, it is not necessary to say anything about the particular form each 'law' takes. We do not, for example, have to say that laws must all take the form of orders.

The recognition theory can therefore allow for the existence of rules of a different sort from the duty-imposing sort required by the idea of law as orders only. Thus it was that Hart concluded that law was best to be understood as a combination of primary, duty-imposing rules and secondary, power-conferring rules (and rules of the 'capacity-creating', 'recognising', 'identifying' type).[23]

How, though, does his theory manage to account for the normative character of law and yet still remain a 'plain fact' theory? Hart finds the answer through the concept of a rule. In an account which denies any normative character of law, rule-governed behaviour can only be described in terms of regularity of behaviour, coupled maybe with hostile reaction to irregularity. Thus, an account, such as Austin's, of rule-governed behaviour in terms of 'habits of obedience' is inadequate at least for explaining how it is that we think that rules provide standards against which conduct can be measured.

Hart introduces that idea through the idea of acceptance. Some people, perhaps most in the Anglo-American system, accept regularities of behaviour as a reason for continuing to behave in that way and as a justification of 'hostile reaction' to irregularity. The simple answer to the question why laws have normative force is that some people, the 'officials' of the system, accept that it has. And we saw, from our discussion earlier on in this chapter, that it is possible for us to describe, as a fact, something that has normative force.

An extreme version of this account is that of Kelsen. He says that law has a normative quality only when cognition of the world proceeds under a certain presupposition about normative force. Thus any talk at all of the existence and validity of law could only make sense to someone, or a group of people, who presupposed the law to have normative force. That must mean that law exists only as the result of a presupposition of people who *accept*, perhaps not consciously, rules of the general character of law as normative.

This idea has force. The propositions that 'Nazi law is not law', or 'South African law is not law', make good sense. Our ordinary understanding of law allows us to assert these propositions. We mean by them that we do not *accept* various rules as having the status and quality of law. In other words, we regard them as lacking the necessary normative force, despite all other appearances to the contrary. On the other hand, this extreme version lacks an explanation for the ordinary way we understand phrases such as 'According to the German law of 1942 ...', or 'South African law requires...', or 'Roman law required that ...'. It is, too, obscure on the status of the curious 'jurist' or 'legal scientist', who seems to be like a person in every respect except for a moral sense.[24]

Hart's more moderate version combines two things. The normative quality of law comes about because officials accept certain reasons for behaviour. This official acceptance binds those who accept it. But, unlike Kelsen, this version allows us to say that officials in fact accept those reasons without our being so bound. We can thus assert the existence of the binding force of law within other jurisdictions – or our own – without being committed to the view that that law has normative force for us. Hart describes this combination of two kinds of way laws can be binding in terms of the difference between viewing the law from an 'internal' and, perhaps, committed point of view, and viewing it from the 'external' and uncommitted point of view.[25]

It is apparent, too, that there is both a moderate and an extreme version of this external point of view. The moderate version acknowledges the fact that others accept certain rules as having normative force, but the extreme version does not, and can only, therefore, view law as having no normative force for anyone. It is an extreme version because it ignores some plain facts about law, namely that certain people *accept* it as having such force.[26]

The moderate version of the internal point of view is the important and relevant one for the present discussion of the plain fact view. We state what the law is by referring to the empirical fact of acceptance by officials of the criteria for the identification of law. It is by virtue of this way of identifying the law that descriptive normative propositions are possible. It accounts for the historical search we carry out when sorting out the plain facts of law. We simply describe what it is that officials currently accept as creating rules of law.

It is clearly the case that this view of the law has widespread acceptance. Let us look at some more examples. The law student, in his first tutorial, is being taught how to find the law in the United Kingdom. He is told, first, that what the United Kingdom Crown-in-Parliament enacts, by an elaborate set of procedures, is law in the form of what are known as statutes. These statutes are identified easily. The student reads them and understands the words in them to be expressive of the rules of law that apply in the United Kingdom. He understands them to be law because he knows that all judges, all lawyers, all policemen, and, in fact, practically everybody in the United Kingdom accepts the practice of Parliamentary legislation as effective in establishing binding rules of law.

The important people who accept these words as law are the judges. Why? In our legal system, they are the people who make the final decisions on the law that the statute expresses. That, of course, does not mean that the statute means nothing until a judge has made some declaration upon it. It is not only the judge who can read what the statute says. Policemen, lawyers, the administrators of various kinds, as well as many other people, go about their daily business and arrange their affairs by reference to and in accordance with the requirements of the provisions in a large number of statutes.

They do this in the knowledge that what the statute expresses is law and that law creates, by virtue of what the words in these statutes express, normative obligations, permissions, and so on, which judges would, if the matter arose for judicial decision, enforce by bringing into operation the coercive powers of the state.

By this, I do not mean to deny that there are any problems at all with this account. I merely emphasise that most of our understanding of law contained in statute proceeds on the basis I have described. Indeed, it is a virtue of the account, expressed in the interpretation of positivism I have offered, that we can go to the law so directly, at least in principle.

A return to plain facts

An appeal to plain fact gives a robust quality to an argument. Why? We saw from the Farmer Jones and Farmer Giles example that plain fact provides a forum of agreement upon which debate may be conducted. The appeal of the idea lies in both certainty and objectivity. The disputants have a reassuring common ground. This comfortable quality that plain fact gives to an argument must be carefully noted. It is something to which critics of Dworkin turn frequently but without analysing what the appeal is.

What is needed in a 'practical' argument, like a legal argument, it is thought, is a set of referents, a set of coordinates, which form the stable base to which all the participants may anchor their arguments. It is this feature that makes law 'solid' and workable. But there are two arguments at work.

First, the 'plain facts' are just there, in the Wills Act 1837, for example, for me, a lawyer, to see that two witnesses are required for my will to be granted probate. I can read. I can see the words of s.9. So can another lawyer, who agrees that these are what the words mean. We know that a judge will read these words, because their meaning is clear and uncontroversial, in the same way. We know the plain facts relevant to the will: that the testator is not insane, that he is not a seaman,[27] that he is like the ordinary man who goes each day into his solicitor's office.

In the ordinary day-to-day way of seeing things, the truth of the relevant proposition of law is without doubt, and it is discovered by these relatively simple empirical means. You look, and the answer is there. This *must* describe a very common means of ascertaining the law. Indeed, if the vast army of lawyers whose task is to advise a client on what he must do, or is permitted to do, or is prohibited from doing, could not advise by using this simple empirical method, then the administration of legal systems would be an altogether different matter.

But a second, practical, argument arises from the empirical possibility of identifying law just noted. It is a *virtue* of the system that, on the whole, law can be so identified. The main virtue is *clarity*. Two people can find a clear and objective proposition of what the law requires. It may not, of course, be understandable to an untrained person. On the other hand, the lawyer can advise, settle, produce compromises, and so on, on the basis of the settled and objective law.

You should see the striking turn the second argument takes. The possibility of a certain and objective ascertainment of the law is now to be seen as a virtue of practical reasoning. It is not only that we report what the law is 'out there' using the methods of empirical science, but also something in the opposite direction. Our idea of looking at law as something 'out there' is kindled by our confidence that there are certain and objective propositions of what law requires. In other words, there is a practical reason supporting the law's identification in the 'plain fact' way. Law is plain fact and it is very beneficial that it is.

A failure to grasp practical reason's way of justifying the 'plain fact' way of looking at law has caused many problems. It is common to condemn legal positivism on the ground that it is lifeless and 'amoral', and encourages the 'legal scientist' to make a 'cold' and 'analytical' appraisal of the facts. From the viewpoint of practical reason, however, the 'lifeless' appraisal makes sense, for it now may be claimed as a virtue of law's ability to coordinate and direct man's affairs that it is identifiable as a 'cold' and 'lifeless' thing. The arguments against identifying law in this way have to be centred on the cogency of the arguments of practical reason for so identifying the law, and not the methodology by which that particular conclusion is reached.

Hart's *The Concept of Law* can be read as a work justifying, as a matter of practical reason, the analysis of law in the way just described. This interpretation of his work is not consistent with his semantic approach, however, because its impetus derives, not from a correct description – a correct 'digging out' – of law-related terms, but from the force of practical reason. He sets up a model of primary and secondary rules whereby the secondary rules of change, adjudication and recognition lift the simple regime of duty-imposing primary rules into the legal arena. This model is justified on the basis that, with the addition of the secondary rules, it remedies the 'defects' of a society which could not change its rules by conscious decision, did not have a system of courts and had no means of determining which were the rules of the system.

Extremely important among these defects is that of the 'uncertainty' of a simple regime of primary rules alone. People would not know which rules were rules of law. They would not know how to plan their lives in accordance with law. This is an intensely *practical* reason for making the identification of law as clear – as plain – as possible. To put the point starkly: Hart's theory of validity, the key concept of which is his rule of recognition, is dependent on its *curing the defect of uncertainty* in the identification of valid law.

Further, of paramount concern for Hart, I think, was that if there were no rule of recognition which could clearly identify what was legally valid, there would be a serious loss to society. The important sense in which we should judge what the state requires us to do by way of the existence of legally valid rules and what, independently, it is morally right for us to do would be obscured. Hart emphasises that the fact that some rule has officially been certified as legally valid should not be conclusive of the question of obedience.

What surely is most needed in order to make men clear sighted in confronting the official abuse of power, is that they should preserve the sense that the certification of something as legally valid is not conclusive of the question of obedience, and that, however great the aura of majesty or authority which the official system may have, its demands must in the end be submitted to a moral scrutiny.[28]

This argument, which appears in Chapter 9 of *The Concept of Law*, is crucial to understanding the complexity of Hart's positivism. The argument links historically to the development of legal positivism as a force in early nineteenth century England. Positivism was a secular doctrine, associated always with the development of liberalism and related doctrines. One of the ideas implicit in it was that people, whether legislators, lawyers or ordinary people, could use the distinction between what the law was and what it ought to be to free the way for critical appraisal, and not wholesale acceptance of judicial decisions and legislative acts. (There was, too, an urge to clarify what 'scientifically' the law was.)

It is significant that many of Hart's arguments in that chapter are put forward in the context of his dismissal of claims by some natural lawyers, Gustav Radbruch in particular, that it was the apparent affirmation of legal positivism in the 1930s in Germany that led to the infamous excuse of 'we were just obeying orders'.[29]

Hart's *The Concept of Law* is not explicit in distinguishing these two sorts of argument for its major conclusions. Nevertheless, both arguments are present in the writings of the utilitarian legal philosophers Bentham and Austin, the influence of whose work can so clearly be seen in Hart. Austin, more clearly than Bentham, wanted first to place law on a firmly scientific basis. It is not surprising, then, that the way he wrote made it sound as though he were just describing law as it was 'out there', as an entity to be observed largely in terms of regularity of behaviour.[30]

Secondly, of course, the utilitarians were concerned with matters of practical reasoning. Why be content with the way the world was? The principle by which the greatest happiness of the greatest number should be urged applied itself to the construction of a positivist model of law. They saw that the way forward for this principle was the creation of legislation which could stand objectively 'there' independent of the standpoint from which criticism, based on the utilitarian principle, could be made. Thus, Austin could say 'the existence of law is one thing; its merit or demerit is another'.[31]

In conclusion, there are good reasons for accepting that there is an understandable and usable sense in which law may be seen as 'plain facts'. First, there is a conventional sense in which law is understood as identifiable as a matter of 'plain fact'. Second, there are reasons of clarity and objectivity for justifying that view.

Dworkin says that the plain fact theory, at its barest, is a semantic theory of law, because disputes about law will, in the end, amount merely to being about the correct use of law-related language. This criticism must be tested since it trivialises (perhaps rightly) the plain fact theory. It suggests that disputes over what the law was are, in principle, simply resolvable dictionary-type disputes.

Perhaps the problem should be put in another way. We could say that lawyers, when debating some point of law, are trying not just simply to find out what the correct meanings of words are. They are, instead, trying to make sense of the underlying social phenomena that constitutes 'the law'.

But this is not helpful. In what does the social phenomenon of law consist? How do we 'get to it', as it were? Hart, for example, says in his Preface to *The Concept of Law*:

> Many important distinctions, which are not immediately obvious, between types of social situation or relationships may best be brought to light by an examination of the standard uses of the relevant expressions.

When legal theorists insist on digging out the meanings of legal language in order to cast light on the nature of law, Dworkin accuses them of having succumbed to the semantic 'sting'. This means that the theorist has wrongly assumed that there is a level of agreement upon the correct criteria with which to use legal language. Any apparent disagreement, then, must be resolvable as a matter of research into the question of whether the participants are using the language correctly. If the sources theory is correct, it means that the disputants are in simple disagreement over something about which the sources cannot be ambiguous. Then there is no real disagreement, only a misunderstanding.

The popular appeal of the plain fact theory is variously grounded in a motivation for clarity, certainty and objectivity. If it is wrong, it is much better to make the case against it along these sorts of lines. I think that Dworkin is right to make the best sense we can of the plain fact theory. A moral claim grounds it and not one purporting simply to describe the way we use words to report the underlying 'social phenomena'.

Positivism and 'plain fact' are best understood as practical propositions. Central to the idea of the plain fact theory is the governance of social life through the use of clearly expressed laws. The paradigm of law, according to this theory, is the easily identifiable, objectively ascertainable yardstick by reference to which people may order their affairs. I suggest that this is what positivism is fundamentally about and the way law is popularly understood in Anglo-American jurisdictions.

It is in this light that we can understand best the appeal, particularly for those on the Continent, and, for example, for Kelsen, of law as a 'science'. The 'legal scientist' appraises the 'cold' facts of the law. He describes the 'legal material' and organises it. By so doing he produces an uncommitted, unideological, 'pure' and therefore useful, because neutral, account of the law. The virtue of this is again clarity. Once we know what the law is, we can see clearly what its demands are and what its sources are, and distinguish those from our own personal moral views about what, all things considered, we think we ought or may do. Metaphorically, we accord dignity to the plain fact theory by surrounding it with a moral garment.

Conclusion

I will repeat my view that it is a misunderstanding of Dworkin's theory to suppose that it rests at all on a 'correct' interpretation of Hart's model of positivism. Dworkin attacks the plain fact view of law, on the grounds that it is meaningless to talk of law simply 'out there'. He offers an interpretive account instead. Further, in his view, the best moral sense that can be made of law requires not thinking of law as exhausted by the clear rules. And it is his reasons for this view that constitutes his primary attack on the account positivism gives of legal reasoning.

A consideration of this question is crucial for Dworkin, and it was his criticisms of the consequences positivism had for the day-to-day business of arguing law in the courts that formed the content of much of his early work. In this chapter, I have referred to the thesis as 'judicial positivism'. It is a consideration of his idea of the 'hard case', which is central to his criticisms of legal positivism, to which I shall shortly turn, in Chapters 7 and 8. But it is first necessary to examine the vexed question, present in all of Dworkin's work, over whether arguments in law and morality have any objective standing.

Notes

1. A crude example is *Judging Judges*, by Simon Lee (Faber & Faber, 1988). He thinks that Dworkin's theory is 'unreal' and 'pitched at too high a level of abstraction'. He appears to conclude that all traces of objectivity are thereby removed from it. By employing a metaphor of empirical description, that of aerial photography, he shows that reality in the law for him means empirical certainty. 'My aerial view', he says, 'gives a more complete impression ...' (p. 92).
Sobering for Lee should be the following pronouncement from a United

Kingdom judge who reviewing Lee's book says: 'The irony is that whereas Lee criticises Dworkin for being a 'dreamer' and putting forward theories which lack 'reality' (a favourite word), Dworkin is one of the few writers on general jurisprudence who accepts and engages with the reality of what judges have to do.' Hoffman ends by saying that 'Readers who want to know what judges are supposed to be doing will do better to buy *Law's Empire*'. See Hoffman (1989) *Law Quarterly Review* 144.

2. See Hume, *A Treatise of Human Nature* (1739) Book III, Section I: 'In every system of morality, which I have hitherto met with, I have always remark'd, that the author proceeds for some time in the ordinary way of reasoning, and establishes the being of God, or makes observations concerning human affairs; when of a sudden I am surpriz'd to find, that instead of the usual copulations of propositions, *is* and *is not*, I meet with no proposition that is not connected with an *ought*, or an *ought not*. This change is imperceptible; but is, however, of the last consequence. For as this *ought*, or *ought not*, expresses some new relation or affirmation, 'tis necessary that it shoul'd be observ'd and explain'd; and at the same time that a reason should be given, for what seems altogether inconceivable, how this new relation can be deduction from others, which are entirely different from it.' I have contrasted 'fact' with 'value' in the ensuing discussion in the text, since I think that distinction expresses best the appeal of 'plain fact' as a theory of legal positivism, in which 'fact' is strongly and sharply distinguished from 'moral value'. On the other hand, the idea of the fact's being 'plain' is well captured by drawing a line between *theory* and fact, as opposed to *value* and fact. A 'plain' fact is what observers report as true in identical terms even if they have different theories explaining those facts, or no theory at all. I am indebted to Sheldon Leader for this point.

3. 'In principle' simply means that we know by what means evidence would be adduced in order to confirm a plain fact. We know, for example, that the question whether Cleopatra had a large wart on her left toe is a plain fact type question, as we do regarding the question whether the Prime Minister of the United Kingdom in 100 years' time will have a large wart on his or her toe.

4. Hart, *The Concept of Law*, p. 107.

5. Hart, *The Concept of Law*, p. 245.

6. Neil MacCormick says that he thinks I am right that Dworkin thinks this, but that is why Dworkin's terminology is, as he says, 'tendentious'. It ignores the idea of the 'internal view' that judges must have towards the rule of recognition and the role that view must play in the construction of complex legal arguments in hard cases. But I think Dworkin should be defended here. Pivotal to Hart's project is the separation of law from morality. Hart achieves this by asserting the existence of the acceptance by officials of criteria of identification of the law. It must be one of his central concerns that the existence of that acceptance is a factual matter, in the end to be discovered in the 'settled practices' (Hart's term) of judges. Hart, I think, has been consistent in his account. Take, for example, his reiteration of the positivist nature of his thesis in 'Legal Duty and Obligation', first published in 1966, but substantially revised in 1982, with a section discussing Dworkin's and Raz's accounts of law, in his *Essays on Bentham* (1982)

Oxford, p. 127: 'I have only argued that when judges or others make committed statements of legal obligation it is not the case that they must necessarily believe or pretend to believe that they are referring to a species of moral obligation.' And in the Introduction to his *Essays in Jurisprudence and Philosophy*, published in 1983, he confirms his view on the 'detached' nature of normative legal statements, saying: 'Such detached statements constitute a third kind of statement to add to the two (internal and external statements) which I distinguish. To have made all this clear I should have emphasized that as well as the distinction between mere regularities of behaviour and rule-governed behaviour we need a distinction between the acceptance of rules and the recognition of their acceptance by others' (14). If MacCormick's point is that the 'facts of the matter' here are complex, or controversial, and not 'plain', then his criticism is not of Dworkin's idea of 'plain fact', but of Dworkin's view that conventionalism makes the 'best sense' of positivism. MacCormick has to supply the *sense* of positivism, given that we are to interpret the factual 'detached' statements of judges in a complex way.

Can we both have positivism *and* see legal argument in all the complex ways that seem at first sight much more easily explained in terms of moral argument? MacCormick thinks so. But that is where I see the virtue of legal positivism drain away. We do not have the 'this is where the law stops' clarity (and 'certainty' – see Hart's justification of the rule of recognition). When I first read MacCormick's *Legal Reasoning and Legal Theory* I thought that it was not all that different from what I had been hearing Dworkin argue out at Oxford. Dworkin, naturally, coming from his background in American constitutional law, sees the complexity of legal argument as critical of positivism. Dworkin assumes that the complexity of moral argument is part of legal argument. MacCormick's argument comes from the opposite, more difficult direction, arguing towards the complexity from the point of positivism. To repeat, that journey, to my mind, is a retreat from the central virtue of positivism: not clarity-about-the-question-that-law-is-distinct-from-morality but clarity in working out what the law demands. That is how I read Hart's comments in *The Concept of Law*, pp. 204–5.

It is salutary to see Hart's recognition of the over-complexity of legal positivism if extended to the hard cases. I think that much the best interpretation is that it is *because* of the over-complexity that he prefers to think of judges as law *makers*. In 'Legal Duty and Obligation' he says (161):

'Frequently and in many important cases the law is not clearly settled and dictates no results either way. In such cases in my view, which is hotly challenged by Dworkin and others, the judges have an inescapable though restricted law-making function, which standardly they perform by promoting one or other of those moral values or principles which the existing law can be regarded as instantiating.' Why are they 'law-making' here? What is so significant about the fact that the law is not *settled* that it requires the invocation of some different function? In my view, it can only be that Hart regards plain rules (plain facts) as the central idea of his positivism. And that accords perfectly with the interpretive underpinnings he supplies and which I have already discussed at some length.

130 *Ronald Dworkin*

7. See Hart 'Kelsen Visited', *Essays in Jurisprudence and Philosophy*
(1983) Oxford, p. 286 (and see his Preface, at pp. 14–15).

8. And it is possible to have normative, normative, normative statements and so on. For example, the devout Catholic who says 'in Spain, the
women's movement ought not to campaign for the removal of laws prohibiting abortion.' That is, a value judgment is being made (by the Catholic)
about a value judgment being made (by the feminist group) about a value
judgment (the creators of the law in Spain prohibiting abortion).

9. It is clear that Dworkin does not mean by 'plain fact' any such thing
as a 'brute' fact. His use of the term 'plain fact' appeals to common sense.

10. See Hamlyn, D. *The Theory of Knowledge* (1979) Chapter 5;
Anscombe, E. 'On Brute Facts' (1958) *Analysis* 69; Ayer, A. *The Problem of
Knowledge* (1956) Chapter 2.

11. See Gottlieb's excellent discussion of this point in his remarkable
study *The Logic of Choice* (1968) Allen & Unwin, particularly Chapter 4.

12. See Hart's *The Concept of Law* (1961) Oxford, pp. 181–2. Chapter 9,
entitled 'Laws and Morals', refines the arguments to support his definition
and is a culmination of many of the arguments he advances in his 'Positivism and the Separation of Law and Morals', originally published in *Harvard
Law Review*, vol. 71 (February 1958), and now to be found in Hart's *Essays
in Jurisprudence and Philosophy* (1983) Oxford, Chapter 2.

13. See s.12(1), qualified by the Sexual Offences Act 1967 s.1.

14. *Law's Empire*, p. 429 n. 3 and n. 6. Also, see Dworkin's reply to
Lyons in *Ronald Dworkin and Contemporary Jurisprudence* (1984) Duckworth,
pp. 254–60.

15. Raz, 'Authority, Law and Morality' (July 1985) 69 *The Monist* 295.

16. See Schofield, 'Jeremy Bentham and Nineteenth-Century Jurisprudence', unpublished paper, Bentham Project, University College London.

17. See *Law's Empire*, Chapter 1.

18. See 'Positivism and the Separation of Law and Morals', in Hart
Essays in Jurisprudence and Philosophy (1983) Oxford, Chapter 2.

19. 'I cannot understand how any person who has considered the subject
can suppose that society could possibly have gone on if judges had not
legislated', said Austin in Lecture VI, *The Province of Jurisprudence Determined*, ed. Hart (1954) Weidenfeld and Nicolson (p. 191). Despite these
remarks, Austin was clear that judge-made law was law only by virtue of
what the sovereign had commanded. The judge would, therefore, have only the
weaker discretion to do what it was that the sovereign would have commanded had he been aware of the facts.

20. See *The General Theory of Law and State* pp. 146–53. But this is a
matter that is debated among Kelsenian scholars. See *Essays on Kelsen*, ed.
Tur and Twining (1986) Oxford.

21. Dworkin says in his Introduction to *The Philosophy of Law*, ed.
Dworkin (1977) Oxford paperbacks, p. 7, that the positivists' theory of
judicial discretion is a 'consequence' of their theory of propositions of law.

22. Maybe Hart would endorse the scientific conception of interpretation. The connection with the plain fact theory is that interpretation would
aim at making sense of the plain facts of law presented 'out there'. For
Dworkin, this idea falls down, as we have seen, because it requires, in hard

cases, the construction of more and more abstract conventions, the culmination of which is the idea of soft conventionalism resting on a 'consensus' among officials that the best interpretation be sought. That would amount, I presume, for Dworkin, to the same as saying that that kind of interpretation is creative, not scientific.

23. *The Concept of Law*, Chapter 5.

24. See Raz, *The Authority of Law* (1979) Oxford, Chapters 7 and 8.

25. See MacCormick's helpful discussion in *Legal Reasoning and Legal Theory* Oxford (1978) Appendix pp. 275–92.

26. Hart uses the linguistic distinction between viewing a red traffic light as a 'sign' that motorists will stop and viewing it as a 'signal' *to* stop, to make this point. See *The Concept of Law*, p. 87.

27. Not all wills require two witnesses. Soldiers, seamen and members of the RAF can write wills without witnesses if in circumstances equivalent to 'actual military service'. See Halsbury's Laws of England, Vol. 50, 4th ed. para. 270.

28. *The Concept of Law*, p. 206.

29. See *Essays in Jurisprudence and Philosophy*, Chapter 2, pp. 72–8; and *The Concept of Law*, Chapter 9, pp. 203–7.

30. Compare Bentham's approach, which was much more clearly motivated by his utilitarianism. See Postema, *Bentham and the Common Law Tradition* (1986) Oxford, particularly Chapter 9, 'Utilitarian Positivism'.

31. Austin, *The Province of Jurisprudence Determined* ed. Hart (1954) Weidenfeld and Nicolson, Lecture V, p. 184.

6

Objectivity in law and morality

The problem of objectivity

The problem of objectivity is the major stumbling-block to understanding Dworkin's theory. The vagueness of the penumbra, the
concern with the periphery, the attempt to make sense of what happens in appellate cases, the idea that 'moral' sense be made of the law,
all combine to give the impression that legal argument can be anything
you care to make it. The combination of that with the knowledge that
Dworkin has a theory about rights to equal concern and respect makes
it unsurprising that his theory has been taken by some, especially those
on the political right, to be an excuse for 'putting his own subjective
ideas into the law'.

This caricature is crude. It has the inherent but superficial appeal of
the plain fact theory that law is confined to explicit legislative and
judicial utterances. But we found, in the last chapter, that if we stuck to
that theory little sense could be given to the *legal* quality of argument in
hard cases. We had to say such argument was 'social' or 'moral', or rely
on some other kind of argument. Nevertheless, the appeal of that
theory lay in the objectivity of being able to point to plain facts, in the
form of the requisite utterances, there for all of us to see, plainly.

I have rehearsed Dworkin's arguments for saying that this is an
inadequate characterisation of law. It fails, for him, because it does not
cast legal argument in the best possible moral light. So, it is objected,
the 'subjectivity' of moral judgments makes legal argument subjective
and, therefore, no more sense can be made of it than that legal
argument consists of just 'trading subjective views'.

There are some points here that must be carefully separated.
Dworkin does not equate legal argument with moral argument.
Rather, he begins with the legal data, the pre-interpretive legal material, and then attempts to make the best moral sense of that. So
interpreters of the law are bound, then, by the need to refer to the
actual legal materials. Further, it does not follow from the 'subjectivity' of moral argument that engaging in argument with others about
moral issues is pointless. Indeed, as I think Dworkin well argues, it is

not helpful to think of moral and legal argument in terms of 'subjectivity' and 'objectivity' at all.

Most seminars and lectures that Dworkin has given which I have attended have attracted scepticism from those asking questions about the 'subjective' nature of legal reasoning as he sees it. Recourse has always been made, in making the sceptical points, to the 'reality' of law and the 'obvious' objectivity of legal argument. The general level of criticism on the point of objectivity has, I think, been both diffuse and misdirected.

Scepticism

A sceptic is someone who denies the basis for argument, perhaps on any matter at all, or perhaps only on some particular matter. Dworkin attracts many sceptical responses, mainly due to the perceived 'subjective' nature of his views.

Scepticism comes in a number of different forms and it is important to be clear about these. Consider, for example, the situation in a typical court. The lawyers for each litigant, and the judge, as well as many others, are all participants in an argumentative institution. By that I mean that everybody concerned accepts that the institution has some sort of 'meaning', and that the part each person plays in it has some sort of sense.

Common responses to what I have just said are as follows. First, people will say that the assertion that 'everyone accepts' an institution in some way morally endorses the institution, or what goes on in it, or, secondly, that it makes the assumption that the institution is devoid of internal conflicts or, thirdly, that the analysis provides no room for a person who is part of the institution yet is 'sceptically inside' it, perhaps with a view to changing it. It is apparent that understanding these three responses is helped by the idea of the 'insider' and the 'outsider' to an institution. The idea which this metaphor embraces is commonly used and is, of course, present in the differences between the internal and external points of view as Hart analyses them. It is, too, I think, a significant characteristic of Kelsen's writings in legal theory.[1] Hart's identification of the importance of this distinction marked a step in the development of legal philosophy, although the distinction, as it has variously been used, has assumed too much prominence in sociology and the American Critical Legal Studies movement.[2]

What are Dworkin's positions on these three responses? First, it is clear that his view is that the concept of law, those discrete ideas about which we agree, is an 'insider's' view.[3] He is to this extent like Kelsen who, as we saw in the previous chapter, views law as meaningful only from the point of view of a general presupposition about its normative force.[4] We must draw this conclusion from Dworkin's thesis that 'best' sense of the law means 'morally best'.

The idea that the institution of law may suffer from internal conflicts needs elaboration, because it is one capable of sitting comfortably with a non-sceptical position. If there are internal conflicts in the law, the insider – it will depend who he is – may have a duty to work to resolve them by constructing new means of resolution. That duty arises under Dworkin's idea of the interpretive legal attitude, following from his view that making best sense of the law means making best moral sense. It appears to be a duty that at least some of the Critical Legal Scholars accept and for one, Unger, it is clearly a duty of liberalism.[4] Of course, it may be that, after trying, an insider will conclude that the form of construction would have to be too great to make sense of existing law, say, where a wicked legal system is involved.[5]

A much stronger form of scepticism, however, looks from the outside, and decides that law, as an institution, is *inherently* flawed and conflicting. Insiders, according to this scepticism, will not be able to make sense of it for reasons arising from the nature of law itself.

This difficult view becomes clearer if we think of it in the light of the sense in which Marxism has viewed the idea of law, under capitalism,[6] as an embodiment of capitalist values. According to some interpretations of Marxism, law is by nature unable to subsist with certain demands of human justice. Each attempt to make law more just tends to reinforce an assumption that the legal way, and the capitalist values embodied in it, is the appropriate mode of change. Capitalist values are thus continued and enhanced.

The third form of response is the 'reform from within' idea. This means that it is possible to be a part of an institution while remaining sceptical about its worth. 'Reform from within' is intended to contradict the thesis that being a part of an institution is somehow to endorse it.

It is clearly the case that this – the insider 'mole' – is a possible way to participate in an institution. But it is equally clear that it is of a parasitic sort, since the understanding we have of such a person's role depends on what we understand his non-sceptical role to be. If no one accepts the institution, we just do not have any sense of the appropriate conventions necessary to give the institution an identity. It is the fact that some accept the identifying marks that makes it an institution with its characteristic roles.

One further point should be added. The beliefs people have about the sceptical nature of the roles they play can only be expressed in the activities they carry out. There is such a thing as 'selling out'. Thus, the revolutionary who intends to change the system from within, but who thirty years on has shown little, if any, sign of having tried to bring about change, is someone whose declared beliefs are suspect.

Dworkin makes use of the metaphor of the 'outsider' and the 'insider' to an institutional practice to describe two kinds of scepticism. He distinguishes between 'external' scepticism and 'internal' scepticism. 'External' scepticism of moral values denies that there is any special metaphysical realm of which moral judgments are a description. It is a form of scepticism that is 'disengaged', because it places the sceptic in a position in which he does not have to argue for a position he holds. It is, instead, a matter of mere 'opinion' for him. The external sceptic denies the 'out thereness' of the nature of moral judgment and for this reason it is a metaphysical and not an interpretive position.[7]

Dworkin says that external scepticism is 'external' because it is disengaged. But if such scepticism is true, it does not, he says, affect the question whether one interpretation can be better than another. The assertion of a moral judgment does not require something *in addition* by way of a description of something existing 'objectively' in order for it to have substance. That is not how we understand moral judgments to be. The assertion that, for example, torturing babies is wrong does not require an extra judgment about the objectivity of the assertion. 'We use the language of objectivity', says Dworkin, 'not to give our ordinary moral or interpretive claims a bizarre metaphysical base, but to *repeat* them, perhaps in a more precise way, to emphasize or qualify their *content*."[8]

Dworkin does, on the other hand, allow internal scepticism, which *is* engaged. Someone might be sceptical, in this sense, if she said that an interpretation of *Hamlet* was not possible because, despite what critics have said, that play just lacks the coherency required before interpretation of it can begin. This sort of scepticism clearly comes under the general umbrella of an interpretive attitude. The sceptic is here prepared to grapple with the substance of the arguments about which she is being sceptical. She meets the arguments by declaring those arguments to be mistaken, and that relies on, rather than dismisses, the possibility that some interpretations can be better.

The example of *Hamlet* may afford just one instance of internal scepticism but scepticism could take a wider form. The sceptic may take the interpretive view that some enterprise, say, literary criticism, is a worthless one because it tries to make order out of something that is necessarily conflicting, or that it deals only in fantasy, or serves no useful or important purpose in human affairs.

Dworkin calls this kind of internal scepticism 'global' internal scepticism, because its scepticism is 'global' about literary criticism. And internal scepticism may, too, arise in relation to a social institution such as law. A person might take the view that, on any interpretation, adjudication fails to make sense because its various rules and principles are too fundamentally conflicting to be resolved or made coherent in any way.

But it is this conclusion that is itself representative of an interpretive attitude. It comes under the interpretive umbrella because it is saying: it makes sense to make sense of certain sorts of things but it just does not make sense to make sense of law! That is, for Dworkin, importantly different from reneging on the importance of the questions simply by saying: there is no objective reality there which could possibly make sense of what you are talking about.

Where do Dworkin's arguments on scepticism get us? The crucial point is, I think, that Dworkin disapproves of the casting off of one very important moral responsibility by the simplistic assertion that there is nothing 'objective' in the world by virtue of which moral judgments are only 'opinion'. The moral responsibility is to make one's views publicly accessible. The problem with the metaphysical approach is that it appears to deny any possibility of a basis for *argument*. It thus denies the need for a public stance other than a declaration of what a person is going to do.

This point is significant for Dworkin whose requirement of public officials is that they not only be consistent in their application of principles of law but that they articulate them as well. The internal global sceptic[9] is in the interpretive forum. He is thus open to challenge over the question of whether he has made the best sense of the practice about which he shows scepticism.

But Dworkin is also forthright about the sociology of scepticism. In the practical world of law, not only are there are relatively few global internal sceptics, a belief in external scepticism makes absolutely no difference to legal argument:

... the skeptical challenge, sensed as the challenge of external skepticism, has a powerful hold on lawyers. They say, of any thesis about the best account of legal practice in some department of the law, 'That's your opinion," which is true but to no point. Or they ask, 'How do you know?" or 'Where does that claim come from?" demanding not a case they can accept or oppose but a thundering knock-down metaphysical demonstration no one can resist who has the wit to understand. And when they see that no argument of that power is in prospect, they grumble that jurisprudence is subjective only. Then, finally, they return to their knitting – making, accepting, resisting, rejecting arguments in the normal way, consulting, revising, deploying convictions pertinent to deciding which of competing accounts of legal practice provides the best justification of that practice. My advice is straightforward: this preliminary dance of skepticism is silly and wasteful; it neither adds to nor subtracts from the business at hand. The only skepticism worth anything is skepticism of the internal kind, and this must be earned by arguments of the same contested character as the arguments it opposes, not claimed in advance by some pretense at hard-hitting empirical metaphysics.[10]

Dworkin's invocation of the 'internal' metaphor in relation to legal argument is a little misleading, despite its common use, because it suggests that Dworkin ignores, or that his theory cannot accommodate, what are often thought to be important 'external' questions about law. What he means is that the genuine external critic does not threaten the possibility, or importance, of legal argument. That is his answer to the 'external sceptic'. But what are often thought to be external questions, such as those concerning an investigation of the history or causal conditions of law, are in his view certainly not *irrelevant* to legal argument. Nevertheless, legal historians, or sociologists who deny moral point to their task, will not, in his view, be contributing to making the best sense of law.

Many people fail to appreciate the force of Dworkin's point here. It is that if a 'debunking' of law is argued on the basis of some historical or sociological fact, that debunking only makes sense if intended as moral criticism of law. There is, of course, a form of moral criticism that says that the idea of law should be eradicated altogether. But that, in Dworkin's terms, is *internal* global criticism, because it accepts that law *could* have justificatory force but argues that this law is so confused, or conflicting, or class-ridden, that it lacks that force. That is why it is an insider attack. It is from the point of view of someone who, despite what he says, recognises the force of the need for justifying the application of law.[11]

We can be sceptical about this by denying the possibility of genuine argument about legal and moral issues. Is there really such a genuine subjective doubter? He could not be a lawyer, or a law teacher, of course, for otherwise we would have to rule out of account most members of the Critical Legal Studies movement, who *do* engage in (what they believe to be) arguments about those issues. But there are people who claim themselves to be 'subjective doubters' and it is instructive to consider their point of view and their arguments.

The one right answer thesis

In an attempt to find out what the 'subjective doubter' thinks is an objectively right answer, I shall now consider a thesis, which is not of Dworkin's own making, but which has been ascribed to him. This has become known as the 'one right answer' thesis, and it has caused some merriment among students and some academics. It is fun if we take this theory (it is not Dworkin's, as will become apparent) at face value. It says that for every legal problem imaginable there is an answer, which is right, and which can be found in a statute or a law report.

It is a silly thesis, although it is actually accepted by some first year law students and one or two eccentric lawyers and academics. It is a bibliographical, or arithmetical view of the law, which supposes that legal research is *no more* than looking 'the law' up, like looking up a word in dictionary, and then making the appropriate deductions, or doing the appropriate sums. It is clearly the plain facts theory in another guise. No one who thought carefully about what is going on in legal argument could accept this theory. Why has it been ascribed to Dworkin, especially given that he states so clearly that he believes the plain fact theory to be wrong?

The immediate answer is that Dworkin's theory, requiring moral judgments, is 'subjective' and that any legal argument is therefore as good as any other. The lawyer for each side advances an argument based upon his own moral preferences, constrained, of course, to some degree, by the actual legal materials, in order to 'convince' the judge. The judge would then make a decision based on *his* own moral preferences.

Legal argument, seen in this way, seems essentially a matter of opinion, because there is no way of showing – or demonstrating – which answer is right. Dworkin's reply to this is a purely defensive one. He asserts that it does not follow that if something cannot be demonstrated that it cannot be right. Or, to put it in another way: it is insufficient to say that there can be no right answers just because they cannot by proved or demonstrated.

The argument is, and has always been, purely defensive. He does not provide arguments to say that there are right answers, over and above his arguments to say what the right answers are. He does not think that any such arguments are needed. Attacks on Dworkin's 'subjectivity', too, have only been at this superficial level. (There may be other possible attacks.) But the widespread misunderstanding of this aspect of his theory is based upon a reading of his defensive comments to the 'subjectivity' attack.

Less immediate and more general reasons are that people like arguments that demonstrate, or prove, or otherwise provide a convincing 'knockdown' effect. A theory that legal argument in pivotal cases does not consist of such arguments thus appears weak. But theories cannot be wrong because people just want them to be wrong and so we shall examine the claim that there can be no right answers unless they can be proved to be right. Let us call this thesis the 'demonstrability thesis', although it could equally be called the 'provability' thesis, or the 'knockdown' thesis.

Is the demonstrability thesis true as a description of legal argument? The short answer must obviously be that it is not. Again go to the courts, or look at a random law report. Judges, lawyers, academics and students spend much of their time arguing about what constitutes the right answer in the law. Take a typical sort of legal argument, say, the sort that might appear in a lawyer's opinion written for a client. The clear law will be set out first of all, and then the alternative ways that the law could go in the unclear areas. The lawyer will then construct some sort of argument about what, in his opinion, is a correct statement of the law. I suggest that this is how a lawyer views what he does in writing an opinion.

But someone will object here that the lawyer can only state what *in his view* the law is, so that the document he produces for his client can only be his own opinion.[12] That is perfectly true, but it simply does not alter the picture. That something is a person's opinion is not an argument for saying that he cannot be right (or wrong) according to some standard. Why in law should 'in my opinion' have a different meaning from that which it has in other areas, for example, as in 'in my opinion, the world is flat; the world is round; the sum is correct; the engine has seized'; and so on? What is the difference, as far as *truth* is concerned, between saying 'In my opinion, the defendant is liable' and 'The defendant is liable'? I suggest, in support of Dworkin, none at all. In each case, the proposition is *being advanced as true*. Perhaps the function of 'in my opinion' is to add a polite reminder ("I might be wrong"), or to express diffidence ("It's *just* my view"), or to express authority ("I am an expert"), or to acknowledge the impossibility of demonstration or proof. None of these functions is incompatible with the possibility of the proposition's truth.

A further objection frequently made is the following. True, lawyers and others talk as if there were right answers, but this is only a cynical way of trying to convince others, in particular a judge. There is no 'real' right answer, only one that is put forward to 'persuade', or 'convince'.

But this objection is just self-contradictory. If there could not be a 'real' right answer in these cases then presumably that is generally known, because the cynical scenario sketched here is enacted every day. If it *is* the case, why would anyone be convinced or persuaded by appeals to the correctness or rightness of the arguments? Whatever appeal such arguments have, it could not be to their 'rightness', which leaves us to wonder what appeal such arguments can have. Yet another objection is that although the word 'right' is used frequently in legal discourse, where there is no question of demonstrability, its function is no more than a commendation that this is the law to be applied.

Dworkin rightly, in my view, cuts through these sorts of objections by appealing to the idea of the truth of propositions of law. What are we saying when we talk of a right answer in law, as when we might feel disposed to say that, for example, the appellate court got the law 'right'? He says that here we are talking of the truth of the proposition of law that is expressed in the judgments. The decision is 'right', or 'correct', by virtue of being in accordance with the right or correct or *true* proposition of law.

There is a host of expressions that may be used to denote the truth of propositions of law. 'Correct' and 'right' seem to me to be the most common, but 'appropriate', 'valid', 'accurate', 'the law is that ...", 's.16 requires ...", 'sound', 'good law versus bad law', 'the better view', all do equally well to refer to the truth of the relevant legal proposition, although in slightly different contexts. But it is clear that in each of these cases a reference is made to what the law is according to the criteria of legal argument.

What other conclusion could we come to? Take, for example, clear cases. The Wills Act 1837 requires that, in certain specified formal conditions, two witnesses must sign a will in order for it to be valid. Here, I think, Dworkin's suggestion is sensible. The lawyer, referring to s.9 of that Act and saying that it 'requires two witnesses', or that a will 'is valid', or (advising a foreign client) 'there exists in England a law that says you must have two witnesses on your will', or 'it is a correct statement of the law that two witnesses, etc ...', is, in each case, making use of the following proposition of United Kingdom law: '...in certain defined circumstances, two witnesses are required for a will.'[13]

If we accept this, as I think we should, is there any difference between accepting truth as predicable of legal propositions that are hard and not easy? We can employ our test again of listening to courtroom argument and looking at law reports, and we could add legal textbooks. If the hard cases are not about the truth of legal propositions then we have to understand courtroom argument, and read reports and textbooks, in an odd way. We have first to sift out the easy cases from the hard cases and ascribe truth to the propositions asserted in the first but not to those in the second. It would make a nonsense of the way we look at these things because in fact we take the (as it were) easy propositions along with the hard ones.

Perhaps the point can be best made by using the example of a typical appellate judgment where there are, say, three majority judges, and two dissenting judges, each judgment being slightly different in the grounds given. Consider all the possible ways we can, and do, take such a judgment.

First, it by no means follows that the majority judges are 'right', that is, express the true proposition of law. If they did, it would not make sense to say that appellate courts get the law wrong, which is a kind of criticism inherent to the nature of legal argument. Second, we can, and do, make statements that distinguish between parts of judgments as, for example, when we say that Judge X stated the law accurately in one part but inaccurately in another. Third, we can, and do, say that Judge Y 'got the right answer, for the wrong reason' (and conversely, Judge Z 'got it wrong, but gave the right reasons').

The significance of these possibilities, which clearly exist, is that our concept of legal argument is much richer than a demonstrability thesis of truth could possibly allow. We not only employ the idea of a 'truth' appertaining to both clear and hard propositions of law but, as the third possibility above shows, we can, and do, refer to the appropriateness of the kinds of reasons relating to the truth of propositions of law.

These considerations, too, support the contention that the distinction between easy and hard cases is itself not one that is 'presented' to us in a plain fact way. The distinction between those propositions that are uncontroversially true and those that are controversially true is the *result* of legal argument and not its starting-point.

I conclude that Dworkin is correct in saying that lawyers in the Anglo-American jurisdiction make widespread use of a conception of truth which crosses the division between hard and easy cases and does not depend on some such idea as 'provability' or 'demonstrability'.

Is demonstrability a good criterion of truth?

A much better question to be concerned with here is whether the concept of truth shared by lawyers is a good or sensible one. Given they do employ the concept of truth, it may still be that that concept is confused or wrong, in the same way that it seems reasonable to say that people were once confused and wrong in conceiving of the world as a flat object.

But the word 'good' here can mean two things. First, is a concept of truth that exceeds demonstrability coherent, one which makes sense for people to use in general? We can answer that question by considering, for example, other areas of discourse to see whether there is a general use for it. Second, if the concept of truth can have coherency, does it make good, practical sense for lawyers to employ it?

The simple answer to the first question is that a conception of truth exceeding demonstrability is in widespread use across a number of discourses. Let us take for a start argument of the sort I am presently engaged in. The first sentence of this paragraph expresses, I think, a true proposition. Did it strike you that that proposition could not possibly be true or false just because I could not demonstrate its truth to you? In fact, you will find, on reflection, that many of the propositions which you assert in the course of everyday conversation are ones where you have no means of demonstrating truth but nevertheless rely upon others to understand that you are asserting that certain things are true.

All this is not to deny that the possibility of demonstration exists in legal argument. What Dworkin means by 'demonstration' or 'proof' is some mechanism by which agreement in principle can be secured, in the way in which it is possible to secure agreement in clear cases of law. We agree on paradigms of law, say, the application of s.9 of the Wills Act 1837. By employing the mechanism of legal argument in first finding the statute, then the section, then the words relating to the requirement of two witnesses, we may demonstrate, by the use of this paradigmatic use of legal argument, what the law is.

If this sounds too 'theoretical', compare this with actual practice, for most problems in lawyers' and administrators' offices are settled in this way. If someone consistently denied that the Wills Act was law, that s.9 made no such requirement as to two witnesses, we would simply say that they had misunderstood the paradigm, or that they did not know what legal argument was about, in the same way that we might say that of a person who consistently denied that $2 + 2 = 4$.

But we are, for present purposes, interested in those cases in which there is no such possibility of demonstration. It may, perhaps, help to consider whether discourses other than law require demonstration. Let us, for example, try the demonstrability theory for religious discourse. It seems uncontroversial to say that the person who believes in the existence of God believes the proposition 'God exists' is true. Does it follow that the believer means by this that he must be able to demonstrate the truth of this proposition? Surely not. To some, indeed, it may be thought a blasphemous idea that the truth of propositions about God depended upon demonstration of their truth. But there is a long history of the view that the idea of truth in theological discourse is a special case, more akin to commitment than demonstration (and there is a long history, in this context, of the meaning of the latter).

Can moral, as opposed to purely religious, propositions be true or false? This is a test case for Dworkin because it is a thesis of his that moral reasoning is a component of legal reasoning. There is one sense in which we might say that the truth of some moral propositions is demonstrable, which occurs when we refer to the correct use of words expressing moral disapproval.

It is, I think, true that torturing babies is cruel (*who* could conceivably deny that?). What is more, this truth clearly goes further than being merely a truth about the correct use of the term 'cruel', verifiable, say, by use of a dictionary. Rather, a person who misunderstood that torturing babies was morally wrong would be said not to understand an important, indeed, a paradigm case of immorality. It follows that at least some kind of demonstration of the truth of propositions of morality is possible.

Further, we certainly *talk* as if all sorts of non-paradigms of morality were true or false. The person who believes that killing animals for meat is wrong presumably believes the following propositions to be true: one ought not to kill animals for meat; it is wrong to kill animals for meat; it is immoral to kill animals for meat. In these cases, it is simply false to say that the question is just one of understanding how to use language correctly. A question of moral judgment is involved. Is there, then, a fundamental difference between the torturing babies case and the killing animals for meat case, which lies just in the fact that in the first case demonstration of truth is possible but not the second?

As far as understanding our ordinary moral discourse, as a description of the way we talk about these matters, I do not think so. When we assert matters in morality, as in other areas, we certainly speak as if what we said were true, independently altogether of the question of demonstration.

But we can make short work of any argument that says that we can only have the possibility of truth (or falsity) if the proposition can be demonstrated to be true or false. Consider the thesis itself. It is not amenable to its own standard of truth. *We cannot demonstrate the demonstrability thesis itself to be true.* Consider the following statement of the demonstrability thesis:

<<only propositions that can be demonstrated, or proved, to be true, are capable of being true or false>>

We so clearly cannot demonstrate that to be true that, at the relatively simple level of showing that a non-demonstrable conception of truth is coherent, we cause embarrassment to devotees of the demonstrability thesis. For they rely on the truth of a non-demonstrable proposition of truth to declare that non-demonstrable propositions cannot be true.[14]

This is a dramatic conclusion. It leads us to turn to the second and more important question I posed earlier, whether a non-demonstrable conception of truth makes good, practical sense for lawyers to adopt.

Consider the following questions. What leads people to accept the demonstrability thesis? Does it have anything to commend it? Or, most important of all, is it within our power to adopt it or some other criterion of truth? We can, after all, adopt postulates (or axioms) to guide our reasoning in other fields, such as geometry or economics. Such postulates are chosen not according to whether they are true or not, but for other sorts of reasons, perhaps, say, to give a coherent account of different sorts of phenomena.

We adopt postulates rather than discover them. If they are true they are so by virtue of stipulation rather than anything else, although conclusions drawn from postulates will be true by virtue of valid chains of reasoning. So, for example, the simple postulate 'x = 6' is true by stipulation, but the sum '2x = 12' is true by a simple analysis of the meaning of the sum given that stipulation. 'x = 6' is not true by virtue of anything 'out there' in the world.[15]

The *adoption* of 'x = 6' is, however, open to criticism. Some people might say that the choice of 'x' is confusing because it is ambiguous with 'x' which means 'multiplies'. Or a postulate that stipulated that 'A x A x A x A x A = A^5' might be praised because it produces a workable shorthand. In fact, the criticism of the adoption of postulates is an important part of many areas of social life. This was clear when I discussed, in Chapter 2, the stipulative nature of wartime codes. We adopt certain codes with practical ideas in mind. 'The cat is on the mat' may be an unpractical, unworkable code, because too easily broken, for 'the missile is on target'. And, it seems clear, paradigm cases in the law are true by stipulation.

If practical considerations are therefore the clue to the justification of at least some kinds of postulates, are practical considerations relevant to the adoption of the demonstrability thesis in law, regarding it now as a postulate?

I think, however, that the case to be made for the adoption of the demonstrability thesis in law turns out to be no more than the case for positivism. It is, presumably, that laws should only be seen as 'existing', that is, being true or false, or valid or invalid, when their existence, truth or validity can be demonstrated (say) by reference to actual official practice.

The arguments against this view, however, are arguments which approach the problem of what is a sensible conception of law and legal argument, and not arguments that depend upon appealing to more abstract and controversial theories of truth. In other words, the appeal to the demonstrability thesis as if it were an independent argument is misleading.

A word about 'best' and the idea of 'opinion'

Some people object to the idea that there can be true propositions of law but will accept that there can be 'best' or 'better' answers. A consideration of this view is instructive because it throws some light on the hold that the demonstrability thesis has on people. It is very common, too, for people to say of a non-demonstrably true proposition that it is not true 'but only a matter of opinion'.

But there is nothing to be gained by saying that although a proposition is the best statement of the law it cannot be true. Why not say that the true statement of law is one that expresses 'the best' view of it? What advance on clarity has otherwise been made?

Further, we must not confuse 'doing our best' to produce a correct, true, statement of the law with producing the correct statement, because, of course, we could be wrong. This common confusion shows, I think, the real problem people have with the whole business of undemonstrable truth. How can we *know*, how can we be certain, that the proposition is true, or 'the best'? People want certainty when none is possible. It does not follow that there can be no correct or true propositions. The judge who does his best may get the law wrong, but his best endeavour is nevertheless an endeavour to state the correct proposition of law.

The fact that something is 'only my opinion' does not release it from the arena of truth. It used to be people's 'opinion' that the world was flat, but that opinion turned out, it now seems, to have been false. We form opinions all the time which turn out to be true or false. In fact, the function of the phrase, 'in my opinion' is often used precisely in the recognition of the fact that the speaker recognises that he may be wrong and that therefore the opinion is capable of being wrong or right.

The possibility of a 'tie'

Some people have expressed reservations about what they have seen as an inconsistency in Dworkin's position on the 'one right answer' thesis. This is that in earlier articles and lectures he has allowed the possibility of a 'tie', that is, a situation where a judge may be faced with arguments that are equally balanced on either side.

In such a case, it seems, there are two legal propositions, each supporting the opposite conclusion, so that they are contradictory (for example, 'ultimate manufacturerers are liable in the circumstances' versus 'ultimate manufacturers are not liable in the circumstances'). If they are 'equally balanced' that presumably means that each proposition is either true, which cannot be possible given the contradiction, and falsifies the *one* right answer thesis, or neither true nor false, which falsifies the one *right* answer thesis.

Let us momentarily practise clearheadedness here. I say this because a common 'putdown' of the elaborate Dworkinian theory is that 'Dworkin asserts that there is always one right answer to every legal problem, and that is an absurdity'. Dworkin's thesis is, as I have already explained, a defensive thesis to the criticism that there cannot be right answers in hard cases where there is no 'proof' or demonstration. It does not follow, therefore, that, in his view, there is 'always' a right answer. The defensive nature of his thesis allows for the possibility of ties.

Given this clarification, it is necessary to note a possible interpretation of Dworkin in Chapter 13 of *Taking Rights Seriously*. In this chapter, entitled 'Can Rights be Controversial?", he considers the question of ties. He says that it is possible to imagine an enterprise or practice whose 'ground rules' recognise the possibility of a tie but denies that such ground rules are part of the foundations of legal argument in the Anglo-American system. He was concerned in that argument to counter the criticism that could be made, say, by a philosopher, that it was not possible for there to be one right answer unless there were objective, demonstrable facts that made legal propositions true. In other words, Dworkin was arguing that there is nothing in general philosophical reasoning that makes the idea of there being right answers an *impossible* one in any particular enterprise. The philosopher could not stand outside the enterprise and make these judgments.

This chapter has been taken by some to mean that Dworkin was making a descriptive claim about 'the Anglo-American legal enterprise'. Thus, claims are frequently made in law schools that Dworkin has failed to appreciate that there 'really' are ties, as though the question were one which could be settled simply by looking at cases. I think that this view may have been supported by comments Dworkin has made occasionally in lectures that some legal systems may be so 'sparse', that is, so lacking in the number of established rules, that ties would be 'empirically' possible.

This article, and these remarks, should now be read in the light of Dworkin's later development of the idea of interpretation. Judgments about the objectivity of law are interpretive judgments, and the philosopher who 'stands outside' and declares truth is impossible in any enterprise where it is non-demonstrable, or lacks a 'real' counterpart, is an 'external' sceptic who is disengaged from the interpretive exercise.[16]

The judgment that there are ties in the law is a possible interpretive one. It is just an interpretive judgment that Dworkin thinks is not a good one. His view is, I think, that legal argument, like moral argument, is about decision, and *always* demands the best decision, that being the one that applies the true proposition. The recourse to ties may fall short of the demands of decision.[17] It represents a kind of 'copping out'. Although tossing a coin represents a kind of decision that kind is not one that rates highly in a good interpretation of legal argument.

The following example may illustrate the point.[18] A company runs a competition to advertise its breakfast cereal. A number of questions are set, matching heads to bodies of famous rock stars. There is also a 'tie-breaker' question which does not admit of a demonstrable right answer as, obviously, the questions about the pop stars do, which asks competitors to say in a jingle of a set number of words what the virtues of the particular brand of cereal are.

Five competitors obtain right answers to the head and body matching and, unlike some competitors who have also obtained right answers here, have written their jingles within the word limit. The task is then left to the competition judge to decide between them, on the basis of the tie-breaker, which one should receive the prize on the basis of the jingle.

In other words, the judge has to decide which of the five entries is the 'best' one. There are no precedents, nothing. Yet, would it seem right if the judge were random in his selection? We expect some judgment. Would it seem right if he exercised some sort of aesthetic judgment and came to the view that two tied? Imagine that he does this and asks the sponsor to award two prizes or split the prize but the sponsor refuses. What does the judge do?

The answer in Dworkin's terms is that a proper understanding of the competition is that the best entry must win and that the judge must go back to the entries and decide which one is the best. There is no more to it than that. The best entry is that which, according to the best understanding of the competition, is the best.

The sense of tautology that you may get from this characterisation of what the competition requires only arises because of the level of abstraction. It is not as if there are no criteria other than the judge's feeling or transient taste. Rival interpretations could be: the most poetic, the most 'catchy', the most literate, the one with advertising appeal, and so on. Test the different possible interpretations. What if the judge decided on the basis that a jingle pointing out the dangers to the environment of the sponsor's factory was the best? Or the one that made a political statement in favour of apartheid? Or the one that made a plea for nuclear disarmament?

The point is that the cornflakes judge does not operate, even with this sparse set of rules, as if there were no right answer. He could not, otherwise he would not render a considered decision. The same could be said, we should note, for any *critic* of that judge's decision. So, from the internal point of view, the no right answer thesis is not a plausible interpretation.

The doubt we would feel about these judgments shows that, sparse as the competition rules were, judgments of an interpretive and argumentative nature are perfectly conceivable (and, indeed, one of the reasons why the rules of such competitions often have clauses saying 'no correspondence will be entered into'). What thundering knock-down argument is left to show us that a 'best' answer is impossible?

The duty to construct

Dworkin's dismissal of the 'out thereness' of both the plain fact theory and the demonstrability theory of truth has a moral edge. He wants moral responsibility to attach to people, not to entities existing outside us, maybe unknown to us. One of his most interesting essays is his one on the methodology displayed in John Rawls's *A Theory of Justice*, in which he makes significant analyses of two of Rawls's most fundamental theses, the starting-points of moral reasoning by way of 'reflective equilibrium' and, when political questions are asked, the 'original position'.

'Reflective equilibrium' is the name that Rawls gives to what he regards as the correct method of moral reasoning. It envisages an equilibrium being attained between moral intuitions, or convictions, and abstract positions on general questions of morality (moral theories) that we hold. The 'equilibrium' between the two should be reached by our comparing our intuitions with our structured moral beliefs.

Sometimes our intuitions embarrass our theories, as when our intuition that just wars are morally permissible embarrasses our theory that innocent life must never be taken. The process of reflective equilibrium justifies the moral psychology whereby either the theory is modified or developed in a way that can explain the intuition (say, for example, innocent life must not intentionally be taken, with some attendant theories about what constitutes innocent life and what intention means), or the intuition begins to lose its impact and finally disappears given the coherence of the theory.

Of course, the abstract positions on general moral questions that we hold will make sense of the particular intuitions we have. So the process is ongoing. We modify, or even eventually abandon, intuitions in the light of our generalisations and acquire new intuitions both in the light of theory and new experiences. Arguments we have with others about moral issues should develop in the same way. We test intuitions we hold against general positions we hold. We embarrass others by pointing to inconsistencies between their intuitions and their general positions.[19]

Dworkin's view is that Rawls's description of the method of reflective equilibrium is ambiguous between two models of moral reasoning (which I shall shortly compare). Generally, I think Dworkin's view is that Rawls's idea is insufficiently prescriptive and that it needs more bite than its appearance as a successful moral psychology, one that shows admirably the development of a person's moral beliefs but not clearly why any person should engage in it.

We shall recognise the first model because it is similar to the plain facts view I have discussed so extensively. Dworkin calls it the 'natural' model, because it supposes that reflective equilibrium is fundamentally concerned to expose an already existing set of moral truths, to use the now familiar phrase, 'out there'. The natural model has the following consequence for moral thought. When there appears to be an irreconcilable clash between moral intuitions and moral theory, there is no immediate cause for concern. We assume, under this model, that the solution, the reconciliation, is possible but that we do not ourselves possess the knowledge or mental acumen to make that reconciliation. The solution outstrips us, but that does not matter.

The second model, the one Dworkin favours, is the 'constructive' model. According to this, there is a duty upon us to *make the reconciliation*, and to construct the answer. There is no 'out there' that absolves us from that responsibility.

In an example, Dworkin attempts to bring out more clearly the difference between the two models. Imagine a zoologist who is trying to work out what an apparently prehistoric animal looked like. All he possesses is a carbon-dated pile of bones. According to the natural model, the zoologist can assume that there was an animal of which these bones may or may not be a complete set. An inability to make something out of the bones is not a failure, because that position presupposes that the bones are only *clues* to what actually exists.

But, according to the constructive model, such a position is not possible, for there is no reality 'out there'. Instead, the zoologist must make the best construction out of the bones he has.[20] Dworkin regards moral reasoning as something which people should engage in to make coherent the different judgments on which they act. People must not renege on this responsibility by simply assuming, as the natural model assumes, that moral intuitions can have a 'correctness' that can outstrip their explanatory powers. They are not permitted to say, when faced with prima facie conflicting intuitions (say, about just wars and prohibiting abortion), that some reconciling explanation exists although it has not been, and may not be, discovered by men.

This is a strongly secular thesis, demanding that we act on principle rather than faith, placing responsibility firmly on the individual. Reflective equilibrium is to be understood in terms of ingesting and reworking basic moral intuitions and being prepared to act according to a plan understood to be as coherent as a person can possibly get. He may not get it right, but the duty is upon him to try nevertheless.

The constructive interpretation of the idea of reflective equilibrium is extremely important from the public standpoint, for Dworkin. The duty to construct becomes, for officials, that of 'articulate consistency', the duty to submerge private convictions in accordance with principle. This is possible in a society where there is relative agreement in intuitions, or convictions, about justice, as in the Anglo-American democratic society.

The idea of the construction of moral judgments is important for another reason. In a society of relative agreement, the idea of community is embodied in the idea of public articulation about principles of justice. This is an idea that Dworkin develops in his theory of integrity.

Morality and objectivity

The idea of objectivity in Dworkin arises mainly in relation to the objectivity of legal argument, and consists in the sorting out of true propositions of law. But it is his most central and famous thesis that moral reasoning is an essential part of legal reasoning, so it follows clearly that he believes that there can be true moral propositions.

How does this thesis relate to the duty to construct? I think the example of the competition to find the best jingle for the breakfast cereal helps here. We are struck, I suggest, by the possibility that, even in that trivial case, there is objective decision-making beyond the mere tossing of a coin to decide between the jingles, however bad they were.

In a serious situation, say, where a decision must be made between two people about who is to carry the financial responsibility after a major road accident, that feeling becomes very strong indeed. Yet we do also feel the pull of the question, 'by virtue of what would the correct moral proposition be `correct'?". Where would the true moral proposition *come from?*

I suggest the answer lies for Dworkin in the idea of the construction of values. The position he advocates is between the twin extremes of a pre-existing moral reality and a total subjectivity of values that denies the existence of a common ground of morality upon which we could stand. If it must spring from something, the truth of propositions of morality springs from the importance of morality, from the commitment we should have when asserting propositions about how, morally, we should act. If moral propositions, and hence legal propositions, have to be 'objective' then it is in this sense we have to understand them.

This may seem to some to be irredeemably subjective. But the argument does not force that conclusion. The requirement that moral intuitions or convictions be made coherent is one check, and that check is clearly one that is testable against other people's working out of coherent positions against their own intuitions and convictions. A requirement of publicity still obtains (that is the pull of the type of question which asks, 'where does the proposition *come from*?") although one vastly more complex than correspondence to an independent moral 'reality'.

Convention and consensus

The difference between these two possible bases for morality is important for Dworkin. In his view, that people in general agree that something should morally be done or is morally permissible, cannot be a sufficient justification for doing that thing, otherwise slavery would have been right once. The mistake is the plain fact mistake over again.

Put in another way, moral positivism is not a tenable position.

Of course, the existence of certain conventions may provide a reason for behaving in a particular way as, for example, the convention that you take your hat off in church in order to avoid offending people. But that is not the same as saying that the convention creates the moral rule, except in the misleading and unimportant sense in which we might say 'theirs was a morality of slavery'. The unimportance (and danger) of the use of the word 'morality' in that phrase becomes crystal clear when we use phrases such as 'the morality of the Nazi party was an *immoral* morality'. The relevant distinction here was drawn neatly by Bentham and Austin, who talked of the distinction between 'positive' and 'critical' morality, positive morality being those social conventions created by man, and critical morality being the standards *by which those social conventions could be judged.*

This distinction is importantly present in Dworkin's writings. In *Taking Rights Seriously,* he criticises the conventional rule of recognition theory, in his second attack on the model of rules.[21] The argument in its basic form merely repeats the argument above in relation to the judicial duty to decide according to the law.

Dworkin first argues that that duty cannot be exhaustively defined by the rule of recognition because judges have duties to decide according to law when the rule of recognition has run out in hard cases. Secondly, the judicial duty cannot even be partly defined by the rule of recognition because that would be to confuse positive with critical morality. He uses the example of the vegetarian who declares, in a way which is familiar and intelligible in moral conversation, that we all have a duty not to eat meat, meaning not that there is such a convention but that there are independent reasons why we should be vegetarian.

To the critic who says that Dworkin's argument is correct about the nature of moral argument but not about the arguments needed to establish the *legal,* judicial duty, he simply replies that legal positivism cannot be invoked in its own support.[22] Further reasons to show why the duties incumbent on a judge are not moral duties are required. The assertion that judicial duties are fully defined by convention is insufficient.

It follows that the rule of recognition mistakes part of the domain of the law for the whole because it misses out the identification of the judicial duty in hard cases.[23] Further, it confuses a *consensus* of official (and other) views about what constitutes law with the existence of certain conventions for identifying law. In other words, that the officials of a community recognise criteria for the identification of law should be understood as meaning that they accept independent and critical reasons for recognition and that coincidence in thought shows just that – consensus – rather than uncritical acceptance of a convention.

The objectivity of morality for Dworkin, then, does not depend on an external world of moral reality or on the existence of conventions. It is not, on the other hand, 'totally subjective' because its coherence must be testable in the public domain. It must, too, as we shall see, be subject to the stringent requirements of rationality.

Lord Devlin and the enforcement of morality

The idea of the public accountability of the moral assertions one makes is made very clear in Dworkin's attack on Lord Devlin's thesis that the state has a right to protect its moral 'existence', if necessary by the use of the criminal law.

Lord Devlin propounded this thesis in his famous lecture delivered in 1958.[24] He argued with the case in mind of the legalisation of consenting homosexual acts between adult males proposed by the Wolfenden Committee of the United Kingdom, which had produced a report in the previous year.[25] Devlin's position was that we have to understand that a society like the United Kingdom is made up of various ties and traditions such as, for example, a common morality based upon the Christian religion. Appealing to our conviction that the state has the right to protect itself by using the criminal law to punish treasonable acts, Devlin argued that the state could, in principle,[26] outlaw acts that threatened to undermine the state's moral existence (although he did not himself regard the prohibition of private homosexuality as falling within this ambit).

Well-known difficulties attach to the several theses buried here. One is that many object to the idea that the state somehow has a right to protect itself from moral change. Unlike most critics, however, Dworkin is prepared to see some merit in this particular thesis, that of its focusing our attention on the connection between democratic theory and the concept of a public morality. Dworkin's criticisms instead centre upon the assumptions that Devlin appears to make about what public morality is.

In short, Dworkin's view is that 'the public morality' is vastly more complex than a description of what the public 'feels' at a particular time, and allows for the holding of sincerely-held views of a different and contrary nature. Since this is what 'public morality' means, and not what the man in the 'Clapham omnibus' feels a real sense of 'intolerance, indignation and disgust' about, the idea of the state enforcing 'public morality' is not so simple as to allow the crude expression of public feeling.[27]

Dworkin comes to this conclusion by way of analysis of the idea of a 'moral position'. It is initially an argument about the way we in fact speak in moral discourse, but it is intended, too, to make moral sense. In *Law's Empire*, Dworkin's dismissal of the 'semantic sting' encourages us to look elsewhere than language for the deeper justification.

The answer is not immediately clear from this earlier article, but, read in the light of his later arguments in *Law's Empire* about the idea of community, things become much clearer. The idea of a consensus in which public morality allows for a variation of moral views is one that lies squarely on the idea of a democratic community in which each individual enjoys an equality of respect. That idea itself is the engine for Dworkin's criticism and it is an idea that is not easily to be extricated from Devlin's position that it is society or community that is important. Implicit at least in the Clapham man's vision is an egalitarian premise that the ordinary man's view, about the kind of moral environment in which he wishes to live, be given voice.

Dworkin notes that we can recognise that others have taken a 'moral position' on some matter without ourselves agreeing with that position. Although not mentioned by him in this chapter, it is an idea analogically connected to the distinction he so often uses between concept and conception. Our shared concept of morality allows for different positions to be held by people on what is morally right and wrong and, at the same time, allows for a level of criticism in which people can be said not genuinely to be holding a moral position at all. In other words, we may criticise people not only for being wrong about what is right and wrong, but for being wrong in thinking that the position they hold is a moral one at all.

It is in fact a relatively simple point applicable to all concepts. If we have no grasp of an idea at all, or at the most only a very poor one, we really cannot be said to have any worked out conception. To discuss with such a person some development of the idea would be pointless unless it were to lead that person to understand what the idea was about. To be crude for the sake of clarity, we cannot discuss, for example, the finer points of chess with a person who thinks that chess is draughts.

Dworkin says that there are several criteria that mark out what it is to have a moral position on some matter. We must, for example, produce reasons for our views.[28] These need not be, of course, in the form of a highly abstract and worked out moral theory, but they must be something we are able to give as an explanation of our views. And it goes further than that: to be said to hold a genuinely moral position on something means that some sorts of reasons do not count. He gives, as examples, four instances of reasons that we do not accept, those of prejudiced reasons, mere emotional reaction, reasons based on mistakes of fact and parroting. In other words, if we accept that it is part of the idea of having a genuinely moral position on something that it is to be based on giving reasons, it follows that those reasons must pass through a sieve of rationality.

We can examine more closely the place of reason in morality. Are *prejudiced* views permitted as genuinely moral views? Dworkin is surely right in saying that they are not. The admission of prejudice by someone disqualifies him in our eyes from speaking sensibly on the matter. The man who says, 'I just hate queers' is not someone who we feel is expressing a genuinely moral position.

What I have just said is very bothersome to some people. We must venture once more into the problems people have with objectivity. In the end, it all comes back to the demonstrability thesis and the hold of 'plain facts'. Some will say: 'who is to say what counts as prejudice?' Again, I have to say, in defence of Dworkin, the problem of saying definitely what is prejudiced is not at issue. I can only say: look into your own way of understanding things. Do you really think that there is no such thing as prejudice? If you do, dare I say that you use it as a way of attacking a point of view? Prejudiced points of view are wrong just because they are prejudiced.

Of course, it does not follow that I can make another person's point of view 'prejudiced' just because I say it is. Whether a person holds a genuinely prejudiced point of view is a matter of debate, and often difficult debate at that. But, without entering into any such debate, you must agree, I suggest, that we share a common criterion of criticism which is that a prejudiced position is not one to be taken with moral seriousness.

A more insidious version of the simpleminded 'who is to say what is prejudiced?' is the 'everyone is prejudiced' view which could be no more than rampant scepticism of the internal global sort. If you think that there are prejudiced and unprejudiced views then you do not think that all views are prejudiced. It is as simple as that. If you do think that all views are prejudiced, you should examine what you mean by 'prejudice' and whether you can distinguish it from 'having a view'. After all, Dworkin's point is not about any particular point of view, but about the idea of being in the position of having a view. If that position is prejudiced then we cannot take seriously any view from that position.

Let us now consider the place of the following reason: 'that action just makes me sick'. Is it sufficient to offer a mere emotional reaction to something to establish one's moral position? We often criticise some forms of moral argument as being 'emotive', meaning, I think, that the appeal they make bypasses reason. If it is a legitimate way of criticising a person's moral stance, then it supports the view that reasons, rather than emotions, are an essential ingredient of having a moral position.

But that way of putting it can be misleading, for having a particular emotion may be a way of stating at least part of a reason, as when we say we feel angry about something. And having emotional reactions to some sorts of thing – say, seeing a cat being tortured – is, we feel, right and proper. Nevertheless, a statement of 'feeling' alone is not enough because we always want to know the reason for the feeling or the anger or whatever. In other words, it is the reason that comes first.

If someone claimed that he morally disapproved of blacks and, in response to the question why, said, 'They just make me angry, that's all', we do not think that this is sufficient. In fact, the absence of a proffered reason, or any reason at all that we can think makes sense of the remark, would in all probability make us conclude that this person had a phobia, or an obsession.

What about mistakes of fact? What if a person says that he morally disapproves of the Bush administration because it started the Vietnam war? What is left of his moral view when it is common knowledge that it is based on a false proposition of fact? Rationality requires that some minimum standard of evidence be complied with in any view put forward based on a proposition of fact. What sort of view would it be if it did not need to pass through that sieve of rationality? The Emperor Justinian was said to have disapproved of homosexuality because it caused earthquakes (presumably, an act springing from the wrath of the gods). There is not a shred of evidence to support any connection between the existence of homosexuality and earthquakes. That is why we do not take his remark seriously. We do not take it as the expression of a moral view which we can argue about, in the same way as we might wish to take issue with the protagonist who asserts that homosexuality enhances art or poetry, or conversely, that homosexuality reneges on 'manliness'. These offer plausible conceptions, perhaps wrong, or right, about the moral value of homosexuality. But the Justinian view does not achieve this level: it is not in the forum, as it were.

Parroting is another disqualifier. Imagine someone says that he disapproves of abortion and, when asked for a reason, replies 'because my mother disapproves'. We expect a person's views to be his or her own, in the sense that the person gives them independent endorsement of their truth, and do not merely parrot the views of others. We can, of course, learn from others. It may be, too, that there are religious reasons of the authoritative, and perhaps 'parroting', sort – 'it is in the Bible' – that form a particular and separate category. But in the usual sort of case, the mere repetition of what someone says as a reason for taking a moral position on a matter is not a qualifying reason.

These are four sorts of reasons that Dworkin says disqualify a person's expressed attitudes from counting as a moral position. But there are others we can imagine once we get the idea. We cannot have moral views about inanimate objects, say, earthquakes ('earthquakes are irresponsible, or frivolous'), for example, and our moral conclusions must follow logically from the premises we claim to hold.

And, even if we are not aware of the general premises we hold, rationality requires that all the moral views we have logically cohere with some general position, however sincerely we hold our views.

Rationality does not permit us to hold contradictory views. In general, to repeat, moral positions, like any other position, are hostage to rational enquiry.[29]

We can now return to Lord Devlin, who advocated a kind of 'jurybox' definition of the morality which he considered it prima facie proper for the criminal law to enforce. The man on the Clapham omnibus was to check his (genuine) feelings of 'intolerance, indignation and disgust'. That was all. It did not appear to matter that these feelings were not in accordance with reason.

Dworkin's most important point here is that the idea of a community consensus on morality runs much deeper than a surface description of what people in fact, at a certain time and in a certain mood, think or feel. The idea of consensus, generally, is one that speaks to the level of reason or conviction and crosses surface differences. To those who are suspicious of any attempt to oppose 'the common man's view' with 'reason', which is, implicitly, a crude appeal to democratic values, it will come as a surprise to learn that Dworkin is not opposed to the idea that the community's morality *should* count. 'What is shocking and wrong' about Lord Devlin's thesis, says Dworkin, 'is not his idea that the community's morality counts, but his idea of what counts as the community's morality.'[30]

A note on cultural relativity

One of the most common arguments used to establish that morality is 'subjective' only is the argument from cultural relativity. Other cultures have different values so, crudely, it follows that there is no one 'essential' morality and all values are 'relative'. Advocates of this kind of thinking are fond of saying such things as that slavery in the southern states of the United States in the nineteenth century was 'morally permissible' *for them*, or cannibalism in certain primitive tribes was 'moral' for them, and so on.

This argument can be met in different ways implicit in Dworkin's general methodology. We are already equipped with Dworkin's appproach to moral subjectivity. And we may consider a further refinement. Someone who holds the sceptical view that values are 'subjective' because of cultural relativity is only an internal sceptic because he holds the insider view that values must be transcultural.[31] We can also appeal to the distinction we draw between positive and critical morality. To repeat, we do not have difficulty in saying that the morality of slavery was an 'immoral morality'.

One kind of argument for cultural relativity can be dismissed here, although it is very common indeed. This is the 'who are we to judge?"

sort and it may be useful to label it the 'cultural arrogance' argument. It says that cultural differences are just so great that it is simply arrogant to suppose that anyone can transplant the values of one culture to another. This kind of argument relies on the strength of our dislike of, for example, Victorian missionaries being shocked by African tribal morality and the insensitivity with which judgments were made and carried out, often with appalling consequences.

But a dislike of arrogance should not blind us into supposing that transcultural judgments cannot, in the nature of things, be made. Try it. Do you morally disapprove of slavery? Does it make a difference that it occurs, or occurred, in another culture? I do not mean to ask whether slavery was 'understandable' in such cultures, because the answer to that question may be yes and the judgment that it is morally wrong be no. If you morally disapprove of slavery, I suggest that you do in fact universalise about it. It does not mean arrogance, or even that you should do something about it, or that you should have done something about it if you were 'in' that culture (if such a judgment is possible). It means: do you really believe that these sorts of transcultural judgments are impossible?

Dworkin does not believe in cultural relativity, and his arguments, in addition to the ones mentioned above, are fairly simple. He takes to task a theory of justice, based on a standpoint of cultural relativity, proposed by Walzer.[32] Walzer's view is that there are conventions which are appropriate to each 'sphere' of justice and that the recognition of the coexistence of these conventions is a necessary part of understanding what justice in general is about. As long as what is appropriate to each 'sphere' does not 'spill over' into another sphere, so that the standards of fairness in one do not (let us say) pollute the standards of fairness of another, social justice is maintained.

In support of this view, he examines certain conventions of economic distribution in a large variety of different cultures, from the Trobriand islanders to the Aztec through contemporary United States west coast society. It is a cosy view, because it inhibits conflict through the use of the idea of what is 'appropriate' to a particular sphere.

The criticism Dworkin makes is simple and obvious. Justice is not a matter of convention, or anecdote about other societies. It is a critical idea and transcends matters of following shared understandings. 'If justice is only a matter of following shared understandings, then how can the parties be debating about justice when there is no shared understanding?'[33]

We should be able to understand the criticism in the light now of Dworkin's use of the ideas of concept and conception, but we should see, too, that it is a modern use being made of the distinction between positive and critical morality. If our standards of justice are critical (who could *conceivably* deny that?) then there can only be a limited use, in the construction of a theory of justice, in describing positive justice. And Walzer clearly believes his theory to be critical.[34]

A summing up

It is clear that Dworkin is not a total subjectivist, inserting his 'own values' into other people's lives. That is a crude but very popular view about anyone who expresses views forcefully. It is clear, too, that he is far from claiming there is 'a right answer' to all moral questions buried somewhere if only we could find it.

Is the middle road, built, as I have suggested, on reason and commitment, really possible? You must ask yourself two questions in order to consider the feasibility – and desirability – of this middle position. First, should moral judgments be subject to (although perhaps not necessarily the product of) any form of rational sifting or are they essentially *arbitrary* assertions? Secondly, when you yourself make a genuine – heartfelt – moral judgment do you really believe that what you assert is not true?

We are now armed with Dworkin's views on the interpretive nature of social practices and his views on the objectivity of certain kinds of controversial propositions. We are thus in a position to turn to his treatment of the controversial areas of the social practice of law, namely, the hard cases.

Notes

1. Kelsen's basic norm can be interpreted as giving logical coherence to a person's full set of legal reasons for acting from either that person's 'legal' point of view, or the point of view of the professional, non-committed 'legal scientist'. See Raz, *The Authority of Law* (1979) Oxford: Clarendon Press, Chapter 7 for an excellent discussion.
2. See later in this chapter.
3. See Soper, *Philosophy and Public Affairs* Vol.18 No.3 (Summer 1989) 209–37. Soper thinks that a line can be drawn between the insider as far as the concept of law goes and the insider as far as adjudication goes. He appears to think that Dworkin is right on the first, but that it does not follow, as he says Dworkin assumes, that one must then be an insider on the second. I am unsure simply on the ground that it does not seem sensible to suppose that we can clearly separate 'the concept of law' from the idea of adjudication. See Dworkin's remark in his Introduction to his *The Philosophy of Law* (1977) Oxford paperback (ed. Dworkin) that some theory of adjudication will be a 'consequence' of the positivist theory of law (p. 7).
     See also: Cotterrell, *The Politics of Jurisprudence: A Critical Introduction to Legal Philosophy* (1989) Butterworth 177–81 (and see his review of *Law's Empire* in (1987) *A.B.A. Research Journal* 509 at pp. 519–23).
4. Although Dworkin does not, of course, share with Kelsen any idea of

a morally neutral but 'committed' point of view. See Raz, 'Kelsen's Theory of the Basic Norm', Chapter 7, *The Authority of Law* (1979) Oxford.

5. See, for example, Unger's *Knowledge and Politics* (1975).

6. See Chapter 4, 'Evil legal systems'.

7. See, for example, Pashukanis's theory of the exchange of commodities, in which contract was seen to be at the basis of all law. He thought the law existed 'for the sole purpose of being utterly spent'. *Law and Marxism* (1978) p. 133.

8. It is an argument deriving from Hume that when a person expresses a moral opinion there is nothing beyond his opinion that justifies it. Hume did not say that a person could not have those opinions, however. Dworkin says, rightly, that they still have to argue for them, since scepticism is not a reason for or against given opinions. See further, on objectivity in moral reasoning, Williams *Ethics and the Limits of Philosophy* (1985) Harvard; Honderich (ed.) *Morality and Objectivity* (1985) London.

9. *Law's Empire*, p. 81, his emphasis.

10. The external sceptic must necessarily be 'global' because his belief in the lack of a metaphysical foundation for argument about value crosses all discourses about value.

11. *Law's Empire*, pp. 85–6.

12. See Dworkin's extensive application of this point to the Critical Legal Studies movement in *Law's Empire* pp. 271–5.

13. William Twining has suggested here the useful distinction between the 'cogency' of a lawyer's argument and its 'persuasive' value. The lawyer constructs cogent arguments as a preliminary to persuasion. The distinction preserves our sense that one of a lawyer's main tasks is to persuade, while affirming that while cogency is a strong element of persuasion, it is by no means a *necessary* element.

14. I ignore for present purposes the Wills Act 1963, which allows for more qualifications and allowances in the form a will takes. It does not affect the line of argument here.

15. See *Ronald Dworkin and Contemporary Jurisprudence* (1984) Duckworth, where Dworkin replies to the criticism by MacCormick that there is no 'Archimedian point' from which it can be decided who is right: 'MacCormick has no hesitancy in ascribing objective truth to his *skeptical* convictions. He says, at the end of his essay, that there is no right answer to some of the questions he raises, but he exempts *that* question. Reasonable people disagree about whether moral judgments can be 'really' true. If MacCormick does not allow truth when reasonable people can disagree, and there is no canonical proof, why does he think there is a right answer to the question of moral `objectivity'?" (p. 280). Hart, in his Introduction to *Essays in Jurisprudence and Philosophy* retires into a form of scepticism: 'For though the search for and use of principles underlying the law defers the moment, it cannot eliminate the need for judicial *law-making* since in any hard case different principles supporting competing analogies may present themselves and the judge will have to choose between them, relying like a conscientious legislator on his sense of what is best.' (p. 7) The emphasis is added here to show that the argument appears to be that if reasonable lawyers can disagree about what the right answer in law is, *therefore* there is no 'right' answer and

therefore the judge *must* be making law. This approach begs all the important questions about 'objectivity' in the law.

16. On the other hand, x = 6 could well be. My present point is about the adoption of nomenclature.

17. See the next section on the internal and external points of view.

18. There is an argument that goes as follows. Sometimes *best* decisions cannot be made because they involve the weighing up of incommensurable values. See, for example, Finnis, in 'On Reason and Authority in *Law's Empire*', 6 *Law and Philosophy* (1987) 357,372: '... a claim to have found the right answer ... is senseless, in much the same way as it is senseless to claim to have identified the English novel which meets the two criteria `shortest and most romantic' (or `funniest and best'), or `most English and most profound'." Dworkin's attitude (as has been his attitude to the entire one right answer thesis debate) is defensive: what, he asks, are the arguments for saying that legal judgments of the 'all things considered' sort that are made all the time entail incommensurable values? I am grateful to Brian Dix for pointing out to me the extent of the incommensurability debate. See also Raz and Griffin, 'Mixing Values' *Proceedings of the Aristotelian Society* Supp. Vol. 65 (1991) 83 and 101; Raz, *The Morality of Freedom* (1986) Oxford, pp. 321–66; Regan, 'Authority and Value: Reflections on Raz's *Morality of Freedom*' 62 *Southern California Law Review* (1989) 1,056–75; Raz, 'Facing Up: A Reply' 62 (1989) *Southern California Law Review* 1,218–22; Williams, 'Conflicts of Values' in Williams *Moral Luck* (1981) pp. 71–82; Nagel, 'The Fragmentation of Value' in *Mortal Questions* (1979) pp. 128–41; and Griffin, 'Are There Incommensurable Values?" 7 *Philosophy and Public Affairs* (1977) 39.

19. It is an example that Dworkin used on several occasions during the seminars that he and Gareth Evans gave in Oxford during 1973–4 on objectivity in law and morality.

20. Notice how powerful this theory is in explaining our moral education from when we are very young.

21. The example is a little odd because it does not give us the clearest idea of what construction would be like in the natural sciences. It is odd to suppose that the zoologist *has* to construct an animal of some sort from the only bones he has (a two skulls for feet, a femur head, some connecting thigh bones, for example). The example is too close to the natural model: show what you have in the light of an assumption that there was something out there once against which the different bones *would* make sense. The general point is nevertheless clear.

22. *Taking Rights Seriously*, Chapter 3, 'The Model of Rules II'.

23. See *Taking Rights Seriously*, p. 64.

24. See 'Social Rules and Legal Theory' (1972) 81 *Yale Law Journal* 855–90, which is reprinted in *Taking Rights Seriously* at pp. 46–80. '... positivism, with its doctrine of a fundamental and commonly-recognized test for law, mistakes part of the domain of that concept for the whole." *Taking Rights Seriously*, 47. Also see Chapter 7, 'Can Principles be Identified by the Rule of Recognition?"

25. 'The Enforcement of Morals'. This is to be found in *The Enforcement of Morals* (1965) Oxford, a collection of essays by Lord Devlin dealing

generally with the same theme, although there are certain refinements, none of which affects the attack made by Dworkin.

26. *Report of the Committee on Homosexual Offences and Prostitution,* Cmnd. no. 247 (1957).

27. In his collection of essays, he is careful to point out the important part considerations protecting personal freedom would play in the decision whether to use the criminal law.

28. In later writings, Lord Devlin abandoned the measure of 'the man in the Clapham omnibus' in favour of the jury. The difference is a pragmatic one. The first is theoretical, the second actual, but both point to the same test of conventional morality. See the Preface to Devlin's *The Enforcement of Morals* (1965) Oxford. At p. viii of the Preface, he affirms that, despite criticisms of his phrase 'intolerance, indignation and disgust', he was still unwilling to qualify it, six years later.

29. He allows the case of not having a reason because of its being some major premise that it is just taken to be axiomatic or self-evident as being a reason of a special sort. See *Taking Rights Seriously*, 252: 'The claim that a particular position is axiomatic, in other words, does supply a reason of a special sort ..."

30. Those who are suspicious about the force of rationality might consider whether the alternative is non-rationality (which must include irrationality). This would be, in Dworkin's terms, the position that an internal global sceptic would take. What justifies it?

31. *Taking Rights Seriously*, p. 255.

32. *Law's Empire*, p. 84

33. *Spheres of Justice: A Defense of Pluralism and Equality* (1982) Michael Walzer, Basic Books.

34. *A Matter of Principle*, p. 217. But see, further, my comments in Chapter 11 about the idea of justice as an interpretive concept. I do think it is necessarily the case that, if justice is interpretive of social practices, it is therefore *not* trans-cultural. But what transcultural social practices justice would be interpretive of is a very difficult question.

35. For an interpretation of cultural relativity generally sympathetic to the interpretation of Dworkin I have offered here, see Lyons *Ethics and the Rule of Law* (1984) Cambridge, Chapter 1.

7

Hard cases I

Dworkin has popularised the idea of a 'hard case' in a novel sense. In general, his use of the term refers to those issues faced by a judge or a lawyer which are contentious and potentially litigable. Specifically, a hard case is a situation in the law that gives rise to genuine argument about the truth of a proposition of law that cannot be resolved by recourse to a set of plain facts *determinative* of the issue.

The core and the penumbra

Let us take Hart's famous example of the statutory provision prohibiting vehicles from the park, where there are no statutory definitions and no judicial decisions that guide interpretation.[1] Does it include roller-skates? His answer is that the rule about vehicles is just inherently unspecific about whether roller-skates are included and that a judge could settle matters by declaring a result one way or another, thus making the rule in relation to the roller-skates a 'plain fact' for the future. Every rule, he says, has a 'penumbra' where its meaning is uncertain. Nevertheless, we would not have an idea of what the penumbra was unless we first had a firm grasp of the idea of the core.

It is useful, first of all, to consider whether there can be 'plain facts' of linguistic practice. There clearly are, and I do not think that asserting this fact entails a view that there are 'acontextual' meanings. But, for example, we can dispense with a sceptical response to my assertion, by saying that, in ordinary circumstances, the word 'vehicle' includes a 20-ton lorry. That is so, by virtue of our linguistic practices, meaning simply that an empirical observation of the way in which 'vehicle' is used shows that it is consistently applied to 20-ton lorries. It is not an odd idea. Dictionaries record current usage in precisely this way, and dictionary definitions are right or wrong measured against, speaking widely, empirically observable practice.

This is not to say that there are 'inherent' meanings of words or sentences. That would be an absurd view to take because it is possible to create definitions by stipulation. Indeed, a military code could make use of the most ordinary words and phrases in order to disguise meanings apparent to those privy to the stipulated meanings. Thus the innocuous phrase 'the cat is on the mat' could mean 'the missile is on its way', according to the code book.

Note the use here being made of ordinary linguistic practices to disguise the meanings. Success of the code will depend on there being ordinary linguistic meanings and how well such meanings disguise what is meant as between the users of the code. Thus, 'the cat is on the mat' might be thought too *obvious*, for example, and 'operation off' better, because more misleading to the enemy.

Another argument for saying that there are plain fact meanings is that, more or less, you understand what I am writing. In the last sentence, 'writing', 'am', 'I' and 'what' all have meanings which you understand only by having understood what those marks on paper mean in ordinary circumstances. Understanding a language means, at the very least, being able to conform to the standard linguistic practices. More simply, if you did not understand Sanskrit, and I were writing Sanskrit, you would not understand what I was saying.

Legal and linguistic practices are similar and different. They overlap. The most common form of judicial practice consists of the identification of certain acts or decisions as authoritative, and general legal practice, whether that of the lawyer, or police or administrator, follows. To take the threatening letter example once more, it is by virtue of the plain facts of legal practice that the Offences Against the Person Act 1861 is authoritative. It is not that the facts in that imaginary case recur with sufficient frequency for us to be able to say that recognition of those facts as being contrary to law constitutes a practice. Rather, it is that the facts of identifying certain legislative acts as authoritative recur.

The plain facts theory is the appealing theory that law is identifiable with the clear empirically identifiable facts of legal practice. The law is expressed in language and must rely on plain – clear – meanings. It must, therefore, rely on clear dictionary meanings in the large part. It follows that these penumbral meanings do not come within the law. Why? It is that since, by hypothesis, they are not defined either in statute or in a subsequent judgment, they are not *plainly* vehicles within the dictionary definition. And so, according to the plain fact account, they are not vehicles for the purposes of the statute. In other words, if the law is not clearly identifiable it is clearly *not* law. This is so, if we take the central characterising feature of positivism to be its insistence upon clarity.

To many people, this will seem a startling claim and one they would not want to be a consequence of positivism. Again, is Dworkin's description of legal positivism fair? It is an attempt to make the best sense of Hart's rule of recognition. That test of legal validity was introduced to reduce *uncertainty* as to what the legal rules were.[2] In Chapter 5 we noted the definition of positivism to be, in Hart's own words, the contention that it is not necessary that laws reproduce or satisfy certain demands of morality. I then said that Dworkin, by attributing the plain facts theory to Hart, claims that Hart achieves the distinction by using a distinction between statements of empirical fact – the source of law – and statements of morality.

If law is to be identified by means of empirical fact, then, *a fortiori*, law cannot include value statements and *a fortiori*, it cannot include normative statements of the moral sort. Do statements of the law necessarily include moral statements? No, because the identification of the law requires only reference to the facts of official acceptance of the rules of recognition. This conclusion is one many people are ill-disposed to accept. Neil MacCormick, for example, says that it is simply not true. Law, he says, is identifiable by criteria of recognition and these may use predicates like 'honest' or 'reasonable' or 'fair' and so forth. Further, rules of adjudication may require or permit judges to 'take account of' moral values in their interpretations. None of this, says MacCormick, is excluded from Hart's definition.

But MacCormick steers clear of a precise alignment of what can be clearly defined by a 'pedigree' test with values, in this case Dworkin's principles. For example, he says, attacking Dworkin's idea (see later in this chapter) that the rule of recognition cannot account for legal *principles*:

> There is a relationship between the 'rule of recognition' and principles of law, but it is an indirect one. The rules which are rules *of law* are so in virtue of their pedigree; the principles which are principles *of law* are so because of their function in relation to those rules, that is, the function which those who use them as rationalizations of the rules thus ascribe to them.[3]

But there will always be this disjunction between empirically identifiable *rules* and other 'principles' in describing the fundamentals of legal reasoning if we stick to Hume's principle, and MacCormick clearly does not abandon that.[4]

On penumbral issues, there is no uniform practice among the officials. In Hart's terms, there is no 'concordant' practice, no concordant acceptance of rules of recognition. Is there law there nevertheless? At first sight, on Hart's own terms, there is not. What if there was a split in official practice? That could mean two things. There might simply be *no* practice here, because judges have such widely different views, say, on the question of the extent to which, in the United Kingdom, arguments drawn from the European Convention of Human Rights are relevant in identifying rules of law of the United

Kingdom. But there may be differing *practices* where, say, judges and other officials are equally divided on the question of whether the United Kingdom Parliament could bind itself in law. According to the view of positivism here discussed, what is the law? Either it is both the law that Parliament can bind itself and the law that it cannot, or it is not law at all. On a weakened view of official practice, ignoring Hart's reference to the 'concordance' of the practice, we obtain a virtually nonsensical result for law. In a nutshell, neither rule follows from the rule of recognition.

Under the semantic theory, it amounts to saying that there are two dictionary-type definitions for the one word which is, of course, perfectly possible. Under the deeper plain fact theory, which values clarity, it just does not make sense. Clarity cannot allow contradictory statements of what the law is. The preferred interpretation is then that where there is no concordant practice there is no law on the matter. This is not such a bad result. Clarity is achieved along with, at a non-theoretical level, the separation of law from morality. At the theoretical level, since clarity was thought to have instrumental moral worth, the choice of theory is motivated by a moral concern.

The consequences for adjudication

What implications does the plain fact view of law have for judicial reasoning? The well-known conclusion is that when judges are faced with a case in which there is no empirically identifiable law, no law determines the issue. It follows that, in exercise of his clear legal duty to come to a decision one way or the other, the judge must make his decision on grounds other than legal ones. The phrase so often used in this context is that 'the judge must exercise his discretion' in order to come to a decision.

In Dworkin's view, this is a conclusion that positivists should want. Positivists place a high value on clarity and certainty. In the untidy areas of legal dispute, where it is of the nature of the case that the law is unclear, the positivist should want to say that this is where the law ends. But the appeal of this clarity must be explored. What is the importance of the idea that the law be publicly identifiable?

Clarity in the law occurs in several different ways. Laws may be clear in the sense that a lawyer can understand them when the ordinary layman cannot. The layman, and many lawyers, too, will make no sense of the Settled Land Act 1925 after a gentle afternoon's read. A lawyer, used to the Settled Land Act, which means that he has understood its various purposes and understands how it is adminis-tered in fact, will, if he cannot explain it to his lay client, be able to arrange the client's affairs in the appropriate way.

One way to test the importance of objectivity and clarity is to view the idea from different standpoints. What advantage has clarity to the ordinary man trying to arrange his affairs, for example? Property law is the most obvious area where the ordinary man wants clarity. If the laws are clear he can manipulate them. Clarity means that he knows what will be required of him so that he can arrange his affairs accordingly. Of course, clarity is not the only virtue because the ordinary man has interests, too, in security and stability. In order for him to achieve these conditions, the law needs to be fairly stable as well. If the rules of property change from month to month, then the clarity of the rules will be of little use. On the other hand, obscure rules or deliberately vague rules that, say, permit ownership of property without defining either 'ownership' or 'property' according to 'what is reasonable' in the circumstances, cannot found a base for stability in ownership in property.

But clarity will not be a virtue where closer attention to the sensitivity of circumstances is warranted. Not every area of human life can be governed by the use of clear rules which announce in advance of a situation how matters should be governed. Laws governing the granting of planning consents, for example, cannot possibly achieve this. Constitutional law, and its offshoot, administrative law, concern matters which, from the ordinary man's point of view, are, for most cases, better understood in terms of general principle than clear rules laying out in precise detail what is required or permitted. An appeal to general principle means an appeal to what is more generally permitted or required and transcends the finality of a clear and precise rule which governs the case.[5]

Can we tighten up the different kinds of clarity involved, though? I have earlier declared an interest in the demystification of facts. Accordingly, I assert that there *are* clear rules, meaning that there are uncontroversial propositions of law. Put this way, the issue of unclarity is really the issue of controversy, which simply means that it will be controversial what proposition of law justifies a court's decision.

At least three kinds of controversy can be discerned. The first need not bother us for long at present, although it is important, indeed crucial, for understanding Dworkin's theory. It is that it is possible to raise doubts about even the most fundamentally entrenched facts in the law. A quick route to this conclusion is to consider whether it is likely that we come to face the world without already having some conceptual apparatus, conceptual spectacles, as it were, through which we structure our thoughts.

Why, then, should it not be possible to raise genuine questions about those matters that we ordinarily regard as clear and objectively identifiable rules of law? The idea seems plausible through Dworkin's idea of paradigms in the law and it may profitably be borne in mind at this stage that doubts are at times cast upon settled doctrines of the common law.

The two kinds of controversy apart from this one are immediately more important because they occur in the context of settled, clear rules. The first is that where there is some clear indication that recourse must be made to a value judgment, say, by the explicit use of statutory words such as 'reasonable', or 'fair'. These words import the requirement of a value judgment and not a relatively simple 'reading off' of what the law requires. In these sorts of case, the indication is that it is only in the particular circumstances envisaged by the statute that recourse may be had to this kind of judgment. Thus a 'fair rent' under the Rent Act 1968 is only to be determined after the tenant has fulfilled the precise conditions, both substantive and procedural, outlined in that Act.

Likewise for the common law. The test of foreseeability in tort is housed within a concatenation of differing rules. Thus the definition of 'neighbour' enters at the point of determining liability, and is hedged in by a number of precise rules arising from previous cases, and also at the point of deciding where the cut-off point is for assessing damages. This provision for the making of value judgments in the law is very common. On the debit side, it is unclear in the sense that the layman or lawyer cannot 'read off' the law in any given instance. But the flexibility and potential of the law to be able to deal with the justice of each case is greatly enhanced. And it is not as if the ordinary man, concerned with understanding what is required of him, cannot make any sense in advance of these unclear laws. It is at least clear that these parts, what is 'reasonable' or 'fair' and so on, will be judged according to what is 'reasonable', and 'fair' and so on.

The second type of unclarity to be discussed here is a less obvious type because the situations in which value judgments are to be made are not spelled out. This is where there is a dispute over what the law is where there *is* a settled meaning. Almost any area of law provides examples. The obvious way to produce these is to appeal to the inherent unclarity in the penumbra of an explicit rule, as in the skateboard example, but this approach obscures the fact that the controversies far transcend problems of language. The language is used, after all, to express the law and the arguments employed in courts towards decisions are not merely semantic squabbles.

Dworkin's example of *Riggs* v. *Palmer* is a good one.[6] There the words of the statute were plain. Beneficiaries were to succeed to the property of the testator if the requirements of a valid will were established. The circumstances were that the beneficiary had murdered the testator. The easy way with the case is to say that if the will was valid (it was) the murderer-beneficiary should succeed. But we live in the real world. There must be, at least in the kind of legal system we inhabit, a real doubt about whether in law the beneficiary should succeed.

The unclarity exhibited in this second kind of case is not different in kind from the first. Both are rather on the same scale of clarity, the second type creating much more uncertainty because of the lack of a clear pointer as to when an (overt) value judgment should be made. But it must be that value judgments will be required in each case. In the case of reasonableness in the law of tort, for example, the judge must decide whether or not the plaintiff was a person who could 'reasonably' have been foreseen by the defendant, in the particular circumstances. In *Riggs* v. *Palmer*, the court had to make a decision about whether or not a murderer may benefit under his victim's will. The court did so by making an assessment of weight of the principle that no person is permitted to profit from his own wrong.

There clearly are areas of the law where the law cannot simply be read off. The judge, or lawyer, or citizen, must make some sort of judgment, one which I have called a 'value' judgment. 'Value' here does not necessarily refer to moral value, as we saw with the examples of judgments of value being made in non-moral activities such as chess or even immoral activities such as torture. The important point is that the judgments which need to be made – to provide the answer in the case – are ones that cannot be determined in the clear and objective 'plain fact' way. The required judgment is, instead, the result of a balance between arguments that can point in different directions.

What are the consequences for adjudication on this account? The positivist has two possibilities: he can either deny that there is any law in these unclear cases, or he can say that there is law there but it requires a different method for its identification. These two possibilities may be considered in turn.

Judicial legislation

It may be objected that I have painted the alternatives for the positivist too starkly. I have forced him to concede that the judge either legislates or he does not. Let us focus in on this claim. The point about these difficult sorts of cases is that it really is unclear what the law is or should be. If the plain fact view of law is the correct one, then it follows that there is no law at all where there are no plain facts of the matter which tell us what the law is. Therefore, a judge who comes to a decision in one of these penumbral-type cases is not applying law in the predetermined plain fact sense. The judge is not applying law, because the only law that exists is that of the plain fact sort.

It is important to see the force of this argument. It is what *follows* from positivism. That is not to say that what follows describes or explains what judges do. It is, rather, the reverse that we need examine.

Does what follows from positivism explain what judges do in hard cases? If it is unsuccessful in doing this, it is much the worse for positivism. Let us take the appeal of the plain fact analysis to be clarity in identifying law. It would appear to follow that where clarity ends, so does the law, and so, in hard cases, there is no law.

It may further be objected that it is not correct to call the judge a 'legislator' since this goes the further step of saying that positivism speaks to the role of the judges. This is an important objection. If the judge is not applying law in the penumbral cases what is he doing? Is he bound by law? The answer, it seems, is that he is not. If the statute is not clear on the question of whether a person has committed a criminal offence by taking a skateboard through the park, then there is no law on the matter. What is the law that binds the judge? There is plain fact law on the question of whether a person has committed a criminal offence if he takes a bicycle through the park. Does this have any bearing on the of question whether a skateboarder has committed an offence? The answer, for positivism, taken to be the theory that the law is plain fact law only, must be that it has none at all. The idea of 'bearing on the question' is insufficiently clear to determine whether our skateboarder has broken the law.

If this account is right, the judge must act in a similar role to the legislature, because he must make new law. There is none on the skateboarder question, so he creates new law on the matter. It is 'new' law because there was nothing in the previous law that guided, or constrained, or impelled him to his decision. This conclusion must, then, speak to the judicial role. It means that every time a judge decides one of these cases, which, of course, are the characteristic sorts of case in the appellate courts, he is as unconstrained as the legislature is in creating new law.

Let us go over this point once more. We are considering a strong version of positivism, the one that gains its central appeal from clarity and objectivity in distinguishing questions about legal validity from questions of what it is, on the whole, morally right to do. If there is no clear law directing a judge to a certain decision, there is no law that constrains the judge. He is constrained, of course, in the sense that there are other laws that carve out the hollow area where there is no law. But *within* that area, there are simply *no legal constraints*.

Let us put it yet another way. The idea of constraint by the law in the unclear cases does not make sense because there is, by hypothesis, no law there. The judge is in exactly the same position as the legislator (in relation to lawmaking), therefore. It is clear, always in the plain fact sense, that he has the legal power to come to a decision, but not the legal duty, defined by clear law, to come to one particular decision rather than another.

Those positivists who concede, or even approve, this strong version of positivism will sometimes modify the description of the judge as 'legislator' to the more restricted 'interstitial' or 'deputy legislator'.[7] The idea is that, true, the judge is not constrained by any law, but there are constraints that hedge him in so that he only has a very restricted area in which to legislate. This will take the form of 'filling the gaps'. I am sceptical of this account because if the law is a matter of plain fact only, the idea of a gap really just means: there is no law there constraining the judge.

Let us try it out. The statute prohibits vehicles in the park. It is clear that 10-ton trucks are prohibited, so the judge is constrained from deciding that a truck driver has not broken the law. It is also clear that no one who walks through the park breaks that law. A 'gap' can thus be seen between the pedestrian's non-liability and the truck-driver's liability. What constrains the judge in deciding anything between these two points if the plain fact account is the true one?

In my view, there can be no law applying. What would it be? It is only if we introduce into the plain fact account some idea of laws which 'weigh in on' the matters the judge should take into account that we can say that the judge is constrained. The sort of argument that would go along these lines would invoke the idea of legislative intention. The judge would have to decide according to what the point or purpose of the legislation was, and thus act as if on the legislator's behalf, maybe functioning as an extension to a legislative drafting office. The judge would be suited to extending the legislation in specific areas where matters which were unanticipated by the legislator came before the court for litigation. The skateboard example is one, however, where there is no plain fact access to what it is that the legislature intended. That means that what was intended has to be assessed as a matter of weight. But, to repeat, this idea of weight is inconsistent with the idea of reading off the law, which is, of course, the appeal of the plain fact account.

To make the example more realistic, it is helpful to consider the role a judge has in sentencing. Here there is usually a maximum penalty (and sometimes a minimum) which constrains a judge from imposing a sentence outside these limits. But in the gap left between the limits there is little by way of legal constraint.[8] If the decision is a 'perverse' one, the sentence may successfully be appealed against, but the judge has enormous leeway inside this sole constraint.

Thus, I suggest, it is a familiar idea that judges are *not* constrained by law in some areas of their legitimate decision-making powers. Indeed, for sentencing, for example, there is the strong rationale that individual circumstances vary so considerably it would be undesirable from the point of view of justice to have such plain fact constraints (as opposed to very general guidelines).[9]

The legislative powers of the judge under this plain fact account are extensive. In the gap left open to him he may make new law. In the vehicles case, he is not constrained by law either to decide that a skateboarder has broken the law or that the same skateboarder has acted in accordance with law. At this point in the analysis some may be tempted to abandon the plain fact account as an account of positivism. That is a difficult thing to do, in my view, since the appeal positivism has is its ability to identify laws independently of morality and one reading of a widely understood theory of positivism, that of Hart, creates that ability by linking law to a plain fact account.

A weaker version of positivism, what Dworkin calls conventionalism, is available to explain how arguments of weight may be taken into account by a judge, through analogy and abstraction. I shall discuss that later in this chapter. Nevertheless, it is ultimately dependent for its appeal on the central emphasis it accords the plain facts of convention and is thus sensitive to the criticisms of the plain fact account.

But it would be wrong at this point to abandon the plain fact account so far discussed in its strong form, perhaps conveniently called 'strong positivism'. In the legislative area of the gap the judge cannot be said to be unconstrained. It makes good sense to say that the judge ought to try, as far as possible, to understand the point of the vehicles statute, to make a decision which accords with the sorts of decision that his fellow judges might make, to have a genuine response to the arguments that counsel put before him, and so on.

Strong positivism merely says that these sorts of constraints (which, once pointed out, will be noticed to be strong and pervasive) are not legal constraints, but perhaps moral, or 'social', or 'traditional', or whatever. There is a good point to making this distinction, one that transcends an argument about semantics. To say that in the unclear areas the judges are bound by non-legal constraints is to preserve a distinction that has the merit of making it clear when a judge is making decisions on controversial matters and thus draws our attention to the great discretion a judge potentially has. It has also, I think, the added advantage of directing our attention to the pluralistic nature of the values which we may bring to bear in criticism. Overall, strong positivism's insistence on clarity is instrumental towards these forms of criticism and control.

We can dig deeper. Why should a judge be controlled in his decision-making? The obvious and most general answer is that a judge has a unique constitutional role. This role centrally concerns adjudication. The judge has therefore great power by virtue of his access to initiating acts of state coercion. He is characteristically unelected and he is not, at least, directly responsible to an electorate. Indeed, it is often thought to be a virtue of the judicial office that the judge should not be swayed in his decision-making by popular demand. Rather, it is thought, the judge should be swayed solely by his sense of justice as to the merits of the case before him. In Lord Scarman's words:

> The judge, however wise, creative, and imaginative he may be, is 'cabin'd, cribb'd, confin'd, bound in' not, as was Macbeth, to his 'saucy doubts and fears' but by the evidence and arguments of the litigants. It is this limitation, inherent in the forensic process, which sets bounds to the scope of judicial law reform.[10]

Further, the judge has a special role *vis-à-vis* the legislature. The legislature is the institution in a democracy through which the will of the electorate (to use a popular metaphor) is expressed. The judge, not being elected, must not substitute his own will as against the legislature. To do so would be to 'usurp the function of the legislature'. The judge is, instead, concerned with matters which are subsidiary to the legislature's role, such as adjudicating on the merits of disputes in individual cases.

Here we have a dilemma. We consider it a virtue of strong positivism that it clearly shows us when a judge is out on his own, as it were, independent of the constraints of law. On the other hand, in the explicit recognition that as a result the judge is making new law, like the legislature, we are forced to the conclusion that the judge's characteristic form of adjudicating is directly counter to what we consider an important feature of our democratic procedures – the doctrine of the separation of powers.

There are two further problems in the idea that the judge acts as legislator. Judges do not talk as though they were performing the same function as legislators and, further, if they are legislating, this means that their legislative decisions are being applied retrospectively. Let us consider both these ideas in turn.

Judges' talk

Certainly, judges speak judicially of their being 'bound by law'. This is apparent from courtroom language and the reports of judgments, even in the most innovative of cases. Take, for instance, Lord Atkin's introduction to his famous statement of the neighbour principle in the law of tort: 'who in law is my neighbour?' It would have sounded odd had he asked: 'who in law *ought* to be my neighbour?'[11]

Most people, I find, accept this feature of legal language. The law is full of it. The lawyers make submissions in court about what the law is. The judges come to decisions about what the law is. Always there is the background matrix of law from which both judges and lawyers draw their arguments. At times, when a judge decides that there is no argument that he can extrapolate from this background matrix, he will make a pronouncement about the appropriateness of his judicial role to decide such a matter.

Let us take the example I used earlier, in Chapter 3, of Lord Kilbrandon and Lord Simon in *DPP* v. *Lynch*.[12] In their view, the law did not permit the extension of the defence of duress to the crime of murder. Consequently, the question was one of whether it should so extend, and that was a question to be determined by the appropriate institution, namely, the legislature. To do otherwise, they thought, and said, would have been to outstep the proper function of the court.

Does it matter if the plain fact theory does not account for this feature of judicial language, and the discourse of other groups, such as lawyers, whose roles are parasitic on the judicial function? Perhaps judges are just mistaken about what they are really doing. This is not as fantastic an idea as it seems, because the immediate concerns of judges, in most cases, anyway, relate to judging rather than to providing more abstract accounts of what they do. It is perfectly possible to be skilled at something without being able to provide a coherent account of what we are doing.

Outside the field of law there are many examples, so why should not the same understanding apply to law? Take the sportsman who trains to produce a better performance. Both his trainer and a physiologist can often provide better explanations than he can himself of how he performs. The field of art produces numerous instances. Stravinsky claimed that his music expressed nothing, yet the first performance of his great *Rite of Spring* was thought to express such crudely primitive emotions, ones that it was thought ought not to be expressed, that mounted police were necessary to quell the riots it caused at the Paris Opera theatre in 1913.

However, one problem for the plain fact account is that its appeal to clarity gains another blow. To be able to make this appeal, we are now left, paradoxically, with a lack of an explanation for why it is that we cannot rely on the plain facts of judicial language. A further difficulty compounds matters. From the point of view of a plain fact account, one which purports to get to the 'plain facts of the matter', there comes a set of explanations why it is that judges speak as if the law were already 'there'. These explanations range from that of judges speaking according to the traditions of their calling to more sinister accounts of judges cynically covering up the fact that they are making law. Let us look at these ideas more closely.

What of the idea of judicial language being a traditional mode of expression? Why? One reason could be that judges, certainly in the United States, and probably in the United Kingdom, although admittedly that is not so clear, have been or are conscious of the doctrine of the separation of powers. They endeavoured, at one time, anyway, to express their judgments in terms appropriate to that doctrine: they did not make the law, they only declared what it was.

But this explanation forces us to reconsider the difficulty which we came across when we considered the role of the judge as a legislator. The obvious response is that if we do not think judges should legislate and they do not talk as if they legislate, this is a very good reason for supposing that not only do they not legislate but the doctrine of the separation of powers is alive and kicking in our legal system.

What of the explanation that judges 'cover up', or 'pretend' that the law is there, but in 'reality' know that there is no law there? This is a common response to the claim that judges 'find' the law. But it is too cynical. Are judges lying? For that is what the claim amounts to in its strongest form. Pitched at a lower level, it paints judges to be fools: assailed from all sides by legal arguments which cannot be settled in the plain fact, 'read off', sense, judges nevertheless think that there is a 'read off' sense. That just cannot be true. A day spent listening to appellate court arguments in a real live practising courtroom will convince the reader otherwise.

To paint judges as miscreants, being either liars or fools, must never be off the jurisprudential agenda. Jurisprudence should not be bound by courtroom etiquette. But it is worth briefly considering whether the argument could end there. The judges liars? No. Is our society in such a bad way that there is systematic lying going on among the judges? (A practice, too, that has been consistent for centuries.) Why would the judges lie? To keep the ordinary citizen in the dark about this undemocratic area of lawmaking? But why would judges go to such lengths, namely, the systematic alteration of their discourse, to maintain this subterfuge? It is, after all, not all that difficult to expose.

In any case, criticisms made of judges by the public that they are legislating seem equally to be of decisions where the law *can* be 'read off'. The granting of interlocutory injunctions on matters of great public importance in the United Kingdom were made routinely, at least during one period in the 1970s, because the particular conditions for the grants were met in the 'read off' sense, but nevertheless often meet the criticism that the judges are legislating in such cases. The law reports, too, are not closely read by many apart from professional lawyers. Often their contents are misunderstood, for example, by journalists. This effort to conceal is therefore largely a waste of time.

Retrospective legislation

If judges make up the law and apply it to the parties before them, it must follow that the law is being made after the events occurred and that the parties are made subject to law that was, by hypothesis, not in force when the events occurred. The law is thus applied retrospectively. Strong positivism acknowledges this consequence as an unfortunate but unavoidable consequence of the indeterminate nature of rules. When a state of affairs occurs where there is no rule in the clear sense required for the plain fact theory, the judge simply has to legislate and thus create a clear rule.

But is this fair to the party who loses out? He can say, very plausibly, that he did not break the law because there was no law at the time. That is a powerful argument. There is only one counter to him, an argument which, in my view, is specious. This is to say that, since this was an unclear, penumbral case, and it was by virtue of this fact that there was no law governing the matter, he had no reason to be surprised by a decision either way.

So what has he to complain about? Assuming that he wanted to conform to the law regarding the skateboard, he could not know with certainty whether taking the skateboard through the park was in conformity with law or not. All he can do is take the risk. What difference does it make to his position that he subsequently was fined? The risk was one of which he was or should have been aware.

The answer is that the surprise argument ignores the principle that people should not be subject to retrospective legislation. One argument for this principle – the principle of *nulla poena sine lege* – is that otherwise people would not be able to plan their lives, not knowing whether what they do will later be prohibited (or whether what they do not do will later be permitted). The strong positivist argument about surprise relies on an understanding of the *nulla poena sine lege* principle only in these terms. This interpretation amounts to saying that the state is justified in taking your liberty away, perhaps in the form of property or even your physical liberty, if imprisonment is involved, when you would not be surprised by that action.

But everything turns on the meaning of 'surprise' here. Does it mean the actual psychological state of the person, a mental state description of the outcome of a deliberation between possible actions? Suppose Jake thinks that he has a 50/50 chance of being held to be guilty of theft if he cuts branches from his neighbour's tree, to prevent them interfering with his gutter. His thoughts on this matter are neither here nor there: he is clearly innocent of theft.[13] Simply, his thoughts could not possibly have converted the legal position into a hard case.

The hard case arises because the official practice is either non-existent on the matter, or, which is more likely in a complex area of law, the official practice is not 'concordant'.[14] In these cases the citizen does not have a justifiable complaint if law is applied to him retrospectively. The strong positivists' account must therefore be that the principle of no punishment (or no liability) without law is not infringed when there is no justifiable complaint that the loser was surprised. The principle, in other words, is that reasonable expectations should not be upset, which is not a surprising interpretation for the strong positivist, since the hallmark of his theory of law is the clarity with which the law may be identified.

But there is more to the principle of *nulla poena sine lege* than the protection of reasonable expectations. A citizen has a complaint that even although he was not surprised by later retrospective legislation there was no liability at the time he did the act. The principle connects significantly with the idea of the rule of law, which requires that official acts be in accordance with law. This latter principle speaks to account-ability, not clarity. If the citizen is being made retrospectively liable, it is because there was no law when he did the act that places the special duty upon the legislature to justify retrospective legislation.

The strong positivist interpretation of the *nulla poena sine lege* principle applies most clearly in only certain sorts of cases, namely, those where the laws in question exist mainly to protect settled expec-tations, in some areas of property law (for example, the law of cheques and currency). Here the settled expectations principle looms large and the rule of law principle small. But in other areas, say, in constitutional law, the rule of law predominates. It is no comfort to the prisoner that he must remain in prison as a result of retrospective legislation because his trial for murder revealed a hard case in law and he therefore had no reasonable expectation that he would be acquitted. He can justifiably say that every moment until the decision of the court there was no law declaring that his conduct amounted to murder. That complaint is a rule of law complaint, not one of reasonable expectation.

Can principles be identified by the rule of recognition?

It should be clear by now that the plain fact theory, even improved by its practical justification, does less and less work for us. Let us sum up the problems. Against what I have termed the instrumental virtue of clarity, we find that the plain fact theory does not seem to provide an adequate account of the doctrine of the separation of powers or the rule of law. In addition it does not seem to be able to account for those sorts of legal argument which involve the use of value judgments, because the weight a value should be given could not be specified in any clear test. Examples I gave earlier in this chapter were the applica-tion of standards of 'reasonableness', of what was a 'fair rent', or the particular applications of the idea of 'neighbour', or the well-known principle (of which there are a number of variants) 'no person is permitted to profit from his own wrong'.

But there is a common criticism of Dworkin's view that the weight of the value-laden idea of principles cannot be captured or identified by a factual – or 'sources' or 'pedigree' test – such as the rule of recognition. It is that the rule of recognition can be rejigged so as to include them. Let us examine this claim and see whether the rule of recognition can accommodate principles. I shall preface my analysis with the remark that, in my view, any attempt is doomed to fail because the distinction between plain facts (not brute facts, remember) and value (not moral value) is the distinguishing mark of any positivist theory that makes good sense.[15] Since 'plain facts' are in a different category from values, a plain fact theory of law cannot accord the same status to principles as it does to fact. The same point can be expressed in terms of his conventionalist theory which I deal with in the following chapter.[16]

Can principles be identified by the rule of recognition? In a sense I shall now examine, they clearly can. It is this sense which must be examined in order to see whether it provides the positivist answer to Dworkin's criticism. The rule of recognition, if we remind ourselves, consists of the facts of official practice in recognising certain standards as law. Can the 'facts of official practice' identify what the law is by means of principle? Let us try. Does 'official practice recognises "No one shall be permitted to profit by his own fraud, or to take advantage of his own wrong, or to found any claim upon his own iniquity, or to found any claim upon his own iniquity, or to acquire property by his own crime"'[17] capture the sense in which that principle was used in *Riggs* v. *Palmer*?

Unfortunately, it is not as easy as that. The problem was, of course, that the question was controversial (that was why there was litigation and an appeal). It must be clear from this example that principles will have to be accommodated for in the rule of recognition in a different way. In my view, we can do it only by allowing the rule of recognition to specify principles which 'must (or may) be taken into account'. The *Riggs* v. *Palmer* type of case becomes 'official practice recognises that the court must, or may, take into account the principle that no man may profit by his own wrong'.

It should be seen immediately how much weaker this is. It transfers the question of assessment of the weight of the principle to judicial discretion. The judge is bound, or permitted, to 'take the principle into account' but not bound to take it into account *in any kind of way*. As far as the advancement of clarity is concerned we are little better off, because it is now just as unclear what weight the principle will carry in any particular case. The lawyers on either side of the litigation will be able to use the rule of recognition to inform the judge that he is bound to take the principle 'into account' but that is all. If the judge is found not to have taken it into account at all, perhaps not even considered it, he has not done what is required of him by law. If, on the other hand, he has taken into account and either made it decisive, as in *Riggs* v. *Palmer*, or has given it very little weight, the lawyers can have no complaint in law.

What has happened is that in order for the principle's essentially value-laden element to be incorporated into the factual test of the rule of recognition it was converted into something value-free or 'source identifiable': the judge was required simply to make a value judgment without specifying how he was to make that judgment. Is that what the positivists want? That emendation to the rule of recognition does not achieve much, because it only says that judges may be required by law to make value judgments, and we knew of that possibility when we discussed the force of the use of words such as 'reasonable' and 'fair'.[18]

Perhaps there is a more complicated possibility. Perhaps we can only understand the clear rules in a 'context' or 'matrix' of value judgments. This would mean, I think, that instead of connecting principles with the rule of recognition directly, in the way we have just now done, we connect them by saying that principles are somehow 'higher order' reasons by which we understand the more simple type rules identified by the rule of recognition. Thus, in *Riggs* v. *Palmer*, the rule identified by the rule of recognition is discovered as the result of two stages of legal argument. First, an apparently clear rule is uncovered which prima facie would allow murderers to benefit under their victims' will. Secondly, the law is surveyed and the principle of 'no one may profit from his own wrong' is discovered to be something that the judge must 'take into account' according to the rule of recognition. This second stage requires the judge to interpret the initial plain fact meaning in accordance with the 'higher order' principle.

Superficially, this all sounds reasonable enough. But it does not withstand closer analysis as a defence of positivism. We are attempting to make sense of the positivists' idea of a master rule for identifying law. Have we, by this purportedly more sophisticated method, got any closer? How can the master test identify for us what the correct interpretation of the first stage 'rule' is? That remains a controversial question, one that was hotly disputed in *Riggs* v. *Palmer*. We can, of course, hope to find even higher order reasons which can direct our interpretation of the 'no man may profit by his own wrong' principle, but we will still come back to the initial difficulty: where is the official practice that clearly determines the result?

Taken to its extreme the highest order principle must be one directing judges to decide according to the best interpretation of the existing rules. We can call that the highest order reason supplying the context or matrix for understanding the now merely prima facie clarity of rules identified by the rule of recognition.

But this argument would not save positivism. On the contrary, it destroys it. It would not be correct to use Hart's idea of a rule of recognition here, because it is unlike anything he postulated (remember: it consisted of empirically identifiable facts of official practice 'normally concordant'). We can use the term 'master rule' or 'pedigree', thus making use of the positivists' insistence on the idea of a source test for the identification of law. This 'master rule' may then be reformulated by saying that law is to be identified by the 'best' interpretation of the settled rules. But that yields an even less precise result. Is *that* what the positivists want? It does not provide a clear test of law because the idea of what is best is fundamentally and inherently controversial – witness *Riggs* v. *Palmer*.

Am I wrong in my insistence that positivism requires a test that is clear? It is difficult to see what else would be relied upon in order to achieve the effective separation of law from morals. Consider the most abstract consensus of all, that of officials agreeing that the law must be identified according to the best interpretation. We cannot deny that such a consensus exists. What is the meaning of 'best'? That is fundamentally controversial and it is difficult to see how that must only be understood as excluding what is morally best (or whatever) other than by simple fiat. Positivism cannot win its arguments in that way.

Of course, we could not simply save positivism, too, by postulating as the master rule all the rules and principles contained in the legal system. Apart from the possibility that this defence involves a circularity (for example, the master rule is to be identified by all the rules, principles and so on, which are identified by the master rule), the undeniable appeal of the idea of a relatively simple test for law, as the master rule thesis supports, is completely lost in complexity.[19]

Original intention

Useful insights into the reasons for the wide acceptance of the plain facts theory may be gained by examining what has come to be known, particularly in the United States, as the doctrine of original intention. It is a theory of statutory interpretation which requires judges to interpret the law in accordance with the wishes, or intentions, of the actual founders of the Constitution so far as those wishes may best be historically identified. Of course, since it would be odd if the founders did not intend judges to apply statutes and previous decisions and so on, the interpretation of law will not *just* be that of a historical inquiry into the founders' intentions at the time they were formed, but of the meaning of many later statutes and judicial decisions.

Nevertheless, the doctrine requires that the intentions of the founders be regarded as the primary source of law and that all interpretations of the law should be parasitic upon it. The doctrine exists in two forms, each corresponding to the simpler and the more complex views of the plain fact theory.

The popular representation of the doctrine has a 'folksy' appeal, one that purports to root current legal interpretation in the historical origins of the legal system. It has the same earthy feel as the 'let's get our facts straight' no-nonsense approach of the Farmer Jones and Farmer Giles dispute. This is the doctrine's simplistic side and it is, of course, open to the same objection as the simple version of the plain fact theory: what reasons are there for accepting it? Despite its naïvety the doctrine is popularly accepted in this simplistic form; the law is regarded as 'there' to be 'applied'.

The second aspect is, at this stage, the important and interesting one. The justification given for the doctrine is that it prevents judges from making novel decisions and so contains them within their role as 'neutral' appliers of the law. The doctrine requires simply that the judges make interpretations of the law based on what the founders of the constitution intended. If those interpretations are thus firmly anchored to those intentions, judges cannot then be guilty of imposing their 'own' values on the citizens. This concern is with the perceived role of the judiciary within the matrix of the doctrine of the separation of powers. Note for future use, then, the connection here between the original intention doctrine and a popular precept of political philosophy.

The concern that judges be unoriginal has two important sides to it. The first is with the principle we have discussed earlier that the judge should not usurp the function of the legislature. This is a more publicly acknowledged worry in the United States, where the Constitution allows the judges to declare unconstitutional legislation to be invalid, than it is in the United Kingdom, where the reigning constitutional theory states that the judges do not have that power.

The worry in the United States is that judges will thwart the intentions of a legislature, which represents, after all, the majority of voters. Although the majority's wishes may be thwarted by the judges on matters relating to the protection of minority rights, for example, by striking down legislation reintroducing slavery, this is by virtue only of the Constitution's express permission. Outside these exceptions where minority rights are protected, on the other hand, judges must be as 'unoriginal' as possible.

This principle is relatively uncontroversial. It is inconsistent with the idea of the respective roles of the legislature and the judiciary in the United States that the judges in general should substitute legislation with their own wishes about how things should be run. That is contrary to the separation of powers doctrine.

Imagine a judge, opposed to the construction of a hospital because it is, to him, a waste of public funds, declaring invalid, on that ground, the regulations which create and finance the institution involved in its construction. Imagine a judge who, disliking the present government, declares all legislation emanating from that government as invalid.

These are fanciful examples and judges who behaved in these ways would not remain in office for long. But why? One reason is that it would be hard for such judges to maintain any sort of credibility in justifying their actions. Their efforts would be likely to show inconsistencies. In part, this would be due to the understanding they will have had (given, for example, their judicial oath) when they took office of the nature of the judicial role. The judges would very probably offer only a confused picture. These examples make it most likely to be inconsistent with the role of the judge to decide in these ways.

A second bother with judicial unoriginality has to do with objectivity. The judge must only concern himself with the intentions of the founding fathers as they can be ascertained from the clear words of the Constitution, or from the clear words of either subsequent legislative or judicial acts which are in accordance with the Constitution. The idea is thought to be necessary because it provides a clear check on judicial originality. *How do we know* whether the judge has incorporated his own 'value' judgments into the law? How do we know when he has departed from the clear and explicit words of the Constitution or subsequent legislative and judicial acts?

It can be seen that the original intention approach, when understood according to its first aspect, makes the same appeal to plain facts as positivism does. It is, in fact, positivism under a different description. But we should look at the second aspect of original intention, which is more sensible, because it seeks justification in morality and democracy. The important point here is that it is *not* necessary in order for a judge to pay due consideration to the democratic requirements of the separation of powers to rely only upon explicitly declared legislative intentions. And we should note that this is so even if 'the intention of the legislature' means something determinable only as a historical fact, which Dworkin denies.

Neutrality

The idea that a judge be as 'unoriginal' as possible is not a particularly appealing idea, for we want judges to be something other than automatons, who do more than 'read off' the law. But the same idea can be expressed more palatably by saying that judges should be 'neutral' in their decisions, meaning that the judges avoid introducing their own moral judgments into the law. The idea of neutrality paints a picture whereby the judge behaves, say, as a neutral country does during wartime. He decides without favouring any particular side.

But even the idea of neutrality, as it has been commonly analysed, does not carry great explanatory power. It borrows from the idea of neutrality in areas outside morality, such as the actual behaviour of nations, whereby the neutral country does not play any active part in dealings between other states, or even mechanics, in which the neutral position of the gears means that the engine is disconnected and thus drives nothing.

Consider, though, the neutral country which continues to sell arms to warring country A and continues not to sell arms to warring country B. Being neutral in this situation in fact supports country A. Or, a father who, being neutral in a dispute between his older and stronger son and his younger and weaker son, passively allows the outcome where the older son, by being more resourceful, unfairly comes out on top. Or, a doctor, 'neutrally' applying Hippocratic principles, who cures the injured Gestapo torturer as he would an ordinary person, and thereby permits further torture.

It is clear from these examples that the idea of neutrality must be understood as having point only if it is seen to be more than 'reading off' an independently defined state of affairs. The better idea here is *impartiality*, because that implies a judgment on the merits but also captures the special sense in which a judge should remain distanced from each party to a decision that he makes. It follows that there is no special virtue in 'being neutral', at least not without some justification for not interfering in the particular circumstances.[20]

Judge Robert Bork

One of the best-known supporters of the original intention theory is Judge Robert Bork, largely through his unsuccessful nomination to the US Supreme Court in 1987. It is instructive to examine both his description of the theory and one of his judgments in which he puts it into practice. Bork clearly holds the plain fact view of law and he combines this with a view about judicial neutrality based on the principles of democracy. It is not so clear now what view he holds of judicial reasoning, given what appeared to be shifts of position during the Senate hearings on his nomination. Dworkin has used Bork's views as a vehicle to explain his misgivings about both views of judicial reasoning.

Bork is firmly against the making of moral value judgments by judges when striking out state legislative enactments as unconstitutional. To make such judgments is, in his view, to subvert the democratic model set up by the United States Constitution and this model, he says, supplies the basis of the political legitimacy of the US Supreme Court. He does not mean by this that the democratic model was one of majority rule only, for plainly, some minority rights are protected by the Constitution.

Bork thinks that there are only two proper methods of deriving rights from the Constitution. First, we must 'take from the document rather specific values that text or history show the framers actually to have intended ...', and secondly, we may derive rights from the governmental processes, such as legislation and judicial decision, 'established by the Constitution'.[21] The essential point is the grounding of any argument for a right in a historical fact so that new rights are not created. Thus, he says that 'the judge must stick close to the text and the history, and their fair implications, and not construct new rights' and that the judge, outside areas where 'the Constitution has not spoken', will have no scale but his own value preferences.

How does the theory work in practice? Bork is critical of an argument that the equal protection clause of the Constitution extends to acts of 'private discrimination'. He says that this argument 'fails the test of the neutral derivation of principle. It converts an amendment whose text and history clearly show it to be aimed only at governmental discrimination into a sweeping prohibition of private discrimination.'[22] The doctrine thus limits the judge's power to make decisions based upon more abstract understandings of legislative decisions. The further a judge gets away from the actual words used the more likely it is that he is swayed by his personal views and is legislating against the majority will.

Bork's analysis of the first amendment right to free speech is that the wording only applies to 'explicitly political' speech. He admits that the framers of the amendment had 'no coherent theory' of free speech, but that it was historically clear that they were accustomed to drawing a line between freedom and 'licentiousness' (he clearly had in mind free speech protection of pornography). He thus limits the interpretation of the amendment to the historical core of what the Founding Fathers believed, so as to avoid judicial legislation:

> If the dialectical progression is not to become an analogical stampede, the protection of the first amendment must be cut off when it reaches the outer limits of political speech.[23]

There is a significant qualifier here to the idea of simply reading off the intentions of the Founding Fathers. Bork notes that there may not have been a set of coherent ideas about free speech among them, and thus allows for the creation of arguments by analogy. But these analogical arguments must not be allowed to 'stampede' and must not extend beyond using the 'building blocks' of the historical materials: 'We cannot solve our problems simply by reference to the text or to its history. But we are not without materials for building.'[24]

So it is clear that Bork does not fully believe that the historical materials are enough. We can go further. Presumably, where there are gaps in our historical knowledge we may ask counterfactual questions about what the Founding Fathers, or subsequent judges or legislators, would have thought had they been asked. Take the English Metropolitan Police Act 1839, which makes it an offence to 'repair a carriage' on a street in the London metropolitan area.[25] Is it an offence to repair a motor car?

The defence could be raised that the legislators in 1837 did not intend to make it an offence, because they could not have known what cars were, since they had not then been invented. We may be prepared for the present to allow some sort of question along the lines of what the legislature might have thought had it been confronted with the future existence of cars. Admittedly, it requires some suspension of judgment. What if most of members of the legislative body did not believe such things could be invented? Or what, if it were believed that such things *could* exist, that they were 'unnatural' things, and not at all like carriages? Bork would presumably allow an argument by analogy here. It would not create an analogical stampede to declare cars to be within the statute, because cars are, for the purposes to be discerned from the statute, the same as carriages as far as nuisance is concerned.

Using an argument by analogy, however, masks the difficulties discernible on deeper analysis. As in the last section where we considered whether principles of interpretation could be connected to the plain fact understandings and found that this involved us in difficulties about the level of abstraction, we meet problems. If Bork allows for *any* arguments by analogy then the appeal to plain fact rights in the Constitution is greatly weakened. No plain fact in the Constitution will tell us when we are pursuing an illegitimate analogical 'stampede'. The allowing in of arguments by analogy allows for value judgments at least of the sort that chooses the best analogy. Truer to the plain fact approach would be a total block on arguments by analogy, and the problem for Bork here would be that an analysis of the law that came to that conclusion would not be accepted by anyone.

The right to privacy

Dworkin labels the plain fact, 'read off', form of the original intention theory as 'weak historicism'. Weak historicism just accepts that the law is 'out there'. 'Strong' historicism is the view that there are *good reasons* for accepting the plain fact clauses of the Constitution as exhaustive of the law, one such reason being that acceptance of the view prevents judicial legislation.

This better account is provided by Judge Bork, although as I have pointed out, he relies heavily, too, on weak historicism. Dworkin's criticism of stronger historicism is that it makes sense, unlike weak historicism, but just does not make good sense. Dworkin's criticism of the plain fact theory, in both of its forms, is helpful in understanding the current controversy in the United States about the existence of a constitutional right to privacy.

There is no 'mention' of a right to privacy in the US Constitution. The first reference in published legal discourse was probably in a famous *Harvard Law Review* article, entitled 'The Right to Privacy', by Warren and Brandeis.[26] The argument in the article is fundamentally about the possibility of asserting the existence of rights in the law by means of arguments of principle and coherency, even although there is no explicit mention of such rights in the law. The extrapolation of such rights was nevertheless a workable possibility, and they proceeded to demonstrate it by using the right to privacy as an example.

The article was largely prompted by personal experience of invasion of privacy. Warren and his wife were prominent Boston socialites and the Boston newspapers had reported in great detail a family wedding. Much of the argument is concerned with pointing both to other areas of the law where analogous protections exist such as in rights to personal security, rights against libel and slander and rights to literary and artistic property, and to the development of new 'demands' of society. The development of these demands created a situation where other rights explicitly recognised in the law could be seen in a clearer, because more abstract, light.

The idea of the development of the 'intensity and complexity' of modern life led the writers to assert that solitude and privacy had become more essential to the individual, and consequently a right to privacy existed which, properly understood, was an instance of a more general right 'to be left alone'. So, formerly 'disconnected' rights, each developed to cope with the particular demands of a particular stage of change in society, were now to be seen as connected by being instantiations of a more general right to 'be alone'.

This article is a famous one. Its particular strategy, that of finding more abstract principles upon which to base less abstract propositions of law, is not, however, as radical as is often assumed. Lawyers, not just in the United States, are perfectly familiar with the form of argument and not just in novel cases. Are skateboards prohibited in the park? That depends upon more abstract propositions making sense of words such as 'vehicles', their sense in turn presumably relying on abstract propositions making sense of, for example, the appropriateness of the legislature to produce legislation.

It is not uncommon for a lawyer to win a case because he can find a more abstract proposition which lifts a dispute beyond what seems an irreconcilable conflict of interpretations – one perhaps where a lazy judge might feel inclined to toss a coin – and shows the opposing lawyer's case in a bad light and his own in a good light. It is, I venture to say, a relatively common phenomenon in the courts. The difference between the Warren and Brandeis thesis about the right to privacy and the concerns of the ordinary lawyer is just that the level of abstraction is higher and therefore encompasses many situations which would not normally fall within the purview of any one litigated case. The thesis aims at establishing a general right of privacy right across the board, without concerning itself with the particular ramifications and qualifications in particular cases. Warren and Brandeis are specific about that:

> To determine in advance of experience the exact line at which the dignity and convenience of the individual must yield to the demands of the public welfare or of private justice would be a difficult task; but the more general rules are furnished by the legal analogies already developed in the law of slander and libel, and the law of literary and artistic property.

In *Roberson* v. *Rochester Folding Box Co.*[27] the plaintiff argued that such a right of privacy existed in New York law. Without her permission, the defendants had used pictures of her in an advertising campaign, and in a New York court she sought damages for the distress it caused her and an injunction to prevent further use of the photographs. Judge Parker, who gave the majority decision, denied the existence of such a right. It did not exist in precedent and had not been asserted by the 'great commentators upon the law'. He referred to the Warren and Brandeis article but dismissed the idea of any general such right on what appear to be two grounds. First, the right did not 'exist' in the precedents nor, in fact, anywhere other than in the Warren and Brandeis article and second, the right was too wide and would include all sorts of 'rights' which could not possibly be confirmed by a court of law.

The first argument should now be familiar. It is Dworkin's weak historicism. We can ask the same question as he does. Why would we be disposed to accept the thesis that the only rights that 'exist' within the law are those that are *specifically mentioned*? Why should the determination of an individual's position in the law by a judge be wholly dependent upon whether there is a verbal counterpart in law expressing that right? Put in that way, the theory seems quite arbitrary. But the argument appears in Judge Parker's decision: 'There is no precedent ... to be *found* in the decisions ... Mention of such a right is not to be *found* ... nor ... does its existence seem to have been *asserted* ...'

The more important argument is the second one, that recognising a right of privacy would be too wide. But what sort of argument is that? It appears to assume that some escape from the confining of legal argument to explicit declarations of law is possible. One must conclude this because Judge Parker felt that he had to address the question, and he would not have done so had he thought that the non-existence of an explicitly formulated right of privacy ended the matter. One must be realistic, too. No judge believes that legitimate

legal argument may not search for more general principles to determine the validity of disputed propositions of law. Judge Parker's
pronouncements, when seen in the light of his choice of a narrower
principle rather than the wider one advocated by Warren and
Brandeis, are not then uncharacteristic pieces of legal argument.

The crux of Judge Parker's argument was a *reductio ad absurdum*.[28] If
he recognised the right then absurd rights such as, for example, a right
not to be insulted or a right not to be gossiped about would have to be
recognised. Therefore, the general right to privacy could not be said to
exist. The failure of the plaintiff's case was thus largely due to the
judge's unwillingness or inability to draw a distinction between these
sorts of case and a right not to have one's picture used commercially
without one's permission.

Two years later, the Supreme Court of Georgia decided the other
way in *Pavesich* v. *New England Life Insurance Co.*[29] The plaintiff's
picture was used, without his permission, in a life insurance advertise-
ment, and he succeeded in obtaining an injunction to prevent further
use of the picture. Justice Cobb dealt with the *reductio ad absurdum*
problem by the obvious device of recognising that the right of privacy
would have a demarcation line against other rights, notably the right to
freedom of speech. But this, he thought, should not be a barrier to
recognising a general right to privacy: 'This right to speak and the right
of privacy have been coexistent ... each exists, and each must be
recognized and enforced with due respect for the other ...'

These two cases illustrate the way in which judges differ. Judge
Parker is simply not as skilful as Justice Cobb in handling abstract
matters. The reliance on 'asserted' or 'mentioned' rights is clearly not
a good argument in itself, nor is the *reductio* argument, when useful
and sensible distinctions can be drawn between a right not to have
one's picture used commercially without consent and a right not to be
gossiped about. This is not to say that Justice Cobb's argument is the
best available, but rather that his understanding of the possibility of
arguing for rights in this abstract, or principled, way makes better
sense of legal argument in general. That is the only point I am
concerned to make at present.

Judge Parker has similar concerns to Bork, being wary of 'non-
explicit' rights. Like Bork, he is afraid of an 'analogical stampede'
which it is the point of the *reductio ad absurdum* he provides to avoid.
One suspects the unexpressed worry to be that argument will get out of
hand the further it moves from explicit and demonstrable rights to less
demonstrable legal propositions argued for in more difficult and
abstract ways. From the point of view of a judge, that is a practical
consideration of some importance, for where arguments are less easy
to understand their merits are less easily discernible and there is the
risk of time-consuming and pointless litigation. But the distinction

between good and bad argument cannot be drawn by *fiat*, by a distinction between explicit and implicit rights, or by refusing to argue for demarcation areas between the applications of abstract principle.

Judge Bork has put his theory into practice. An example is *Dronenburg* v. *Zech*,[30] in which he upheld as constitutional the US Navy's policy of mandatory discharge for homosexual conduct. He rather grudgingly recognised a right of privacy in some limited areas by virtue of express recognition but said that he could not 'extend' that right to protect a homosexual naval clerk. Dronenburg had argued for the general right to privacy which protected him from having his private sexual conduct taken into account in considering his dismissal. He cited a number of precedents that applied that right to what he claimed were relevantly the same circumstances. For example, he cited *Griswold* v. *Connecticut*,[31] in which the US Supreme Court held, on the basis of a right to privacy, that a statute forbidding husbands and wives from buying contraceptives was unconstitutional. He also cited *Eisenstadt* v.*Baird*,[32] in which the Supreme Court struck down a statute forbidding the distribution of contraceptives altogether, on the ground that no ground of difference could 'rationally' explain the different treatment accorded married and unmarried persons under the statute.

The argument is simply that these cases instantiate a more general principle relating to a legal right to engage in sexual acts for non-procreative purposes unqualified by the marital relationship between the parties. Bork's answer to this argument illustrates his original intention approach. He says he cannot find an *articulation* of this general principle:

> In this group of cases, and in those cited in the quoted language from the Court's opinions, we do not find any principle articulated even approaching in breadth that which appellant seeks to have us adopt. The Court has listed as illustrative of the right of privacy such matters as activities relating to marriage, procreation, contraception, family relationships, and child rearing and education, It need hardly be said that none of these covers a right to homosexual conduct.[33]

This is the plain fact, weak historicist, theory in all its glory. Judge Bork concludes that there is no right to engage in homosexual conduct simply because there is no verbal counterpart in the cases. The argument is given a little more substance when he gives other reasons for sticking to verbal formulations, namely, that the legislature's intention would otherwise be thwarted, and that the legislature has the sole, because democratic, right to determine the legality of private sexual conduct.

But not all that much more. One would have expected something along the lines of his fears about analogical stampedes, well echoed in the Supreme Court's decision in 1986 declaring as constitutional a Georgian statute making sodomy an offence. In *Bowers* v. *Hardwick*, Justice White, delivering the opinion of the Court, said:

> The right pressed upon us here has no similar support in the text of the Constitution ... And if respondent's submission is limited to the voluntary sexual conduct between consenting adults, it would be difficult, except by fiat, to limit the claimed right to homosexual conduct while leaving exposed to prosecution adultery, incest, and other sexual crimes even though they are committed in the home. We are unwilling to start down that road.[34]

It is difficult to see why different arguments could not apply to the other cases of sexual conduct. However, more specific arguments about what kinds of sexual conduct may be legally prohibited by a democratically elected legislature were discussed in Chapter 4, because they are concerned, not with versions of the plain fact theory, but with, in Dworkin's terms, the duty the state has to treat its citizens as equals.

But the original intention theory requires more analysis and that will be relevant to understanding the inadequacies of the plain fact theory and thus relevant to the concerns of this chapter. I raised the question earlier whether being true to the intentions of the legislature required following the plain fact theory and said that did not seem to follow. Nevertheless, the idea of legislative intention *means* something. Is there a way of understanding what it is that does not require us to look at a plain fact conception of it?

The concept of legislative intention[35]

To accept this last possibility is to accept a conception of legislative intention that is more sophisticated than that of a crudely descriptive 'psychological group fact'. But can 'legislative intention' mean more than that? Judge Bork and Justice White appear to use the idea in that way, as though there were a historically existing intention belonging to the legislature at a specific time.

Dworkin is critical of the idea in the context of constitutional interpretation although an easier route to understanding him is in the context of the plain fact theory, for that in the end is what the original intention theory is. The astounding thing about the theory is that it could ever be taken seriously by anyone. The reason it has been taken seriously is the concern with judicial neutrality (in the United Kingdom, the concern that judges do not 'usurp the function of the legislature'), but once we can see that concern as a separate concern, one not necessarily connected with a plain fact, 'read off' theory, we can abandon it.

Dworkin's view is that the idea of legislative intention is a metaphor for drawing our intention to the important fact that the legislature has a right to legislate. If we ignore that right or give it little weight we are making a serious mistake about the nature of our legal system. In a law school tutorial, or a court of law, reference to a statute means reference to what has been decided by the appropriate, if you like democratic, forum, for creating new law.

Let us consider the original intention theory literally. The first question is clearly: whose intention? In legislatures such as those in the United States and the United Kingdom a large number of people are responsible for the production of legislation. Foremost are the members of the legislative assembly who vote in accordance with the appropriate procedures. But there are other groups. Law commissions and various other similar sorts of advisory bodies produce draft legislation for consideration which is eventually passed in verbatim form. Do the intentions of the people on these bodies form part of the legislative intention?

Sometimes it helps in ascertaining the meaning of some technical pieces of legislation to understand the problems, not with which the legislature grappled, but with which the particular body was concerned. Much legislation is debated in small committees created by the legislature in order to discuss technical or other points in greater detail than would otherwise be possible in the larger chamber. Often these committees accept the advice of specialist persons or bodies as to what should be placed in the proposed enactment. Are these, too, to have their intentions included as part of the intention of the legislature? It would be necessary, in other words, to have some sorts of limitations upon the numbers of people who could be said to have formed the 'legislative' intention.

But how would these limitations be made? We could suggest that one necessary condition for inclusion within 'legislative intention' could be membership of the legislative assembly, although it not easy to say why. After all, we are looking for 'the legislative intention' and to say that it is simply the intention of a definite group of persons looks tautological because there are the above plausible contenders, especially where the legislation is technical and not understood in its finer points by the average member of the legislative body.

Difficulties immediately get in our way with even this limitation, however, because it will be necessary to have rules to tell us which intentions count and which do not. Is the legislative intention to be that of only those who voted for a measure? Surely, to carry the argument on in this literal way we do have to make such a stipulation, for otherwise we have to say that those who voted against the measure intended the law to have the meaning that it does in the end have. Further combinatorial difficulties are created among those voting for the measure, where personal intentions differ on various points in the legislation, where, say, some members intend that certain provisions be understood in one way and others in another way. Do we take the largest of these groups? Or the majority? Or a representative opinion gleaned from, say, the three largest groups none of which forms a majority within the group voting for the measure?

The difficulties compound. A legislator could vote for a measure of which he knows barely anything with the intention of acting in accordance with his party's policy. Or he could understand the point of the legislation but vote for it simply because it will have the unintended effect of furthering his own business interests. How could we possibly include this kind of mental state within the idea of 'the legislative intention'?

It is clear that the problem here is making the assumption that 'legislative intention' is a mental state and then trying to fit into that assumption all the various contradictory possibilities. It is a good example of what Hart called the fallacy of the 'growth of theory on the back of definition'.[36] If the definition is wrong in the first place, no amount of theory to explain away anomalies not at first sight covered by the definition will make the definition right.

There is no sense in talking of one intention which a group of people have because our intentions relate to the acts only we ourselves can carry out and so I cannot intend that another person do something and so *a fortiori* I cannot intend that a group do something. It follows that a group of persons cannot have the same intention, only similar intentions. The idea of a single group psychological state thus cannot supply the drive for the idea of legislative intention. It is clear that the idea has appeal only in the same way that the unsatisfactory 'plain fact' view of law in general has had such widespread appeal. It is now time to abandon it.

Summary

Where do we go from here? An acceptance of Dworkin's theory of law as integrity is not compatible with an acceptance of law as plain fact. We can see two versions of the law as plain fact, one which places a 'virtue' on plain fact. It is time to explore two further questions. First, does the plain fact theory have a different aspiration from Dworkin's concern with justification of judicial decision-making (grounded in morality)? That is, could Hart's theory, as well as some other theories, be saved by saying that their primary consideration is to provide some other account of law than one justifying judicial argument? Secondly, if justification is properly a major concern of the legal theorist, what other kinds of theory are available? In the next chapter, I shall mainly examine the second question because of Dworkin's criticisms of two alternative theories he calls, respectively, conventionalism and pragmatism.

Notes

1. Rules of statutory construction are much less help than commonly realised. The so-called 'literal' rule will be invoked by one counsel to counter the so-called 'mischief' or 'golden' rule used by the other counsel. There is no rule formally recognised by the courts offering a reconciliation of the different rules. But Cross has attempted to formulate a rule. In *Statutory Interpretation* 2nd ed. (Bell and Engle) (1987), he argues towards a fusion of the three rules. He says the literal rule has been treated too literally; that it has been applied as though there were a 'true', contextless, meaning. To introduce context, the mischief rule must be 'insinuated into' the literal rule. Further, when the literal rule, so interpreted, leads to some absurdity or inconsistency, the words of the statute may be modified, in accordance with the golden rule, so as to avoid the absurdity or inconsistency, but no further.

2. 'The simplest form of remedy for the *uncertainty* of the regime of primary rules is the introduction of what we shall call a `rule of recognition''. Hart, *The Concept of Law*, p. 92.

3. See *Legal Reasoning and Legal Theory* (1978) Oxford, p. 233.

4. See *Legal Reasoning and Legal Theory* p. 244, where MacCormick distinguishes between principles and rules: '... the principles interact with the rules, underpin them, hedge them in, qualify them, justify the enunciation of new rulings as tested out be consequentialist arguments, and so on.' It is more helpful to leave this common criticism by positivists, such as MacCormick, to the later section entitled 'Can Principles Be Identified by the Rule of Recognition?'. Several more of Dworkin's distinctions still need to be introduced and detailed discussion requires both an introduction to his idea of judicial discretion and further development of his idea of the 'rule of recognition'.

5. The same observation must be true for the judge and lawyer as it is for the ordinary layman. In the areas of property and commercial law precise guidance is helpful, but in constitutional and administrative matters it is a hindrance.

6. *Riggs* v. *Palmer* 115 N.E. (1889) 188.

7. See, for example, Hart: 'For though the search for and use of principles underlying the law defers the moment, it cannot eliminate the need for judicial law-making, since in any hard case different principles supporting competing analogies may present themselves and the judge will have to choose between them, relying like a conscientious legislator on his sense of what is best and not on any already established order of priorities

among principles already prescribed for him by law.' (Preface to *Essays in Jurisprudence and Philosophy* (1983) Oxford, p. 7).

8. In *Read* v. *Secretary of State for the Home Department* [1988] 3 All E.R. 993 the implication of the judgment of the House of Lords is that a sentence imposed that is not in accordance with sentencing 'guidelines' is nevertheless a sentence within the law. Read had been sentenced to twelve years' imprisonment in Spain for an offence the sentence for which, if it had been imposed in the United Kingdom and in accordance with United Kingdom sentencing guidelines, would have amounted to only two to four years, although the maximum penalty under the Act which provided for the offence was ten years. Under The Repatriation of Prisoners Act 1984 and the international Convention on the Transfer of Sentenced Persons 1983, Read could be repatriated to a United Kingdom prison, although the prison term was to be that determined by Spain unless it was 'incompatible' with 'United Kingdom law'. The House of Lords confirmed Read's sentence as one of ten years, subtracting the time he had already spent in the Spanish prison. Twelve years was incompatible with the United Kingdom maximum, but ten years was held to be compatible with the sentencing guidelines of two to four years.

9. An exception here is the requirement that a court must disqualify from driving, for at least one year, any person convicted of drunken driving unless there are 'special reasons' for not doing so. Road Traffic Act 1972 s.93.

10. See *Lim* v. *Camden Health Authority* [1979] 2 All E.R. 910, 914.

11. *Donoghue* v. *Stevenson* [1932] A.C. 562, at 580. Maybe we could try 'Who, in law, *ought to be considered* my neighbour?' which does not sound odd. But that is because it is consistent with there being an answer within the law (try: 'Who ought to be considered as the murderer?').

12. [1975] 1 All E.R. 913, 942 (Lord Kilbrandon); 939 (Lord Simon).

13. See The Theft Act 1968. Theft, which includes destruction, can only be of 'property' and that does not include things 'picked' from trees unless done for 'a commercial purpose'. See s.4.

14. See Hart, *The Concept of Law* p. 107.

15. Kelsen's theory may be seen to raise a problem since, relying on the distinction between the 'is' and the 'ought', he declared that the law's normativity – its characteristic of directing action – was dependent on the law's existing within the world of 'oughts'. Laws existed in the world, not of 'causality', but 'imputation'. But his theory still made the determination of law dependent on a master test, the basic norm, which could be described as a clear presupposition of validity. The significance of the basic norm in legal theory is that it marked the step towards understanding the relevance of acceptance of standards as the essential part of legal argument. Its obscurity lies only in Kelsen's non-specification of the reasons for the acceptance of those standards. There is no obscurity in the root-of-title conception of being able in all cases to identify law by reference to a clear master rule.

16. He extends what he calls 'soft' conventionalism, which includes all the possible rules to govern all possible cases, to its logical conclusion: that the convention that tells judges to decide between them in any case is the one that includes a judgment about value. It is the rule that says: 'decide in

accordance with the *best* rule to cover the case'. This is my paraphrase of his argument on soft conventionalism 'collapsing' into integrity. See *Law's Empire* pp. 127–8.

17. See *Riggs* v. *Palmer* 115 N.E. (1889) 188, 190.

18. The position of what are known as 'persuasive' precedents, where judgments of judges in other jurisdictions are *taken into account* fits best with the way I have suggested principles may be captured by a rule of recognition. They are 'persuasive' and not 'binding'.

19. This tactic against Dworkin's dismissal of the rule of recognition theory is one that Rolf Sartorius once attempted. See 'Social Policy and Judicial Legislation' 8 *American Philosophical Quarterly* 151 (1971).

20. For excellent discussions on the problems raised by the idea of neutrality, see the article by Montefiore in the book he edited, entitled *Neutrality and Impartiality* (1975) Cambridge, p. 1, and Raz, *The Morality of Freedom* (1986) Oxford, Chapter 5.

21. Bork, 'Neutral Principles and Some First Amendment Problems' (1971) 47 *Indiana Law Journal* 1, p. 17. Note his curious doctrine that rights are derivative from the democratic process, and exist in order to ensure the democratic process continues. The idea of the one man/one vote principle does not, in his view, express the equal worth of individuals, but exists, rather, to ensure that the democratic will of the majority is not frustrated. Here, as elsewhere, Bork's analysis is superficial. He does not examine the question why the will of the majority is so important. One obvious explanation is that it offends some dimension of equality if the will of a minority prevails, as in a totalitarian regime. See also Dworkin, 'The Bork Nomination', (1987) 34 *N-Y Review of Books*, no. 13 p. 3 (also in 1987 9 *Cardozo Law Review* 101–13); 'The Bork Nomination: An Exchange' (1987) 34 *N-Y Review of Books* no. 15, p. 59; 'The Bork Nomination' (1987) 34 *N-Y Review of Books*, no. 17, p. 60; and 'From Bork to Kennedy' (1987) 34 *N-Y Review of Books*, no. 20, p. 36.

Bork's views have apparently changed recently, some changing during the Senate hearings, but I describe his views at the time in which they are relevant to Dworkin's comments on them.

22. *Indiana Law Journal* 16.

23. *Indiana Law Journal* 27.

24. *Indiana Law Journal* 22–3. The flavour of his thinking has not changed much, though. See his *The Tempting of America* (1990) Sinclair-Stevenson. For example, he says of the distinction between 'concepts' and 'conceptions' that it '... is merely a way of changing the level of generality at which a constitutional provision may be restated so that it is taken to mean something that it obviously did not mean' (213–4).

25. S.54 of The Metropolitan Police Act 1839 states 'A person is liable on summary conviction to a penalty if in any thoroughfare or public place in the Metropolitan Police District or in any street elsewhere in England and Wales to the annoyance of the inhabitants or passengers he ... makes or repairs any trailer, cart or carriage except in cases of accident where repair on the spot is necessary.' 'Carriage', incidentally, now includes a motor vehicle and a trailer, by virtue of The Road Traffic Act 1972 s.195, but that does not affect the argument.

26. Samuel Warren and Louis Brandeis, 'The Right to Privacy' *Harvard Law Review* (1890) Vol. 4, 193.

27. 171 N.Y. 538 (1902).

28. He also employed the familiar argument that recognition of the right would result in 'a vast amount of litigation'.

29. 22 Ga. 190 (1904).

30. 1984 741 Federal Reporter, 2nd Series.

31. 381 U.S. 479, 85 S.Ct. 1678, 14 L.Ed.2d 510 (1965).

32. 405 U.S. 438, 92 S.Ct. 1029, 31 L.Ed.2d 349 (1972).

33. At 1,395–6.

34. 106 S.Ct. 2841 (1986) at 2,846.

35. See McCallum, 'Legislative Intention' in *Essays in Legal Philosophy* ed. Summers (1967) Blackwell, for an excellent discussion.

36. See Hart's 'Definition and Theory in Jurisprudence' in *Essays in Jurisprudence and Philosophy* (1983) Oxford: Clarendon Press, Chapter 1, p. 25.

8

Hard cases II

We may now consider more sophisticated analyses of what happens, and what should go on, in cases where there is genuine disagreement about the truth of propositions of law. Again, we must appreciate that, corresponding to the different senses of positivism that I outlined in Chapters 5 and 7, there may be different perspectives or concerns in the identification of hard cases. Here we will be concerned with Dworkin's own focus on the aspect of judicial reasoning.

What, though, are we to make of those theorists who claim that judicial positivism is only part of, and peripheral to, concerns of a more universal kind, such as that of 'a descriptive theory, offered to historians to enable a discriminating history of legal systems to be written' and 'without intent to offer solutions ... to questions disputed among competent lawyers'?[1]

The phenomenology of judicial reasoning

There are two main objections to the above account of the plain fact theory. Each objection contests the other. The first states that positivism is not 'primarily' concerned with 'the phenomenological aspects' of the tidying-up process of law by the courts. This has been the approach, I think, of Hart in response to Dworkin's criticisms of his theory. It relies on being able to draw a distinction between questions about the nature of law and questions of a professional type about what the law is in a particular jurisdiction. In Hart's case, it relies, too, on a particular view of the role of definition. The second objection comes from those positivists who take strong discretion to be a *virtue*.

A question about the nature of law might be asked by an anthropologist or a visiting Martian. Either might want to know what the differences and similarities were between, say, custom, morality and law. A Hartian type response would be in terms of the analysis in *The Concept of Law*. It might begin by drawing the anthropologist's attention to the many similarities there are between morals and laws, for example, the overlapping content and the common language of rules, and the rule-related ideas of rights, duties, obligations, permissions and so on. The anthropologist will then be told to look for a combination of effective rules of both the duty-imposing type and the type that sets up rule-creating and rule-applying institutions. He will also look for the existence of officials who administer these institutions and learn the criteria by which these officials make decisions as to what the laws are.

Gradually, in learning the Hartian model, the anthropologist will discern differences between morals and laws. In general terms, laws will consist of those rules in society which can be created, extinguished and modified. They will also be identifiable by reference to the practice of a particular class of people, the officials of the system, who administer the necessary coercive acts which make the system effective. Law is to be distinguished from morals by its more intimate connection with the state by virtue of legislation and adjudication, and the formal method by which it is to be identified. In short, law has to do with officialdom, in a way that morality does not.

This would be the short answer to the questions the anthropologist might ask. The answer is a universal one in the sense that it is not about any particular legal system. It purports to say not only, of course, that law and morality are to be distinguished, but that they are to be distinguished in a particular way in every society. Compare this approach to what I have called the professional question. This asks, for example, 'what is the law regarding vehicles in parks in the English legal system?' It is legal system specific and situation specific. It directly asks a professional question. The lawyer need not be interested in the difference between law and morality. He wants to know how to find the answer to a specific question, maybe one concerning the conflict of laws. He has to know, for his own professional concerns, what the law is in a particular legal system.

Hart provides an answer to this question although it is implicit rather than explicit. The law on vehicles in the park in England is to be found by looking to the rules of recognition of England, that is, to the plain facts of official practice there. Statutes are identified as law and the vehicles in the park provision is found in a statute. Since the plain fact meaning of 'vehicle' includes a 20-ton truck, the answer to the professional question is found.

Drawing this distinction between these two sorts of questions shows how it is possible to emphasise different questions in legal theory. The anthropological type of question is different in emphasis to the professional one. An anthropologist wants to be equipped with some intellectual framework in making comparative studies on matters where there are close connections, but also dissimilarities, between various social phenomena. This is not to say that he must 'impose' these, nor say that there are no alternative frameworks. But the minutiae of particular laws will not concern him to the same extent as a professional lawyer. Therefore, using this distinction, a positivist of the Hartian sort could say that the particular phenomenology of particular laws of particular legal systems is not as important as being able to provide a broad canvas that can provide a general and universal account of law.

This defence of the Hartian account coheres with Hart's idea of definition for social phenomena such as law. 'Defining' is not a useful concept in this area, since it suggests something watertight, something that would provide a portmanteau-type phrase which would give a 'definitive' account of, say, what was 'essential' to law, in the same way as definition may be given of a triangle as 'a three-sided figure bounded only by straight lines'. Instead, only the central, significant, features can be given ('the central characterising features'). Questions raised about social phenomena which possess only some of these features can then only be answered in terms of comparison with the central case, say, by pointing out the similarities along with the dissimilarities.

The theory of the central case works well for law. Puzzles raised by the existence of international law, or primitive law, can now be answered by comparison with the chosen central case, in Hartian terms, the central model of the modern municipal legal system in the form of the model of primary and secondary rules. Carrying the argument into the adjudicative sphere, what actually goes on in courts is not a major worry for his theory. He does not have to answer that question in a 'definitive' way. The question of whether skateboards are prohibited from the park in England is a question like 'is international law law?' The answer is, yes, for some purposes, no for others.

This answer is only a weak one if you assume, as it may be reasonable to assume, that answers to questions about what the law is in a particular legal system require a definitive answer, one way or another. The emphasis for a practising lawyer within a particular jurisdiction is on that approach, and it is clear that Hart thinks too much emphasis can be placed upon it. I think his view is summed up in his claim that:

> Of course, it is good to be occupied with the penumbra. Its problems are rightly the daily diet of the law schools. But to be occupied with the penumbra is one thing, to be preoccupied with it is another.[2]

There is appeal to this defence of Hart when you consider the huge differences between legal systems in the minutiae of their criteria for identification of the law, their methods of adjudication, and so on. It seems reasonable to say, in defence of the Hartian approach, that the provision of a schema for answering professional-type questions is sufficient. In Hart's case, the general characterisation of legal argument as being concerned with the rules of recognition satisfies the requirement, and further elaboration is unnecessary because that is not a primary concern of the general theory. Dworkin's answer lies in his distinction between the 'force' and the 'grounds' of law.

Conventionalism

We should now turn to examine the idea that strong discretion is a *virtue* of positivism. In the previous chapter, it was convenient to regard hard cases as those cases where the rules of law, identified descriptively, 'ran out'. This view of hard cases is the one encouraged by the various forms of positivism: where there are no plain facts of the matter, there is, *a fortiori*, no law, and the judge has a discretion to make up new law. The way we came to this conclusion was by an examination of what the plain facts of law consisted in. We found, by employing, for example, Hart's idea of a rule of recognition, that the plain facts of law, at least in the United States and the United Kingdom, consisted of certain practices by officials through which we could identify, in a clear and objective way, what the criteria of legal validity were.

From this direction of approach, the emphasis is upon hard cases as those that lie in the penumbral area of human language. It is a short step from this to the view that hard cases are peripheral to more important issues and are interesting as a part of 'phenomenology' but not from any more important point of view. Under this account, 'hard cases make bad law' is a phrase that makes very real sense.

But the embarrassing question that Dworkin asks of the plain fact account is 'why accept it?' And we saw that, in fact, people such as Hart and Kelsen, and even Judge Bork, do supply reasons for acceptance. Hart's and Kelsen's concerns, while different in many ways, were united in the concern for preservation of individual moral judgment against the moral judgment of the state; Bork's concern was for the neutrality of the judge and the preservation of democratic rule.

It is now necessary to examine Dworkin's idea of conventionalism which, in his view, makes the best sense of positivism. The argument is a little complicated because, I think, the sense in which positivism is best understood is not necessarily the way its proponents understand it.

But the form, at least, of this argument should not cause difficulties. After all, it is possible, and routine, for people to defend propositions with arguments which are not the best ones, and I think that this is notably true in the case of legal theory. Legal theory and argument must be about more than the description of plain fact. This is not to say that there is no sense at all in which the 'plain facts' of law can be said to exist. They clearly do in some sense and their existence allows us to understand how it is possible for a layman to mug up a little area of law armed only with a statute.

But we must ask a question about the practical importance of accepting that view. There must be *some* virtue in accepting that the 'plain facts' view of law is correct. That virtue is not present in an account of law which purports merely to describe law. I have indicated that in fact Hart and others, such as the utilitarian positivists, and judges such as Bork, saw that virtue in, above all, clarity and certainty.

It is important, then, to distinguish *conventionalism* from the plain fact account. Conventionalism does not make any semantic or descriptive claims, but rather argues that the best interpretation of legal practice is that it is a matter of respecting and enforcing legal conventions. These legal conventions we can think of as identifiable, mainly, if not solely, by reference to the plain facts of legal practice. I have suggested the instrumental appeal of clarity as the hallmark of the plain fact approach.

What appeal does conventionalism have as a consequence? Dworkin says that law as convention serves the ideal of 'protected expectations' by giving a 'fair warning' to people about what the law requires and permits.[3] It is, in other words, clear to people what is and what is not law. The fact that a judge, when faced with a penumbral type case, cannot appeal to law under this account actually supports the ideal of protected expectations.

In the skateboard-type case, the ordinary citizen, trying to arrange his affairs, can, under the conventionalist view, do so with relative ease. A skateboard is not clearly prohibited, so it is not prohibited at all by law. A judge cannot, therefore, when faced with one of these sorts of situation, appeal to previously existing law when coming to his decision about the matter.[4]

But the idea of a gap in the law should not be a bother to conventionalism, for conventionalism defines law in terms of the plain fact of agreement and where there are no plain facts to see, the existence of hard cases is itself a plain fact. Everything is thus out in the open, and the judges cannot be charged with interstitial decision-making. When convention runs out the law cannot be appealed to, and this serves the ideal of protected expectations, because the judges cannot 'then pretend that their decisions flow in some other way from what has already been decided'.[5]

How do we now deal with hard cases under this account? As is well known, the idea of hard cases is crucial for understanding Dworkin. Many critics have said that the idea is not a good one, for all cases can be 'hard'. The idea takes some getting into, but for present purposes, they are those cases that arise where there are no plain facts of the law which determine the issue either way. The idea first arises in Dworkin in relation to his criticisms of positivism and the idea of a hard case is best approached from this standpoint. It also has more ready appeal. Hard cases are the penumbral areas of meaning under this account. Take the case of vehicles being prohibited from the park. It is in the penumbra of the word 'vehicle' whether a skateboard is a vehicle or not. Under the conventionalist account, which protects the ideal of protected expectations, there is no law in the hard cases. It will be seen that the idea relies on drawing out the consequences of the conventionalist-plain fact account, because the hard cases are those where there is unclarity and thus uncertainty.

But there are other conceptions of hard cases. Certainly some positivists would not accept the above account, because it produces the result that a significant forum of legal argument, namely, the courts, does not discuss questions of what the law requires or permits, rather than what ought for various reasons to be made into law. My view is that those positivists who rely for plain fact clarity in order to distinguish questions of legal validity from questions of morality are nevertheless bound to this view. You only need to go back to the vehicles example. There is no plain fact that skateboards either are or are not vehicles. It follows that it is not clear what the law says. That must be so under any sense of clarity, since the penumbral meaning allows either the result that the plaintiff or the prosecutor wins, or that the defendant wins. That situation must be one of paradigm unclarity.

But some positivists, such as Austin (and Kelsen), are robust in their drawing out of the consequences of their positivist theories. Austin is clear in saying that judges make new law rather than find it (in his clearly empirical sense), which means that he was not prepared to say that the law was somehow there despite not being clearly ascertainable empirically. Positivists have a virtue – clarity – to which they should consistently stick.

We should consider, however, another kind of hard case, the one where, although the identification of the law is not clearly ascertainable, there are propositions of law that as it were 'hover' around clearly ascertainable propositions. So, for example, a purported proposition of law such as 'skateboards are prohibited in the park' hovers around the clear proposition of law that 20-ton trucks are prohibited. In this kind of hard case, the judge must choose between the different 'hovering' propositions. But how?

One way to decide would be to modify the plain fact view of law, although this will mean abandoning the virtues of clarity that that account has. We could now say the law consists of not only the plain facts of law, but in addition, all the hovering propositions that can come within some more abstract convention that includes the plain facts of law. At the level of the plain facts of 20-ton vehicles being permitted in the park, and the hovering propositions that skateboards are both prohibited and permitted, no answer is forthcoming. A more abstract level, however, reaches to different plain facts of law, where, say, there is a convention that judges decide cases that are unclear in favour of the defendant (a principle of construction of penal statutes, for example).

At this level there may be conflict, say, where the statute only created a civil duty, and it is unclear whether the rule that criminal statutes should be construed in favour of the defendant extends to civil matters. And, at an even more abstract level, there may be a convention that, in civil matters, statutes should be construed so as to achieve their purpose. Here, as always, there will be possible conflicts. What if there is more than one purpose which may be ascribed to the statute? In the end, to preserve the idea of convention it will be necessary to fall back on the most abstract convention of all: judges must follow the best understanding of what the law requires.

It is clear that it will always be possible to draft a more abstract proposition of law with which judges will agree and which a particular judge may call upon to decide an instant case. To repeat, the idea of convention can be maintained into the realm of the hard cases by the method outlined above (called by Dworkin 'soft conventionalism'). Judges agree that judges must follow the best understanding of the law. No one could sensibly dispute that. We can, therefore, describe the convention as a plain fact view.[6]

But what is the virtue of this view? Clarity, except at the highest and most unusable level (judges must follow the best understanding of the law), has gone, and thus the instrumental virtues of keeping one's distance from the state (Fuller's 'consistency of dealing' between state and citizen, and Hart's insistence that what the state demands must not be conclusive of the question of obedience) and the ideal of 'settled expectations'.

Is the distinction between law and morality maintained, though? Remember: positivism insists on a distinction being drawn between questions of legal validity and questions of how we ought, morally, to act. That at least is clearly expressed in Hart, Kelsen and Austin, three of the best-known positivists. But what is the value of that distinction? Surely, clarity. And, since we have seen that to have gone, what is the point of clinging to the distinction?

We should persist, however. Let us not embrace soft conventionalism because it takes us towards conclusions that are ultimately inconsistent with 'hard' conventionalist claims. How should a conventionalist judge decide hard cases? The obvious answer is that, when there is no convention informing him what the litigant's legal position is, he should come to a decision which is 'consistent' with the relevant previous judicial and legislative decisions. In this way the ideal of protected expectations is served. Litigants can count upon a judge deciding in a way that is most consistent with that ideal, which would mean that a close look at the strict conventions, at what has clearly been decided, will give a lead as to what is required or permitted in the difficult, hard cases.

But Dworkin says that conventionalism is not a very good explanation of our legal practice because it relies on an inadequate idea of consistency. In order to protect people's expectations, conventionalism would have to adopt what he calls consistency of 'strategy' which would amount to a strict consistency with previous decisions. Why? Because the previous decisions will have been relied upon and the ideal of protected expectations will require new decisions by judges to be consistent with the previous decisions. Negatively, conventionalism claims that the conventions exhaust a person's legal rights, and so any decision must be consistent with those previously defined rights.

But strategic consistency is a poor conception of consistency in legal argument, says Dworkin, because it ignores the idea of consistency in principle. Any good lawyer recognises that there are wider issues at stake in many legal arguments beyond establishing bare 'strategic' consistency with past cases. Sometimes it is necessary to depart from convention when there is a greater issue at stake, one where the ideal of 'protected expectations' may have to be weighed against some other ideal.

This argument is a very similar argument to that used in collapsing conventionalism into soft conventionalism. The idea of consistency in principle emphasises the importance of elements in legal argument that match in weight the ideal of protected expectations, as the idea of soft conventionalism emphasises the possibility of choice of level of abstraction. As far as an explanation of our legal practices goes, conventionalism fails to grasp the complexities of legal argument, especially of some of our most important and landmark decisions.

In Dworkin's terms, 'Consistency in principle ... requires that the various standards governing the state's use of coercion against its citizens be consistent in the sense that they express a single and comprehensive vision of justice.'[7] A way to test the claim that consistency in principle is to be preferred to consistency in strategy is to ask yourself the following questions. From your own experience of legal argument is there a single and comprehensive vision of justice which the law should express? And, if so, is that the ideal of protected expectations? Is the distinctive feature of legal argument that it only impels judges to act to protect expectations, or is there a distinctive form of legal argument which permits that ideal to be weighed against others?

Can we explore the idea of conventionalism further? It is useful to provide a short summing up at this point. Dworkin has criticised the plain fact account of law, primarily on the ground that it does not make sense. This seems a bald criticism only because it is so obvious. Try it again. Why should we accept that the law's demands are just those that appear as the 'plain facts' of law? Why should the highly important question of justification of the use of state coercion depend upon simply pointing to a historically describable state of affairs?

Once we accept that there must be a point to resting the justification upon historically describable facts, it is a reasonable step to assuming that one reason may be to enshrine the ideal of protected expectations. Conventionalism serves that ideal rather well, although we feel uncomfortable at the idea that legal argument is solely to be thought of as directed at the production of *consistent* decisions.

Some readers at this point may be perfectly happy at this description of legal argument as consistency only, however. But is it true that consistency is enough? Does a good lawyer have *just* to produce consistent decisions? In the decomposed snail case of *Donoghue* v. *Stevenson*,[8] widely held to be an imaginative and innovatory (and good) decision, the House of Lords invented a new relationship of liability between manufacturer and consumer.

But it was not quite invention. It was true that the House of Lords did not decide consistently with previous conventions. These clearly did not allow ultimate consumers to sue ultimate manufacturers because of the absence of any contractual relationship. But Lord Atkin's judgment attempts a coherent connection with past decisions. It makes sense. And subsequent commentators, academic and judicial, have thought that the decision of the House of Lords made sense in principle, even if there was no 'consistency of strategy'. The approach was to say that the courts had, in many particular instances, given remedies for the kind of harm done to the woman made ill from the bottle's contents, for the kind of wrong done by the fizzy drink manufacturer, even although there were no formal precedents.

Lord Atkin engaged in the same abstract sort of reasoning as Warren and Brandeis:

> ... the duty which is common to all the cases where liability is established must logically be based upon some element common to the cases where it is found to exist ... in English law there must be, and is, some general conception of relations giving rise to a duty of care, of which the particular cases found in the books are but instances.[9]

What is notable about his judgment is his awareness of the abstract nature of the route he was taking. Although it does not seem to me to be a necessary feature of this kind of creative argument that the participant have a conscious realisation of what he is doing, it does nevertheless appear to be an ability that great judges have.

There have, of course, been criticisms of the reasoning employed by Lord Atkin, mainly along the lines of the slender authorities he relied on (for example, his reliance upon a very wide statement in a case called *Heaven* v. *Pender*[10]). But the point I am concerned here to make is not vitally dependent upon Lord Atkin's decision being right, but upon whether the general method he employed was right. A conventionalist has to say that the decision was wrong because it did not consistently apply the convention that, in the absence of a contractual relationship, there could be no remedy. This line was, in fact, taken by a dissenting judge, Lord Buckmaster, who criticised the majority decision because it was 'simply to misapply to tort doctrine applicable to sale and purchase'.[11] He apparently thought that this was a sufficient argument to deny the woman her claim. How should we compare the reasoning of Lord Atkin and Lord Buckmaster? In some circles, Lord Atkin is thought to be entering a fairyland of abstraction.[12] In others, Lord Buckmaster is rigidly favouring a demarcation between tort and contract in the face of the demands of justice. Do we have to say that Lord Atkin has simply got his jurisprudence wrong, that is, that he has completely misunderstood his role as a judge?

These positions make a caricature of judicial reasoning. A more subtle account, free of the shackles of conventionalism, allows us to say that, for example, although Lord Atkin gave less weight than he might have to the role of the legislature in matters of manufacturer–consumer relations (because of the consequences of this important decision), he nevertheless had a superior conception of the point of legal argument than Lord Buckmaster.[13]

Convention to achieve co-ordination?

Although the protection of expectations is one obvious justification for following a plain facts view of law, it is not the only one. Some writers have suggested that the most important reason is co-ordination, having in mind 'prisoners' dilemma'-type situations, where the best solution can only be achieved by acceptance of a common standard, rather than by individual, but perfectly rational, action. Here what may be important for a judge is not strategic consistency with previous decisions, but, at least for some cases, the creation of a new convention for co-ordinative purposes. For example, a judge may be justified under this new rationale in declaring cheques to have the same legal status as money[14] or, perhaps, declaring landlords to be the legal owners of tenants' fixtures.

But does this modified explanation gain us much? It achieves more flexibility, because judges need not stick to strategic consistency where a problem of co-ordination arises. It may even be that the idea of co-ordination can be stretched to cover cases like the decomposed snail case. We would then understand the new convention imposing a qualified liability directly between ultimate manufacturers and ultimate consumers to create co-ordination between these two groups. But that would stretch the idea too far, Dworkin says, because it would collapse the idea of co-ordination, which is primarily about achieving what individuals cannot on their own achieve, into the idea of regulation of any group activity whatsoever. Since governance of human life by conventions is just the regulation of group activity, we gain nothing by extending the meaning of co-ordination here. What we are instead looking for is the idea of flexibility, and if this is the important idea, as Dworkin says, we should embrace that idea and abandon conventionalism.[15]

The real problem with conventionalism

Conventionalism requires only that for a convention to exist on some point of law, there is a bare agreement among lawyers. Thus, the justification of the rule that says that the clear words of a statutory provision are law is simply, under conventionalism, that lawyers are agreed on that fact. This is the 'plain fact' point about conventionalism. The convention is defined by agreement, and agreement alone. Once we are reminded of this, it becomes clear why the co-ordination rationale has appealed to some writers (but shows the difficulties, too, in extending that rationale to the decomposing snail case: what was the content of the bare agreement of the members of the House of Lords?).

But the idea of 'bare' agreement constituting the core of legal argument precludes any depth of argument. Understanding this point is of fundamental importance to understanding Dworkin and it is a theme throughout his work. A dramatic way of putting this point is to note the difference between a proposition's being true by convention and its being true by independent conviction. We all agree that it is wrong to torture babies, but the arguments that it is wrong relate to the substance of the act, not the fact of there being a convention that babies ought not to be tortured. Our convictions that babies ought not to be tortured depend upon the substance of the argument, not on the fact that others agree with us. Importantly, that others agree with us plays no part in our conviction, and the idea of people agreeing on this matter amounts to no more than saying that people coincide in their views on this matter.

This example drawn from the nature of moral argument by Dworkin is intended to introduce the idea that it is by reference to the substance of the arguments that legal argument, especially in hard cases, has important character. For example, in the decomposed snail case, we are to view each judgment as one reporting the judge's convictions about the responsibility of ultimate manufacturers, rather than a report of the judge's views on what decision would be most consistent with previous law.

Here, it is much more edifying to talk, when judges agree on a matter that goes to their convictions, of a *consensus of conviction* rather than an agreement. And it makes better sense to suppose that it is judges' convictions that are at work here because that would explain more clearly why there are often very slight but important differences of opinion between judges over matters where the end result – the judgment or the decision – is the same. It makes better sense, too, of the sorts of reasons that judges give for their views. Judges report their beliefs about what the right decisions are in terms vastly more complicated than an arithmetic of conventions. Mostly their arguments are ones conducted *within* the rules, not *about* them.

Taking this position does not deny the relevance of conventions in law, or indeed, in other areas where social rules are applied. It is clear that an important part of legal argument, especially where problems of co-ordination occur, is simply the pointing to the existence of the appropriate convention. And among ordinary social conventions, we can obey rules not because we think they are justified (or have any independent 'meaning'), but just because we do not wish to offend those people who think they are justified. A non-believer might doff his cap in church for just that reason, for example.

Pragmatism

If more flexibility is needed, why not abandon conventionalism? Conventionalism is rigid in two sorts of way. First, it does not seem to provide an explanation of our current legal practices simply because our general understanding of legal argument is more complex than a 'reading off' of conventions. Even when we beef that notion up, by introducing the ideas of consistency of strategy and co-ordination, we are left with no more than an arithmetic of rules. Second, conventionalism does not provide us with a sufficient range of justifications for our legal practices because it relies upon the central idea of law as the historical facts of bare agreement among lawyers as to what counts as law.

Dworkin's abandonment of conventionalism is important because it represents his departure from positivism. Conventionalism is, in his view, the best form positivism can take, and it loses out on the two dimensions of description and justification of our legal practices. (It is at this point that the defender of positivism should make his defence. Is conventionalism the best account of positivism? How sound are the reasons given by Dworkin for abandoning it?)

What might we consider in conventionalism's place? His answer is that the requirement of greater flexibility that even amended conventionalism would not allow could be met by what he calls pragmatism. This doctrine is put forward as a better theory – one that better explains and justifies our legal practices – than conventionalism.

Pragmatism offers the greatest scope for flexibility. It denies that past decisions create any rights which bind the judge. It is, therefore, what Dworkin calls a 'sceptical' conception of law. Pragmatism is to be seen, then, as the opposite of conventionalism. Judges may now act with the maximum flexibility in deciding what is the best decision, not being bound by any conventions.

In practice, however, pragmatism would be less radical because judges would in many cases look to past decisions in order to work out what the best solution was. Thus, the best decision may be just to continue past practice, the difference with conventionalism being that a judge would not be bound by any past decision to follow it or even take it into account.

Since Dworkin talks of past 'political decisions' not being binding upon a judge, he presumably includes legislative enactments as not creating rights. The idea of pragmatism is, then, a very radical idea in principle. But, of course, in working out what was the best decision, so often recourse would have to be made to the content and status of past decisions. Judges may well adopt the view that past decisions of the legislature should be strictly followed because that is in the best interest in the long run for society. And they might take only a slightly less strict view about the common law.

The theory just described articulates a view of law shared by a number of radical commentators on law in the United Kingdom, in particular that of Griffith in his popular book on the United Kingdom judiciary, *The Politics of the Judiciary*. In that book he criticises judges for being biased towards 'law and order', meaning that, despite what justice demanded, especially in the field of employment law, judges would seek justifications which stood on the side of what had been previously decided. Griffith's view is that the United Kingdom judiciary as a whole is heavily biased in favour of management, against strikes and the working man, and that this bias is assisted and reinforced by recourse to conventions of past judicial behaviour, these conventions themselves created by subjective conservative preferences.

What Griffith means is that where the 'law' and justice clash, justice must prevail, and that 'law' refers to judicial conventions alone. But he does not appear to envisage alternative ways of conceiving of law other than by convention, or judicial decision-making in accordance with anything other than what Dworkin calls 'bare consistency'.

Does the idea of pragmatism help here? In Griffith's case it encourages the rather easy thinking about law that says 'I don't like this law, so it ought not to be followed'. What the law should be becomes solely a matter of one's own subjective political preferences arrived at without reference to the law as it already stands. That is the feature of pragmatism which promotes willingness to abandon settled rights in favour of what is best for the future.

The problem of rights

If judges are to take into account past political decisions, what precisely is the force of those decisions? If the judge is not bound to follow past precedents, then it cannot be correct to say that people have rights created by such precedents. The judge will always have the power to depart from precedent when that is necessary to achieve flexibility and there would be no argument that had the force, as the assertion of a right has, that the need to be flexible must give way to the need to recognise a right.

But, Dworkin says, the less radical working of pragmatism in practice will mean that judges will act in most cases 'as if' people had rights. Would this matter? Is there a significant difference between people's having rights and judges acting 'as if' they had rights? Well, yes. If flexibility means that judges can ignore a person's claim to be treated in accordance with precedent then that person cannot have a right. The right exists only in so far as its recognition is in accordance with a decision that is the best practical one for the community. That is to say that it has no independent existence.

There are two ways 'as-if' rights could be maintained in the community. First, the judges could deceive people into thinking that they had rights, and that arguments in court were about rights that people brought with them to court, supported by the precedents. Worse, I think, would be the case if judges deceived themselves that people came to court with rights that could be ignored whenever community interest required it. Second, if it were widely understood that community interest came first and that rights argument, when the crunch came, was a sham, there would be little incentive in many (I suspect, important) cases for people to go to litigation. Why? Because the effect of such cases would be to create new rules for the future, not enforce pre-existing rights.

This account does not fit well with the way we think about law. We believe ourselves to have legal rights which pre-exist legal decisions about those rights. You may be sceptical about this conclusion, at this stage, in relation to hard cases but not, I venture, in relation to easy cases. You have, I suggest you believe, legal rights in relation to the coins in your pocket, the clothes you wear, your employer, your working conditions, the police, the tax authorities, and so on. In order to understand the thrust of Dworkin's theory it is important to appreciate that this simple and unanalysed idea of legal right is both widely held and perfectly intelligible.

I am aware, however, that the idea of rights throws many people into paroxysms because of its ideological connotations. To some it imports an assumption of middle class complacency, of bourgeois individualism and materialism. To others it imports too much of the wrong kind of freedom and, at worst, anarchy. To yet others, calling themselves utilitarians, rights have only a shorthand meaning expandable into claims for society as a whole.[16] Yet to others, it imports a loose understanding of the complexities of moral language, whereby 'first order' assertions about rights have a function which, as a 'second order' understanding shows, is fundamentally meaningless. Others, of course, are sceptical about everything including their own existence.

I suggest that we place this all to one side at this stage. The difficulties raised are answered by Dworkin in his extremely important discussion on 'external' and 'internal' scepticism in *Law's Empire*, although he has a clear understanding of the difficulties involved throughout his work. We only want at this stage to see whether this theory of pragmatism is concordant with the way we think law is used and justified *in our own lives*. I find it difficult to believe that, in the United States and United Kingdom jurisdictions, someone could seriously believe that he had *not* one legal right.

Pragmatism is better than conventionalism because it allows more flexibility in determining a better society. The conventions were a bind on judges, holding them too much to the past. Pragmatism allows judges to make all sorts of judgment about sensible and imaginative ways the community might develop.

The idea of pragmatism does not prevent legislatures or judges from making decisions for the improvement of society and this is the strength pragmatism has over conventionalism, which ties decision-making just to the bare conventions. But pragmatism only recognises previous decisions according individuals 'rights' as instrumental to making society better and that account does not, in Dworkin's terms, take rights seriously.

The fundamental reason that Dworkin has for abandoning conventionalism and pragmatism and for embracing the idea of integrity is that it is only by linking legal argument with the idea of genuine political *community* that law can have a properly moral content. Conventionalism justified community coercion by reference to bare agreement. Pragmatism's more flexible justification made no real sense of a group's past history. Integrity, on the other hand, both united the past and the present and incorporated the fraternal idea of treating all members of the same community as equals. It was this idea, too, as we saw in Chapter 4, that was at the basis of Dworkin's analysis of the ideas of democracy and judicial review.

Hard cases as 'pivotal' not 'penumbral'

We have now seen some of the problems thrown up by the so-called hard cases both in the course of the historical development of positivism and in the forms of reasoning engaged by judges in the Anglo-American context. There has been an important change of emphasis. Our introduction to the idea of hard cases was through the factor of uncertainty brought about by imperfect human foresight, and the inherent vagueness of natural language. The hard cases were thus to be viewed as penumbral and peripheral to the core and central emphasis on law as objectively determinable plain fact.

The focus of attention for positivism is clarity. As we have seen, this focus relegates attention away from the hard cases. Their interest to the positivist is peripheral. But clarity and respect for the ideal of 'protected expectations' are not the only virtues. Let us take the following tack and make the focus of our attention the penumbral, hovering cases. Immediately, we are faced with the problem of making sense of what goes on in the courts, for it is in them that the hard cases are fought (as well as classrooms and law reviews). It is in the courts that we learn what are the arguments that count towards certain decisions rather than others, what rights and duties citizens have, and so on. It is understanding this focus of interest that is the key to understanding Dworkin's legal philosophy, for he considers these sorts of case to have a 'pivotal' significance rather than a peripheral one, as 'pivotal cases testing fundamental principles, not as borderline cases calling for some more or less arbitrary line to be drawn'.[17]

What arguments support this view? The main one is practical. It is from the courts that we obtain the arguments relevant to the direct application of state coercive power. Each day, in all the courts, a vast number of decisions are made which result in the use of state coercion to reduce personal freedoms and to redistribute property. The arguments bringing about these decisions are patently not of the plain fact sort and are represented by an argumentative attitude rather than the application of deductive rules implied by the plain fact approach.

'Easy' or 'clear' cases

If it is right that hard cases are pivotal rather than penumbral, what is the status of clear cases? The short answer is that the assumption that a case is clear is the result of a process of reasoning and not the start. The penumbral nature of a legislative enactment, according to Hart, for example, is defined by the existence of the core: without the core we could not have a penumbra. But hard cases are hard only because there are genuinely competing arguments as to what is the best understanding of the law. The easy cases are just those cases where there are no such doubts.

The assertion that there are cases in which there are no doubts usually meets a sceptical response. But the answer lies in a simple appeal to your own understanding of legal argument. There are laws which are not open to doubt. The maximum speed limit on motorways is an example. It is just that it is a mistake to suppose that such examples of clear laws are raw 'plain fact' data from which we proceed to understand difficult cases. We regard laws such as the maximum speed limit as having a paradigmatic status as law, and we would think that any understanding of law that denied them this status would not be a competent one.

Mistaking paradigms of law for the plain facts of law is one of the most serious errors in Anglo-American jurisprudence. The 'folksy' appeal of the original intention theory as propounded and used by Judge Robert Bork is an example of the error. In *Dronenburg*, for example, the clarity of the previous law and its contrast with the 'unclarity' of its extension of a right of privacy to homosexual relations was, for him, a reading off of what the plain facts of law required. No plain facts said that Dronenburg's homosexual conduct was protected, so Dronenburg was not protected.

But it became apparent that Bork failed to understand that this clarity of the previous law was the result of his view, shared within a consensus, that certain ways of making law, say, by way of legislation, or by judicial decision, dependably create law. In fact, he gives good reasons for asserting the plain fact view, although he offers them rather as an afterthought. These are that the legislature consisted of a representative majority view and judges were bound to defer to it.

The idea of 'paradigms' might strike some as very strange. If there is a consensus, a plateau of coinciding views about what constitutes law, then surely this plateau serves to inform us about what is uncontroversially law in a plain fact way. But to deny the 'reasons behind the law' ignores the crucial fact that consensus is a *coincidence* of views, each of which provides a separate justification. Again, the view that there are specific, clear rules of law is a result of particular views, not the starting-point of those views.

One very important result of the distinction between plain fact and consensus and the consequent idea of paradigms of law is that the idea of law is freed of rigidity. Paradigms have their point because they act as stable plateaus from which we can make sense of the shifting arguments about them. In this sense, someone who rejects a paradigm makes a mistake for, as Dworkin says, 'paradigms anchor interpretations'.[18]

On the other hand, because of the idea of consensus, paradigms are not rigidly unchangeable. It will always be possible for someone with very different convictions about, say, justice, or fairness, to conclude that what is uncontroversially accepted as law ought not to be so accepted, and so be able to persuade us that our views should change. As views change, the consensus shifts and the paradigm changes. Judge Bork's view that plain facts drive the law does not allow for this possibility; the 'law', for him, is just 'there'. And is it not simply true that a shifting of paradigms as to what counts as good law describes the development of the common law, marked significantly by the decisions of great cases?

The existence of paradigms of law really bothers some people. One of the criticisms that the Critical Legal Studies movement makes is that the paradigms of law creation in our legal system are weighted towards supporting middle class interests and capitalist aspirations. They are particularly critical of the movement in legal education towards the economic approach to law, for example.[19] Another criticism is that there are paradigms, those of 'liberal individualism' and 'altruism', which are fundamentally in conflict, although contemporary legal argument attempts to minimise the conflicts for ideological purposes.[20]

For some members of the movement at least, it appears, formal analyses of legal argument are worse than worthless because they only serve to strengthen the existing paradigms of legal arguments, by strengthening the prevailing middle class capitalist leanings of the system.[21] At best, legal analysis is only worthless because it tries to do the impossible of reconciling the irreconcilable.[22] But a more rigorous understanding of the complexities of legal argument, in which it is understood that laws, including legal paradigms, are changeable, should lead these critics to the sophistication in criticism they are seeking. For the Critical Legal Studies scholars just assume that there is *no* argument worth joining. But they should appreciate that it does not inexorably follow that, if you join in legal argument, you are encouraging the *present* system. The recognition that there can be different, and controversial, kinds of argument that are characteristically legal does not mean that 'the law' represents a chaotic and conflicting set of norms based on different class interests.

To conclude, then, Dworkin provides us with a new focus in law. At first sight, this focus is upon the hard cases, now to be characterised by the examination of areas of law which are controversial in a more fundamental way than the characterisation of such areas as peripheral, or penumbral to more important laws. At second sight, a deeper understanding shows us that, because of the consensus nature of legal paradigms, it is possible for all cases to be hard cases, and that the real focus is not on the difference between what is clear or unclear, but upon the quality of the underlying legal argument justifying the invocation of the coercive powers of the state.

The different senses of 'discretion'

Dworkin has been cited on numerous occasions for having drawn attention to different senses which the idea of discretion has in our legal system. His first article[23] was on this topic and it is interesting to see how he has developed the ideas that he first discussed there into his later work, in particular, his 'Is Law a System of Rules?'. Despite the large number of approving citations in books and articles, it seems to me that the different senses which he is very careful to elaborate in this article are nevertheless widely misunderstood. The reason is the one that bogs many people down with his theory: the apparent lack of 'objectivity'. The problem of objectivity explains the popularity of the 'plain fact' theory, too, I think.

It is a widespread feeling, throughout the Anglo-American legal systems, that the existence of official discretion to make decisions is undesirable, even dangerous, because it implies 'subjective' licence and lack of control. But the notion of discretion has not, I think, been adequately understood. I think that this has been particularly so in the case of administrative lawyers seeking to control the discretionary exercise of powers of officials making administrative, as opposed to judicial, decisions. The problem of control is too often unclearly and unhelpfully posed as one of whether the matter should be one controlled by 'law' or by 'discretion'.[24]

Dworkin concentrates his analysis on distinguishing several different senses of discretion and it is disappointing that administrative lawyers have not seized upon his analysis. There are some modern trends the other way and these are to be encouraged.[25] In a sense, modern administrative lawyers have been too practical because they jump immediately to focus upon the question of remedy. As a result, they obscure from view the reasons that lead them to suppose that the officials in question really do have excessive powers. Wide powers mean that alternatives such as special review bodies, or more tightly drafted legislation, or, very commonly, more 'public accountability', should be introduced.

But all of these methods of constraint make two assumptions. One is that widely worded grants of power ('the Minister may, if he thinks appropriate ...', etc.) really do grant the wide powers they are often assumed to.[26] But that will not be the case if the width of the powers is determined not by what seem to be 'given' by the plain words but by legal argument. The question would be: what is the extent of the Minister's powers? and not: given that the powers are so wide, how best are we to approach the question of containing them? The mistake made here is to think of the law as somehow 'given', and I have already discussed this at some length.

A less obvious assumption is that it is not necessary to spell out why officials should not have wide powers. This sounds odd because it is reasonable to assume that, on the whole, it is undesirable that very general powers be in the hands of officials. This in part explains why a rather empirical approach is made towards dealing with the problem. Given that official discretion should be 'controlled', what is the best way of going about it?

It is not surprising, then, that the approach has a descriptive as opposed to a normative slant. The question has become not: what are the relevant arguments for defining an official's discretionary powers? but: what are the best techniques for containing official power? This latter question tends to hide the normative assumption against wide discretionary powers by concentrating on different techniques of *control* and not on the force of argument. Why not the 'techniques' of argument? Of course, the techniques of 'control' (let us say, as opposed to *argument*) may assume major importance when the official concerned is a policeman, or a social worker, but it is a distortion to suppose that all official action should be viewed in this way.

Dworkin's analysis of the idea of discretion shows how distinguishing between these questions matters, because the essential idea for him is for discretion to be centrally seen as *judgment*. Officials, specifically judges, must exercise appropriate judgment when exercising discretion, and that judgment must be of a public nature responsive to public argument. The appropriateness or not of a particular judgment made in the exercise of discretion is one that can be tested and controlled by legal argument.

Of course, this is not to argue that it is practically feasible for all decision-making to be controlled by application to the courts. Clearly, some sorts of decisions are not primarily about the rights of citizens but primarily about the best way of carrying out certain policies, say, on urban planning. But understanding the difference in the kinds of decisions and the kinds of discretion which are relevant to them relies largely on understanding what kind of discretion is appropriate to judicial decision-making. At the baseline in our Anglo-American jurisdiction, decisions affecting citizens' rights are thought to be within the range of the courts' purview at the very least, obviously so in the United States and maybe only increasingly so in the United Kingdom.

The upshot of this is, I suggest, that tribunals and other bodies set up to control the use of official discretion must reflect the discretionary judgment of the courts and differ only where the special subject matter of the body requires it to carry out its specific purpose. If we think of discretion as judgment, this conclusion is an easy one: judgments made by officials of the state must be made in accordance with appropriate criteria, and can be wrong. The idea of discretion as licence carries no weight.

Discretion analysed

There are three senses of 'discretion' analysed by Dworkin, two 'weak' senses and one 'strong'.[27] The first sense is the one I have already referred to, that of judgment. A sergeant, for example, 'may have been left a lot of discretion' when, say, he is instructed to select his five most experienced men. We mean here that although he has not been given instructions any more precise than this, he has to exercise judgment in deciding which of his men have the most experience. An understanding of this sense is crucial to understanding Dworkin, and his example is helpful.

It is, of course, possible to say that the choice for the sergeant is difficult, or that it cannot be determined by any special test. It is clear, too, that we can criticise his choice. We can criticise him for a lack of judgment, as well as for disobeying a clear rule, as we would, for example, if he chose not to select his most experienced men, or chose only two men, or even chose only women. This sense of discretion permeates the common law, and examples of it should be familiar to anyone. One of these is encapsulated in the famous example of the judge's discretion in this sense in declaring a skateboard to be a vehicle for the purposes of the statute prohibiting vehicles from the park. It was discretion of this sort that the judges exercised in the right of privacy cases already discussed, as well as in *Donoghue* v. *Stevenson* and, indeed, *in most cases coming before the courts*.

But a full discussion of the importance of discretion is not possible without distinguishing this first weak sense from the 'strong' sense. This occurs in the situation, in Dworkin's words, where a person 'is simply not bound by the standards set by the authority in question'.[28] We now imagine the sergeant simply being ordered to pick any five men for patrol he chooses. Here the particular qualities of the men are not specified and the sergeant has a 'strong' discretion in making the choice.

The contrast between these two senses is important and has caused a number of difficulties in understanding Dworkin. He is at pains to stress that strong discretion 'is not tantamount to licence' and that a proper judgment be made, for example, not one that is stupid, malicious or careless. It is just that his decision is not controlled by a standard furnished by the particular authority in the context of which the question of discretion is raised. If the sergeant is bound by standards in this sort of case, too, how can the distinction between weak and strong discretion be as sharp as Dworkin appears to maintain?

This characterisation of the difference is, I think, unfortunate. To say that the area of strong discretion is that where the 'particular' authority has not 'furnished' the standard looks very like saying that the judge has strong discretion just because there is no pedigree test identifying the standards he is to apply. And if we are to agree to *that* we are bound by definition to say that positivists remit us to a theory of strong discretion in hard cases. A positivist might well deny the validity of Dworkin's move because it is circular and may reasonably demand a stronger argument to lead him to suppose that positivists are bound to accept strong discretion in hard cases.

For reasons such as these, his argument has received the criticism that in fact the idea of discretion is not amenable to the sharp distinctions he maintains and exists rather as a gradation from a very weak discretion ('are skateboards vehicles?'), through less weak versions ('what is *reasonable* restraint of trade?'), to a strong discretion ('the Minister may, *if he sees fit ...*').

But this criticism, common though it is, does not help. It is, in part, like collapsing the distinction between youth and maturity by pointing out the gradation between the two. Granted the gradation, what follows? That youth and maturity are the same? Of course not. I think, too, that the distinction between the first weak sense and the strong sense serves a useful purpose in our understanding of the legal process, which I shall attempt to show shortly. If it can be shown to have an independent purpose, then the distinction should provide some non-tautological support to Dworkin's view that positivists can only support a theory of strong judicial discretion.

In any case, the positivist can be embarrassed if one simply asks him what the test is by which legal standards binding judges in weak discretion cases are identified. My experience is that a positivist only produces arguments of the conventionalist kind. He constructs more and more abstract conventions justifying what I termed the 'hovering' propositions in hard cases. He will end up with the soft conventionalist approach: his 'test' will amount to 'being in accordance with the best sense which can be made of the standard furnished by the particular authority'. This test will be of such a complex and abstract nature that connection with the point of adopting the conventionalist approach will be all but lost.

The judge has a weak discretion where he has to come to a decision about what is 'reasonable' in the circumstances, like the sergeant who has the weak discretion to decide who of his men is the most experienced. In these sorts of case, it is clear what the 'standard furnished by the particular authority' is. But these sorts of case are not the most common kind and the more obvious and problematical case is where a judge must make a decision of the analogical sort, say, where he must decide whether a skateboard is a vehicle or whether a right to privacy of unmarried heterosexual couples extends to homosexual couples. The judge has a weak discretion here and there just is no 'standard furnished by the particular authority'. It surely cannot be an authoritative legislative enactment or judicial decision which simply declares that the court must apply the intention of the legislature, or enforce the citizens right to a fair decision.

Dworkin can, in other words, stick to his original position. This is that positivism cannot both have a relatively simple pedigree test for law and, in addition, claim that when a judge faces a question such as the right to privacy question in the homosexual hard case he is bound by law. In order to avoid becoming stuck in the quagmire of soft conventionalism, the positivist must deny the existence of weak discretion altogether. He cannot say that there is weak discretion just because that denies that the standards were 'furnished by the particular authority'.

We can make use here of Dworkin's analogy with art. It is helpful, in an intuitive kind of way, for understanding the distinction between these two crucial senses of 'discretion'. The analogy with art raises its own problems, but I believe the analogy helps.

Let us take the musicologist of Chapter 3 who wishes to compose a symphonic movement to complete Schubert's Unfinished Symphony. Does this project make sense? The short answer is that it does, because this sort of thing has been done before in all fields of art. Novels, poems and plays have been completed by persons other than the authors. Whether or not the piece uncompleted by the original artist counts as 'true' art or 'part of the work', and so on, should not concern us here. Rather, what in general is the way in which the musicologist should go about his task?

I shall make the following suggestions. He would have to be aware of Schubert's style of composing and the genre of the classical symphony, before studying the particular nature of the first and second movements and the sketches for the third. He would have to know the key in which they had been written and, further, be aware of the various themes and tempos. Most important, he would have to get a 'feel' for the character of these movements. Then, in the light of all this, he could begin to write a further movement.

This example is helpful because it shows that it is possible to exercise a certain freedom, a discretion, while at the same time being bound by certain general standards. A musicologist could be criticised, as indeed musicologists have, for being unimaginative ('not equal to the original creator's powers' is usually unfair) or for failing to capture the correct sense or 'feel', because they do just that. But there is no question that there is any *pedigree* test by which the appropriate criticism should be made. There is no 'standard furnished by the particular authority in question', either by the rules of harmony or laid down by Schubert himself. The idea, in fact, seems anathema to art because it appears to deny the idea of creation. True, it may be because of this that some people might wish to deny the force of this analogy with art.

But it pays to press on. Let us take another musicologist, or even someone who knows little about music, who wishes to finish the Schubert Unfinished Symphony. He has never listened to Schubert and does not know what a key signature is, or what writing in the classical genre means. He nevertheless writes a piece of music which he entitles 'Schubert: the Unfinished Symphony, final movement', and scores it for guitars, drums and a 1,000-strong male choir accompanied by bagpipes on a five note tone row. It is easy to conclude here that he has not written the third movement, but a completely different work. This is not to say that it would be *impossible* to use this scoring, or even to depart from the classical tonality, for it to count as the last movement of the Symphony, just that it would be extremely unlikely given this second musicologist's lack of knowledge about Schubert's music.

The second musicologist shows us how the work of creation can be consistent with being bound with certain specific, but not pedigree-defined, standards. The second musicologist is, of course, bound by standards set through a different dimension. Assuming he is serious, he will consider himself to be bound by certain standards of his art. But he fails to achieve what he claims to achieve, the finishing of Schubert's symphony, because he ignores important standards appropriate to that task.

Some people find the excursion into art, regarded by so many as a purely subjective experience, too remote from the concerns of law. But it is instructive to ask yourself why if that is your view. Can legal argument be creative? Ask some lawyers who are experienced in courtroom legal argument and you will soon find that it is a highly creative business. Are the great legal judgments creative? It is very difficult to argue that they are not. We can resort to denying that 'creative' judgments are in accordance with law, as Dworkin says the positivists must argue if they are not to become caught in a maze of soft conventionalism. And is it a satisfactory reply to say that all creative judgments are not about law at all? If we do not think that is satisfactory, then I suggest that we are drawn to the idea that the musical analogy brings out so well: that it is possible to be both constrained and creative at the same time. It is precisely this idea that the idea of weak discretion is supposed to capture.

This combination of creation with constraint makes it possible to see why 'discretion' and 'law' are not opposite, mutually contradictory ideas. It shows that the question which is frequently posed by administrative lawyers in England, 'is the matter one controlled by law, or is it a matter of discretion?', is misconceived.

A second 'weak' sense of discretion

Dworkin isolates a second weak sense of discretion which refers only to the fact that an official has the authority to make a decision. This sense should be unproblematic but it is frequently confused with the first weak sense. The second sense means only that the official has the authority, as when we say that the sergeant has the discretion as to which experienced men he chooses. It is clearly different from the first sense, because we can say of his decision that, although it stands (he has the discretion to decide), he exercised it badly (his use of discretion showed that he has bad judgment). In other words, we can recognise that a decision can both stand and be a bad one.

This phenomenon is, of course, very common in law. The High Court's ruling stands, until overturned by a higher court, by virtue of rules that give its decisions that power. There are good practical reasons for that. Law is an eminently practical enterprise. Decisions must be made and carried out even when there is a possibility that they may be wrong. Hence we should have no difficulty in saying: 'this is the law, because it is decided so by the House of Lords, but I think it is wrong, because it was based on faulty reasoning'. It is not only academic writers who say this sort of thing (too little academic legal writing is characterised by the approach, incidentally). Lawyers often argue that previous decisions of courts were wrong in law, and put those arguments to judges in real cases.

The idea can only be made sense of if we recognise the distinction between the court's discretion to decide, willy-nilly, and its discretion, in hard cases, to *make a judgment*. The distinction creates some difficulties for positivism, too, because the decision of the highest court supposedly provides the test of pedigree. If the Supreme Court or the House of Lords comes to a decision, that is the law. How can it then make sense to say both that it is the law and that it was wrong in law?

There is one answer but it employs Dworkin's distinction rather than shows it to be otiose. This is that the decision is wrong because an authoritative previous ruling was not considered by the court. In other words, the decision was a *per incuriam* decision. But this is not a satisfactory answer, because *per incuriam* decisions are relatively rare (or rarely admitted) and criticism of the legal basis for the decisions of final courts ranges far wider than the use of the *per incuriam*-type criticism would allow. Lawyers and academic writers do not usually criticise judgments because crucial precedents have been overlooked, but for much more complex reasons, reasons of the sort that are enmeshed in different levels of abstraction and which attempt to make sense of the law as a whole.

A preliminary conclusion

I have described the plain fact theory, warts and all, with a view to seeing both its initial appeal and its serious limitations. One of the problems with presenting it as starkly as I have is that, properly understood, it carries very little persuasive value. How could anyone ever have accepted it? Has Dworkin been jousting with a straw man? Is there really no better form of positivism existing, which can resist Dworkin's attacks?

To sum up once more. The plain fact theory says the law exists 'out there' independently of theory. No one should accept that theory. Nevertheless, there are significant signs in Anglo-American jurisprudence that people have done so and still do. Dworkin rejects it because he does not see the point of it.

The plain fact theory can be given point in the form of conventionalism in the ideal of protected expectations. But, Dworkin argued, this did not make the best sense of law because it was too inflexible. Abandoning the idea that law could be identified in any conventional way at all in pragmatism, however, produced flexibility at a cost. That was that we were forced to abandon the idea of any person having a right to be treated by government as part of a community in which the past is connected to the future in a consistent and coherent way.

The major disadvantage with conventionalism was that it could not cope with the bridging of the gaps between historically identifiable conventions. The postulation of 'higher' and more abstract conventions only supplied solutions ambivalent between litigants, unless the idea of the 'best' convention were supplied and that, as we saw, was not answerable in an historical way. The major disadvantage with pragmatism was that it denied the intimacy of connection between what had gone before in the law and present decision-making. Both theories ignored the fundamental feature of legal argument that we take for granted in all legal argument: that any proposition of law we assert must 'cohere' with all other propositions of law.

From his argument that law must have point, Dworkin asserts that penumbral decisions are not linguistically penumbral, nor phenomenologically peripheral, but highly significant. The hard cases bring to the surface the reasons why we should accept the easy cases as easy. The requirements of consistency and coherency in decision-making mean that the best decisions in such cases must be consistent in principle with those reasons.

But let us remember the philosophical foundations of Dworkin's approach to understanding law. He takes explicit positions on the troubled problems of objectivity and subjectivity of judgment. Many, if not most, of the difficulties in understanding him rest upon the fetishistic hold of the plain fact theory in, I regret to say, its primary and primitive sense, as something 'objectively' 'out there'.

Integrity and equality

The connection between equality and his criticisms of both conventionalism and pragmatism is very important in Dworkin's work. After all, what *makes* integrity is its ability to achieve coherency in principle by keeping its commitment to treating people as equals. Both conventionalism and pragmatism fail because they are, consecutively, too rigid and too arbitrary to require government to speak with one voice to all citizens. We have seen, too, the way Dworkin develops the connection between the idea of community and the treatment of the citizens who compose it through the idea of integrity. But what does 'treating people as equals' really mean? It is this very abstract idea of 'treating people as equals', one of Dworkin's most fundamental ideas, which must now be examined.

Notes

1 See Finnis, *Natural Law and Natural Rights* (1980) p. 21.

2 Hart, *Essays in Jurisprudence and Philosophy* (1983), p. 72.

3 Hart's doctrine of 'fair opportunity' is an important parallel here. See his *Punishment and Responsibility* (1968) Oxford.

4 Dworkin adds sophistication to the plain fact, conventional view here, by asserting the existence of implicit conventions in addition to the explicit conventions constituted in the plain fact account as bare agreement among lawyers. Implicit conventions, he says, consist of 'the set of propositions that follow from the best or soundest interpretation of the convention ...' p. 123. This is an unfortunate addition necessitated by his having abandoned the 'plain fact' approach for conventionalism. The strength of conventionalism lies in its protecting, as he says, the ideal of protected expectations. It achieves this by adopting the 'plain fact' approach. The ideal is not supported by the idea of implicit convention if *that* idea relies on the 'best' approach because that will involve controversy – unclarity – in determining what is 'best'.

Perhaps Dworkin just means that agreement includes those propositions that are entailed by what is clearly agreed, but where the entailment is not appreciated, or is overlooked. This would be the case where what is entailed comes under a dramatically different description, for example, where a new invention clearly comes under the agreed rules. The prohibition in The Metropolitan Police Act 1839 against repairing vehicles in public places clearly includes cars although no one could have agreed that 'vehicles' would include cars in 1839 because cars were not invented then. (See my earlier discussion of this point.)

5 *Law's Empire*, p. 118. Should the ideal be served by requiring judges to engage their own convictions as little as possible and be as deferent as possible to the legislature? Dworkin says that the judge might still be mistaken, and even if correct about what the current legislature thinks, that decision will not have been announced in advance.

6 See, for an interesting interpretation of the idea of conventionalism in Dworkin, Simmonds, 'Why Conventionalism Does Not Collapse into Pragmatism' [1990] *Cambridge Law Journal* 63. The arguments there, however, do not depend on Simmonds' interpretation of conventionalism being the same one as Dworkin's. Note here that Dworkin's description of conventionalism is a *possible* model of law based on his making the best sense of 'the ideal of protected expectations'.

7 *Law's Empire*, p. 134.

8 [1932] A.C. 562. See also Chapter 2.

9 [1932] A.C. 562, 580.

10 (1883) 11 Q.B.D. 503.

11 [1932] A.C. 562, 577.

12 See the 'skinhead' school of jurisprudence referred to by Hoffman, J. in his review of Lee's *Judging Judges* (1989) *Law Quarterly Review* 144.

13 But see MacCormick's extensive discussion of this case in his *Legal Reasoning and Legal Theory* (1978) Oxford, particularly pp. 104–28. He disagrees with Dworkin (and me) about the plain fact view of law making the best sense of positivism's intentions. It is not difficult for him, therefore, to proclaim that abstraction, in a dimension such as Lord Atkin's, is *part* of positivism: '... the decision contended for is thoroughly consistent with the body of existing legal rules, and is a rational extrapolation from them, in the sense that the immediate policies and purposes which existing similar rules are conceived as being aimed at would be *pro tanto* controverted and subjected to irrational exceptions if the instant case were not decided analogously with them' (p. 120). But *other*, rival, abstractions or contractions (Lord Atkin *versus* Lord Buckmaster) are possible. What is the practical virtue in this mess of conflict of preserving the distinction between law and morality? It is clear that MacCormick accepts that positivism must have practical, that is, moral virtue and, indeed, that is one of the fundamental theses of his book. Discussing Hart, he says, 'What must be essential to the 'internal aspect' of the rule of recognition is some conscious commitment to pursuing the political values which are perceived as underpinning it ...' (pp. 139–40) and further: 'It is not that moral reasoning is a poor relation of legal reasoning. It is rather, if anything, that legal reasoning is a special, highly institutionalized and formalized, type of moral reasoning' (p. 272).

How does he choose one abstraction over another? By another, higher, abstraction? *What are the criteria of choice?* Note his desire to *make sense* of the law. Coupled with his view that legal reasoning is centrally *committed*, how does his theory maintain its positivist stance with credibility? 'The formulation ... of statements of principle in law is one way of making such values relatively more explicit. But observe, this is not necessarily nor even usually a matter of making explicit what is already known clearly; it is a matter of *making sense* of law, as much as of finding the sense which is already there' (p. 234).

14 See *D. & C. Builders* v. *Rees* [1966] 2 Q.B. 617.

15 See Gerald Postema, 'Coordination and Convention at the Foundations of Law', 11 *Journal of Legal Studies* 165 (1982); Leslie Green 'Law, Co-ordination and the Common Good', *Oxford Journal of Legal Studies* 3 (1983) 299.

16 I refer here to some popular ways of thinking. There are, of course, less stark descriptions of these views. See, for example, Campbell *Left and Rights* (1983) and Lukes, *The Socialist Idea* (Kolakowski and Hampshire, eds.) (1976), Chapter 6.

17 *Law's Empire*, p. 43.

18 *Law's Empire*, p. 73.

19 See Chapter 9.

20 See, for example, Kennedy, 'Form and Substance in Private Law Adjudication', (1976) 88 *Harvard Law Review* 1685 ('The explanation of the sticking points of both the modern individualist and altruist is that both believe quite firmly in both of these sets of premises, in spite of the fact that they are radically contradictory' p. 1,774 n. 99), and Unger, 'The Critical Legal Studies Movement' (1983) 96 *Harvard Law Review* 561 ('Conventional legal doctrines try to suppress or minimize the ... conflicts' pp. 647–8).

21 See Kennedy, 'The Political Significance of the Structure of the Law School Curriculum' (1983) 14 *Seton Hall Law Review* 1, and his *Legal Education and the Reproduction of Hierarchy* (1983).

22 A good start to understanding the Critical Legal Studies movement are the symposia in (1984) 36 *Stanford Law Review* Nos.1 and 2, and (1984) *Texas Law Review*. Also, Kennedy and Klare, 'A Bibliography of Critical Legal Studies' (1984) 94 *Yale Law Journal* 461 and Kelman, *A Guide to Critical Legal Studies* (1987) Harvard.

23 'Judicial Discretion' (1963) 60 *Journal of Philosophy*, pp. 624–38.

24 See Gidon Gottlieb's valuable discussion of this point. See *The Logic of Choice* (1968) Unwin, p. 119.

25 Jeffrey Jowell and Anthony Lester, 'Proportionality: Neither Novel or Dangerous' in J.Jowell and D. Oliver eds., *New Directions in Judicial Review* 1988 *Current Legal Problems Special Issue*. J.Jowell and A. Lester 'Beyond *Wednesbury*: Substantive Principles of Administrative Law' (1987) *Public Law* 368. Note Denis Galligan's reference to 'principles of good administration' in his extended review of Wade's *Administrative Law*, entitled 'Judicial Review and the Textbook Writers' 2 *Oxford Journal of Legal Studies*, p. 257 (1982).

26 See *Associated Provincial Picture Houses Ltd* v. *Wednesbury Corporation* [1948] 1 K.B. 223.

27 See *Taking Rights Seriously*, pp. 31–3.

28 *Taking Rights Seriously*, p. 32.

9

Treating people as equals

I said, in Chapter 2, when I was discussing Dworkin's methodology, particularly in relation to his idea of making 'the best sense' of law, that the abstract principle driving his political philosophy was that 'people should be treated as equals'. It is necessary always to go back to this ruling idea in interpreting Dworkin. It is an attractive one for the obvious reason that, it being so abstract, almost no person could rigorously dissent from it, although most people could offer dramatically different rival conceptions of the basic idea.

The abstract principle of equality is important for Dworkin throughout his work. It affects the way he interprets utilitarianism, which spills over into his ideas of the justification of reverse discrimination, of fundamental constitutional rights, of procedural rules in evidence and the criminal law. And, most importantly for understanding his highly sophisticated theory of the foundations of liberalism, the principle governs the distribution of resources through the idea of the envy-eliminating market.

Dworkin's political philosophy consists, then, of a carefully worked out conception of the idea that the state must treat people as equals. In brief summary, he says that the metric for distribution must be economic resources, first, because that assumption lies behind any judgment about the comparative worth of human lives and second, because treating people as equals means allowing them to live their lives freely within the resources available to them. Equality is thus an idea inseparable from liberty. Further, since a person's right to liberty is 'parametered' by this just distribution it means, according to Dworkin, that people living ethically conflicting different lives within equality of resources can each approve the political scheme from each ethical perspective.

But this short summary is a taste only and we must turn first to the content, at the most abstract level, of the idea of treating people as equals. The problems in this idea, and Dworkin's treatment of it, will occupy us for the remainder of this book.

Problems of equality

A useful introduction to the idea of equality is Bernard Williams'
subtle and important article 'The Idea of Equality'.[1] It seems to me
that both Williams and Dworkin are in substantial agreement about
the initial force of the arguments for equality, and is helpful to examine
Williams' article in some detail.

Do we need to justify the injunction that people should be treated as
equals? There are two important reasons why we should. The first is
that the idea of equality is bandied about in political debate in a loose
and unexamined way. Popularly, equality is thought to be the enemy
of liberty. So, for example, those who advocate 'equality' often advocate the reduction or restriction of private medicine or private education, on the ground that benefits will be spread more equally by a
publicly ordered distribution. The popular criticism is that such a
public distribution denies people the choice to make their own decisions on medical and educational matters.

The argument that a person's liberty to choose what he does is part
of what makes him a person has a powerful hold on us. On the other
hand, the apparent counter argument of the egalitarian – why should
one person's liberty be obtained at the cost to another's? – also has a
powerful hold.

This apparently irresolvable conflict between equality and personal
freedom has the effect of making people take sides.[2] It is possible to
discern a connection between the political left and equality, whether it
is moderate as welfare liberalism or extreme as communism, and the
political right and personal freedom, where there are also moderate
and extreme versions. The seeming conflict is unfortunate because it is
by no means clear, even on a superficial analysis, that freedom and
equality are incompatible. Dworkin goes further than anyone else in
saying that both are inseparable notions. To him, each idea emphasises an important aspect of the other.

It is critical, therefore, that one is not swayed by popular
understandings of these terms. The idea of equality is normative in
an important and pervasive sense. There could be no point in trying
to capture confused, albeit popular, understandings within an analysis
of the idea.

The second reason is that the idea of equality, as Williams points
out, seems either too strong or too weak to be able to do much work.
The strong sense is that used when, as the French revolutionaries
declared in art.1 of the Declaration of Rights, it is held that 'men are
born and remain equal'. The statement seems patently false in
respect of ability, wealth, status, good looks, height and even weight.
Noting this feature, Jeremy Bentham remarked at the time in his
well-known contemporary work *Anarchical Fallacies* that it would

follow that lunatics could lock up sane people, and idiots would have a right to govern![3]

To make more sense than this we should turn to a weaker sense of equality which says that human beings are equal *qua* human beings, that is, in Williams' terms, they are equal in sharing a 'common humanity'. This rescues the strong sense from absurdity although it also means that we are not given a clear lead as to how to treat humans as humans. We are, rather, merely being reminded of the fact that all people are equally human.

It is important here to consider the view of some contemporary philosophers that the idea of equality provides no substantive justification for treating people in any way. Take the views of Joseph Raz, which are representative.[4] He distinguishes three senses of weak equality. First, equality as what he calls merely a 'closure' principle, which marks off a general rule as applying only to those instances that come within it, as for example, in the statement: 'every human being is equally entitled to education'. This, he says, states nothing more than that human beings are entitled to education, with the reminder that is only the quality of humanhood that is relevant. The work of the phrase, in other words, is done by the idea of being human.

A second sense is more fruitful. This is where claims to equality refer to an actually existing inequality of distribution, such as, for example: 'human beings have a right to those things that others have but they themselves do not have'. This sense Raz thinks has more promise. It comes closer to expressing the sentiments of the signatories to the French Declaration of Rights. But, Raz points out (as have many others), this principle can be satisfied by a levelling down rather than a levelling up.[5] Really, stripped of its rhetoric, the principle is saying no more, and of course no less, than that humans have a common humanity.

The idea of equality does not, in his view, refer to any more substantial idea of equality which could rescue us from a levelling down solution. This second sense is a very important one to appreciate, I think, because it illustrates a not very rigorous but popular criticism of socialism. It is that socialism, by aiming for equality, is prepared to level people *down* and, in doing so, sacrifices the important value of freedom. More, however, of this shortly.

The third sense is one that Raz refers to as 'rhetorical' equality. According to this sense, reference is made to equality with good rhetorical effect ('we are all equal – as human beings') but without a substantial intellectual foundation. He is not against this rhetorical use if it works to bring about a better community but thinks that it is, nevertheless, an intellectual fudge. In his view, again shared by many others, the statement that 'all human beings are entitled to equal respect' could just as well be rendered as 'being human is a ground for respect'.

He gives the example of a person who is deceitful to one child but not another, or breaks a promise to one but not another. In each case, he says, the wrong is a wrong which can be described independently of how the *other* child or person is treated. In each case it is wrong to be deceitful or to break promises.

He says that this fudged idea of equality might nevertheless serve the rhetorical purpose of showing a person's inconsistency. It might, too, have the instrumental effect of reducing envy and therefore of promoting stability. Bentham, for example, certainly thought that the main reason for treating people equally was to reduce envy and dissatisfaction, and thereby maintain what was very important to him, a secure and peaceful society.

I think we must be aware of these criticisms because of how common they are. But you should see their triviality. Were the French revolutionaries really appealing to nothing when they used the word 'equality'? Of course not. They were saying that it is wrong for some people to have more than others just by virtue of luck, class or status. These attributes, they were saying, are irrelevant considerations when it comes to the way people should be treated because people have *equal* status as human beings.

Is saying this to ignore Raz's argument that, by using the idea of equality, the French revolutionaries were open to the response that their claims could be met by the levelling down of the French aristocracy? No. The demand for equality was not intended as 'treat people in an equal way' but 'treat people equally *as human beings*'. These two injunctions must be fundamentally different. Treating people in an equal way treats people as numerical units and is, therefore, neutral over whether there should be a levelling down or a levelling up. But the injunction to treat people equally as human beings could not permit a levelling down.

Of great importance to Dworkin is the distinction he draws between the twin ideas of treating people 'as equals' and giving people 'equal treatment'. The primary idea, he says, is that of treating people 'as equals', and the idea of 'equal treatment' only derives from the former. Giving equal treatment to human beings would mean giving as much by way of resources, say, to a handicapped person as to someone who was not handicapped. It would not, in other words, be sensitive to the differences between people. Indeed, it is the confusion between these two very important and different senses of equality that leads people to reject equality as a moral ideal.

If the injunction that we should accord primacy to treating people as equals is deemed to be the most abstract injunction in political philosophy, we will be led, Dworkin says, to saying that handicapped people do not have a right to equal treatment but, rather, a right to *unequal* treatment. The handicapped person, according the primary abstract principle, must be entitled to more in the way of resources to compensate him (as far as resources can compensate) for his handicap.

> If I have two children, and one is dying from a disease that is making the other uncomfortable, I do not show equal concern if I flip a coin to decide which should have the remaining dose of a drug. This example shows that the right to treatment as an equal is fundamental, and the right to equal treatment, derivative. In some circumstances the right as an equal will entail a right to equal treatment, but not, by any means, in all circumstances.[6]

The success of equality-cynical arguments comes from drawing too marked a separation between 'equality' arguments, which permit us to drop equality in favour of 'closure' principles, and 'human being', or 'person' arguments which are thought to be sufficient in themselves. But the moral force of equality is to show the unjustifiable distributional differences between human beings. It must secure the idea of equality and 'being human' in one bundle. I think that another way of making this point is to say that any worthwhile, non-closure, sense of equality supports not only distributive but substantive reasons for reordering society. In this way, the levelling down argument of Raz, and others, is shown to be pointless.

Williams expands on the idea of common humanity. Just giving reasons for discriminating between people is not enough to satisfy the requirements of common humanity: relevant reasons must be given, and morally relevant reasons at that. To assert that blacks should be discriminated against simply because they are black sounds, as he says, an arbitrary assertion of will, like the emperor Caligula executing anyone with three 'R's in his name. Drawing upon what I said in the previous paragraph, this in itself is not a reason connected with how a person should be treated. We can go further with Williams. The idea of being human has a point. Each person should, equally, be identified as an end, with purposes and feelings of his own, and not as an instrument of another's will.[7]

The chief problem in the idea of equality concerns, of course, the filling out of how people should be treated as 'ends'. Williams finds the solution in the idea of the opportunities open to a person. Respecting a person means seeing that person from the 'human point of view'. So we distinguish, for example, between the person and the particular status, or 'title,' he has. A failure in society occurs, Williams thinks, when people no longer distinguish the title from the 'man who has the title'. The hierarchical society which ignores the distinction is poorer because the view becomes accepted that titles, and status, are foreordained, or inevitable. Further, in such societies, an important problem is that people lower in the hierarchy endorse their own lowly status as acceptable, in the same way as those above will endorse their previous lowly status before as in the proper order of things. Everyone accepts 'their lot' as inevitable.

But, of course, all sorts of goods in society are limited and so it will, necessarily, be the case that a hierarchy, although not necessarily a pre-ordained hierarchy, will form. How, then, to give equality any bite here? Williams thinks the idea lies in a properly understood equality of opportunity. Equality of opportunity is frequently and wrongly understood just to mean that status should be open to all, without any other qualification, and that conception leads to a complacency about the existing state of affairs. For example, it is perfectly true that anybody may apply to Eton. The problem is that equality of opportunity is impotent unless it is understood to include the real possibility that status or titles are available to all human beings equally.

Williams thus draws the connection between equality of opportunity and equality of persons. The argument depends first on distinguishing people from their status and seeing people from 'the human point of view', and second upon seeing that people may, as a result of their environment, in which they are denied goods, not have a real possibility of attaining status further up the hierarchy. We have, in Williams' words, to be able to abstract people from their 'curable' environments.[8] Williams concludes:

> [A]n ideal of equality of respect that made no contact with such things as the economic needs of society for certain skills, and human desire for some sorts of prestige, would be condemned to a futile Utopianism ...[9]

Here, I think, are the beginnings of the idea drawn out by Dworkin eventually into equality of resources. The levelling down consequence of the Raz argument cannot do justice to equality. That concept is properly to be understood as treating people s ends by enabling them to have *real* opportunities to make something of their lives.

Equality and utilitarianism: double counting

Dworkin has a unique and striking view of the relationship between rights to equality and utilitarianism. He is the only philosopher who has, I think, linked them in such a fundamental way. It is extremely important for understanding his general positions in political and legal philosophy to see the connections he makes between both rights and utility and the pervasive but, I think, not yet fully developed idea of interpretation.

We can begin be reconsidering what utilitarianism is. We need not, at first, be too sophisticated because Dworkin aims to capture what is intuitively understood by the utilitarian maxim that governments should aim to maximise the average welfare of their citizens. There are, of course, well-known difficulties in the basic idea, to which are provided equally well-known answers. For example, the idea of welfare sometimes is intended to refer to well-being in the form of pleasure or happiness. Such was the view of utilitarianism argued for by Bentham, which was based upon a view of the psychology of human motivation. Sometimes, however, welfare has been considered as well-being measured in other sorts of ways, for example, in terms of the success a person makes of his life, that success judged either from that person's point of view (or that person's point of view if he were fully apprised of the circumstances) or from an entirely objective viewpoint.

Without, therefore, being too concerned, until the next chapter, about the filling out of the idea of 'welfare', we can see that essential to utilitarianism is the aim at the maximisation of some form of what is considered to be good, measured over the whole of a community. The link here between arguments of utility and policy arguments is obvious. To remind ourselves of the relevant distinctions, as I discussed it in Chapter 3:

> Principles are propositions that describe rights; policies are propositions that describe goals.[10]

> A goal is a non-individuated political aim, that is, a state of affairs whose specification does not in this way call for any particular opportunity or resource of liberty for particular individuals.[11]

The maxim of 'the greatest happiness of the greatest number', Dworkin says, owes its 'great appeal' to the inherent egalitarian premise that no person is weighted in the greatest happiness calculation than anyone else:

> Utilitarian arguments of policy, therefore, seem not to oppose but on the contrary to embody the fundamental right of equal concern and respect, because they treat the wishes of each member of the community on a par with the wishes of any other ...[12]

The idea of equality is here drawn from the non-specificity of persons in utilitarianism. John Rawls famously remarked that utilitarianism was 'no respecter of persons', which is to point to a malign side of the doctrine.

The best-known criticism of the doctrine draws upon this malign characteristic by pointing out that a utilitarian calculation, say, one involving large imbalances in wealth, could justify great misery among a few people in order to achieve a marginal gain in overall happiness for a large majority of people. This possibility has turned many people away from utilitarianism. It does not permit the idea of rights against a majority decision where doing what the majority wants would, in fact, increase overall welfare. And it does not, further, give any real weight to the idea of the equality of persons. Their position is 'equal', yes, in numerical terms, but, as the usual criticism goes, the idea of each person's right to equality cannot be used to justify a constraint upon a decision made which will increase overall welfare. On equality, Bentham was notably consistent. The idea was only relevant to calculating a distributional pattern which promoted stability and security by reducing envy.[13]

Dworkin, on the other hand, points to a benign side to utilitarianism. According to this theory, the greatest happiness is for the greatest *number*. People are distinguished in this calculation only by the fact that they are numbers or points or receptacles of pain and pleasure. Benignly, in other words, people are to be treated impartially and no person is to count for more than one and no one to count for less than one. This phrase was one of the appealing maxims of the doctrine.

It is difficult not to agree with Dworkin on this point historically, since the growth of utilitarianism accompanied a parallel growth in liberal and egalitarian reforms. And the force of the argument that there is an equality premise contained in the utilitarian numerical calculation, admittedly of the 'closure' sort identified by Raz, is strong. Dworkin's argument is, therefore, a striking one because it is at odds with many interpretations of the doctrine.

It is an interpretive idea which Dworkin examines in a specific way. His interpretation of practices of pursuing community goals makes the best sense of them. It is as follows. The appeal of utilitarianism lies in its condemnation of the view that any form of life is inherently more valuable than any other. The wishes of each member of a community are to count on a par with the wishes of any other member. So, for example, if a community has only enough resources to give medicine to only some of its members, the sickest must be treated first. Or, if more members of a community want a new swimming pool than would prefer a theatre, the swimming pool comes first. No sick person should be preferred because he is worthier of more concern and the wishes of the theatre-lovers are not to be preferred because theatre is a more worthwhile interest than sport.

Dworkin teases this 'no person to count more than one' premise out. He distinguishes between a person's personal and impersonal, or external, preferences. A person's personal preferences are those which relate to his own life only. His impersonal, external, preferences relate to the way he thinks other people should live. Dworkin says that the satisfaction of impersonal preferences 'corrupts' utilitarianism because it violates the important idea that no one's preference is to be assessed in terms of its worth. If impersonal preferences are taken into account, it must mean that double counting is involved. A person in stating his preference for how another person should live can negate the effect of that other person's preference, as well preserving his own preference for how his own life should be led.

Let us look at some examples. Someone who has a dislike of homosexuals votes, along with a majority of people, for the imposition of criminal sanctions on certain kinds of homosexual activity. Legislation is created, police do their work, and a minority of people live more miserable lives than they lived before. At first sight, the utilitarian calculation has worked because the majority is now happier because homosexuality is publicly recognised as a less worthwhile life and, we shall assume, that happiness, because of the number involved, outweighs the increased misery felt by homosexuals. But, according to Dworkin, this is corrupted utilitarianism at work. The egalitarian element has been violated because votes have been made on the basis of a judgment about the worthwhile nature of the lives of others.

Of course, in the real world, it is going to be very difficult to separate personal and impersonal preferences because often both will be expressed in a single statement. Take, for example, the white law school candidate who has a preference for all-white law schools. He has two reasons. If there were all-white law schools it would raise his chances of becoming a lawyer. His second reason is that he does not approve of blacks doing professional jobs. What is the double counting? His vote for all-white law schools is one for himself and legitimate *in utilitarian terms*. That must be the case. There is nothing in the idea of the egalitarian maximising of average community welfare that rules out this vote, so long as the blacks have an equal vote. In a majority system, it is just true that some people have to miss out. But his vote could also be one that is wholly motivated by prejudice. Then, his vote acts to neutralise what some other person, in this case a black voter, prefers for his own life.

There is a problem here about the substantive moral arguments supporting the prohibition on double counting. What if a person votes for a political decision, not because that decision will affect him personally but because he disapproves of the way of life of others and thinks such a way of life should be legislatively suppressed. What is the wrong? Is it that he will effectively cancel out the vote of a person who wishes to live the life of which he disapproves? That would mean that people are only entitled to vote for those things which affect them. The mirror similarity with Mill's distinction between self- and other-regarding action is striking. You are not entitled to vote where that vote has an effect (a 'cancelling out') on someone's else's vote. Mill's account was similarly formal and Mill offered the substantive argument by emphasising the importance of the cultivation of individuality.[14]

How does Dworkin use this idea of equality captured in the idea of utilitarian, goal-based theories of community? It is not fully clear how he moves from the closure sense to a more substantive sense. Let us examine this closure sense again. The fact that utilitarianism does not distinguish between people, and thus identifies people equally, means simply that it is a doctrine about people, according to the closure sense. The doctrine does not use the idea in the substantive sense in which I discussed it in the last section. The doctrine says that governments should maximise the happiness of the greatest number and this, it must be pointed out, is even consistent with the idea that *not all* need count when the greatest possible happiness is in question.

I do not think this criticism is bothersome for what Dworkin wishes to achieve. We have, though, to accompany Dworkin in an intuitive jump to saying that the equality idea is a substantive and non-numerical one. At the end of his article 'Equality of Welfare' he reconsiders the idea of egalitarian utilitarianism, pointing out that it could not 'purport to supply all of a plausible general political or moral theory'. The reasons he gives are that:

> The egalitarian utilitarian would have to explain why it is not as good to aim at maximum average misery as maximum average happiness, for example, or why there is anything to regret in a natural disaster that kills thousands though it improves the situation of a few.[15]

Why does he say this? It is because egalitarian utilitarianism aims at the maximisation of welfare based on a number principle ('no person to count for more nor less than one') and does not value welfare as a good in itself. It is just a reference to one of the empty senses of equality as defined by Raz. Dworkin thinks that the explanation for what is wrong with the two situations he envisages lies in further political principles, one of which clearly he would endorse, one 'which holds that those who aim at others' misery or failure do not show the others the concern to which human beings, at least, are entitled'.[16]

Is such an appeal to intuition here a poor argument? After all, the doctrine of utilitarianism has a certain unsophisticated appeal, apparent in its most popular maxim. What, you have to ask yourself, is its real appeal?

Dworkin thinks that best grounds we have for instituting the well-known fundamental rights in a liberal society, the sorts of rights usually collected under the title of a 'Bill of Rights', is that they are learned by experience to counteract the effect of double counting which, in the real world, can hardly fail to occur. So, for example, the rights to freedom of expression and to free choice in personal and sexual relations, in Dworkin's view, may be defended because in these areas of human activity, the political process will not usually be able to make the necessary discriminations in order to eliminate the different views about the worth of these activities.

Dworkin does not elaborate on this important idea beyond showing the general character that justifying fundamental rights should take. It is interesting to note the contingent, historical nature of his case for fundamental rights. These are justified, first, by reference to communities which actually do have practices of making political decisions by reference to community goals. In that sense, they are contingent and historical. Second, they are justified in 'trumping' such goals, not because they embody a 'fundamental' right to be treated with equal concern and respect, but because history has proved that if communities are constrained in a fundamental way from pursuing certain kinds of goals, the right to equal concern and respect is *more likely* to be respected. 'Fundamental' here refers to the nature of the constraint rather than the intrinsic quality of the right itself.[17]

This contingent feature of fundamental rights is very important, to Dworkin, for the following reason. It means that the establishment of fundamental rights to freedoms are independent of each other, each being dependent upon judgments of the antecedent likelihood of political decisions based upon corrupted community goals. If this is true, then there is no substance to the charge often made against liberals that it is inconsistent for them to accept a general right to freedom of speech but not accept a general right to freedom of property. Since, as Dworkin says, and is clear from his commitment to the most abstract principle of equality, there is no general right to freedom *simpliciter*, it follows that there is no inconsistency. The arguments for maintaining a right to freedom of speech because of the antecedent likelihood of corruption will be of a different historical character from the arguments for instituting a fundamental right to property. There we must agree with Dworkin, at least as far as the general character of his argument goes, that some limitations by a community on rights to property do not obviously show a denial of a right to equal concern and respect.[18]

A paradoxical element of *Taking Rights Seriously* is the tension between the strong 'rights as trumps' anti-utilitarian strain of the work and the apparent endorsement of this egalitarian version of utilitarianism. The striking interpretation he offers of utilitarianism is reconcilable with the idea of rights as trumps and so we must conclude that the anti-utilitarianism strain is antagonistic only to 'corrupted' utilitarianism. But it is wrong to suppose that Dworkin endorses even an uncorrupted form of utilitarianism. To repeat my remarks in Chapter 3, rights only assume importance in a community whose practices include justifying political decisions by reference to communal goals. From the distinctions he draws between the ideal real world and the ideal ideal world, it is clear that in the latter world, utilitarian arguments have only a restricted role to play. And that is to say that utilitarianism cannot tell the full story.[19]

Economics and the Chicago school

We are now armed with an introduction to Dworkin's views both on equality and utilitarianism. We must now examine his attack on a theory, which has gained widespread acceptance, about the relationship between legal and economic argument. It will be instructive to do this for two reasons. First, we need an introduction into terms and concepts of economic thought in order to understand Dworkin's political theory of equality of resources. Second, it is helpful for us to understand that the attack he makes on a particular economic theory is not intended to be dismissive of what he clearly believes to be a fertile relationship between economics and law. Indeed, his attack on the Chicago school of law and economics is an attack based, as we would expect, on the abstract principle of equality, and is directed against a highly unconstrained form of utilitarianism. That attack leaves untouched the egalitarian utilitarianism which we have already examined, although we have already noticed that Dworkin thinks that version of utilitarianism to be incomplete.[20]

We first need some definitions. In many ways, it is best to start with the idea of the market. One reason is that, for Dworkin, the abstract principle of equality finds its best expression here in justifying questions of distribution. And for the Chicago school, and economists of many other hues, the market constitutes the central concept of their discipline.

The idea of a market is a model and it does not therefore need to exist in the real world. But it is not, therefore, a difficult idea. We need a model, something to which we can refer, in order to understand that what occurs in the real world could be otherwise. Think about it. We need the idea of a 'perfect' market in order to be able to understand what a market 'imperfection' is in the real world. It is no answer to the criticism that a market is distorted or imperfect (perhaps because of the existence of monopolies) simply to say that the market is 'just like that'. You should note that it only makes sense to make this latter criticism because we are comparing the real market with our model of a monopoly free market.

But, further, to understand the idea of market we have to appreciate the directly practical aim of much of the thinking in economics. Economics is thought of as a practical subject, directed to decision-making. In this respect it is like law. As a result, and to a greater degree than law, it must take short cuts. It does this by making certain psychological assumptions about people which are, many respects, patently false, but which are nevertheless sufficiently appealing to be workable.

An important assumption, for example, is that people are 'rational self-maximisers', that is, they always act so as to maximise the satisfaction of their preferences. We could call this the assumption of rationality. We can link this idea to that of the ideal market and say that people, ideally, will make decisions in the market-place with the intention of satisfying the maximum number of their preferences.

Many of the working propositions of economics depend upon assumptions that exist in a strange category which is partly to do with ethical attractiveness (the autonomy of the market, the workability) and partly to do with untested empirical propositions (such as rational maximisation or the declining marginal utility of wealth). Models of economic activity, because models, cannot be directly tested against empirical data. On the other hand, economic models are intended to be workable, and so the major assumptions about human psychology and motivation have to have some empirical link with what is actually true.

We can trace the development of one or two of the ideas from preference utilitarianism. Economists can bypass, with relative ease, the problem of the measurement of what is of value in a person's life, by talking of the 'satisfaction of preferences'. People state what it is they want and are assumed to be the best judge of their own interests.

A couple of bonuses come with this assumption. Using the idea of what people are prepared to give up, measured in currency, for what they want, interpersonal comparisons become possible. Further, making people the final judges about what is good for them, or what constitutes the best life for them, is a pleasantly liberal assumption which many people are inclined to accept.

The market-place provides the mechanism for cashing in these bonuses. If a person is willing to forgo the satisfaction of one kind of preference in order to have another preference satisfied, we can measure the value of the satisfaction he wants namely, by what economists call 'lost opportunity'. Someone who trades his teddy bear for a book of poetry values the book of poetry more than the teddy bear. He has, in other words, increased his wealth. It does *not* follow, note, that he has increased his welfare.

Currency permits a more generalised account of the measurement of wealth. A and B swap a typewriter and a book. A would be willing to hand over the book and accept the typewriter but B uses the typewriter and he feels that just having the book is not sufficient. He says that he will trade only for the book and £10. He calculates that he will have the book plus enough money to put a deposit down on a new typewriter. A accepts this, because he is willing to give up this sum of money as well as the book, because he wants the typewriter and he is willing to forgo both the book and the opportunity costs (say, a restaurant meal) in order to get it.

We achieve the commensurability of values here by just comparing the choices people are prepared to make. We see what they are prepared to give up in order to get something they value. Since generally people are willing to give up things for currency,[21] and currency for things, the numerical count of the currency provides a guide to what is valued and by whom.

This is not to say we are free from difficulties, but it is a start. Obvious difficulties must arise from the separation of value, what people actually want and believe is worthwhile in their lives, and the idea of having the means to acquire it, known by economists as 'wealth'. Roughly sufficient for our purposes, a person's wealth is his stock of possessions which have a market value.

The idea of the market is best expressed, in my view, through the economists' concept of 'paretonism', named after the Italian economist Vilfredo Pareto.[22] Paretonism has great ethical appeal because it derives its force from the importance of both personal well-being and personal autonomy. It provides a criterion, combining these two aspects, for measuring increases in welfare or utility. Situation B is 'pareto-superior' to situation A if in situation B at least one of the parties is better off and neither of the parties is worse off. a 'pareto-*optimal*' situation envisages the end of a possible chain of pareto-superior changes whereby there is no further situation where one party would be better off without the other being worse off.

Paretonism provides a measure for marginal increases in utility or welfare. No one is worse off and at least one is better off. According to the theory that the greatest number should be better off, the criterion must measure some increases in utility. It does that at the same time as nodding in the direction of personal autonomy. Two people enter the market and leave with at least one of them better off and neither of them worse off. The appeal of paretonism is that the market appears to achieve a nice balance between overall utility and personal autonomy.

Of course, in the real world things are very different. But the ideal market, as I described it before, does have a use. What, then, is the correct characterisation of that ideal? Generally, economists define a perfect market in the following way. A perfect market transaction is one where the parties bargain to mutual advantage, measured against the choices of the 'rational maximiser', or they bargain, at least, to the advantage of one and with no disadvantage to the other; the market is not 'distorted' by, for example, the existence of a monopoly; the parties have 'perfect knowledge'; and there are no 'transaction costs'.

Given this widely accepted definition, it is plain to see that the problem with paretonism is that in the real world, because of various market *im*perfections, pareto-superior situations occur with relative infrequency, the more usual situation being that one party is left worse off after a transaction. Because of this fact about real markets, there will be a large number of pareto-optimal situations in the real world, because mostly no further market move can be made without some party becoming worse off. In short, in the real world, there will often be some loser, maybe a third party, in any market transaction.

But the idea of paretonism, with its inborn ethical attractions, is not used by the Chicago school economic lawyers. They use an alternative criterion of *wealth* maximisation, as opposed to welfare maximisation which attempts to overcome the practical difficulties in real markets. Such a criterion was first proposed by Kaldor and Hicks[23] and states that a decision, or policy, is wealth-maximising if the amount of wealth created by the decision is enough to compensate those who are left with less wealth after the decision. There is no requirement that those who lose wealth in the process should be compensated.

The criterion is a formal description of what we understand as cost-benefit or cost-effective analysis. A factory moves to another town to avail itself of the cheaper labour and land prices. The town it moves from suffers financial loss but the factory and businesses in the new town gain enough financially from the move for it to be possible, in principle, to compensate the loss of wealth to those who lost out in the move. The move is a cost-effective move.

The idea is an important one because it places emphasis on efficiency. It directs our attention very precisely to the fact that more wealth can be created by certain sorts of decisions even though those decisions place some people at a disadvantage. It is an important idea also because it is workable. That must be an argument in its favour. If we accept that it is, at least, one factor in favour of a decision that it produces more wealth, the cost-effective criterion is helpful. It is not a criterion which says what, overall, should be done. It just tells us what the cost-effective move is.

A useful way into the idea is to see the Kaldor–Hicks criterion as paretonism shorn of its distributional aspect with its measure of welfare replaced by that of wealth. Immediately we have done this, though, we see how radically different a criterion it is. It is much less attractive ethically, although, as I have said, there is no immediately obvious reason why we should think of it as telling us, overall, what should be done. Wealth, measured in currency, must replace reference to welfare because the extent to which one party is better off has to be measured against the extent to which the other party is worse off.

The criterion appears to assume that increases in wealth overall will bring about increases in welfare. Wealth replaces welfare on the assumption that wealth has the potential for increasing welfare although, of course, not necessarily that of those who lose out in the wealth created by the Kaldor–Hicks move.

We need one more definition to understand the Chicago school. This is the 'theorem', very commonly used by lawyer economists, known as the 'Coase theorem', named after an economist from Chicago.[24] The idea is that whatever legal rights the parties have before going to the market they will bargain (in the perfect market, remember, they are 'rational maximisers') for the most economically efficient result. For example, A is a neighbour to B's glue factory. Let us say that, according to the law of nuisance, B has the legal right to pollute the air. The theorem states that in the perfect market, independently of the initial assignment of legal rights, A and B will bargain to produce the most efficient result. A, but only if he is willing to forgo the lost opportunities, will pay B to reduce the pollution by the amount which will enable B to reduce the pollution and still make a profit. With a different assignment of initial rights, whereby B is entitled to pollute only to the extent to which he pays compensation to A, B will reduce his pollution to the extent to which his payment to A does not prevent him from making a profit. Either assignment of legal rights, in other words, does not affect the overall efficiency of the outcome.

This theorem has fundamental importance for decision-making in the real world where, of course, markets are imperfect. In particular, the lawyer economists focus on the imperfection of what they call 'transaction costs'. In the pollution case, for example, there will, in all probability, be many people in A's position and the costs of the negotiations leading to the separate bargains between these people and B and the costs of the creation of the contracts will be large. The initial assignment of the legal rights under the law of nuisance, in the real world of transaction costs, will affect the efficient outcome of bargaining because in many cases, one can easily imagine, people in the same position as A will be deterred by such costs from even beginning to negotiate.

We can now concentrate on Dworkin's target, which is Richard Posner's theory of law. It can be explained with relative brevity. Posner, along with other members of the Chicago school, proposes that, in order to produce efficiency, judicial decisions in hard cases should 'correct' any inefficient allocation of resources which is brought about by imperfections in the market. It may be that efficiency in the perfect market requires B to reduce his pollution but that transaction costs prevent that. The answer is simple. The court bypasses the business of transaction costs and just imposes the efficient result. The only cost is court time which is much cheaper than the numerous contracts which would otherwise have to be formed.

A famous judicial formulation of an economic test for working out liability, and one which has been seen by Posner and others as confirming the incidence of judicial decision-making in economic terms, was that by the United States judge Learned Hand. He devised a test of 'reasonableness' to govern the distribution of liability in tort cases. It is sometimes known as the 'least cost avoider' test. A litigant had acted 'unreasonably' when he had done something which caused loss to another and which it would have been cheaper for him to have avoided than it would have cost the victim to avoid it.[25]

From what we know of Dworkin's theory already, we can guess how his arguments will go. What is striking about the view is its application to judicial decisions. We do not find it a particularly difficult idea to see the sense in market intervention by the legislature to prevent costly transactions. But we may feel, with Dworkin, that courts should, and do, deal with altogether different sorts of decision. Obviously, Dworkin attacks Posner's theory from the point of view that economic efficiency is one particular form of community goal and ignores litigants' rights to decisions when such rights are properly argued for from the integrity of the law. The arguments are essentially those attacking what I shall call 'undistributive' utilitarianism.

Posner tries to give more substance to his claim but ends in a muddle. He notes that the Kaldor–Hicks criterion lacks the immediate ethical appeal of the Pareto criterion. But, recognising the lack of ethical charm of the former, he is prepared to use it as an 'administrable approximation' of it:

> While Kaldor–Hicks is not a Pareto criterion as such, it will sometimes function as a tolerable and, more to the point, administrable approximation to the Pareto-superiority criterion.[26]

The entreaty here is to the workability of the efficiency criterion and to the connection between wealth and welfare. He has in mind the idea, as Dworkin describes it, of aiming at the maximisation of wealth as a 'false target'. In the real world, Posner is saying, aim at wealth and you will achieve welfare.

So, by using the idea of opportunity costs measured by units of currency the theory of wealth-maximisation purports to resolve, in a practical way, the problems of incommensurability of welfare. But, says Dworkin, since wealth itself can only be instrumental to welfare (he says that it is 'an empirical question') the maximisation of wealth by the courts must be a false target. That may be a justifiable way of aiming towards welfare in the real world, although it appears to assume that the legislature will then redistribute court-created wealth to produce welfare. But, in any case, if a court has the choice between the false target, wealth, and utility, whatever could be the reason for choosing wealth over utility?

In a nod towards the autonomy component of paretonism, Posner says that parties to litigation accept, or consent, in advance to the outcome of the court case, because they have consented in advance to allocation of rights according to the wealth-maximising principles:

> The notion of consent used here is what economists call *ex ante* compensation. I contend ... that if you buy a lottery ticket and lose the lottery ... you have consented to the loss.[27]

But, as Dworkin must be right in saying, the idea of consent, which is intended by Posner to import the idea of a genuine exercise of autonomy and is itself a problematic idea, is being confused with fairness. Posner seems to envisage *actual* consent, saying that his own arguments improve on the kind of fictional consent of Rawls's original position because the consent under wealth maximisation is concerned with actual people making choices under what he calls 'natural' ignorance.

But there is *no* actual consent in the case of litigation and so the argument must rest on either self-interest (which clearly fails) or fairness. The analogy with the lottery is a most unfortunate piece of advocacy on Posner's part, too, because it is a partisan appeal to what he thinks the business of litigation is. If the question is one of fairness, therefore, Posner's argument for the justice of wealth-maximisation is a circular one. He cannot import fairness into the model which he intends to use to show us that wealth-maximisation is fair.

I do not think that, as far as understanding Dworkin's attack on this aspect of the economic analysis of law is concerned, we need go much further.[28] I recommend Dworkin's two articles 'Is Wealth a Value?' and 'Why Efficiency?' for a very full and considered attack on Posner's theory and on Calabresi's part defence of court wealth-maximising on the ground that the best solution is one which trades efficiency against justice.[29]

The economic analysis of law, in this very common form, is utilitarianism of a sort particularly vulnerable to criticisms strung along the dimension of equality and fairness. There is just no distributional element in it at all. It is not like the egalitarian utilitarianism which Dworkin posits, because while that places value on the maximisation of welfare, it requires that average welfare be measured over the whole of the community, in accordance with the principle that people should be treated as equals. That means that there is a distributive element, the 'no person is to count for more, nor less, than one' principle.[30] In other words, says Dworkin, Posner 'cannot claim a genuine Pareto justification for common law decisions, in either hard or easy cases. His relaxed version of paretonism is only utilitarianism with all the warts.'[31]

Equality and legal argument

We have seen how the important idea of integrity, for Dworkin, links with the idea of equality through the intermediary of fraternity and community. The state must treat its citizens as equals because that is the idea that gives fullbloodedness to the idea of a community where every person counts. The idea of treating people as equals requires that in the ideal ideal world the state must speak equally, and justly, to all.

In the less than ideal world, the ideal real world, judges must assume a scheme of rules that speaks equally. They must attempt to construct a coherent set of principles that is capable of justifying all decisions that are part of law's huge empire.

Dworkin has, on many occasions, applied the Herculean technique to various areas of both United States and United Kingdom law. Examples are cases relating to the abolition of slavery,[32] reverse discrimination,[33] free speech,[34] criminal procedure,[35] right to privacy,[36] and abortion.[37] It would make this book too long, and destroy its purpose, if I tried to do justice to the subtlety of his arguments in all these cases. I have already discussed part of his analysis of the cases on the right to privacy.[38] A number of his analyses read like clear and liberal judgments by Supreme Court judges. One, in particular, I would commend to you is his admirable analysis of the constitutionality of abortion and the then impending case of *Webster* v. *Reproductive Health Services*.[39]

Reverse discrimination

I shall examine one of these analyses, the problem of 'reverse' or 'affirmative' discrimination. This problem can be stated in a fairly simple way and shows very clearly how Dworkin sees political argument, involving moral judgments and rival moral conceptions of equality, as an integral part of the legal argument.

First, we must understand the legal setting. The Fourteenth Amendment of the US Constitution provides that no state shall deny any person the equal protection of its laws. A reverse or affirmative discrimination programme gives preferential treatment to a minority group. The aim is to raise the status of the group in the community and thereby reduce overall community prejudice to it. The question is whether the Fourteenth Amendment prohibits such programmes where permitted by state law.

The question is not whether such programmes would actually work to reduce community prejudice. That question is the subject of much empirical debate. Obviously, if a programme of reverse discrimination *in fact* would not reduce prejudice it could not be justified. Instead, the question is whether such programmes are justified in principle. In other words, is it a violation of the equal protection amendment just to have such programmes, irrespective of whether they work or not?

My experience is that many people do not separate these two questions with any clarity. They think that there is nothing left to the question of equality if the programmes can be shown not to work. But this is a silly way of dismissing the question for programmes of different kinds might be devised that did work and the mere fact that they worked would not be a sufficient justification. If a person is genuinely denied his right to the equal protection of the laws, then the question of whether as a result of the denial of his right some good community goal is advanced is irrelevant. The question is, instead, to be settled as a matter of *rights* to equal protection of the laws.

Note how the question is both a legal and a moral one. In deciding whether reverse discrimination is legally justified, we have to enter a debate about what equality requires. In the discussion that follows, bear in mind the positivist view of law. A common criticism of Dworkin is that the 'inherent vagueness' of legal terms such as 'equal protection of the laws' prove his theory *wrong*. The criticism is that such terms cannot be 'filled out' by any argument of a sufficiently controlled kind to merit being described as 'legal'. Let us see.

The state law of Texas, as it stood in 1945, provided that only whites could attend the University of Texas Law School. After prolonged litigation, in 1949 this law was struck down by the Supreme Court as contrary to the Fourteenth Amendment.[40] This decision would be accepted by most participants to the debate on reverse discrimination as right. The Texas law was a law motivated by racial prejudice and denied blacks, simply because they were black, the same chances that whites had to become lawyers.[41]

We should compare this case with the following.[42] State law permits a law school entry programme that allocates a number of places to some people, largely on the ground that they are a member of particular minority groups. They have to have sufficiently good academic records to enable them to take the course, but apart from that, their entry is unaffected by the average grade required for entry to the course by those not members of the minority groups. It follows that there will be some applicants, not from minority groups, who fail to be admitted, even although their average grades are higher, perhaps considerably so, than that of the average grade of the minority intake.

Is denying these applicants a law school place denying them their rights of equal protection of the laws? In other words, does the decision on the Texas University Law School apply squarely to their case?

The answer lies in the idea of equality. What does 'equality' mean? Dworkin says that all citizens, as we have seen in both his legal and political philosophy, are entitled – have a right – to 'equal concern and respect'. We have seen how the idea of a 'right to equal treatment', for him, is derivative from the 'right to equal concern and respect'. Let us try out these distinctions. If a person is entitled to 'equal protection of the laws' it is reasonable to suppose that means that laws must embody the principle that people have a right to be treated as equals under the law. The principle must be that laws *must not be prejudicial*. Or, another way of putting it, the laws must not be constituted so as to put people at a disadvantage for some irrelevant, arbitrary, and therefore insulting reason such as that their skin is coloured black.

I suggest that this is a very straightforward understanding of the Fourteenth Amendment. It is, if you like, a reading of the words that casts them in their best moral light. How does it apply to our reverse discrimination programme? Is the majority applicant with higher grades denied an opportunity to attend law school on an insulting ground? Well, why has he been denied the opportunity? It is because a programme aiming at reducing racial prejudice has been instituted and he happened to be a person who is at a disadvantage as a result.

What is insulting about that? Many people are disadvantaged through social policies and no one accepts that social policies are *only* justified when no person is disadvantaged. It would be ridiculous to suppose that the Fourteenth Amendment protected equality of treatment. If it did, not only would it not make sense, it would be utterly unworkable.

Let us try it again. Is the majority applicant denied his right to equal concern and respect by being denied a law school place? He has been considered along with everyone else. His grades are found to be below the cut-off point for majority applicants, which is what the discrimination programme institutes. Is it implicated here that he is inferior? No, the policy affirms the equality of both the majority and minority groups. Less worthy of respect? No, the policy affirms equality of respect. Less worthy of concern than minority applicants? No, because the policy does not deny that applicants from the majority group should be admitted.

This argument is appealing. There is an absurdity in applying a case of clear racial prejudice in Texas to prevent, as a matter of principle, a programme designed to *reduce* racial prejudice. Other policies do not cause these difficulties about discrimination. Take, for example, a highway which has to be constructed across the path of a number of houses, which have to be demolished. The owners are disappointed, they are disadvantaged, they lose out, but they are not insulted or denied an equality of respect.

In one way, the property owners have a stronger case than the loser in the reverse discrimination case because they have, at least, rights to their own property, whereas in the normal case, no one has a right to a law school place. But even then, that right is one that, at best, gives a right to compensation, not to a right which would see the highway scheme abandoned.

Of course, I am envisaging a highway scheme of a properly administered sort. Fourteenth Amendment problems would clearly arise were there state laws requiring that highways be routed through black areas just to avoid inconvenience to whites, or, in this case, vice versa.

I have expressed the crux, I believe, of Dworkin's affirmative action argument to show the connection between a (compelling) conception of equality and legal argument. But I have cut some corners and, in what remains, I shall show how the affirmative action arguments bring out some important points about his view of utilitarianism and double counting.

It seems that Dworkin allows for an uncorrupted utilitarianism which works to produce an unjust result. Say, for example, that it was a commercially wise decision, as it may have been, to produce only white lawyers in Texas immediately after the World War II. Or, that alumni gifts to the University of Texas would fall dramatically if blacks were admitted and the consequences of that could outweigh any damage done to blacks as a result of continuing discrimination.

These commercial policies *could* be approved by unprejudiced, personal votes. Obviously, in the end, these conclusions will be dependent on prejudiced thinking. But it is perfectly possible that a majority of personal votes could support a policy of this discriminatory sort. But, contrasting 'ideal' arguments against utilitarian arguments, Dworkin says that the University of Texas could not produce an 'ideal' argument for its discrimination, one that would justify discrimination by arguing that it would lead to a more just society. On the other hand, reverse discrimination programmes can, since their purpose is to reduce prejudice of minority groups.

This account is revealing. It shows, I think, the interpretive character of Dworkin's account of rights 'as trumps'. To say that the best form of utilitarianism is uncorrupted utilitarianism, because it takes into account what I have called the 'numbers' view of fairness, is not to approve utilitarianism. Rights act as a constraint on community practices where those practices include justifications for decisions aimed at improving community goals.

The account is important for understanding how a community might legislate on the question of sexual practices, including the consumption of pornography. A majority might wish, voting personally, for a particular kind of community 'cleanliness' or 'moral environment'. At what point is the line between personal and impersonal preferences crossed? We might want to draw that line along the distinction – also rough – between public and private behaviour, taking the robust line that only a perversely sensitive person could object to minority sexual activity taking place out of sight. This was, for example, the line the Williams Committee took in 1979.[43] Or, following the

Millian tradition, we might try some definition of 'harm', perhaps to include, as Raz does, the idea of restriction of autonomy.[44]

In *Law's Empire* there is a more fully worked out justification of the idea of reverse discrimination, although it is consistent with the arguments so far described. Dworkin does not explicitly mention the idea of personal and impersonal preferences. He prefers, instead, the idea that there are certain 'banned' sources of *prejudice* (which, I think, must be understood as including the idea of external preferences). Simply, we must not allow prejudiced decisions to play any part in decisions affecting people. That is the ruling idea. It is to be preferred, he says, to the idea that discriminations made on the basis of certain racial characteristics, such as being black, must always be 'suspect', for historical reasons. And it is to be preferred, too, to the idea that, in most cases, such categories of classification are simply to be banned.

Why is prejudice the ruling idea? True to form, Dworkin thinks that banning categories of classification cannot be properly understood unless the principle that they are wrong because they are prejudiced is made clear. We can (and do), he says, properly introduce classifications which distinguish between people by their characteristics, even although these are inherent characteristics over which they have no control. He says '... [I]f race were a banned category, ... then intelligence, geographical background, and physical ability would have to be banned categories as well.'[45]

The idea that it is *prejudice* at work here will, of course, supply us with a list of categories which we will regard as suspect. History tells us that where some form of racial discrimination exists there is very likely to be prejudice at its basis. But since it is prejudice driving condemnation of discriminatory classification, where prejudice is *absent*, so is the condemnation. In other words, any set of 'suspect classifications' may be rebutted where it can be shown to be based (genuinely) on people's unprejudiced preferences, or shown that the justification is unprejudiced. The result is that, in a reverse discrimination case, Dworkin argues that the argument that classification on the basis of race is *in itself* wrong (the 'banned categories' view) is untenable because the only principled argument in support of it would be that '... people must never be treated differently in virtue of properties beyond their control'.[46] It follows that, if there is no prejudiced reason behind introducing the reverse discrimination programme, from which unfortunate majority applicants suffered adverse consequences, the appeal to prejudice (as opposed to some other argument[47]) lacks any power at all. Again, to use Dworkin's term in his earlier writings on reverse discrimination, where is the 'insult'?

A brief summary

We have examined, by way of general introduction, the idea of equality and settled upon a so far relatively unanalysed conception of 'common humanity' as the main thrust of that idea. We have examined, too, Dworkin's important distinction between the ideas of 'treating people as equals' and 'according people equal treatment'. The idea of treating people as equals is at the root of his criticism of the Posnerite school of the economic analysis of law. This criticism is made in the context of communal practices of justifying political action by reference to the maximisation of community goals. So Dworkin's argument is an interpretive one, interpretive of that context. His answer is that unconstrained pursuit of a community goal, such as wealth maximisation, does not make good sense. Likewise, in his particular application of the idea of constrained utilitarianism to the problem of reverse discrimination, he argues that prejudiced voting is not permitted as it constitutes an unfair 'double count'. On the other hand, if a background political justification is striving for communal goals, as it appears reasonable to say is actually the case in the United States and the United Kingdom, those goals that are not founded on prejudice, or contempt for others, are justified.

It remains for the next chapter to see how Dworkin has developed the idea of 'treating people as equals'. His approach is pragmatic. He assumes that we should treat people as equals and then views the problem as one of distribution. How should a government, as far as is practically possible, reorder society so that people are treated as equals? What, in other words, should it attempt make them equal in?

Notes

1 Williams, B. 'The Idea of Equality' in *Philosophy, Politics and Society, second series*, ed. Laslett and Runciman (1962) p. 125.

2 Political commentators are characteristically caught in the stranglehold grip of the socialism–capitalism dichotomy. Those on the political right pretend that there are no inconsistencies in popularly understood capitalism (lack of freedom for some) and no good in socialism (equality for all). Left wingers assume that there is little, if any, value in freedom because they equate it with the freedom to 'exploit'. That is why socialism so often appears puritanical and capitalism selfish.

3 See Waldron, ed. *Nonsense upon Stilts. Bentham, Burke and Marx on the Rights of Man* (1987) Methuen, p. 51. Williams says that because people's empirical differences so clearly affect their capacities Kant was wrong to assert a universal moral capacity derivable solely from the status of personhood. The Kantian principle, too, he says, is a secular analogue of the Christian conception of respect. It is empty to conclude, he says, that men

are equal in their moral capacities. See 'The Idea of Equality'.

4 See Raz, J. *The Morality of Freedom* (1986) Chapter 9 'Equality'. Also, Lucas, J. *On Justice* (1980) Chapter 9 'Justice and Equality'.

5 Dworkin notes this feature obliquely in his article 'Equality of Welfare', which I discuss at some length in Chapter 11. See also later in this chapter and his remarks in 'What is Equality?' Part 1: Equality of Welfare', *Philosophy and Public Affairs* (1981) 185, at 245.

6 *Taking Rights Seriously*, p.227.

7 See Nagel, T. *Mortal Questions* (1979) Cambridge, Chapter 8 'Equality', p. 106. Nagel suggests that we should look at morality from the perspective of the person who has the most 'unacceptable' point of view. 'It is this ideal of acceptability to each individual', he says,'that underlies the appeal of equality' (123). He gives the example of two children, one normal and the other handicapped, in a family which has few resources. A move to the city would be unpleasant for all except that proper medical facilities would be available for the handicapped child. A move to the country would mean less strain on the family's resources and it would mean that the normal child would have a more agreeable life than the handicapped child whose disagreeable life will only be rendered less disagreeable by the medical treatment available to him if the family moved to the city. As far as equality is concerned, Nagel says that the move to the city is required because of the urgency.

8 See O'Donovan, K. 'Affirmative Action' in *Equality and Discrimination: Essays in Freedom and Justice* ed. Guest and Milne (1985) Franz Steiner p. 77 at p. 81. She argues, in defence of reverse discrimination, that the debate is really about equality of opportunity.

9 'The Idea of Equality', 130.

10 *Taking Rights Seriously*, p. 90.

11 *Taking Rights Seriously*, p. 91.

12 *Taking Rights Seriously*, p. 275.

13 See Fred Rosen's interpretation of Bentham. He says that Bentham thought that only 'diminishing returns' were to be obtained by inequalities. Rosen, *Jeremy Bentham and Representative Democracy. A Study of the Constitutional Code* (1983) Oxford.

14 See Mill, 'On Liberty', in *Utilitarianism, On Liberty and Considerations on Representative Government* Everyman (1972). Mill's distinction is general enough for the analogy I have drawn here! Throughout 'On Liberty', Mill uses different words to describe the distinction and there is an obvious latitude in the idea. Other-regarding actions are those which do harm to others (73), injury to others (115), encroach on the rights of others (121), injure certain interests of others (132), inflict loss or damage (135), involve falsehood or duplicity (135), are selfish abstinences from defending others against injury (135), breach a duty to others (135), infringe the rules necessary for the protection of fellow creatures (135), violate distinct and assignable obligations (137), occasion perceptible hurt to any assignable individual (138), are prejudicial to the interests of others (149), or are hurtful to others (149).

15 See 'Equality of Welfare', 245.

16 See 'Equality of Welfare', 245.

17 See *Taking Rights Seriously*, p. 277–8.

18 See *Taking Rights Seriously*, p. 278 and *A Matter of Principle*, Chapter 2 'The Forum of Principle' esp. p. 58 and pp. 65–9. Also see 'Social Sciences and Constitutional Rights – the Consequences of Uncertainty' *Journal of Law and Education* 6:3, 10–12 (1977). See, too, *Lochner* v. *New York* 198 U.S. 45 (1905) in which the Supreme Court struck down New York's maximum hours for bakers under a supposed right to liberty to contract (mentioned by Dworkin in *Taking Rights Seriously* at p. 278).

19 See Dworkin's remarks in Magee's *Men of Ideas*: 'Isn't it absurd to suppose that pleasure (or happiness, or the satisfaction of desires) is a good in itself? So if we really do think that the general welfare is an important consideration in political affairs we must find a better explanation of why. I think we can find a better explanation in the idea of equality ... The apparent opposition between rights and the general good ... is just an opposition on the surface.' Magee, *Men of Ideas*, p. 225.

20 See last section.

21 This will depend upon such factors as the general use, the relative stability, confidence, and enforceability of contracts involving money, and many other ones, of course.

22 He wrote *A Manual of Political Economy* (1909).

23 The criterion is based upon two important papers: Kaldor, 'Welfare Propositions of Economics and Interpersonal Comparisons of Utility' (1939) 49 *Economic Journal* 549–52; and Hicks, 'The Valuation of Social Income' (1940) 7 *Economics* 105–24.

24 See Coase, 'The Problem of Social Cost' (1960) 3 *Journal of Law and Economics* 1–44.

25 See *United States* v. *Carroll Towing Co.* 159 F.2d 169 (2d Cir. 1947). Judge Learned Hand said there that the defendant was negligent if the loss caused by the accident, multiplied by the probability of the accident's occurring, exceeded the burden of the precautions that the defendant might have taken to avert it. Also see Posner, 'A Theory of Negligence' 1 *Journal of Legal Studies* 29 (1972); also Brown, 'Toward an Economic Theory of Liability' 2 *Journal of Legal Studies* 323 (1973). In the next chapter a non-Posnerian interpretation of this test is considered.

26 (1980) *Hofstra Law Review* Vol. 8 487–507, 495.

27 Posner, (1980) *Hofstra L.R.* 487 at p. 492.

28 Let us say we accept Dworkin's analysis of the relationship between courts and legislatures and consider that the function of courts is to decide the rights of the parties and not to decide upon matters concerning the creation of more wealth for society as a whole. Do we have to accept that the economic lawyers' analysis is wrong?

Some lawyer economists recognise the problem in the following way. It is, I think, unsatisfactory. The tactic is to recognise that people feel a sense of grievance when efficient results do not benefit them and to weight those grievances with a wealth component, which economists call 'demoralisation costs'. An example, bringing out its essential nature, is that of the litigant who goes to court because he believes his rights have been infringed and then discovers that a wealth efficient decision is imposed. His 'demoralisation' is 'costed' in some weighting factor but he loses out in the calculation of overall efficiency. He still has a grievance. As you can see, this cannot get around the problem because the grievance is not satisfied. This must follow from the use of the efficiency criterion that the economic lawyers use. The net benefit is not used to compensate those left worse off after the decision.

29 See Calabresi, G. 'About Law and Economics: A Letter to Ronald Dworkin', *Hofstra LR* 8: 553 (1980), where Calabresi answers Dworkin's article criticising Posner, 'Is Wealth a Value?' now in *A Matter of Principle* (1986) p. 237.

30 And something else to give the idea of equality more than just a closure or 'numbers' content.

31 *A Matter of Principle*, p. 283.

32 See 'The Law of the Slave-Catchers', *Times Literary Supplement*, 5 December 1975, p. 1,437; 'Justice Accused', *Times Literary Supplement*, 9 January 1976.

33 'The *Defunis* Case: The Right to Go to Law School' (1976) 23 *New York Review of Books*, no. 1, p. 29 (Reprinted in *Taking Rights Seriously*, ch. 9 at p. 223 as 'Reverse Discrimination'); 'The *Defunis* Case: An Exchange' (1976) 23 *New York Review of Books* no. 12, p. 45; 'Why Bakke Has No Case' (1977) 24 *New York Review of Books*, no. 18, p. 11 (Reprinted in *A Matter of Principle*, at p. 293 as 'Bakke's Case: Are Quotas unfair?'); 'The Bakke Case: An Exchange' (1978) 24 *New York Review of Books* no. 21 and 22, p. 42.; 'The Bakke Decision: Did It Decide Anything?' (1978) *New York Review of Books* no. 13 p. 20 (reprinted in *A Matter of Principle*, at p. 304 as 'What Did *Bakke* Really Decide?'); 'How to Read the Civil Rights Act' (1979) 26 *New York Review of Books* (reprinted in *A Matter of Principle* at p. 316); 'Let's Give Blacks a Head Start' *The Times* 12 December 1981, p. 6.

34 'Journalists' Right to a Fair Trial', *The Times*, 30 November p. 17; 'The Rights of Myron Farber' (1978) 25 *New York Review of Books*, no. 16, p. 34 (reprinted in *A Matter of Principle*, at p. 373 as 'The Farber Case: Reporters and Informers'); 'The Rights of Myron Farber: an Exchange' (1978) 25 *New York Review of Books* no. 19, p. 39; 'Is the Press Losing the First Amendment?' (1980) *New York Review of Books*, no. 19, p. 49; 'The Press on Trial' (1987) 34 *New York Review of Books* no. 3, p. 27; 'Time's Settlement' (1987) 34 *New York Review of Books* no. 4, p. 45; 'Time's Rewrite' (1987) 34 *New York Review of Books* no. 6, p. 45; 'Reckless Disregard: An Exchange' (1987) 34 *New York Review of Books*, no. 13, p. 3; 'Devaluing Liberty' (1988) 17 *Index on Censorship*, no. 8, p. 7; 'The Ragged Banner of Liberty' *The Independent*, 8 September 24 (a summary of the *Index on Censorship* article).

35 'Principle, Policy, Procedure' in *Crime, Proof and Punishment: Essays in Memory of Sir Rupert Cross* (London: Butterworth, 1981), p. 193.

36 'Reagan's Justice' (1984) 31 *New York Review of Books*, no. 17, p. 27; 'Reagan's Justice: an Exchange' (1985) 31 *New York Review of Books*, no. 2, p. 38; 'The Bork Nomination' (1987) 34 *New York Review of Books* no. 13, p. 3 (Also in *Cardozo Law Review*, 1987, p. 101); 'The Bork Nomination: an Exchange' (1987) 34 *New York Review of Books* no. 15, p. 59; 'The Bork Nomination' (1987) 34 *New York Review of Books*, no. 17, p. 60; 'The Great Abortion Case', 36 *New York Review of Books*, no. 11, at p. 49 and see 'The Future of Abortion' 36*New York Review of Books* no. 14 at p. 47.

37 'The Great Abortion Case', 36 *New York Review of Books*, no. 11, at p. 49 and 'The Future of Abortion', 31 *New York Review of Books* no. 14, at p. 47.

38 See Chapter 7 in relation to the idea of 'original intention'.

39 His analysis of the case appears in *The New York Review of Books*, Vol. XXXVI, no. 11, at p. 49 as 'The Great Abortion Case'. See also, 'The Future of Abortion', 36 *New York Review of Books*, no. 14, at p. 47.

40 *Sweatt* v. *Painter* 339 U.S. 629, 70 S.Ct. 848.

41 Of particular importance, at this stage in the development of this argument, was the fact that in Texas, the law school of the state university had a unique standing in preparing candidates for admission to the bar. Given this standing, it was impossible in fact for separate black educational facilities to be equal. This policy of admissions is assumed, or argued, to be a necessary element in an 'affirmative action' programme which will improve the position of minority groups in the legal (or medical, (etc.) professions). It is necessary to point this out to show why the later case of *Brown* v. *The Board of Education* 347 U.S. 486 (1954) still had something to decide.

42 Dworkin's important remarks about reverse discrimination are general statements about political and legal philosophy and so I have described the general case of reverse discrimination programmes. I have included the idea of argument in the context of the Fourteenth Amendment to illustrate how a moral, political argument can, at the same time, be a legal argument. Dworkin has discussed two cases on the constitutionality of such programmes, at some depth, however, the *Defunis* and *Bakke* decisions. See 'Why Bakke Has No Case' (1977) 24 *New York Review of Books*, no. 18, p. 11, reprinted in *A Matter of Principle*, at pp. 293–303, as 'Bakke's Case: Are Quotas Unfair?'; 'The Bakke Decision: Did It Decide Anything?' (1978) *New York Review of Books*, no. 13, p. 20, reprinted in *A Matter of Principle*, at pp. 304–15, as 'What Did *Bakke* Really Decide?'; Chapter 9, 'Reverse Discrimination', of *Taking Rights Seriously*; and particularly *Law's Empire* pp. 387–97.

43 *Report of the Committee on Obscenity and Film Censorship* Cmd.7772, HMSO, London, 1979. Dworkin thinks that what he calls 'the Williams's strategy' is wrongly based on the idea that what is important, or unimportant, about the banning of pornography revolves entirely round the question whether community goals are enhanced. Although he is in favour of a number of conclusions of the Report, he does not think the goal-based strategy is sufficient to support them. Goal-based justification, he says, '... has the weakness of providing contingent reasons for convictions that we do not hold contingently' (*A Matter of Principle*, p. 352).

44 See Raz, *The Morality of Freedom*, 1986, Chapters 14 and 15.

45 *Law's Empire*, p. 395.

46 *Law's Empire*, p. 394.

47 See *Law's Empire*, p. 397. Note Dworkin's discussion of the case of *Regents of the University of California* v. *Bakke* 438 U.S. 265 (1978). Dworkin suggests that a possible line Bakke (who was a majority, white applicant) might have taken was that the Davis medical programme did not consider the impact of the quota system upon *his* group in assessing the contribution to the general welfare by having a greater number of qualified black doctors.

But, he says, 'Hercules would decide (I believe) that this claim is confused: a quota system gives the same consideration to the full class of applicants as any other system that relies, as all must, on general classifications.'

10

Equality of what?

Dworkin, more than any other contemporary political philosopher, has taken on the pivotal issue in liberal–democratic thinking of defining equality, and forcefully developed that idea to produce a bold and striking theory. Equality is central to Dworkin's political philosophy and forms a major focus in his legal philosophy. The connection with law is that making the best sense of the law means making the best *moral* sense of it and *that* means making the best sense of it in terms of equality. We have seen in the previous chapter how Dworkin's particular conception of the concept of equality lies in the idea of treating people 'as equals', as opposed to treating them 'equally'. It is this latter, very abstract idea that Dworkin develops.

This chapter proposes to examine his current thinking on equality. It is at yet in the stage of development and takes us at first some way from legal philosophy. But because the arguments of equality are relevant to the determination of legal rights and duties, his legal and political philosophy are fused firmly together.

The development of his thinking already suggests ways in which legal arguments may develop, in particular in connection with the growth of economic analysis. In *Law's Empire*'s most difficult section, he outlines a possible mode of reasoning which tracks contemporary economic analyses of the law of tort, in particular the torts of nuisance and negligence. The result is an analysis of the 'neighbour' principle which connects legal rights and duties with a result conducive to both economic analysis and the abstract principle of treating people as equals. I shall examine this at the end of the present chapter. But I am aware that to get to it requires taking a tortuous route.

The background to this development takes us into the question he raised in two extremely difficult but important papers he published in 1981.[1] He has since refined and expanded his views in a dense but brilliant article, 'The Place of Liberty', published in 1987.[2] I have drawn, too, from a number of unpublished papers and seminar materials, as well as from my sense of his theory as I have heard it develop at seminars he has given. Assuming that we accept that people should be treated as equals, the question he raises is: what resources should people be entitled to, in the ideal society where people are treated as equals? In a nutshell, equality of resources is Dworkin's conception of treating people as equals.

A preliminary intuitive account

Dworkin's concerns are with the reconciliation of the twin liberal ideals of equality and liberty. How do we preserve individual liberty in requiring that each individual be treated equally – as a human being? Dworkin's conclusions are highly original. At first blush, they are a mixture of socialist equalising and *laissez-faire* economics. That is so because we are used to thinking that theories of liberalism make sense only on the assumption that equality and liberty are polar opposites. Dworkin's strong defence of equality, on the contrary, is at the same time a strong defence of liberty.

How does he claim to achieve this? In what follows, I shall describe what I believe to be the main stages of his highly compli- cated theory. As I have said, his own description of his theory, contained in three articles, is dense and extremely difficult. He mixes brilliant intuitive insights with obscure passages of explanation. Much of it is intuitive, which should not bother us too much, I think. We are aware of the method he employs of the constructive form of Rawls's 'reflective equilibrium'. On the other hand, much of the discussion enters the technical world of economics. One gets the feeling sometimes that philosophy ought not to have to be as difficult as this. (But is there a single reason why philosophy should *not* be as difficult as this?)

Dworkin does make sense of many of the arguments that we do, in fact, take for granted in our day-to-day understanding of political affairs. In particular, the intimacy of the connection he makes between market economics and liberal egalitarianism is extremely important and constitutes, in my view, a large step forward in political thinking.

I propose, given the difficulties, to present his theory by offering first an intuitive and journalistic overview. The first general insight is this. Resources are a major source of freedom. They are not the only one, but certainly a major one. Generally speaking, we are more free the more resources we have. But note the following, at least for the real world. We have more resources if we are talented and fewer resources if we are handicapped. In other words, the more talented and the less handicapped you are the more freedom you have.

Let us refine the idea of freedom. Is it an important idea? Yes, because if you are free to develop and shape your life in accordance with your own convictions and ambitions you live a better life. In fact, it may be that it does not make much sense to say that you can live a life, properly called *your* life, that has been shaped for you by, as it were, external forces.

There seems to be, then, a distinction, in the real world, between those aspects of you which are part of your capacity to form ideas and convictions about how you would like to live your life and those aspects which are a help or hindrance to living that life. The aspects will include access to physical resources as well as talents and handicaps.

Let us now apply the principle that people are equal as human beings. We do not distinguish between people on any basis other than our concern for their humanity. You will recall our discussion of this aspect of equality in the last chapter. Are talented or handicapped or rich or poor people any better or worse *as human beings*? Are people of different castes, or of different coloured skins, or of different sex or of different heights better or worse because of these attributes? If we endorse the principle that we must treat people as equals, clearly the answer is no.

In other words, the person we are getting at in the fundamental idea of treating people as equals is a disembodied person, which is not at all an odd idea. If we think that the colour of a person's skin is irrelevant in taking into account his *humanity*, we just ignore that bodily attribute.[3] More directly: if you think that a person is inherently entitled to more respect just because he has talent, or just because he is a member of a particular caste, consider whether you accept the principle that all people should be treated equally as *human beings*.

Let us now turn to the twin ideas of equality and freedom. If the government must treat its citizens as equals, what should it do in the absolutely ideal world? Dworkin says that it should, crudely, make them equal in their freedoms, as far as that is possible. Treating a person as an equal means treating him in such a way as to give him maximum freedom to develop his life in accordance with his convictions. But it must follow that the freedom of each person is to be limited to the extent that person's exercise of freedom reduces the amount of freedom of another. That *must* follow from the initial abstract injunction that people be treated as equals.

Here we should connect freedom with the question of distribution of resources. No person or group of persons should be granted disproportionate freedom in the use of resources because the effect would be to *take away* freedom in the use of those same resources from other persons. At first sight, then, any justification for allowing unequal use of resources compromises equality.

But if the disembodiment of personality is taken seriously, we have to make up for the potential freedoms lost by the handicapped person. We have to equalise him upwards. Think about it. If he is as much a *person* as someone who has average potential, he loses out. Treating him equally as a person must mean distributing to him sufficient resources to bring him, as nearly as possible, to the level of potential freedom of the average person.

The logic of equalising must now be carried fully through. Someone who is talented has potentially more freedom. He can move through the real world more easily and will find it easier to acquire more resources, say, by the more skilful use of the resources he already has. But if it is true that he is just as much a person as a handicapped or averagely competent person, then he gains, just by virtue of his talent, an unequal share of resources. That means that that when he uses his talents (because, of course, he might not choose to) the freedoms gained which are attributable to talent alone (remember, we are in the absolutely ideal world) represent an unequal share of the total freedoms (as it were) available.

You can see the intermeshing of equality and freedom here. Neither is a prerequisite to the other. We cannot know whether a person is being treated as an equal until we know the freedom to which he is entitled. We cannot know whether he has sufficient freedom until we know that he is being treated as an equal. They are, according to Dworkin, two sides of the same coin.

An important point should be clarified about this general, and admittedly journalistic, account before going on to see how Dworkin has developed it. It is that a person's resources are those measured over that person's whole life. In a nutshell, your life begins at birth and ends at death. During that time, you have resources of all sorts. You can make a large splash at the beginning and have fewer freedoms later on. You can restrict yourself at the beginning and have greater freedoms later on. You can make gambles and either win or lose. Or you can choose to use as few of your resources as you like. It is in these ways that you develop your life. It follows that, at any particular time, some people will have, as a matter of their own choice, more freedoms than others. In other words, any idea of equalising resources will have to take into account the amount of resources people have as measured over their whole life, not just at any one time.

Dworkin's key idea here is that equality demands that each person's freedoms, measured over his life, should be quantified against what his having that freedom costs other people in having *their* freedoms. How, though, can we make real sense of this measurement of relative freedoms? Dworkin suggests that the idea of the economic market provides an answer in the idea of relative cost. We distribute freedoms so that no person 'envies' (in the economic sense in which we assume that each person wishes to maximise the freedoms open to him) any other person's freedom. And we then allow bargaining to take place through the market-place in order to reflect the different choices that people make over their lifetimes.

A problem arises in the setting up of the circumstances of bargaining. This is that the idea of the market presupposes a number of things, such as (the most obvious one) *people* to bargain. To get the idea of the cost of each person's life to other people, the idea of 'a market' is not in itself enough. We have to specify the conditions under which market transactions are properly conducted.

What does this mean? It means that the idea of a person is 'prior' to the market. Contrary to Posner's claim, the market does not allocate rights but is itself determined by them.[4] What is important to the person is to be specified in the conditions (the baseline) under which the market operates (remember that we are talking about the absolutely ideal world). What is important to the person? Well, obviously, personal security. You cannot enter the market if you are prevented by physical coercion. Further, the market must operate consistently with the injunction that people should be treated as equals. That means that market transactions that, for example, resulted in a racially prejudiced distribution would be inconsistent with the baseline. And further, if the market cannot ensure bargaining that is consistent with that baseline through technical reasons ('externalities' in economist's terms) then it might be corrected so as to produce the result consistent with equality that would have come about but for the technical difficulties (remember the Coase theorem).

On the other side of this coin, however, is the injunction that people should have the maximum potential for freedom possible consistent with the principle of equality. This principle has two aspects. First, people's choices should be authentic choices. They should not come to the market manipulated into making predetermined choices, nor should they make their choices in a state of ignorance. They should not, in other words, have come to the market without having had the chance to form their opinions and convictions about what they want to do in conditions of freedom. Also, the market should not artificially restrict the availability of what is bargained for, or otherwise place any restrictions on their subsequent use.

Here is an important point. If freedom is part of the conditions for the market, how can we make sense of bargaining in the market *for* freedoms? Those freedoms have to be determined before the market can even take place.

It is a recognition of this problem which, I think, makes Dworkin look in two directions. One is backwards, towards the idea of certain fundamental freedoms necessary to determine genuine equality. The other is forwards, towards the idea of resources. Resources represent only a potential for freedoms. In other words, there is a distinction between resources and the freedoms necessary for the economic market, although resources represent one kind of important potential for freedom. The distinction is important because resources are the subject of bargaining *after* the baseline for the market has been put in place.

What, more precisely, are resources? They must include wealth, namely all those tangible and intangible assets with which a person may trade. But they must also include talents and, conversely, we must say that handicaps represent a lack of resources. This is not, actually, such a difficult or strange idea. Our talents are part of our potential freedoms, as much as our bank balance. So, we make people equal in resources, with the appropriate emendations in relation to handicaps (by giving handicapped people what they would have been able to get without the handicap) and talents (by taking from talented people all those things that they acquired solely through talent). We then arrange the market so that it works in accordance with the principle of equality which, remember, includes the principle that the market transactions assume maximum freedom.

What are advantages of this – obviously ideal – way of looking at things? I think Dworkin intends there to be two main ones. First, the theory combines the insights of socialism, that men are inherently human beings, independent of their particular circumstances, with the insights of a popularly understood libertarianism, that men are best when they are free to make their own lives according to their own lights. It achieves this without falling into the obvious pitfalls of both socialism and libertarianism, namely, that socialism supports an unwarranted restriction of freedoms, a 'levelling downwards', and libertarianism supports the unjustifiable promotion of the liberty of a select few. The second insight, I think, is that it provides an ethical basis for market mechanisms, and suggests ways in which the market should be corrected in accordance with that ethical basis.

But this account is, as I have said, only an intuitive overview, and I should now proceed to examine in detail, first, how Dworkin makes his case for equality of resources and why it is preferable to equality of 'welfare'. The answer to this question informs as to how equality of resources differs from utilitarianism. Secondly, we must look more closely at the principles to be embedded in the market baseline, in particular what Dworkin calls the principle of abstraction. Thirdly, we must look at Dworkin's application of this ideal theory to the real world that you and I live in and look, particularly, at his important idea of the 'liberty-deficit'. Finally, and most importantly for this current study, we must see how Dworkin relates the ideal of equality of resources to legal argument.

The argument for equality of resources: the unintelligibility of equality of welfare[5]

Here is the problem. The idea that everybody should be equal in welfare is initially attractive but, on closer inspection, incurably problematic. If people are to be treated as equals, what should they be made equal in? Happiness? Wealth? Pleasure? Success in a chosen field? Beauty? Health? Luck? What they want? Plots of land? Each of these things raises its own problems. Some things are unattainable by some people, others are not attainable things. That is why some people say that the idea of equality is a myth, as I discussed in the previous chapter. But some of these things are attainable, like success or happiness, and the means to attaining them are possible. A government cannot endow people with success or happiness but it can provide, by way of distribution of resources, in the form of goods and services, the means to these things.

'Welfare' is a collective name for most of those things of the above list that are attainable by people. Roughly, and as an introduction to the idea, it means 'wellbeing'. The question of the principles we should use in making people as nearly equal in welfare as possible thus makes some sense. It means that a government would have to ask what constituted welfare for different people and then distribute resources so that people were, as best as could practicably be secured, equal in that welfare.[6]

The idea of 'reasonable regret'

Dworkin considers three ways in which we might consider the idea of welfare. We might think of it as the achievement of success in some area whether it is to do with our own or other people's lives. Or, we might consider it to be the attainment of some sort of conscious state, such as pleasant feelings, as the early utilitarians thought it to be. Or, we might think welfare to be some form of either of these two possibilities, but add the rider that the judgment of a person's success or his attainment of a particular conscious state is one to be judged objectively, say, in face of a denial by that person of his level of welfare.

Dworkin's most detailed discussion of the problem is on the question of the equalising of success in personal preferences. He draws a number of distinctions of striking originality and importance in the making of judgments about people's lives. The impressionistic 'feel' it has arises only because of his use of the method of reflective equilibrium. He is appealing to your intuitions and your task, if you disagree, is either to deny (genuinely) that you have such intuitions or point to some theoretical incoherence in the conclusions he draws.

He concentrates his study on the idea of welfare upon how a

person's life rates in terms of its 'overall success'. It entails a more serious account of what is of value, what he calls 'critical' value in a person's life. It is by his idea of the critically valuable life that Dworkin dispenses with much of modern utilitarian thinking and welfare economics on the ground that it is concerned only with lives of relative success. He says: '... the language of preferences (or wants or desires) – seems too crude to express the special, comprehensive judgment of the value of a life as a whole.'[7]

But how do we measure overall success so that we can do the equalising? Dworkin tries several tacks. Just asking a person what value their life is to them will not always yield the right result. What of the 'miserable poet' who thinks life is not worth living because he has not produced a great poem? Dworkin suggests that we could make some judgment about the particular talents the poet has and ignore his judgment as to whether it was good for him to have had them. This may allow us to say – as it seems right to say – that there is value in the life of the miserable poet who judges his own life to be a failure.

But this sort of judgment will not, he says, work for the ordinary case. Take two people, Jack and Jill, who live similar, ordinary sorts of lives and are successful although not highly talented. The relevant difference between them is that Jack thinks his life is valuable while Jill thinks her life is humdrum. If overall, critical success is to be measured by their relative judgments of value, then more resources have to be given to Jill because her life, in her view, is not as successful overall measured against Jack's.

Dworkin says that this result is counter-intuitive. By whatever means the judgment is made,[8] the result will be dependent upon Jack's and Jill's *beliefs*, not on the actual differences in their lives. We need, in other words, a degree of objectivity.

Dworkin suggests the idea of 'reasonable regret'. Jack and Jill should judge their lives by asking themselves whether there is something that they could reasonably have had which would have made their lives overall more successful. 'People have lives of less overall success if they have more reasonably to regret that they do not have or have not done.'[9]

It is easy to guess how Dworkin intends the argument to go. The idea of 'reasonableness' imports an independent yardstick meaning that we cannot make people equal on the criterion of their *own* judgment of overall success alone. Take Jack's point of view. He regrets not having more resources in order to take up motor racing. How does he decide that it is a 'reasonable' regret?

It would seem odd if he could simply refer to his aspiration in order to have more resources justifiably transferred to him. The requirement of 'reasonableness' seems right, too, because he could not 'reasonably' request resources for some monstrously expensive project such as, say, the building of a colossal monument to himself. Dworkin's conclusion is thus:

> ... that reasonable regret cannot itself figure in the distributional assumptions against which the decision whether some regret is reasonable is to be made.[10]

Jack and Jill, like most people, both regret that they have had fewer rather than more resources. But how do we determine what is 'reasonably' more? How could Jill compute what she could reasonably have more of in relation to Jack in order to be equal in having a life of overall success? That is only possible, says Dworkin, by making use of some scheme of *fair* distribution of resources in which the judgment of overall success is not included.

Dworkin's argument is not powerful here. It clearly depends on the idea that if one person gains in resources another loses. (And this is supported by his later theory of opportunity costs.) 'Gains' and 'loses' here refer to gains and losses measured against an imagined equal distribution of resources. It follows that each person who makes a judgment about his own life can, according to Dworkin, only do so in relation to an assumption about the fairness of equal distribution.

Why should this follow? I can see that any judgment about the distribution of resources requires an overall judgment about the total resources available. If I judge my life to be a failure unless I can build a monument as high as the Empire State made of diamonds, I must realise that success is impossible because of lack of resources. But why should I regard the idea of 'reasonableness' in 'reasonable regret' as referring to *equal* resources?

Let us try the argument again. True, diamond Empire States are out. *But almost anything else is in.* Take a group of people of assorted talents and virtues. Some are hard-working, some are intelligent or talented in other ways, some are both hard-working and talented, some are not particularly intelligent and do not have much ambition. Let us make judgments about their lives. Let us say that the hard-working talented ones are much more likely to live better, more worthwhile lives. We look to the total resources available and distribute them according to the principle that people should be equal in the value of their lives as judged by themselves. Let us say that the least talented and unambitious admit that they will not make much of their lives, however much money they have. Nevertheless, they can make something more of their lives if they have a certain minimum amount. The talented and hardworking need more money to achieve the lives they envisage for themselves.

We do not *need* a metric of equality of resources here, except for ease of accounting, in the same way as it is wise to have one unit of currency in a fiscal system. Take Guy, Keith and Nicola. Guy is talented and hard-working. Nicola is intent on sexual scheming and needs little except new clothes. Keith likes darts and drinking, and needs more than Nicola but less than Guy. They all recognise these differences between themselves. We give Guy one half of the total of resources, Nicola one eighth and Keith three-eighths.

We achieve equality of overall success. Why not? All three are agreed, and that corresponds, too, with an objective judgment we make about the three lives. We grade the lives and carve up the resources. Where is the *equality* of resources metric?

Dworkin's response to this, I imagine, would be that we are not here talking about equality because the picture I have drawn typifies non-egalitarian distributions. Take a father who divides pocket money among his children. Sarah gets more because she spends wisely, Kevin gets less because he squanders his money. Sarah does not get more than what an equal distribution would be. She just gets more than Kevin. The baseline for distribution is what each child will make of the resources made available subject, of course, to the overall amount that the father is willing to make available.

Nevertheless, I think it follows that Dworkin fails to *derive* equality of resources from showing that equality of overall success can only be understood on an equality of resources metric. All this is not to say that equality of resources is wrong. There may be other grounds for supporting it. One attractive one is that it comes closest to including within the abstract principle – that people should be treated as equals – an explanation of our intuition that people should be left alone to do what they like with their lives.

We have to know at least that there are some resources available. (Chad, for example, has the lowest proportion of resources as a nation per head of population. It may be that we cannot even begin to talk of the equalisation of welfare in that country, apart from the logistical problems of distribution, since there might not be enough food to go round every inhabitant.) But that is a long way from saying that everyone has an entitlement to an equal amount of resources.

Also the idea of fairness does not do the work here required of it. It may be fair that Jack and Jill receive equal resources and it may be fair that Jill receive more because her life (subjectively or objectively) is of less value than Jack's, or she enjoys it less than he does. That would depend on the correct conception of fairness and that will be, of course, for Dworkin and perhaps for the reader, a conception that equal resources are fair. But that conclusion does not follow from the impossibility of an equality of welfare without an equality of resources.

We could try the following argument in Dworkin's defence. Since we are discussing the concept of equality the conception of fairness within that discussion capitulates to 'fairness as equality'. But that must, I think, beg the question. True, equality of welfare seems to require a criterion of distribution of resources. But the mere fact of 'being in the argument' about equality cannot ensure an equality outcome and we must not be persuaded by our intuition alone that if equality of welfare is wrong equality of resources must be right.

We must assume, then, that Dworkin means that equality of welfare fails through lack of an independent metric of resources. This is a striking way, I think, of arguing that welfare is not subjectively measurable between people, and that another metric, not necessarily of resources, would be required. He then adopts what appears to be the next best candidate. And, as I suggested in my intuitive overview of his theory, a particular attraction of this is its potential for distributing potential freedoms – resources – and that produces a neat synthesis of equality and freedom.

The economics of equality of resources[11]

As I have said, much of the argument in the previous section reminds us of the kind of debate that is often carried on in discussions on the value of utilitarianism, in particular on the question of the incommensurability of values. But it should not be confused with that sort of debate, for Dworkin, it should be remembered,[12] has a unique conception of what utilitarianism, properly understood, is. Utilitarianism is a a form of welfarism, which is the sort of theory that considers welfare to be of central importance. The utilitarian form aims at the maximisation of welfare, although there are some variants. According to Dworkin, 'teleological' utilitarianism regards welfare as a good in itself and so sees sense in its maximisation,[13] but 'egalitarian' utilitarianism is a conception of equality whereby making people equal in welfare is seen as the relevant good.

This 'egalitarian' utilitarianism is the interesting one for Dworkin. He says there are a number of difficulties with it. One is that it is ambivalent between preferring maximum average happiness and maximum average misery. Why? Because the utilitarian part is concerned with welfare and the egalitarian part is concerned with making people equal. So there is no principle within this form of welfarism for separating the situation where everyone is equal in a low degree of welfare but where there is more welfare overall.[14]

Our intuitions seem to balk at the idea that we should increase population in order to obtain more welfare at the expense of lowering the general standard of living. 'Teleological' utilitarianism can get round that problem by saying that levels of welfare are intrinsically important, irrespective of distribution.

But the more telling objection is simply that egalitarian utilitarianism is vulnerable to the charges already laid against the possibility of equalising people in welfare, whether it is some form of success or enjoyment. This cannot be achieved without knowledge of the availability of the means to this welfare and some independent criterion of distribution.

Equality of resources is Dworkin's conception of treating people as equals. It is, of course, an ideal conception and is concerned with the articulation of the principles according to which our political institutions should be organised.[15] The ruling idea is that a person's resources should be measured by what it costs others for him to have:

> Under equality of resources ... people decide what sorts of lives to pursue against a background of information about the actual cost their choices impose on other people and hence on the total stock of resources that may fairly be used by them.[16]

This is fundamentally similar to the idea of 'opportunity cost' familiar in economics but, of course, there is here the more explicit link to an important moral premise of equality. Each person's treatment as an equal in equality of resources must always be measured in terms of the cost to equality of resources of other people. It is natural, therefore, for Dworkin to say that equality of resources presupposes an economic market of some sort.

It is important to follow his development of the idea by which equality of resources might be reached. There is no further argument, other than the ones we have already looked at, for equality of resources. He is only concerned to see how an equality of resources would be achieved and I shall trace his project in what follows. But he exposes a number of important problems in the idea of the ideal market, problems which speak to the rift between right and left wing contemporary political debates on the relative importance of liberty and equality.

The auction

Dworkin proposes an imaginary auction as a model whereby equality of resources might be achieved. Immigrants to an uninhabited and economically rich island take part in this auction. According to the model and consistent with their being treated as equals, the immigrants arrive at the island in full knowledge of the nature of the auction and of the economic riches of the island, and capable of making authentic choices. Naturally, no immigrant has come to the island with extra resources. Accordingly, each immigrant is given an equal number of some form of currency (Dworkin suggests clam shells) and bids for various goods, including plots of land, on the island. Even the size of the various goods, or the plots of land, will be determined by the bidding.

The bidding continues until a stage is reached where no one 'envies' any other person's bundle of goods. Dworkin introduces the envy test as follow: 'No division of resources is an equal division if, once the division is complete, any immigrant would prefer someone else's bundle of resources to his own bundle.'[17] This envy test is an economic, not a psychological test, of widespread use in economic thinking. It is a shorthand way of testing a situation to see what the rational self-maximiser would have achieved.[18]

It is important to see throughout what job the principle of treating people as equals is doing here. It explains the envy test (because no person is to remain envious of another's goods). Further, it governs the assumption that people come to the auction as equals, so that no one person begins from a superior position of resources or superior knowledge. These seem to be eminently reasonable stipulations, because otherwise people in such positions would have advantages over others.

According to Dworkin, the equality principle also creates the conditions for the conduct of the auction. Imagine that the division of the goods on the island is the result of a pre-division by some person. That person, say, divides the land up into plots the size of football pitches. The auction is held and, as a result, no person envies any other for the bundle of goods that she holds.

The result would be that the plots of land contained in the bundles are weighted in favour of the football-size plots as opposed to any others that could have been made. That is why, he says, there should be a requirement built into the auction that the size of the divisions should themselves be open to auction.[19]

Similarly, the auction would be similarly weighted if the auctioneer had traded the island's resources for a large number of equal bundles of – to use Dworkin's examples – pre-phylloxera claret and plovers' eggs. The envy test would be met, but there would be an inherent weighting of the auction towards the particular tastes of the auctioneer.

It is important to see, too, the position played by taste and luck. The goods available on the island may not appeal to the taste of everyone and it may be a matter of luck what tastes could be satisfied. So if there were only pre-phylloxera claret and plovers' eggs available it could be a matter of luck to the person who liked such things but not the person who did not, although the latter would not be able to claim, under equality of resources, that the division of the resources under the auction was unfair.

Luck would be relevant to the popularity of tastes, too. Sometimes, it is lucky that not many people share the same taste and that means that the price is low because the demand is low; other times, the price will be high because there is no popular demand that works economies of scale in production. Again, under equality of resources, these considerations do not affect the fairness of division by the auction. In other words, a distribution could not be challenged as unequal on the ground of the contingent facts of the goods available and the varieties of taste.

The hypothetical insurance market

The envy test is important. It checks that people are being treated as equals because it disallows as an equal division of resources any division which leaves a person preferring another bundle to his own. Crucial for the economics of equality of resources is Dworkin's distinction between 'option' luck and 'brute' luck. 'Option' luck is the sort of luck we might have in gambling, or in playing the stock market, whereby we take a deliberate risk in relation to something. 'Brute' luck, on the other hand, is merely a matter of how risks fall, such as the bad luck we would have if a meteorite fell on us.

Dworkin thinks that 'option' luck is consistent with equality of resources, and indeed, it is a fundamental idea in his development of the idea of personal liberty. People should be permitted to take risks of certain sorts and to reap both the lucky and unlucky consequences. The gambler who wins made a deliberate choice to take a risk and the true cost of that risk is to be measured against what it costs those who have chosen a safer life. The price of that safer life is forgoing any chance of gains. The gambler who loses has at least been in the position to take a risk, with consequent possible gains. He has thus paid the price, losing, for having had the chance to gamble.

Dworkin concludes that there is no general reason why risk-taking should be limited, although he thinks that there could be qualifications such as those based on paternalistic reasons, or reasons of political morality (for example, you should not take a gamble with slavery).[20]

But Dworkin does not think that brute luck is consistent with equality of resources, simply because brute luck is not a matter of deliberate choice. The problem may be dealt with, however, through insurance which will convert brute luck into option luck.

In the simplest case, we can buy insurance to protect our property against theft, for example. We pay a premium, the price of which buys us restitution in the event that our property is stolen. That price is the amount which an insurer would be prepared to accept in order to bear that risk, so the true cost of the insurance is measured as a matter of actuarial calculation against the loss of resources of the insurer in the event of theft.

This relatively simple idea is the key to an elaboration of a hypothetical insurance market carried out by Dworkin to justify compensating brute bad luck. The problem with much brute luck is that it occurs before anyone is near the position of being able to take out insurance to convert it into option luck. In fact, there is usually a cruel catch-22. Those people who have had really bad luck because they are born, say, with spina bifida disease would not be insured because there is no insurable risk and, even if there were, they would not be able to afford the premium.

In the ordinary case, before a handicap strikes, it is often a relatively simple matter to calculate the risks of such an occurrence, especially where the risks are equal. This possibility poses no problem for equality of resources, Dworkin says. In the case where people could not have insured, a counterfactual solution is possible. What insurance would people have bought had they known of the risks? He says that this will give us a workable baseline from which to work out a premium. Further, this will be so, even though people differ in the risks they are willing to take and the insurance premiums they would be prepared to pay. People would, he says, make roughly the same assessment of the value of insurance against handicaps such as blindness, or the loss of limbs, that affect a spectrum of different sorts of lives. He does not think that it would be necessary to 'personalise' insurance for each individual.

The possibility for this kind of compensation for handicaps is there in principle, according to Dworkin. He does not think that it would be possible to find an alternative that would have fewer practical difficulties. Clearly, he thinks that the great merit of the hypothetical insurance form of compensation is a *principled* one because it measures the cost of the system in terms of the equality of resources:

> ... there is no reason to think, certainly in advance, that a practice of compensating the handicapped on the basis of such speculation would be worse, in principle, than the alternatives, and it would have the merit of aiming in the direction of the theoretical solution most congenial to equality of resources.[21]

Back to the immigrants. It will thus be by means of a compulsory insurance levied upon the immigrants that those of them who come to the island with handicaps, or who later develop handicaps, will be compensated for their brute bad luck. This will then place them in the situation of having the same resources (or as near to the same resources as money can compensate) as those of the immigrants who are not handicapped. The cost will, of course, be the combined levies.

It follows that the resources owned by each immigrant will be equal but less than they would have been in the community before the hypothetical insurance system was installed, although, of course, no person will be in unequal position through brute bad luck. And that is morally justified according to the most abstract principle that the state must be organised so as to respect the rights each person has to be treated as an equal.

In order to compensate handicaps in people it is not necessary, Dworkin says, to have some idea of what constitutes 'normal' powers. The enormous difficulties inherent in that idea are not necessary in the hypothetical insurance system. There the market determines which handicaps – the instances of brute bad luck – people would be prepared to insure against because their preferences will be tied to the cost. That market will, therefore, determine an upper limit on the handicaps that are compensable.

Why? Since the ruling idea is that a person's resources should be measured by what it costs others for him to have, the upper limits will be determined by factors such as the risks people would be prepared to take and the premiums they would be prepared to pay given the resources available. It would, perhaps rather unexcitingly, be a matter solely of actuarial calculation.

Similar sorts of argument are available for those who lose out relatively in the labour market. Here, too, Dworkin thinks that a hypothetical insurance market can set a premium which measures, in terms of costs to others, how much a person should be compensated for his lack of talents. We simply imagine the immigrants know their talents but do not know the resources available and thus the likely income levels. They then insure themselves against not having the job which they believe their talents would warrant. At the high end, the insurance premium for *not* having Mick Jagger's sort of job would be very high, because almost no one would be able to achieve that job and so there would have to be a large payout. In fact, only people like Mick Jagger would be able to pay that premium. But further down the scale of skills, it will become much more sensible to insure for, says Dworkin, 'Many more than twice as many people have the abilities necessary to earn the amount earned in the fiftieth percentile than in the ninety-ninth percentile of a normal income distribution'.[22]

By this means we are able to calculate the amounts per person by which a talent-led economy falls short of an ideal distribution. Could we devise a redistributive tax scheme under which those with less than average talents are compensated? How would we pay for it? A flat rate tax, at the level of the average under-employment premium, would be unfair, says Dworkin, because rich people would pay the same as poor people.

Given a number of refinements, however, premiums graduated to match earnings would be acceptable. The declining marginal utility of money, affecting the amount people would be prepared to pay for insurance against not having high paying jobs, and the fact of cheaper premiums at the lower end, would make the insurance scheme more efficient (because the hypothetical insurance firms could make more of a profit).

Further reductions in cost could be achieved by, first, placing the onus on people asking for the more expensive insurance to show that they were not mistaken or dishonest about their talents and, second, by co-insurance, the requirement that people pay a proportion of the difference between what their talents can produce and the level of employment they have insured against not having.

Does this system of tax make sense? If the idea of equality requires that people do not earn less solely through lack of talent, it seems that the principle demands that the more talented you are the more tax you should pay. But note that in the hypothetical insurance market someone like Mick Jagger need not take out an insurance premium, because his talents are sufficient to do without insurance. The hypothetical scheme, in fact, does not appear to account for the very feature it is supposed to. In short, the hypothetical insurance tax scheme cannot fix levels high enough to make the less talented as well off as the very talented. There will, therefore, be a failure in the envy test: people will still envy the talent-earning capacities of the most talented (further down from the most talented, of course, the closer redistribution will get to equality of talents).

Dworkin's answer to this is that the envy test cannot be expected to eliminate differences between people in the way they are actually born to be. He compares two worlds. First, there is the world in which people know of their disadvantages in relation to the talents and ambitions of others and suffer. Second, there is the world in which people do not know of their disadvantages in this way but have an equal opportunity to insure against the disadvantages. Dworkin says the second world is better, saying that the hypothetical insurance argument aims to reproduce the consequences of the second world, as far as it can, in the real world:

> It answers those who would do better in the first world (who include ... many of those who would have more money at their disposal in the second) by the simple proposition that the second is a world that, on grounds independent of how things happen to work out for them given their tastes and ambitions, is more nearly equal in resources.[23]

But this does not mean that wealth differences should be eliminated. That would affect everyone *and distort true opportunity costs*. We cannot argue for a community in which we all have Mick Jagger's income. The closest we could get to that is to say that no one should have that income, so that each of our incomes moves relatively closer to his.

Mick Jagger might not now do what people want him to do, and thus people's choices to listen to, and watch, Mick Jagger will be affected. This political aim would be 'choice insensitive' and the point of the hypothetical insurance market is to make people's choices relevant to the setting of the tax level. We cannot permit that, says Dworkin, for that '… is exactly why the immigrants chose an auction, sensitive to what people in fact wanted for their lives, as their primary engine for achieving equality'.[24]

Dworkin thinks that the dislike of wealth differences is a response to the present society in which we live, in which wealth is admired for its own sake. He suggests that a society of equality of resources, run along his lines, whereby there are wealth differences, but which reflect different ambitions and tastes, would not give rise to the same attitudes and motivations.

Liberty and equality[25]

Vital to Dworkin's conception of equality as equality of resources is his view that we must distinguish the person from his particular circumstances. What does this mean? It helps to go back to the idea that people should be treated as equals and to the idea of the 'common humanity' of people as proposed by Bernard Williams and discussed in Chapter 9. People are alike in their being 'human' so that physically handicapped or talentless people must be treated as 'equals', as equal in humanity, as the non-handicapped and talented.

On the other hand, people differ in their ambitions and tastes and these differences go right across the spectrum of talent and handicap. People can do things. They can further their ambitions and cultivate and develop tastes. But to treat people as equals only requires that they be given the capacities, by way of equality of resources, to do these things. In other words, Dworkin assigns tastes and ambitions to the person and the person's mental and physical powers to his circumstances:

> The distinction required by equality of resources is the distinction between those beliefs and attitudes that define what a successful life would be like, which the ideal assigns to the person, and those features of body or mind or personality that provide means or impediments to that success, which the ideal assigns to the person's circumstances.[26]

In other words, equality of resources stops short of compensating people for their particular tastes and ambitions but requires compensation for lack of talent and physical incapacity.

It stops short because of liberty. Dworkin's project is, as we have seen, to locate liberty in the idea of equality,[27] and that project requires separating out, as it were, that bit of equality that treats people as part of 'common humanity' from the attributes of a person that are capable of development and fulfilment. It would be a wrong part of the equalising process to make people equal in their achievement of their ambitions (equality of overall success). It would be an *illiberal* interference with the development of personality.

If I am right here, I have located the real argument for equality of resources. I have already argued that it does not follow from the collapse of equality of welfare for want of a resources metric. Its real appeal, I suggest, lies in its providing a footing for the development of individual personality.

To repeat: equality of resources is the correct principle of distribution within a political scheme pledged to treating people as equals because 'common humanity' requires that people be put in a position equal with others in order to be free to conduct their lives in a way they wish.[28]

It is necessary now to turn more specifically to what happens once there has been an initial distribution of resources at the auction. Dworkin amends the envy test to apply, not to the bundle of resources that a person has at the moment the auction is finished, but to the bundle of resources that the person has over his whole life.

There is a radical consequence of the compensable nature of talent. It means that no person should be allowed to reap the benefits of his endeavours where the benefits are attributable to his talent but not his ambition. In Dworkin's terms, a distribution of resources is faulty when it becomes 'endowment sensitive' rather than 'ambition sensitive'. Why? The answer goes back to the envy test. A person who, through his talents, achieves a greater share of a community's resources will be envied by other members of the community.

A note on convictions

In his later Tanner lectures,[29] Dworkin considers the criticism that his theory requires too much of a distinction between those parameters of a person's life that he assigns to personality, such as ambition, and the circumstances that a person finds himself in. Is there a relevant difference between personality and circumstance, as he claims?

He considers the objection that there is no relevant difference between personality and circumstances. His answer is that your views, your convictions, about the way you should lead your life, should not be regarded as 'obstacles' in the way of your leading a good life.

My views express what I believe to be truths about the way my life should be led and it would be perverse to suppose that they therefore acted as a limit upon my choices. True, my views limit my choice in one way. I do not choose what I do not choose to do! But, Dworkin says, that is nothing to do with the 'metaphysics' of choice, but is simply an expression of 'the logic of ethical life'.

Let us try this argument yet again. Why is talent not part of personality? Could we be *ourselves* without it? Our convictions express our view about the right way to lead our lives. They 'parameter' them as much as our talents. We could be without them too. Why not compensate a person for his lack of them?

What is Dworkin's argument again? Is it just appeal to intuition in the reflective equilibrium way, that convictions about what the good life is just do not fall into the category of the limits or parameters of the good life? Imagine my convictions to include the belief that violin playing to the best of my (considerable) talents is what constitutes the best life. What would it mean to say that I am not to be compensated for these convictions? To lead my life in accordance with my convictions I need more resources than Dworkinian equality of resources allows (time, an adequate violin, teachers).

Let us try it again. My objection is that my personality, in the convictions I hold, are part of the circumstances in which I live. I must, if I am to be compensated for my circumstances, be compensated, too, for my convictions. Dworkin denies this. He says that our views about what constitutes the good life cannot be regarded as handicaps (unless we thought them wrong, in which case they would not be our views).

What if they are wrong? What if I am wrong in thinking that the right life for me is that of violinist? I am not sure if Dworkin would admit the sense of that question. The argument is difficult here. It appears to rest on the intuitive rightness of one's convictions not being handicaps, or a matter merely of luck. Perhaps that is the real answer: that one's convictions are not a matter of luck. But, then, Dworkin says: 'I can decide not to do what I believe to be best for me, but I cannot decide not to believe that it would be best.' That sounds as though it *were* a matter of luck!

Further on in the Tanner lectures, he seems to offer a separate argument that 'Convictions are part of us not part of our situation ...'. But it seems reasonable to ask in reply: why should not talents be part of *us*?

It may be useful here to return to the striking and intuitively appealing claim that handicaps and talents are a matter of *luck*. Our convictions are not a matter of brute luck, but circumstances are, so circumstances must be adjusted in accordance with the abstract principle of equality so as to compensate the handicapped and tax the fruits of talent. We have no problem with the idea of a person who, through bad luck, suffers some handicap. That we can easily agree, from the abstract principle of equality, requires a different allocation of resources from the total available. It is the *luck* of it that does the intuitive trick. Why should a person be worse off than anybody else through bad luck?

If we stick to the logic of this approach, we must be struck by the argument: why should a person command *more* of the total resources available merely because by *luck* he happens to be more talented than other people? That must offend the abstract principle of equality, too.

I find this argument highly compelling. Now, let us move to other aspects of the personality (because it is clear that talent is part of personality). The appeal of Dworkin's distinction between talents and ambitions must lie in the fact that ambitions are not due to luck, but to something else, something which, I suspect, he would confirm as a virtue.

Methodology: the bridge argument and the market baseline

We have seen, in my introductory intuitive account to Dworkin's idea of equality of resources, that the immigrants' auction must presuppose liberty in the very idea of bargaining so as to equalise resources. It follows from this, he says, that liberties are not to bargained for in the auction or the subsequent market transactions. In other words, liberty has a more fundamental position than a tradable commodity. That is why, he says, it is wrong to suppose that several famous debates, some fought in the US Supreme Court, were merely debates over the correct *compromise* between liberty and equality, as though liberty were no more than what people happened to regard as in their interest. Rather, liberty must be in place, before the arguments about equalising can make sense. That, in Dworkin's view, accords sense to certain fundamental liberties while denying that there is a general and overriding right to liberty.

But this is already too cryptic and we are leaping ahead. What, first, are the constraints, based on liberty, which Dworkin says must be added to the market baseline? The overriding idea, against which every aspect of the market must be tested, is, of course, Dworkin's foundational principle that people must be treated as equals. Dworkin calls this the bridge argument linking his foundational requirement to all that goes on in the market. In other words, we must select the baseline constraints to the market that best give effect to this foundational principle.

One constraint is fairly straightforward. There must be a constraint of freedom to protect personal security. Dworkin leaves development of this idea for future discussion and obviously thinks that there are market-independent reasons – consistent, of course, with treating people as equals – for constraining liberty in order to protect personal security. But there are market reasons, too. We cannot enter the market in many situations where our personal security is jeopardised.

Given this principle, Dworkin introduces the existence of the wide principle of 'abstraction', which asserts the intrusive presence of liberty into the baseline and includes the idea of 'correction'. This principle

> establishes a strong presumption in favour of freedom of choice. It insists that an ideal distribution is possible only when people are legally free to act as they wish except so far as constraints on their freedom are necessary to protect security of person and property, or to correct certain imperfections in markets ...[30]

The principle of 'correction' referred to here is a practical principle for the application of the principle of abstraction to situations in the real world. We cannot assume, especially in the real world, that the market will always achieve results that are consistent with the foundational principle of treating people as equals. We need to permit a correction of the market outcome to take account of this. Dworkin's principle here is very similar to the principle contained in the Coase theorem which we examined in Chapter 9, although, I think, wider in scope. It is available to mimic an ideal market outcome in a real world where 'externalities' thwart people's ambitions and projects. It can be used, too, for situations where such ambitions and projects require co-ordination rather than bargaining, situations where the aim is only to make things work more smoothly (for example, where choosing what side of the road people should drive on).

The point of the abstraction principle is that it sets the conditions for discovering *true* opportunity costs. That is why, in Dworkin's view, it is so much part of the idea of equality. If people are not free to make discriminating choices the real cost to others will be revealed. Imagine, for example, that, before the auction, the auctioneer divided the land on the island up into football field sized lots, or traded all the goods on the island for champagne and cigars. This would show a failure of flexibility, making the array of goods very much less sensitive to the plans and preferences of the immigrants.

Dworkin says that this principle of abstraction bears importantly on the question of whether, if a majority of people want a religious or sexual orthodoxy, there should be an enforcement of that orthodoxy. He thinks that the principle generally supports the liberal view that the state should be neutral between people's moral views, even when there is a majority preference.

Why? Because the idea of opportunity cost is neutral between the *kinds* of lives people wish to lead. Just as a person will find it prohibitively expensive to spend his life amassing the works of Picasso, so will a person who wants to surround himself by a culture that is culturally and sexually orthodox. Of course, in a community where there is a predominant culture of orthodoxy it is likely that living an unorthodox life will be more expensive. That is the other side of the coin. No minority can be assured of a social culture which is congenial to them. If equality of resources were committed to producing a culture in which lives were supposed to be, as Dworkin says, 'equally easy to live', then it would have become an equality of welfare.

Two other principles are of great importance. These are the principles of 'authenticity' and 'independence', both of which spell out more precisely requirements of the principle of 'abstraction' – the presumption in favour of freedom of choice.

Any person who comes to the market must be able to make authentic choices. Obviously, if he has been duped, by lies, or misleading advertising or, indeed, brainwashing, the lifestyle he chooses will not be the one he would have chosen had he been fully free. In his duped state, the lifestyle he chooses will, according to Dworkin, not be properly costed against the choices of others in the market. That is, given the principle of abstraction, the baseline will have to fix some point at which people's personalities are sufficiently developed to make the sorts of free judgments required.

Dworkin develops this idea as one of the grounds for freedom of speech. Freedom of speech is linked to the formation and development of personality. Only in a culture where ideas are tested against others, and *a fortiori* where people have a right to express their views and attempt to persuade others, will the appropriate conditions for the development of the 'authentic' personality be achieved. Indeed, Dworkin thinks that this is such an important aspect of the ascertainment of true opportunity costs (and thus the equalising process) that only in matters of personal security should the right to free flow of opinions be abridged (the 'clear and present danger' test of the US Constitution).

We need to bear in mind the bridge argument in order to understand the principle of independence. The bridge argument, if you remember, requires that all principles governing the market baseline must be consistent with the foundational principle that people should be treated as equals. Simply, the independence principle requires that markets reflecting prejudice or contempt for people are faulty.

Imagine that white immigrants, who form the majority, are prejudiced against blacks and, for that reason, buy up large tracts of land for the express purpose of keeping blacks out of white areas. Dworkin says that there is nothing in the principle of *abstraction* that would prevent this. Nevertheless, it is forbidden by the foundational principle that people should be treated as equals.

This principle of independence can be relevant in two ways. First, it must be written into the baseline so as to remove distortion of opportunity costs. In other words, the auctioneer is to disallow bids based upon prejudice. But second, even markets operating on an unprejudiced baseline will need to be corrected *after* prejudiced bids have been discounted. In the real world, the principle of independence will have to operate alongside the principle of correction. Sometimes, the market will have to be bypassed just in order to achieve the result that would have been achieved had prejudice not infected the transaction.

There is an important and difficult point to note here. Dworkin does not think the elimination of prejudice is a matter of the *ad hoc* patching up of a corrupt market. The insertion of the requirement of independence into the baseline shows, in his view, that the elimination of prejudice is fundamental to the achievement of equality of resources, showing that being prejudiced is the same in status, although not remedy, as being physically handicapped.

It will not hurt to summarise Dworkin's theory yet again. We equalise people in resources by a market device, using the envy test, in order to measure what people wish to do by what that will cost others, who are equally people. We distinguish people as people, independently of those aspects of them attributable to sheer luck, such as handicaps and talent, leaving them only distinguishable on their convictions and ambitions. In judging what the cost to others will be of what they have, we assume that each such person should have physical security and the conditions for free development of personality, and be free from prejudice. We assume that the overriding principle is that people should be treated as equals, and so that in the real world the market can be corrected in accordance with that principle.

A theory of improvement

Of course, the theory so far advanced describes a utopia – an ideal ideal world. For that reason, many people would like to say that it is useless. Why talk about an imaginary world? That is just philosophers' dreamings. We live in the tough, real world where people are prejudiced, mean and stupid and where unjust decisions are made. Why not get down to improving *that* – our kind of world?[31]

This very common response to the kind of theorising that I have been discussing is utterly misguided. We cannot *understand* the idea of our real world being 'tough', 'prejudiced', 'mean', 'stupid' and 'unjust', *unless we understand alternatives where people are not like this*. We must have some idea of what would count as a 'just' decision, for example, to say that 'in the real world' a decision is unjust.

Dworkin's theory is as ideal as any theory of market economics. We understand the imperfections of the market dominated by monopolies, only because we have in mind some ideal market in which there are no monopolies. It is no answer to an economist who is giving advice about why and how monopolies should be controlled to say that his project is misconceived because, actually, there *are* monopolies. He knows there are.

The preliminary intellectual point aside, however, it can be of exasperatingly little help to say, of some institution in the real world, that it needs radical overhauling in comparison to some imaginary model. Dworkin is aware of this problem. He needs some means by which he can attach his critical model to a programme of reform in the world in which we actually live. He attempts to do this by his important idea of an 'equity deficit' which represents the difference between the circumstances of a person in the ideal world and his circumstances in the present real world.

In the real world, Dworkin says that there will be two sorts of equity deficits. First, resource deficits, by which people will have fewer resources than they would have been entitled to under an ideal egalitarian distribution. That is a fairly straightforward idea. However, second, there will be what he calls 'liberty deficits'. These will arise because of some failure, again in the real world, of the baseline principle of abstraction. What is important for Dworkin about this idea is that it is possible for a person to be worse off *vis-à-vis* other people in liberty, but no worse off in relation to them in resources.

Take, for example, a general prohibition on the use of marble for satirical sculpture. Such a prohibition is forbidden by the principle of abstraction, which assumes freedom to do with resources what people want (otherwise true opportunity cost is not ascertained). But the value in the marble to the satirist sculptor is not the same as it is to the person who wishes to construct a marble bath. The sculptor desperately wishes to make satirical points. And that difference in value cannot be measured in money terms. Nor can it be measured in *welfare* terms, if we are to accept, as Dworkin does, that the equalising of people in welfare fails through the lack of an independent metric. (His way, as I have pointed out, of arguing that interpersonal comparisons of welfare are not measurable.)[32]

It is obviously not possible to hold a comprehensive immigrant-type auction in the real world. So we must, according to Dworkin, measure our improvement of society by measuring the reduction of both resource and liberty deficits. Could we devise some general test of reduction? What about a *resource* form of utilitarianism? But this will not work, says Dworkin. Just an increase in community resources when there is no worsening in any person's liberty-deficit would still allow for some people being worse off. That cannot be permitted within Dworkin's scheme because it would be contrary to the foundational principle that people should be treated as equals.

What about a 'dominating' test, namely, one that reduces equity deficits of some people without increasing the equity deficits of others?

This is a subtle test. Note how it differs from the Pareto test of improvement in welfare favoured by many economists. There could be an improvement as far as equality is concerned without an improvement in welfare. Indeed, an improvement in equality might mean the reduction of welfare for, say, some rich people, if redistribution is required to fund equality-justified welfare schemes:

> Even though they limit freedom, they leave no one worse off, with respect to the value of that freedom, than he would be in an ideal situation. So dominating improvements in equality are much easier to achieve, and are therefore of much greater practical importance, than Pareto improvements.[33]

But we can go further, says Dworkin. Some non-dominating improvements (in other words, reductions in equity-deficits which result in the increasing of equity-deficits for others) are possible. If, for example, there were no new liberty-deficits, and the resource-deficits of the worst off were improved then, he says, that might be justified at the cost of some resource deficits being increased.

Dworkin produces a rule of thumb type guide to the kinds of political decisions that might be made. But he does not think that a 'general and comprehensive' formula is possible and prefers a fresh inspection of each non-dominating claim. It bears some similarities to the Rawlsian 'difference' principle, according to which any improvement in the worst-off is a gain in justice but, as Dworkin says, is 'more guarded'. (And, of course, is overtly different in the sense that Dworkin's rule of thumb is based squarely on a foundational principle, that of treating people as equals). It is this:

> << non-dominating gains are justified where no one's deficit loss is greater than the largest deficit gain to a member of the most disadvantaged class>>

But we must note the extremely important rider Dworkin adds here. It is that no programme of improvement in his view is justified if it introduces, as he says, 'new and significant' liberty constraints. Why? The argument is startlingly simple. It is just that liberty and resource deficits are *incommensurable*. It is not possible to measure, in terms of improvements towards equality, the loss of, say, free speech, in terms of an increase of rice for the very poor.

But, as Dworkin points out, we do live in the real world. Is it really the case that restrictions on freedom cannot be justified in bringing that world closer to the ideal?

His answer is no. Any person who has some liberty taken away in the cause of improving equality will be 'victimised'. Dworkin is, unfortunately, at his unclearest here. Not every loss of liberty will be a case of victimisation, because no person is entitled to more liberty than the ideal distribution would allow. But beneath that level it seems right to say that people will be victimised, because any person suffering from a liberty-deficit suffers a loss of freedom to do something that would contribute to a more just society.

Consider our satirical sculptor. Or the man who wishes to make political speeches. If they are prevented from pursuing their desired activities they are unable to work towards a world where decisions about resources are made in conditions of freedom (that is, in accordance with the principle of abstraction). Decisions will be less authentic, according to Dworkin's justification of free speech in terms of the baseline principle of authenticity.

The implications for the real world are difficult, as we would expect. But Dworkin considers three cases in which the principle of victimisation would be helpful.

The first one is that of the justification for placing financial constraints on the promoting of political candidates. In the United States there was a statute passed by Congress which limited the amount any one person could lawfully spend to advance the interests of a particular political candidate.[34] In *Buckley* v. *Valeo*, this statute was declared to be unconstitutional by the Supreme Court on the ground that it violated freedom of speech as guaranteed by the first amendment.[35] Under an ideal egalitarian distribution, Dworkin thinks that such a restriction would be unjustified. If you will remember from Chapter 4, in his view, the freedom to be able to influence political thinking is a significant freedom of a properly democratic community. In the *ideal* society, where there is equality of resources, no person will be able to amass such an amount of resources as to have a disproportionate political impact. Things are different, however, in the real world, where vast differences of income permit some political candidates to make a disproportionate impact. In Dworkin's view, the financial constraints placed upon political candidates were justified. Since they did not impose restrictions on freedom that were less than would have been permitted under an ideal egalitarian distribution they were not, therefore, instances of victimisation.

The argument works most easily for this case of political constraint because it concerns solely a financial constraint. But Dworkin tests the argument against two other areas of concern: restrictions on freedom to use private medicine and restrictions on freedom of contract. If private medicine was abolished, as political parties do, from time to time, promise, this would reduce the freedom of rich people (and people on company insurance schemes) to choose their doctors and times of treatment. The test Dworkin proposes – the victimisation test – is whether the freedoms so reduced would take these people's freedoms *below* what they would have under an ideal distribution.

Dworkin thinks that there are a number of answers to this question and that this fact in itself speaks to the practicality of the victimisation test. Two possible sorts of ideal distribution might be possible in the real world. First, a comprehensive private system combined with government insurance for what the average person would be prepared to insure. Second, something like the British system, whereby there is the National Health Service combined with the availability of private medicine.

If we assume that the National Health Service would not be improved by abolishing private medicine, then we could compare the National Health Service alone with either of these two possible ideal distributions. Then we could ask whether, compared with these, we would obtain better care, or faster service for less than life-threatening illnesses, or more choice for particular doctors. If the answer is yes to each of these three questions then we would have to conclude that the government was victimising people by outlawing private medicine and leaving only the National Health Service as it presently stands.

Dworkin gives the example as an illustration of a way he sees his theory of improvement working. It is not intended to exclude other possibilities. He says that the government might abolish private medicine in favour of a more close-to-ideal version of the NHS, or it might limit queue-jumping.

Dworkin also considers restrictions on freedom of contract, such as those imposed by New York State in the 1900s on bakers' employees' hours and conditions of work (for example, bakers were forbidden to work for more than sixty hours each week). These legal restrictions were declared unconstitutional by the Supreme Court in the well-known case of *Lochner*.[36] His answer is that it seems right that freedom of contract should not be restricted, because it victimises the employees. On the other hand, he does not think that the *Lochner* decision was right. It did not, for example, deal in sufficient detail with such matters as health and safety, and paid no attention to questions of equality of bargaining power.

But there is a much more fundamental reason, in Dworkin's view, for criticising the Supreme Court's decision. Here we have to turn back to the idea of judicial integrity discussed in Chapter 3. Dworkin reminds us that the Supreme Court is not the legislature and that it must, therefore, assume that New York State was continuously carrying out a policy of treating *all* of its citizens with equal concern and respect. This assumption is an assumption of principle. The court had to interpret the legislation, in other words, on the assumption that the employees who lost jobs as a result would be treated in a way that compensated for that loss of income and status. To interpret the legislation in any other way would, in Dworkin's view, have been to judge it according to the *policy* contained in it. In other words, Dworkin is saying that the Supreme Court was usurping the New York State's legislative function and, in fact, declaring that State's policy to be unsound.

The neighbour principle and the law of tort

We have now had an inkling of how Dworkin's theory of equality of resources touches real, live legal argument. We should remind ourselves of his interpretive approach. He wants to make the 'best sense' of legal argument. The best sense means the best sense in terms of political morality. It is clear that, for him, moral judgment is not an interpretive exercise. So, the best sense that can be made of legal practice must be traceable to the moral picture of the ideal ideal world. I say 'traceable' because the existence of the real world means that there will be an intermediate theory of improvement which translates the ideal world into a programme for reform.

Ideal and real world improvements

We come to a difficulty in interpreting Dworkin. It is clear that he thinks that utilitarianism, even in its very best form ('egalitarian utilitarianism in the resources space'), is not the correct theory of justice in the ideal world. Why? Simply because it can justify making some people less equal if average equality (of resources) is increased.

On the other hand, we discover that Dworkin thinks that, in the real world of the US and UK legal systems, the political 'culture' is predominantly utilitarian, that is to say, community goal oriented. We are now required, by Dworkin, to make best sense of this real practice of utilitarianism by, for example, interpreting the pursuit of the goals as constrained by rights. This is the force behind his idea of 'rights as trumps' over utilitarian goals.

I do not think that there is a problem here. After all, Dworkin's theory of improvement acknowledges the force of obligation to a 'good faith' attempt by government to approximate to an ideal distribution (what he calls the 'most defensible egalitarian distribution' in the real world). We saw this in Chapter 4.[37] If it is utilitarianism of some sort, it is, for example, right for him to defend reverse discrimination programmes on the basis that utilitarianism is – in the uncorrupted version he advocates – correct.

But there may be areas of law where a direct application of the ideal theory of equality of resources could be applied. And it may be that now Dworkin would wish to defend reverse discrimination programmes on the basis of a more direct application of equality of resources, independent of speaking to constraints on community goal seeking. Such an argument might go (if we remember the principle of independence): minority groups are handicapped by coming to the market with fewer freedoms than others by virtue of prejudice. Redress requires a redistribution of a kind such that they are placed in the position that they would have been in had there been no prejudice. That argument is sketchy, but plucks at the intuition that black people should be compensated, an intuition that sits more squarely with the egalitarian thrust of Dworkin's political theory than his justifying the community *goal* of bringing about a fairer society.

Equality of resources and tort law

Dworkin has, however, attempted to apply equality of resources to tort law. He has noted, as many have, the intuitive appeal of the idea that judges' decisions may be assessed usefully in terms of their economic impact. But he does not think, also capturing the intuitions of many people, that cost–benefit, utilitarian accounts, of the Posnerian kind, for example, are right, for the reasons we looked at in the previous chapter. In his articles attacking Posner, his central theme is that utilitarian, or wealth-maximising, criteria ignore the central place to be accorded in our legal system to legal rights.

He returns to the question of the economic analysis of tort in Chapter 8 of *Law's Empire*. It is the most difficult chapter of that book. Here he takes another tack by adopting a more general criticism of utilitarianism that it does not account for our strong intuition that a certain amount of self-interest is important in our lives. If we were really required to act in accordance with welfare or wealth-maximising criteria, he says, 'personal autonomy would almost disappear in a society whose members accepted the market-stimulating duty, because the duty would never sleep.'[38] In any case, for Dworkin, that onerous duty does not make sense of the idea of the importance of living one's *own* life.

Here arises a crucial point in Dworkin's work which has yet to be developed, namely, the difference between citizen and community. The duty of the government, on behalf of the community, is to treat *all* of its citizens as equals. Our 'familiar convictions', says Dworkin, support a division between private and public responsibility. While the public responsibility is towards all citizens equally, the private responsibility is only towards those with whom we have relatively immediate contact, our 'neighbours'.

What is the connection between the citizen's duty to treat people as equals and the state's? The citizen's duty is limited to his neighbours, and I think we should assume that Dworkin would draw the connection as one of agency. In relation to the treating as equals of non-neighbours, as it were, the state acts as agent for the citizen. This interpretation would certainly cohere well with the corporate type of responsibility which Dworkin ascribes to the state in *Law's Empire*,[39] and we should also note that there is, according to Dworkin, a continuity of ethical endorsement between the citizen and the political structure.[40]

Further, given that integrity expresses the duty that the government 'act with one voice' to all its citizens equally, we can see how the division of responsibility works in relation to the legal rules governing the division of property. In the case of clear rules, the citizen can consider himself *entitled*, by virtue of integrity, to act as he pleases within those rules:

> a citizen can suppose himself entitled to act for himself or others he chooses, as a member of a community of principle whose schemes secures, according to the latest public settlement, what it deems are the conditions for a permissive, self-interested attitude.[41]

However, in hard cases, we must accept that the governing principle of equality must be behind the determination of the outcome. Because of this, the citizen's attitude must be egalitarian rather than permissive. Unsurprisingly, Dworkin says that it is 'market-simulating' rules that will provide the best conception of equality compatible with both the duty of equality on the part of the government and the duty of equality in the private sphere.

How does he achieve this? He assumes that equality of resources is the best conception of equality, so his view is that when abstract legal rights compete, as they do in hard cases, the market-simulating model should be used. This means that cases should be examined according to a principle of comparative harm, whereby harm is measured economically by asking the question: who will lose more in resources?

Of course, the idea needs qualifying, but we can see that the general principle is that of the type of market outlined by Dworkin in his 'Equality of Resources' as refined in accordance with principles of abstraction, correction, authenticity, independence and non-victimisation. But the idea, he says, gives us the main outlines of a partial theory of personal responsibility.

If we can assume rough equality of resources,[42] in those areas of accident involving damage to property, equality of resources is the engine to providing the best resolution to hard cases, by awarding damages to the party whose equilibrium of resources under a just distribution has been upset by his neighbour. Dworkin says that 'we do have sufficient general knowledge ... to make the principle of comparative financial harm workable enough in most cases'.[43] The practical elaboration may require legislation (of the market-mimicking, Coasian sort) but Dworkin thinks that his thesis explains such ideas as reasonableness, contributory negligence and 'the other baggage of the law of tort'.

The intuitive idea is this. The torts of nuisance and negligence limit the impact of inequality when people's projects – their exercise of autonomy – intersect. Here we can see a more appealing interpretation of the Learned Hand formula.[44] If you are required by the courts to pay damages on the least cost avoider test, it is not that you are being made to fulfil a utilitarian duty due to the whole of the community, but that you are, so to speak, being made to repair the cost to your neighbour's equality of resources. You are, in accordance with a sensible requirement to treat your neighbour as an equal, being made to restore his resource equilibrium.

Conclusion

We have now got to a position where we can see the map of equality of resources and, in this last instance, the area of the common law. The question, equality of what? is answered by: equality of resources. We saw, however, that the idea was not as simple as it first appeared because of the constraints placed upon it by the requirement that, in the end, people are to be treated as equal in their humanity. That requirement led to the irrelevance of certain types of circumstance in calculating equality of resources, for example.

It remains for Dworkin to explain and justify a scheme of government which accords with this abstract, constraining principle: that of treating people with equal concern. His analysis of how we measure equality needs to be broadened into an analysis of why people should be treated as free and equal human beings. He requires, in other words, a theory of the fundamental principles of liberalism, and it is to that topic that I now turn.

Notes

1 'What Is Equality ? Part I: Equality of Welfare' (1981) 10 *Philosophy and Public Affairs* 185–246; 'What Is Equality ? Part II: Equality of Resources' (1981) 10 *Philosophy and Public Affairs* 283–345.

2 'What Is Equality? Part III: The Place of Liberty' (1987) 73 *Iowa Law Review* 1–54.

3 Some idea of disembodiment is implicit in Rawls's original position. We get the idea of the person who does not know he is black, or what his intelligence is, and so on. We could argue, of course, that this is just simple lack of knowledge, imposed by the artificial restraints of the original position. But that explanation does not quite capture the intuitive insight of the original position, which is to say that people *matter* independently of their skin colour, intelligence, and so on.

4 See Charles Fried, *Right and Wrong* (1978) Harvard, chapter 4, particularly pp.100ff.

5 The arguments in this section are largely to be found in 'Equality of Welfare', but a certain amount is drawn from notes taken at seminars, particularly the New York University Law and Philosophy seminar, chaired by Dworkin and Nagel, September – December 1987.

6 He says that 'a distributional scheme treats people as equals when it distributes or transfers resources among them until no further transfer would leave them more equal in welfare'. 'Equality of Welfare' 186.

7 'Equality of Welfare', 210.

8 Dworkin suggests that they try comparing their own lives against what would have been their ideal life given the right circumstances, or against a life devoid of value. But the counter-intuitive results that Jack and Jill come up with different evaluations of their lives judged overall does not go away.

His argument is obscurely expressed here. It invites the simplest and most obvious objection. Why cannot a judgment be made about the relative worth of the two lives? After all, one of us may be prepared to make the judgment that Jill's life would be better, because she has, say, 'aspirations', and so she should 'reasonably' have more to regret if she cannot fulfil them. 'Reasonableness', let us say, imports a value of striving. Jill should be 'equalised' with Jack by giving her more resources.

The objection needs journalistic expression. Crudely, why should equality ignore judgments made about the quality of people's lives? What is it in the nature of equality that stops that? I can make judgments about Jack and Jill. Jill has a potentially better life because she regards the kind of life that Jack leads as humdrum. Therefore, we give her more money so that she can try to fulfil her aspirations.

Is Dworkin's point that since Jack and Jill have equal talent, Jill could not have a better life and therefore that the only difference between them is that Jill is dissatisfied? If that is the case, that awaits the arguments against equalising enjoyment which Dworkin says is beset with the same problem of there being an independent yardstick in 'reasonableness'.

9 'Equality of Welfare', 216.

10 'Equality of Welfare', 219.

11 This section is largely drawn from 'Equality of Resources'.

12 See Chapter 9, the section entitled: 'Equality and utilitarianism: double counting'.

13 In Dworkin's language, 'the stipulated function of the stipulated conception of welfare is something good in itself that ought to be produced for its own sake.' 'Equality of Welfare', 244.

14 Dworkin also says that egalitarian utilitarinism cannot explain what is wrong with a natural disaster which kills thousands but improves the situation of a few.

15 'Our interest', he says, 'is primarily in the design of an ideal, and of a device to picture that ideal and test its coherence, completeness, and appeal.' 'Equality of Resources', at 292.

16 'Equality of Resources', 288.

17 'Equality of Resources', 285.

18 See Chapter 9, 'Economics and the Chicago School'.

19 What is known as a 'Walrasian' auction.

20 He suggests we modify the envy test to include option luck as follows: '... resources gained through a successful gamble should be represented by the opportunity to take the gamble at the odds in force, and comparable adjustments made to the resources of those who have lost through gambles.' 'Equality of Resources', p. 295.

21 'Equality of Resources', 299.

22 'Equality of Resources', 323.

23 'Equality of Resources', 331.

24 'Equality of Resources', 330.

25 The arguments in the next section are largely drawn from his 'What Is Equality? Part III: The Place of Liberty' (1987) 73 *Iowa Law Review* 1–54.

26 'Equality of Resources', 303.

27 See the next section entitled 'Equality and liberty'.

28 Consistently with that principle, of course. A person cannot use his freedom to limit another's, obviously.

29 *The Tanner Lectures on Human Values* XI (1990) University of Utah Press. I discuss these lectures at some length in Chapter 11.

30 'Equality of Resources', 25.

31 Magee, in his dialogue with Dworkin in *Men of Ideas*, makes the same sort of objection to the idea of Rawls's 'original position'. At p. 216, the following exchange occurs:

Magee: 'But all this [theory], it seems to me, bears excessively little relation to the historical realities out of which actual societies emerge, and which therefore shape them, and the social realities in which actual individuals find themselves – and therefore the real factors to which political philosophies need to relate.'

Dworkin: 'We're not concerned with the historical question here. We're concerned about which principles are *just* ...'

In other words, the riposte to the argument that Dworkin or Rawls are utopian is to say, of course they are. *That* is the point, to set up a model by which we can test and criticise the practices of the real world.

32 See 'The Place of Liberty', 41: 'Equality of resources leaves no basis for interpersonal comparison of liberty deficits rising from the same constraint.'

33 'The Place of Liberty', 42.

34 Federal Election Campaign Elections Act amendments of 1974, Pub.L. No.93–443, 88 Stat. 1263 (1974).

35 424 US 1 (1976).

36 *Lochner* v. *New York* 198 US 45 (1905).

37 See earlier, Chapter 4, 'Principles of democracy'.

38 *Law's Empire*, p. 294.

39 *Law's Empire*, pp. 167–75.

40 See the next chapter.

41 *Law's Empire*, p. 300.

42 See 'Equality of Resources', 386.

43 *Law's Empire*, p. 308.

44 See the previous chapter.

11

The basis of liberalism

We have considered in detail Dworkin's very important ideal political scheme of equality of resources. We have seen that it is guided by the important foundational – humanistic – principle that people should be treated as equals. But we have also seen that there is a need for a fully worked out division between the public and private responsibilities of people. We have seen that distinction worked out by Dworkin in a number of different contexts. It is inherent in his rejection, in the ideal ideal world, of utilitarianism, even of the egalitarian sort. It is inherent, too, in the argument for a participative political equality of influence, as opposed to impact. Dworkin develops the idea of the division in a brilliant attack on the contractarian account of liberalism in his Tanner lectures. But it is necessary, first, to understand what is the substance of recent debates on the justifications for liberalism, and second, to understand the nature and significance of the contractarian approach.

An introduction to thinking about the foundations of liberalism

It is important to appreciate the intellectual difficulties of liberalism. It is intended to be more than a set of discrete beliefs, say, about rights to personal freedom, or to the treatment of people as equals, or to the exercise of personal morality. Liberalism is these things, true, and can be loosely summed up as tolerance. But it aspires to be a justified doctrine of beliefs. No liberal, just as no conservative, wishes to hold a set of beliefs that could be shown to be contradictory, for example, or could be shown to have unacceptable consequences.

This much, I think, is obvious. But the particular problem with liberalism lies in its requirement for tolerance. It means that a true liberal must accept that other people may do, say or think things of which he himself disapproves. This is, at first sight, contradictory. How can Algernon approve of X, when, as Algernon knows, X entails the possibility of Y, and Algernon disapproves of Y?

The answer is not easy in theoretical terms, and in social life it becomes even more difficult. It means the doublethink of feeling the importance of, say, individual freedom, and then permitting its abuse. You see the problem all the time in political life. It is relatively easy for a government to reach over the protecting arm of tolerance and appeal directly to the widely, and perhaps rightly, perceived wrong of some action, in order to gain political support for banning it. The argument for tolerance, so often in such cases, either seems weak when it is at its strongest, or it is supported by the unsatisfying utilitarian argument: 'if the government got into the habit of doing this, it would be a bad thing'.

The problem of liberalism is, then, that it appears two-faced. It seeks a moral justification for ignoring certain sorts of immoral conduct. Before seeing how Dworkin proposes to provide a solution, it is helpful to give a short review of ways in which answers have been sought to the problem.

One very common view is that liberalism follows from the perceived impossibility of the objectivity of moral reasoning. The argument goes (I emphasise that this view is extremely common): 'My moral view is my own personal opinion only, and therefore I have no right to enforce it upon another person. It follows that everyone is entitled to his own personal point of view. It further follows that the state must be tolerant toward everyone's views.' This view is untenable, because it is dependent on the views about subjectivity previously shown to be wrong. It is in any case self-defeating, because it *enforces* tolerance.

Another view, not common now, but very common among young people in the 1960s, is a variant of the view just expressed, and shares, like it, the liberal intuition about tolerance. Instead of accepting the dilemma that you might not approve of conduct that must be tolerated, you were urged to approve it. What you did was to be tolerated not just because it was an exercise of your freedom, but because it *was actually good*. You were to approve lifestyles that were supposed to seem only at first sight tedious, such as commitment to leather sandal-making. Or, you were to 'see' that acts, which you might formerly have thought of as immoral, such as drug-taking or 'free' love, were not immoral. This 'hippy' liberalism takes tolerance to its extremes, extending beyond the simple endorsement of the exercise of freedom, to the acts resulting from that freedom.

There are, of course, various problems with the view. The main one is that it is too hopeful and, in a crude curtailment of discussion of the argument, is not one which most liberals would want. Liberalism wants to keep alive personal moral criticism of the actions of both ourselves (which 'hippy' liberalism, to be consistent, must presumably deny) and others.

Hippy liberalism does, however, escape the crude assumptions about the subjectivity of moral opinions, and its amiable and attractive side includes the injunction that we should, at least, take an active and approving interest in the activities in which other people engage. That is an endorsement of the imaginative possibilities of liberalism, in which we must view our lives as experiments in living.

But it would be wasteful to explore hippy liberalism any further, since it was constituted by a set of very informal attitudes. It may, in any case, be a contradiction to suppose that you can endorse all actions.[1] It gives us this pointer, however. It suggests that liberalism ought not to detach itself from the question of what constitutes the proper sort of personal ethical life that citizens should lead. This is an important point because usually anti-liberal and conservative theories are critical of liberal theories just on the ground that they are what is often called by political philosophers 'anti-perfectionist', meaning that liberalism permits societies in which citizens can, as a matter of right, live morally poor, 'imperfect' lives, without any criticism or better ideas being offered to them.

Influential among these critics has been a group of philosophers known as the 'communitarian' critics of liberalism. They have criticised liberalism on a number of grounds, several of which can be described generally as follows. Liberalism, in preaching the virtues of tolerance, relies too heavily on 'the priority of the individual and his rights over society'.[2] The criticisms focus on the idea that individuals cannot, for a variety of reasons, some 'metaphysical', some solely moral, be thought of as 'atomistic' beings independent of their existence within a community. The idea is that, in some important sense, an individual's good life cannot be separated from the good of the community (and vice versa).[3]

The arguments are too diffuse to be examined in detail here. For what is not clear is that liberalism depends on any idea that community values are not important (depending, of course, on what they are) or that, in any society, individuals can only be seen as 'atomic' units.[4] Nor is it clear that people's having rights is inconsistent with community goals.

An elegant attempt at defending liberalism against the charge that it is neither concerned with the quality of individual lives nor provides an adequate account of community is made by Joseph Raz.[5] His attempt denies the primacy of rights to liberalism, but it does, too, accord very special weight to the idea of personal freedom. He argues that the possibility of an autonomously led life requires that there exist within society an 'adequate' range of options. If there is only one option, or only an extremely limited range of options, then lives cannot be lived autonomously. Raz offers as an example of a life where there are clearly inadequate options that of a man who is kept in a pit. He is given sufficient food to survive. He is free to do what he likes except that he is not allowed to get out of the pit. Another example Raz gives is that of the 'hounded woman'. The woman lives on an island and there are sufficient resources to survive. Unfortunately, there is a large and ferocious animal on the island, too, who hunts the woman, so that she has to spend most of her time and energy escaping from it.

Raz's view is that valuable lives consist in the pursuit of projects and commitments to various 'forms of life' and, since such projects and 'forms of life' are frequently supported and identified by public institutions, the state has an integral role in the enhancement of autonomy. The state *is*, then, concerned with 'perfect' forms of living but not with particular ideals, for that would offend the principle of autonomy.

The difficulty with this view is in the idea of tolerance it assumes. Can a 'comprehensive' moral view such as this allow for incompatible forms of life? The answer is yes. Raz says that the life of the 'perfect' nun, for example, is incompatible with the life of the perfect mother. This follows from the fact that no one can be *both* a nun *and* a mother (at the same time). But each form of life is compatible in the sense that from one perspective, within one single comprehensive ethical view, each life can be judged a perfect life, given the initial choices. Each life can, therefore, be compatibly 'tolerated' within the scheme.

But forms of life incompatible with the driving principle of Raz's scheme cannot be tolerated, surely. Imagine an autonomous choice to choose a non-autonomous life (as in some ways of living as a nun). There is clearly a difficulty here. How can the endorsement of autonomy permit a non-autonomous life within one comprehensive view? Raz senses that his form of liberalism withers where it is most needed, for he rules out certain incompatible forms of life. We are not required, in his view, to tolerate forms of life that are 'repugnant'.

It is not surprising that he leaves the argument there, for he must sense that his theory, while providing a coherent and comprehensive view, does not solve the central and pressing problem of liberalism. On what grounds must we support the toleration of conduct that is repugnant to, or 'discontinuous' with, our own personal ethical convictions?

Discontinuity theories

The 'subjectivist' foundation, and the twin comprehensive foundations of the hippy and Raz, are unsatisfactory. What other possibilities are there? The major one, discussed in modern liberal theory, is that of 'contractarianism', whereby the rights of individuals to conduct their affairs arise by virtue of, and solely from, an arrangement of government. The rights are derived from this arrangement and, important to this account, there are independent reasons for accepting the arrangement. The grounds for the rights, and the grounds for accepting the arrangement that gives the grounds for the rights, are regarded as two different sorts of justification.

Dworkin's own liberal theory is best understood by considering his distinction between what he calls 'discontinuity' and 'continuity' theories of the foundations of liberalism. The contractarian theory just described is a discontinuity theory. The discontinuity is between a person's personal ethics – what Dworkin describes as 'first person' ethics, or 'well-being' – and 'third person' ethics, or 'morality'. Thus, contractarian theories allow for first person ethics to provide the justification for the existence of the contract, and for third person ethics to be justified only by reference to the contract itself.

Dworkin says that the paradigm for a social contract theory is an ordinary commercial contract. There are different personal reasons why we might enter into such a contract but the rights and duties are established not by those reasons but the contract itself. It means that the contract acts as an artificial social construct from which rights and duties flow.

Dworkin cites Rawls as having the most sophisticated version of the discontinuity strategy. Rawls's view is that the basis of liberalism must be sought in an 'overlapping consensus' among different comprehensive ethical views.[6] In other words, at the basis of liberal political principles could only be a shared assumption that these were required in order to provide for co-operation in society where there were different ethical views. Such liberal principles are not, as Rawls has said, to be thought of as a mere '*modus vivendi*', that is, as necessary to ensure self-interest, but as a moral basis for liberalism. People should come to see that the liberal principles connect to each person's different moral interest.

Dworkin thinks that Rawls's theory is sophisticated because it connects morality in the personal perspective ('well-being') with the political perspective, unlike many other social contract theories, notably, I suppose, Hobbes's, whose social contract was derived purely from self-interest.[7] It is difficult to go much further with Rawls, because there are difficulties with the idea that the will to endorse the Rawlsian contract goes beyond a *modus vivendi*. One can easily imagine the same kind of contract being endorsed by self-interested parties, as by those whose desire is for a morally based set of political principles. Co-operation is not clearly *not* neutral between self-interest and morality. On the other hand, it is clearly not antagonistic to personal morality and so Dworkin's interpretation (and Rawls's interpretation of his own position) cannot be ruled out.

But the rights and obligations that people have, under Rawls's scheme, derive from a perspective that is not personal, because it is founded in the idea that people of different convictions about personal ethics should endorse liberal perspectives for reasons other than those to be found in their personal ethics. That, at least, Rawls is clear about: that the political principles of liberalism are not to be drawn from any comprehensive theory.

Personal ethics and liberalism

Dworkin's project, on the other hand, is to make a bridge between personal and political ethics, so that ethics is part of liberalism's foundations. He agrees that the personal perspective is everything the liberal political perspective is not. We are not neutral and impartial, as liberalism claims the state should be, but committed and attached.

The distinction between the continuity and discontinuity strategies is helpful. It serves to distinguish the theories I mentioned earlier. What is the status of the confused argument for liberalism from the basis of the supposed subjectivity of moral judgments? It purported to derive neutral principles from the nature of moral argument itself. Put at its best, buried in its premises is a proposition about mutual respect: since I can no more prove my moral assertions to be true than you can, our moral assertions shall have equal weight. If this is so, then it is a continuity theory.

But another interpretation might find tolerance to rest upon self-interest. We could say that because of the non-provability of moral propositions, we should deal with others at arm's length to ensure that they keep at arm's length from us. That interpretation makes out the connection between one's personal ethics and the political perspective to be discontinuous.

What about the hippy liberalism to which I referred? That clearly is a continuous theory because it requires you to adopt as part of your personal ethics the personal ethics of everyone. That is why it is confused. Nevertheless, its strategy is to encourage everyone to extreme tolerance through the development of each person's personal ethics.

Raz's theory is a continuity theory, too. The political perspective is defined by a personal ethics which places very great weight upon the principle of personal autonomy. That principle must be endorsed by the state in the form of tolerance of a plurality of different exercises of personal autonomy. In other words, state tolerance follows from a personal ethics placing great importance on personal autonomy.

Contractarianism and categorical force

We are now in a position to be able to examine Dworkin's continuity version of liberalism which, for the political sphere, he calls 'political equality'.[8] Dworkin says that there are three major problems which any theory of liberalism will have to face, those of the visionary appeal such theories should have, the promise they have of attracting a consensus about them and, in particular, what he calls their 'categorical force'.

These problems arise from the difficult problem in liberalism of drawing a line between the personal and political perspectives. In the first place, since it is *premised* on the idea of people having different views in their personal ethics, on what constitutes the good life and personal well-being, how can any such theory hope to have either visionary appeal or consensual promise?

At first sight, the premise of difference seems to deny the possibility of people being equally struck by an equality vision of the future. What appeals to one person's personal convictions will not appeal to another.[9] Further, if that is the case, what is the hope for being able to attract a consensus about the idea? Dworkin goes so far as to say that it is unrealistic to suppose that political liberalism can gain a consensus yet.

There is a particular problem in the idea of the categorical force of political liberalism. From what basis can we claim justification for the moral strength of the principles? If people have different ethical views, views which may be partial and committed to different forms of life, how can independent moral force be accorded to the neutral and impartial liberal principles?

These three questions, concerning visionary appeal, consensus and categorical force, usefully throw into relief the difference between the continuity and discontinuity strategies. Take, for example, the visionary appeal of a discontinuity theory. Since it assumes different ethical views, it is difficult to see what visionary force it can have. Its appeal is not supposed to lie in any person's particular personal ethical perspective. In what, then? The best will be in some idea, such as Rawls's, of 'mutual respect and cooperation' but, as I have already pointed out, that idea is only hopefully something beyond self-interest (and self-interest, we assume, is not the same as personal ethics).

A similar problem arises with categorical force. From what moral perspective does this come? The short of it is that no one is going to accept as binding upon him a proposition which is not part of his personal ethical perspective. The discontinuity strategy assumes different ethical perspectives, so that the categorical force can only arise from the contract. Here we can return to the paradigm of the ordinary commercial contract, in which the rights and duties flow from the contract and not the personal perspectives of the parties.

Dworkin produces a devastating argument here. It is simply to remind us that there *is no social contract* matching the commercial contract. It is an 'insane' theory, he says, that there was ever actually a contract between citizens to form a state. No obligations of the commercial contract sort arise in advance of the contract coming into existence, not even where such a contract is clearly about to be made. The categorical force, then, of discontinuity theories cannot be located within the structure from which the rights and duties are supposed to flow.

Where could they come from? We can turn to the test whether discontinuity theories have 'consensual' promise. Perhaps visionary appeal and categorical force arise from the promise, or prediction, that consensus may, in the future, collect around a structure that ensures 'mutual respect and cooperation'. This, I think, is the most promising case for discontinuity. We consider ourselves as under an obligation to work towards a state in society where citizens act together in a state of co-operation and stability.

But there are problems with this view, according to Dworkin. What would be the moral motivation behind working and arguing for the only consensus likely to be successful, when it was almost wholly at variance with your own personal ethical perspective? Further, would the matter be merely a prediction of what was more likely to succeed as a consensus, a structure you endorse, or some other you do not? If so, the following odd situation would emerge. You would have, as a matter of categorical force, to urge a structure which you did not endorse as part of your personal ethics, because it is only marginally more likely to succeed than the structure you could endorse. That must be wrong. The assignment of categorical force here is too casual.

The discontinuity theory fails, according to Dworkin, because it cannot account adequately for the three features which he, reasonably, says are necessary for a successful liberal political theory. But what about the continuity theory? This fares much better on visionary appeal and categorical force. Both are derived from the personal ethical perspective, so that a person can be called upon to endorse from his own perspective the political structure proposed. There is no need to pray aid from an intermediate stage similar to the commercial contract.

Of course, many will have difficulty with this idea in Dworkin, because of the supposed problem of objectivity. What hope is there, ever, that the categorical force for liberal principles can arise from personal ethical perspectives? Perhaps moral views are too radically different,[10] for the continuity project to be successful.

There are two ways in which we might take this objection. First, it could merely express the simple view that moral argument, say, about the categorical force of political principles of liberalism, will always be controversial. We saw how Dworkin deals with that problem in Chapter 6. As I said there, in Dworkin's view, lack of demonstration of truth is not an obstacle to moral argument.

But second, it could express a more complex view that the controversy is such that *argument* is not possible, that the incompatibility is of a nature that not even modes of argument are shared. I think that this view is that of people who talk of the presence of irreconcilable conflicts (a 'contradiction' of principles, as opposed to 'competition') in society. They mean that conflicts exist which are simply not resolvable. This view is more sophisticated than the 'subjectivist' view, because it can allow for moral controversy, but asserts that, in some societies, the controversy can be irresolvably deep, where arguments necessarily pass one another.

But I take it from Dworkin's position on cultural relativity,[11] and his remarks on the 'internal scepticism' of the critical legal scholars,[12] that he would not accept these objections. So, the situation remains, for Dworkin, one where there *is* the possibility of argument, and the categorical force of the political liberal principles will spring directly from the (right) personal ethical perspective. It is not an argument against *this* view that people might disagree, therefore. To point to the fact *that people will disagree* is merely, I take it, in his view, to make a statement of the sociology of moral argument.

But, how can categorical force derive from the personal ethical perspective really? After all, our personal perspective is coloured, as Dworkin points out, by ideas of partiality and attachment, not the ideas of impartiality and detachment required in political liberal principles. It was, in fact, this apparent contradiction which, in his view, sent the contractarians to formulate their discontinuity strategy.

It is instructive to look at two ways of answering this question, each of which Dworkin believes to be unsatisfactory. One is that we could, using the idea common in political philosophy, say that in matters of state, the 'right' takes priority over the 'good'. In other words, perhaps in politics where, as Dworkin says, 'the stakes are higher', morality should be given exclusive force over personal well-being.

But he does not think this argument is sufficient. It is no more than an assertion because it offers no independent reason why morality should have sovereign force in the political sphere. Particularly, he says, the ideas of personal well-being and morality are not independent. The idea of fairness, for example, allows partiality towards friends and family, so that within the idea of fairness, as it were, is the idea that friends and family are important.

So there may be a bridge between the sorts of principles he wishes to endorse at the political level and the personal ethical perspective. The connection requires a deeper analysis of the relationship between fairness, justice and impartiality, on the one hand, and the personal perspective, which Dworkin later gives. But it is not enough, he thinks, simply to insist that, in the political sphere, the right takes priority.

A second way of looking at the question of reconciling the two perspectives might be to adopt the same sort of interpretive approach that Dworkin uses in his legal philosophy, in *Law's Empire*. The idea for justice, he says, is in Rawls. It is that a political conception of justice gains its categorical force, as well as its consensual promise, when its principles are 'latent' within a political culture. These latent principles may be extrapolated by making an interpretive judgment about our society, one that makes the best sense of the principles of justice actually accepted.

The idea is attractive. It suggests a way of producing one single theory of justice from a number of different, overlapping ones. But Dworkin says that he 'doubts' this possibility because of the problem of 'fit'. Let us assume, for a start, there is a certain degree of consensus on what the correct set of political principles are, say, in the United States. On some matter, however, at least two stories 'fit' equally well with what is accepted. One is that the underlying theory is, broadly, justice as fairness. The other is, again broadly, that political matters should be decided on the basis of justice as utilitarianism. What, on these matters, is the latent theory of justice?

Dworkin says that the question cannot be decided without circularity. He says that a legislator could not decide which was the better of the two doctrines, justice as fairness and justice as utilitarianism, without relying on a further and more abstract theory of justice to decide that question. And it would be that further theory of justice from which categorical force would be claimed:

> At some point we must rely on what (we believe) is *true* about matters of justice in order to decide which interpretation of our own traditions – which way of telling our story – is best.[13]

The argument here is very difficult to understand. We rely on moral propositions we believe to be true (about rights, perhaps) in order to 'make sense' of existing legal practices, according to Dworkin. Why not, in the same way, make sense, by virtue of true propositions of morality, say, that justice is fairness (the argument here necessarily must be crude because schematic), of existing practices of justice?

Is Dworkin's argument just that justice is not an interpretive concept? He says, rather lamely, that 'latency' cannot be the source of categorical force. Here, I think, a problem may arise in Dworkin's work, which I noted in relation to the distinction he draws between the 'grounds' and 'force' of law. Presumably, in the legal system I endorse, because it supplies for me the moral 'force' of law it supplies, too, categorical force. That force must, in one important sense, be 'latent' in the community because I endorse the community practices.

Why not for justice? The discrepancy for Dworkin is striking because so much of his methodological approach can be seen as an extensive development of Gallie's idea of the essentially contested concept. And that idea sprang from an analysis of justice as a paradigm of such a concept.

We may gain some clue from remarks Dworkin makes in *Law's Empire*, where he states that justice is the 'most distinctly political' of the moral ideals, although his remarks are suggestive rather than fully supported:

Interpretations of justice cannot themselves appeal to justice, and this helps to explain the philosophical complexity and ambition of many theories of justice. For once justice is ruled out as the point of a fundamental and pervasive political practice, it is natural to turn for a justification to initially nonpolitical ideas, like human nature or the theory of the self, rather than to other political ideas that seem no more important or fundamental than justice itself.[14]

A digression on personal ethics

It will be useful, again, to sum up Dworkin's idea of liberal equality. The beginning idea is equality of resources which is measured on the 'envy' test. That means that people are to be made equal on the basis of their 'impersonal' resources. Because, in the real world, people differ in their 'personal' resources and luck, liberal equality requires a means for compensating these inequalities. Dworkin's suggestion, as we have seen, is that we use a system of redistributive taxation which can mimic a hypothetical insurance market which links the cost of compensation to the total available resources (its true cost to other people).

A person should be free to use his resources as he wishes. In other words, a genuine understanding of treating people as equals (the 'principle of abstraction' operating through the 'bridge principle') means that invasions of liberty are invasions of equality as well. Of course, invasions of liberty will be justified where that is necessary to protect an egalitarian distribution of resources and will include, for example, the protection of personal security. Invasion of personal liberty on other grounds, such as intervention to prevent private sexual behaviour, will not be justified, however.

The political equality implied by equality of resources means that only equality of 'outcome' is justified, not equality of 'impact'. It follows, says Dworkin, that democracy is defined by outcome as well as by other things flowing from the worthwhile life. He sees political activity as flowing naturally from personal moral experience and this idea is his answer to the charge that his theory lacks the dimension of community. Democracy means more than just the formal opportunity to vote. It requires the much richer idea of politics as a theatre of moral commitment and debate.

Above all, the idea of equality of resources removes the idea that people should be made equal in welfare. That idea places too little weight on the responsibility that people have for carving out their *own* lives from the resources which have, justly, been distributed to them.

In his Tanner lectures, Dworkin seeks, among other things, to answer two pressing difficulties with his idea of equality of resources. First, the idea does not have immediate intuitive appeal. This is simply because most of us do not think of resources as a good in themselves but as instrumental to some version of welfare we accept. A theory that places so much weight upon resources is, therefore, suspect.

Secondly, although we might agree with Dworkin's conclusion that tolerance and the strict observance of neutrality is required at the political level, that idea is too austere to govern our treatment of other people at the personal level. We make judgments about people according to their individual moral characteristics. We favour or condemn other people according to the virtues we perceive in them. We form commitments, too, that seem blind to the virtues of equality. If so, why should such a sharp demarcation be drawn between the public and private spheres? As we saw, it was this dilemma that has drawn philosophers to the idea of the social contract.

Dworkin's solution to these two problems is to argue for a conception of personal ethics which is intended to justify the inclusion within it of a political conception of justice. It is an argument of great importance for him in his ambitious project of making personal and public ethics continuous within one comprehensive vision of the morally right way to behave.

Critical well-being

Dworkin begins by introducing the idea that what is important about one's life is constituted not by what one *wants*, what he calls 'volitional well-being', but by one's 'critical well-being'. The difference is this. 'Critical well-being' is what you should want as opposed to what you actually want, which is 'volitional well-being'. The idea of the satisfaction of wants, such as pleasure, is too unstructured, and insufficiently complex, to explain the judgments we make about what is good in life.

Dworkin's analysis here is obvious. We do not think that what is worthwhile is *constituted* by simple want satisfactions of whatever kind. As he says, your life is not better because certain of your wants, such as being able to sail better, are satisfied, or your life is not worse because you suffered in the dentist's chair. There are some wants, however, which do matter for your life in the relevant way. Dworkin suggests one such as *wanting* to have a better relationship with your family. And the only way to distinguish between those wants that are important and those that are not is by abandoning the simple idea of want satisfaction, or 'volitional well-being', as constituting what is important.

Dworkin does not think that this distinction commits him to a distinction between 'subjective' and 'objective' wants. Clearly, it does not, even granted the general unease his methodology has about the meaning of that distinction. But, to employ the terminology, 'subjectively' I can distinguish between those wants I have that express volitional interests and those that express critical interests. Dworkin's distinction is only a graphic way of distinguishing between what I consider important and what I do not.

The distinction is important for Dworkin. But it is not clear how much it can do for him. We can use the distinction across a subjective and objective distinction, too. And if that is right, it must mean that we can say of a person, not that *he* was mistaken about some judgment about what was important *for him*, but that, overall, he judged wrongly. That is to say, a person can make a wrong judgment about what is important in his life, not from the perspective of his own personal ethics, but from an independent – 'objective', if you like – standpoint.

Dworkin rather downplays the idea of objective 'success' theories of welfare in 'Equality of Welfare'. He dismisses it, you will remember, on the ground that objective theories assume a resources metric, like the subjective theories.[15] We can agree with that, but the result must be only to shelve the idea. In relation to the volitional-critical distinction, it becomes clear that the 'subjective' approach is crucial. Buried in the idea is the liberal assumption of personal autonomy. So, it appears, the important thing about the distinction is not what first seems like a statement of general ethical psychology but a judgment whose importance arises primarily from the fact that it is a judgment *personal* to the actor.

I am not sure whether that matters. After all, Dworkin is using the method of reflective equilibrium and the direct appeal to intuition here is not inconsistent with that. His project, too, is to provide a link between personal ethics and a liberal political structure. He has given reasons why he thinks that people should have liberty within equality of resources elsewhere, and the appeal here to personal autonomy is no more than a reference to that. On the other hand, we must note that the distinction between critical and volitional interests does less work here than seems at first.

The good life constituted by performance

We can be agreed, then, that what is important to a person's life is what is important as judged from the perspective of that person. Dworkin goes on to draw some very useful distinctions. First, he distinguishes between the 'product' value of a life, measured by what that life produces, and a life's 'performance' value, measured by how a life is lived. A life of good product value would be something like Mozart's life, because he produced great works of music, or Alexander Fleming's life, because he discovered penicillin.

A life of good performance value, on the other hand, would be one where a person responds to his circumstances in, as Dworkin says, an 'appropriate' way. We can see what he means. A composer might live a life both of performance and product value. We might say that his life, lived as a performance, achieves value from the *way he lives it*, quite apart from a judgment that *what he produced* is of value.

Employing the idea of critical well-being, Dworkin now says that idea makes most sense only on a judgment about the performance value of a life. If we only judged lives according to their product value, as he says, most of our lives would be 'puny' compared, say, to that of Mozart or Fleming. Under the performance model, however, the response to life is parametered by each person's particular capacities. The goodness of a life is not judged in the shade of that life's 'product' but in terms of how it has been lived. Under this account of critical well-being, the brilliant person produces something better than I do, but the value in his life is measured against his response to his circumstances. You can see that here Dworkin is drawing upon the same sort of argument that led him to devise a tax on talents. At root, it strikes at rewarding people for what is merely a matter of luck. It is true, of course, to the liberal tradition of regarding this sort of *desert* as having no place in the distribution of resources.

The parameters of the good life

What is the role of endorsement of what is of value in your life? Dworkin suggests that the important idea for critical well-being is that the good life is one that you endorse. Further, it does not make terribly good sense to say that your life has value without endorsement, because the good life is one that is constituted by your doing what you critically believe you ought to be doing. In other words, endorsement is 'constitutive' of leading a good life.

This makes sense because it is an odd idea to suppose that we could lead a critically good life which we do not endorse, although you should note that Dworkin relies again here on the liberal idea implicit in the idea of critical, as opposed to volitional, well-being, that a person's own judgment of what counts as critical well-being is sovereign. The force of the argument really derives from the tautology that employing the liberal premise creates. That is, if a person's life is good because he responds to it in the way he believes is right, then it is not surprising that the goodness of his life is dependent upon his endorsement, or belief, that it is right.

What would be an alternative? Dworkin suggests that endorsement could have value in its being 'additive' to whatever else is of value in a critical life. But, as you can see from my previous argument, that idea is going to have very little value on the performance model if, indeed, it has any meaning at all. Dworkin says the additive view fits the product model much better. A person who values what he has produced has additional value in his life, thereby, than someone who does not.

The idea is bizarre for the product model, in my view. Dworkin drops it, by reason of his preference for the performance model. Let us say that Mozart's life is the better for his having endorsed his products, as it were, than if he had merely produced the works for money and neither one way nor another thought of them as otherwise worth doing. Does that make much sense? Does it really make any difference to the value we place on Mozart's life whether he valued what he produced?

I do not think so and I think that is another way of saying that the 'added' value could only come from judging a life by its own internal convictions, which is to confirm Dworkin's analysis of the performance model. He gives the example of Fleming's janitor who disobeys his instructions and omits to throw away the mouldy culture dish from which Fleming discovered penicillin. Fleming's janitor's life had product value. Would it make the slightest bit of difference that he had endorsed his breach of duty?

We continue with distinctions. Dworkin now distinguishes between 'transcendent' and 'indexed' accounts of the good life. A 'transcendent' account measures a person's life independently of a person's circumstances. The simplest form is hedonism. If life is to be judged good according to how much pleasure it has in it, then two lives can be compared at a transcendent level. The life with more pleasure in it, independent of circumstances, is the better life. If two people have an equal capacity for pleasure and equal means of fulfilling it, one who lives twice as long as the other has a better life measured in in terms of pleasure. As Dworkin says, mortality places a drastic limit.

It can be seen that the transcendent account fits the product model best because if the value of a life is independently measured by the value of its 'product', it follows that there are values of measurement which transcend particular lives. Dworkin thinks that the vulnerability of the transcendent view shows that the product model should be rejected:

> It seems absurd that the kinds of experiences or achievements that make up a good life for a human being to lead could remain transcendently the same, no matter what his circumstances of technology or cultural heritage or political structures or anticipated life span or economic resources.[16]

We should compare this transcendent account of the good life with an 'indexed' account which *does* tie what is of value in life to the particular circumstances of a person. Here is a move of some importance for

Dworkin's project. A failure to achieve through circumstances, he says, is not a 'limit' to my well-being but a 'parameter'. The good life is 'parametered' by circumstances.

This distinction takes into account the difference between transcendent and indexed ideas of the good life. If we understand what is of value in life to be transcendent of particular circumstances we shall, of course, view circumstances as limiting what is of value. But if we view what is valuable in life as linked fundamentally with the circumstances we are in, then our judgment of what is of value is indexed.

We can begin to guess where Dworkin is leading. Which features of a person's circumstances set the parameters? They must include all those things which enter into the judgment about whether a life has been critically worthwhile. For example, they will include a person's character and his volitional interests. They will also include his critical interests, for they will provide the background against which he enacts his life.

That seems clear. More problematic is Dworkin's claim that the parameters will also include the expected length of life. Since we have ruled out transcendent judgments about a person's life, the value in what a person does, in the only life for him to lead, will be parametered by some expectation about life-span, say, the upper end of the average life-span of the present generation. Only under this assumption, says Dworkin, can we make 'critical' sense of saying that it was a misfortune for a person to die young. That expresses a judgment about that person's missing out on a life we would have expected.

Presumably, Dworkin's point is that under the transcendent or product views we would counter-intuitively conclude that had Mozart died when he was fourteen, since he had already produced a number of great pieces of music, there was no great value lost by his early death. But that is not counter-intuitive because we would have hoped for more of value to have been produced by Mozart measured in product or transcendent terms. And at the other end of the age spectrum, we feel that, for some people, there was more that they could have done which would have made their lives more of value.

I employ here, of course, our intuition that both product and transcendent values are not insignificant in making judgments about the value in people's lives. What I am employing here is the anti-liberal objective strain of thinking to which I referred earlier. Certainly, for Mozart, the critically good life for him was to be judged against the backdrop of his *own* convictions about what was important to him (his art) and his *own* understandings of the time available to him.

But it is not true to say that, even taking into account a liberal premise, there is *no* room for the product sense of what counts as value. Mozart presumably aimed at producing what, independently of how he judged it to be, actually was good art on the product model. We can agree that Mozart's convictions about the worthwhile life constitute a significant parameter on the final judgment. But those convictions themselves will contain a judgment about what constitutes a valuable life. It is difficult, therefore, to see how this would fail to include a judgment, a conviction, about his life judged upon a product model.

What about resources? Dworkin says that they must be a parameter for otherwise we would be committed to the absurd idea that the only critically good life would be an immortal life with limitless resources.

Justice and personal ethics

Now we come to the conclusion of Dworkin's lengthy discussion of philosophical ethics. Do we say that a person's life is critically good measured against the resources he actually has? No. We can say that a person's life was not a good one *just because he had too few resources*. Here is the nub of the argument. It is now clear where Dworkin is going:

> the best life for a particular person, we might say, is the best life he can lead with the resources that *ought* to be at his disposal according the best theory of distributive justice.[17]

This is an arresting conclusion. It means that justice enters ethics by limiting the amount of resources a person can have to live a good life because, you will remember, the measure of equality of resources is its true cost to other people. Dworkin claims here that there is in this idea a shadow of Plato's claim that justice is always in a person's interests.[18]

What is congenial about Dworkin's conclusion is that the answer to the question of whether I have lived a good life ties the question of the ideal performance of my life to that of justice. For example, I cannot regret not having done well at politics if it is clear that I could only have done so had I an unjust amount of resources. Or, says Dworkin, I cannot be (rightly) pleased by having lived well despite my having had only a pauper's share of resources.[19]

We are now in a position to see the connection between personal ethics and the claims of liberal equality. Justice enters the personal sphere because it sets the parameters of that sphere. My own ethical life is coloured by the justice of the distribution of freedoms, particularly in the area of resources. Crudely, I cannot escape the effect justice has on my own ethical life, measured as a matter of critical performance (from my own point of view). Justice and my personal ethics cannot be separated. That means that a proper concern for my own personal ethical life must lead me to a proper concern for the just distribution of freedoms in the community.[20] The continuous link between personal ethics and the political structure is, in Dworkin's view, thereby established.

It may be instructive to see how far this conclusion departs from the contractarian line which Dworkin sees himself attacking. Let us go back to what he sees as the paradigm of the contractarian argument, which is the ordinary commercial contract. The contractarian line says that the rights and duties arising under the contract are independent of the personal ethics of each party. That is how the contractarian justifies the neutrality of political liberalism without any inconsistency with personal ethics.

But, if we are to employ the metaphor of a contract, and it is no more than a metaphor, then we can see that it only makes sense to talk of contracts if we endorse the institution of contract-making and contract-enforcement. We see the *ethical* sense of them. (We *need* not, I know. We *can* claim that contracts are merely institutions which in the long run fulfil our non-ethical self-interest.) In other words, it is not too difficult to give personal ethical justification to the contract's neutral way of distributing rights and duties.

But I do not think that these remarks touch Dworkin's project. His attack is against a line of specific contractarian thinking that really does regard the line between personal ethics and political liberalism as genuinely discontinuous. Despite his generous efforts to make the best sense of Rawls's idea of an 'overlapping consensus', in looking for an interpretive account of justice 'deeply embedded' in a pluralistic community, Dworkin does not succeed in rescuing him.

The way Dworkin denies the contractarian line is to say that the contract can only make sense seen as a striking way of showing that the sense of justice which sets the limits to our personal ethical convictions is the same sense which orders the principles of liberal equality.

A short summing up

Dworkin's most recent remarks in political philosophy have tied together several loose strands of political thought present in his writings. Two major requirements are posed by his theory of law if he is to be successful in his claim that legal argument is a species of arguments of political morality. First, a connection must be shown to exist between the meaning of a coherent argument of justification at the hands of a judge and a general and ideal theory about foundational moral principles.

Second, a connection must be drawn between these foundational moral principles and a general theory of distribution. This requirement arises, I think, because any legal system of which Dworkin urges us to make 'interpretive sense' should, for legal arguments to make full justificatory sense, exist in a community in which there is some semblance of justice. I mean by 'some semblance' sufficient adherence to principles of justice, in a community, to provide the sense and will for following the guidelines of improvement.

I conclude that Dworkin is on his way to drawing satisfactory theories for these two ideas. His desire for a holistic picture of citizen, state and law is a relatively rare one in the Anglo-American academic, legal and political culture, in which the contemporary virtues appear to encourage scepticism, deconstruction and relativism. But his idea of integrity combines the rational requirements of coherence with, of at least equal importance, a moral requirement. That requirement is the idea that people should be treated as equal in their humanity. In all cases, then, in the real world, all decisions that affect other human beings must be consistent with that motive. They are otherwise, in Dworkin's views, *unjustifiable* decisions.

That is a reasonable requirement. It is sufficiently abstract both to attract support and sufficiently concrete to provide a method of argument in real legal cases (subject to the more immediate requirements of integrity). So Dworkin is largely successful in making the first connection between legal argument and foundational moral principles.

It is too early to say whether he has succeeded in the second. An attraction of his theory of distributional equality is the central weight he gives to the idea of the costs imposed on other people, equally human, by the exercise of individual liberty, and its obvious practical impact through market mechanisms. But success in developing the more technical aspects of defining the market baseline may prove elusive. If it does, failure would suggest that the strong intuitions many of us have both that equality of welfare is impossible *and* that the market has an ethical base are, in fact, false.

Notes

1. Although the endorsement of 'A's action in doing X', and the endorsement of B's action in doing non-X', is not obviously so; nor is the endorsement of 'A's action in doing X, at time T_1' obviously contradictory of the endorsement of ' A's action in doing non-X at time T_2'.

2. See Charles Taylor, 'Atomism' in *Powers, Possessions and Freedoms: Essays in Honor of C.B. Macpherson*. ed. A. Kontos, (1979).

3. Note Margaret Thatcher's well-known statement that 'there is no such thing as society, only individuals and families'. What is interesting is that she should think this to be a central tenet of conservative thinking, when the communitarians in the United States, who are largely conservative in outlook (they would share many of Margaret Thatcher's convictions),

urge the opposite view, that individuals cannot be separated from the community in which they live.

4. For an excellent account of how two of the leading communitarians, Sandel and McIntyre, misunderstand liberal aspirations, see Gutmann, 'Communitarian Critics of Liberalism', *Philosophy and Public Affairs* (1985) 308–22.

5. See Raz, *Morality and Freedom* (1986) Oxford: Clarendon Press. See also my review of his book at (1987) 103 *Law Quarterly Review* 642–7.

6. See Rawls, *A Theory of Justice* (1972) Oxford: Clarendon Press, pp. 197–8 and 221–4. Also his 'Kantian Constructivism in Moral Theory,' 77 *Journal of Philosophy* 515 (1980); 'Justice as Fairness: Political not Metaphysical' 14 *Philosophy and Public Affairs* (Summer 1985) 223; 'The Idea of an Overlapping Consensus,' *Oxford Journal of Legal Studies* 1 (1987); 'The Priority of Right and Ideas of the Good' 17 *Philosophy and Public Affairs* (Fall 1988) 251.

7. See Thomas Hobbes, *Leviathan*, chs. 13–15.

8. In what follows, I have drawn from his *Tanner Lectures* on moral philosophy (1990) University of Utah Press and seminars he has given both in Oxford and at University College London since then. Given the late date of publication of these lectures I have had to rely largely upon an early draft which retains the power of the published work.

9. Dworkin thinks that it may be that Rawls's appeal to his overlapping consensus as being more than a *modus vivendi*, by his appeal to something in the personal ethics of everyone participating in such a consensus gives visionary appeal. Dworkin says that there is 'plain nobility' in the goal of mutual respect and co-operation.

10. In Raz's terms, 'strongly' pluralistic.

11. See Chapter 6, 'Cultural relativity'.

12. See earlier, Chapter 6, 'Scepticism'.

13. *The Tanner Lectures*, p. 34.

14. *Law's Empire* p. 425 n. 20.

15. See 'Equality of Welfare', 225.

16. This is taken from a draft of the Tanner lectures. See *Tanner Lectures* pp. 62–6. He says, at p. 63: 'It seems irresistible that living well, judged as a performance, means among other things living in a way responsive and appropriate to one's culture and other circumstances. A life of chivalrous and courtly virtue might have been a very good one in twelfth-century Bohemia but not in Brooklyn now.'

17. This is taken from one of Dworkin's drafts for the Tanner lectures. I believe it encapsulates the major thesis of the latter half of his published lectures. *Tanner Lectures* pp. 98–104.

18. Dworkin says he is tempted by something more complex than Plato's claim which he says can be 'relaxed' into: '...the critically ideal life, for any person, is the critically best life he could lead, in his circumstances [or] otherwise, if he had at his disposal the material and other resources that the best theory of justice entitles him to have' (Draft lectures).

Plato, in *The Republic*, Chapter 14, makes Socrates define justice as a virtue in the individual. The idea is that justice is an internal order of the soul which will bring about right behaviour: 'The just man does not allow the several elements in his soul to usurp one another's functions; he is indeed one who set his house in order, by self-mastery and discipline coming to be at peace with himself ... Only when he has linked these parts together in well-tempered harmony and has made himself one man instead of many, will he be ready to go about whatever he may have to do, whether it be making money and satisfying bodily wants, or business transactions, or the affairs of state' (*The Republic of Plato* trans. Cornford (1941) Oxford: Clarendon Press, pp. 138–9).

19. This example is not so intuitively obvious. I suppose that one's pleasure in that is the perverse one of having borne up well in unjust circumstances. Is that so different from someone from a poor country, but one where resources are justly distributed, saying 'I made the best of a bad lot'?

20. Remember that this was Dworkin's conclusion from his examination of the idea of community. See Chapter 4.

A bibliography of Ronald Dworkin

'Judicial Discretion' (1963) 60 *Journal of Philosophy* 624–38.

'Does Law Have a Function? A Comment on the Two-Level Theory of Decision' (1965) 74 *Yale Law Journal* 640–51. Previously printed under the title 'Wasserstrom: The Judicial Decision' (1964) 75 *Ethics* 47.

'Philosophy, Morality and Law – Observations prompted by Professor Fuller's Novel Claim' (1965) 113 *University of Pennsylvania Law Review* 668–90.

'The Elusive Morality of Law' (1965) 10 *Vanderbilt Law Review* 631–9. Capsule form of what has been written in: 'Philosophy, Morality and Law – Observations prompted by Professor Fuller's Novel Claim' (1965) *University of Pennsylvania Law Review* 668–90.

'Lord Devlin and the Enforcement of Morals' (1966) 75 *Yale Law Journal* 986–1,005. Reprinted in *Taking Rights Seriously,* at pp. 240–58 and in Wasserstrom, R., *Morality and the Law* (Belmont: Wadsworth, 1971) at pp. 55–72.

'The Case for Law – A Critique' (1967) 1 *Valparaiso Law Review* 215–17.

'The Model of Rules' (1967) 35 *University of Chicago Law Review* 14–46. This article is reprinted as 'Is Law a System of Rules?' in Summers, ed. *Essays in Legal Philosophy* (1968) Blackwell at pp. 25–60, and as Chapter 2, 'The Model of Rules I', in *Taking Rights Seriously* (1977) Duckworth at pp. 14–45, and also appears in Dworkin, ed. *The Philosophy of Law* (1977) Oxford, at pp. 38–65.

'There Oughta Be a Law' (1968) 10 *New York Review of Books,* no. 5, p. 18.

'On Not Prosecuting Civil Disobedience' (1968) 10 *N-Y Review of Books,* no. 11, p. 14. Reprinted in *Taking Rights Seriously,* ch. 8, pp. 206–22.

'Morality and the Law' (1969) 12 *N-Y Review of Books,* no. 10, p. 29. Reprinted in *Taking Rights Seriously,* ch. 1, at pp. 1–13.

'Taking Rights Seriously' (1970) 15 *N-Y Review of Books,* no. 11, pp. 23. Reprinted in *Taking Rights Seriously,* ch. 7, and in

Simpson, A.W.B., *Oxford Essays in Jurisprudence* (Oxford: Clarendon Press, 1973) at pp. 202–37.

'Rights and Interests' (1971) 16 *N-Y Review of Books*, no. 4, p. 44.

'The Jurisprudence of Richard Nixon' (1972) 18 *N-Y Review of Books*, no. 8, p. 27. Reprinted in *Taking Rights Seriously*, ch. 5. at pp. 131–49.

'Americans at Table', *The Times*, London, 23 May 1972, p. 17.

'Safeguards in Court', *The Times*, London, 3 July 1972, p. 15.

'Social Rules and Legal Theory' (1972) 81 *Yale Law Journal* 855–90. Reprinted in *Taking Rights Seriously* at pp. 46–80.

'Fact Style Adjudication and the Fourth Amendment' 48 *Indiana Law Journal* 329.

'Did Mill Go Too Far?' (1974) 21 *N-Y Review of Books*, no. 17, p. 21. Reprinted in *Taking Rights Seriously*, ch. 11, at pp. 259–65.

'A View of U.K.: Reports of Immanent Death Are Greatly Exaggerated', *Sunday Times*, London, 11 May 1975, p. 13.

'The Law of the Slave-Catchers', *Times Literary Supplement*, 5 Dec 1975, p. 1,437.

'Hard Cases' (1975) 88 *Harvard Law Review* 1057–1109. Reprinted in *Taking Rights Seriously*, at pp. 81–130.

'Justice Accused', *Times Literary Supplement*, 9 January 1976, p. 35.

'The Defunis Case: The Right to Go to Law School' (1976) 23 *N-Y Review of Books*, no. 1, p. 29. Reprinted in *Taking Rights Seriously*, ch. 9 at pp. 223–39, as 'Reverse Discrimination'.

'The DeFunis Case: An Exchange' (1976) 23 *N-Y Review of Books*, no. 12, p. 45.

'Journalists' Right to a Fair Trial', *The Times*, 30 November 1976, p. 17.

'Why Bakke Has No Case' (1977) 24 *N-Y Review of Books*, no. 18, p. 11. Reprinted in *A Matter of Principle*, at pp. 293–303, as 'Bakke's Case: Are Quotas Unfair?'.

'Social Sciences and Constitutional Rights – The Consequences of Uncertainty' (1977) 6 *Journal of Law and Education* 3–12. Also published under 'Social Sciences and Constitutional Rights' (1977) 41 *The Educational Forum* 271–80.

'Seven Critics' (1977) 11 *University of Georgia Law Review* 1,201–67.

'What Moral Philosophies can Learn from the Law' (1977) 7 *University of Maryland Law Forum* 115.

'No Right Answer?' in *Law, Morality and Society: Essays in Honour of H.L.A. Hart* (Oxford: Clarendon Press, 1977) pp. 58–84. Reprinted under 'Is there Really No Answer in Hard Cases?' (1978) 53 *University of New York Law Review* 1–32, and in *A Matter of Principle* at pp. 119–45.

(ed.) *The Philosophy of Law* (Oxford: Oxford University Press, 1977).

'The Bakke Decision: Did It Decide Anything ?' (1978) 24 *N-Y*

Review of Books, no. 13, p. 20. Reprinted in *A Matter of Principle*, at pp. 304–15, as 'What Did *Bakke* Really Decide?'

'The Bakke Case: An Exchange' (1978) 24 *N-Y Review of Books*, nos. 21–2, p. 42.

'Soulcraft' (1978) 25 *N-Y Review of Books*, no. 15, p. 18.

'The Rights of Myron Farber' (1978) 25 *N-Y Review of Books*, no. 16, p. 34. Reprinted in *A Matter of Principle*, at pp. 373–80.

'The Rights of M.A. Farber: An Exchange' (1978) *N-Y Review of Books*, no. 19, p. 39.

'Liberalism' in Stuart Hampshire, *Public and Private Morality* (Cambridge, Mass.: Harvard University Press, 1978) at pp. 128–33. Reprinted in *A Matter of Principle*, at pp. 181–204.

'Political Judges and the Rule of Law', *Maccabean Lecture in Jurisprudence* (1978) 64 *Proceedings of the British Academy*. Reprinted in *A Matter of Principle*, ch. 1, at pp. 9–32.

'Some Views of Mrs Thatcher's Victory' (1979) 26 *N-Y Review of Books*, no. 11, p. 26.

'How to Read the Civil Rights Act' (1979) 26 *N-Y Review of Books*, no. 20, p. 37. Reprinted in *A Matter of Principle*, at pp. 316–31.

'How to Read the Civil Rights Act: An Exchange' (1980) 27 *N-Y Review of Books*, no. 8, p. 44.

'Is the Press Losing the First Amendment?' (1980) *N-Y Review of Books*, no. 19, p. 49. Reprinted in *A Matter of Principle*, at pp. 381–97.

'Is Wealth a Value?' (1980) 9 *Journal of Legal Studies* 191–226. Reprinted in *A Matter of Principle*, at pp. 237–66.

'Why Efficiency?' (1980) 8 *Hofstra Law Review* 563–90. Reprinted in *A Matter of Principle*, at pp. 267–89.

'Dissent on Douglas' (1981) 28 *N-Y Review of Books*, no. 2, p. 3.

'An Exchange on William O. Douglas' (1981) *N-Y Review of Books*, no. 9, p. 52.

'Lets Give Blacks a Head Start' *The Times*, 12 December 1981, p. 6.

'Do We Have A Right to Pornography?' (1981) 1 *Oxford Journal of Legal Studies* 177–212. Reprinted in *A Matter of Principle*, at pp. 335–72 and under 'Rights as Trumps' in Waldron, J., (ed.) *Theories of Rights* (Oxford: OUP, 1984) at pp. 153–67.

'The Forum of Principle' (1981) 56 *N-Y University Law Review* 469–518. Reprinted in *A Matter of Principle*, at pp. 33–71.

'Principle, Policy, Procedure' in *Crime, Proof and Punishment: Essays in Memory of Sir Rupert Cross* (London: Butterworths, 1981) pp. 193–225.

'What Is Equality ? Part I: Equality of Welfare' (1981) 10 *Philosophy and Public Affairs* 185–246.

'What Is Equality ? Part II: Equality of Resources' (1981) 10 *Philosophy and Public Affairs* 283–345.

'Natural Law Revisited' (1982) 34 *University of Florida Law Review* 165.

Humanities in Review (1982) Cambridge

'Law as Interpretation' (1982) 9 *Critical Inquiry* 179–200.

'What Liberalism Isn't' (1983) 29 *N-Y Review of Books*, nos. 21–2, p. 47.

'In Defense of Equality' (1983) 1 *Social Philosophy and Policy* 24.

'Why Liberals Should Believe in Equality?' (1983) 29 *N-Y Review of Books*, no. 1, p. 32. Reprinted in *A Matter of Principle*, at pp. 205–13.

'To Each His Own' (1983) 30 *N-Y Review of Books*, no. 6, p. 4. Reprinted in *A Matter of Principle*, at pp. 214–20.

'Spheres of Justice: An Exchange' (1983) 30 *N-Y Review of Books*, no. 12, p. 43.

'A Reply by Ronald Dworkin' in Cohen, M. (ed.) *Ronald Dworkin and Contemporary Jurisprudence* (London: Duckworth, 1983) pp. 247–300.

'Reagan's Justice' (1984) 31 *N-Y Review of Books*, no. 17, p. 27.

'Reagan's Justice: An Exchange' (1985) 31 *N-Y Review of Books*, no. 2, p. 38.

'Art as a Public Good' (1985) 9 *Art and the Law* 143.

'The High Cost of Virtue' (1985) 32 *N-Y Review of Books*, no. 16, p. 37.

'Law's Ambition for Itself' (1985) 71 *Vanderbilt Law Review* 173–87.

A Matter of Principle (Cambridge, Mass.: Harvard University Press, 1985).

'A New Link in the Chain' (1986) 74 *California Law Review* 103.

'Report from Hell' (1986) 33 *N-Y Review of Books*, no. 12, p. 11.

Law's Empire (Cambridge: Harvard University Press, 1986).

'The Press on Trial' (1987) 34 *N-Y Review of Books*, no. 3, p. 27.

'Time's Settlement', (1987) 34 *N-Y Review of Books*, no. 4, p. 45.

'Time's Rewrite' (1987) 34 *N-Y Review of Books*, no. 6, p. 45.

'Plea for a Philosopher', *New York Times*, 22 July 1987, p.A.26.

'The Bork Nomination', (1987) 34 *N-Y Review of Books*, no. 13, p. 3. Also in (1987) 9 *Cardozo Law Review* 101–13.

'Reckless Disregard: An Exchange' (1987) 34 *N-Y Review of Books*, no. 14, p. 54.

'The Bork Nomination: An Exchange' (1987) 34 *N-Y Review of Books*, no. 15, p. 59.

'The Bork Nomination' (1987) 34 *N-Y Review of Books*, no. 17, p. 60.

'From Bork to Kennedy' (1987) 34 *N-Y Review of Books*, no. 20, p. 36.

'What Is Equality? Part III: The Place of Liberty' (1987) 73 *Iowa Law Review* 1–54.

Philosophical Issues in Senile Dementia, 1987, Office of Technology Assessment, US Congress. US Government Printing Office

'What Is Equality? Part IV: Political Equality' (1987) 22 *University of San Francisco Law Review* 1–30.

'Devaluing Liberty' (1988) 17 *Index on Censorship*, no. 8, p. 7.

'The New England' (1988) 35 *N-Y Review of Books*, no. 19, p. 57.

'The Great Abortion Case' (1989) 36 *N-Y Review of Books*, no. 11, at p. 49.

'The Future of Abortion' (1989) 36 *N-Y Review of Books*, no. 14, at p. 47.

'Liberal Community' 77 *California Law Review* no. 3, pp. 479–504.

A Bill of Rights for Britain. Why British Liberty Needs Protecting. (London: Chatto & Windus, 1990).

The Tanner Lectures on Human Values XI (1990) Salt Lake City, Utah: University of Utah Press

'Equality, Democracy and Constitution: We the People in Court' 28 *Alberta Law Review* 324 (1990).

'Bork's Jurisprudence' *University of Chicago Law Review* (1990).

'The Right to Death' (1991) 38 *N-Y Review of Books*, no. 5, at p. 14.

'A Harmful Precedent' (1991) 28 *Index on Censorship*, nos. 4 and 5, at p. 2. Reprinted as *No News is Bad News for Democracy*, in The Times, 27 March, 1991.

'The Reagan Revolution and the Supreme Court' (1991) 38 *N-Y Review of Books*, no. 13, p. 23.

'Jurisprudence and Constitutional Law', forthcoming in the *Encyclopaedia of the American Constitution* (1991).

'Pragmatism, Right Answers and True Banality', forthcoming in *Pragmatism in Law and Society* (1991) Boulder, Co: Westview Press.

'La Cour Supreme', forthcoming in *Pouvoirs* (1991).

Index